LONG TIME GONE

Neighbors
Divided By Civil War

D1565875

LONG TIME GONE

Neighbors
Divided By Civil War

LES ROLSTON

MARINER
PUBLISHING
Buena Vista, VA

Copyright © 2009 by Les Rolston
Wilderness Map Copyright © 2009 by Rick Britton

1 3 5 7 9 10 8 6 4 2

Library of Congress Control Number: 2009920572

Long Time Gone
Neighbors Divided by Civil War
By Les Rolston

Edited by Andrew Wolfe
Includes Bibliographical References

p. cm.
1. American Civil War 1861–1865 2. Rhodes, Elisha Hunt, 1842–1917,
biography 3. Sheldon, James Rhodes, 1840–1928, biography 4. Infantry,
United States Army 1861–1865 5. Infantry, Confederate States Army
1862–1865 6. History, Georgia 18th century 7. History Rhode Island
18th century 8. Rhodes family genealogy 9. Sheldon family genealogy 10.
History, Thomasville, Georgia 1820–present 11. History, Pawtuxet, Rhode
Island 18th century to present
I. Rolston, Les 1954—, II. Title.

ISBN 13: 978-0-9820172-7-2 (softcover : alk. paper)

ISBN 10: 0-9820172-7-8

Cover Design by Beth Wilkins
Book Design by Tracy Lee Staton

Mariner Publishing
A division of Mariner Media, Inc.
131 West 21st ST.
Buena Vista, VA 24416
Tel: 540-264-0021
on the web: MarinerMedia.com

Printed in the United States of America

THIS BOOK IS DEDICATED TO MARY

This book would not have been possible without the love and encouragement of my wife and best friend. Through endless rewrites, reworkings and restarts, Mary believed in this project. Whether offering suggestions or criticisms, her love of James and Elisha's story eventually equaled my own.

Thank you Mary.

FAMILY LORE

"She gave 12-year-old James a dollar and put him on a train to Boston to find a job. On the train he met a man from Georgia who was so impressed with the young boy that he told James that he would give him a job on his plantation in Georgia."

Irving Sheldon, recalling his mother's tale of his grandfather, James Rhodes Sheldon

"When I was a little boy I would climb into bed with Grandma and Grandpa before they got up, and he would tell me yarns about a young soldier he called 'Johnny Mud' who was in the Civil War."

Frederick Miller Rhodes, Jr., grandson of Elisha Hunt Rhodes

TABLE OF CONTENTS

ACKNOWLEDGEMENTS

This book would not have been possible without the kindness and generosity of countless organizations and individuals. Thanks to James and Elisha's friends everywhere. Among them are: The Thomasville Genealogical & Fine Arts Library, The Thomas County Historical Society, The Rhode Island Historical Society, The Warwick Public Library, The Providence Public Library, Ms. Susan Dunn, Ms.Cynthia Trainor, Mr. Dick Weeks, Ms. Judy de Lisle, Ms. Margaret Chevian, Ms. Sherry Harrell, The Jefferson Davis Memorial Historic Site, Mr. Gregg A. Mierka, Mr. Horatio Rodman Rogers, Ms. Drusilla Sheldon, Mr. Irving Sheldon, Mr. Robert Rhodes, Mr. Chandler Cheek, Mr. Simeon Smith, The Knoxville Civil War Round Table, The National Park Service, Ms. Mary Johnston, Ms. Kathy Holland, Mr. Terrance Strater, The Rhode Island Civil War Round Table, Mr. Patrick Schroeder, Mr. John Heiser, Mr. Alan Pitts, Mr. J. Tracy Power, Mr. Mark Dunkelman, Mr. Henry A. L. Brown, Reverend Evan Howard, Mr. William S. Smedlund, Mr. John Cox, Mr. Bruce Allardice, Mr. David Richards, Ms. Doris Davies, Ms. Kerry Sheridan, Mr. Kenneth Carlson, The Rhode Island State Archives, Mr. Wayne Motts, Ms. Sonita Cummings, Mr. Niles Madsen, Ms. Nicole Dufresne, Ms. Mary Anne Quinn, Ms. Deborah Rock, Mr. John Griffin, Ms. Margie Bonnes, Ms. Marian Johnston, Ms. Janet Lee Rotondo and Bonaventure Cemetery.

My sincerest thanks goes to Andy Wolfe of Mariner Media for his priceless editing and advice; to Rick Britton for his superb Civil War history knowledge. A special thanks goes to Ms.Tracy Staton for her wonderful book design and for putting up with the author's constant phone calls and endless stream of changes. I also thank Ms. Beth Wilkins for her innovative cover design. I cherish you all as friends as well as professional advisors. I am indebted to all of you for believing in this book.

Les Rolston
2009

AUTHOR'S NOTE

In 1999, I sat fishing beneath the Pawtuxet River bridge. Watching the water pour over the little waterfall, I thought of how James Sheldon and Elisha Rhodes must have spent many an afternoon on the same spot, watching the river being carried into Pawtuxet Cove into Narragansett Bay and the great Atlantic beyond. I didn't catch a fish that day but I decided to write this book.

I began my research armed only with the knowledge that Sheldon and Rhodes lived next door to each other as boys, and grew up to face each other as enemies in a vicious war. I soon discovered that Thomasville, where James spent his pre-Civil War years, was founded to a large degree by two Pawtuxet men. Intrigued, I was equally surprised to learn that few people in Thomasville knew this today. Thus the story of James Sheldon and Elisha Rhodes became entwined with that of Pawtuxet, Rhode Island and Thomasville, Georgia. James' brothers Israel and George also served in the Union army — a true example of "brother versus brother" in the Civil War.

In researching the life and Civil War exploits of Elisha Hunt Rhodes, I had available to me his wonderful illuminating diary which was published as *All For The Union* by Orion Books and beautifully edited by his great-grandson, Robert Hunt Rhodes. Bob has been extremely cooperative in helping me with my own book and I am indebted to him for his kindness. My other resources included a narrative and the Rhode Island Adjutant General's Report of the war. I used newspaper articles, official reports and letters written by soldiers in his brigade, division, and corps. Spelling and punctuation has been corrected in many cases. I made no attempt to delve into the relationships James and Elisha may have had with the girls they left at home during the war, although evidence indicates that these relationships did exist. My story is one of boys from a small seaside village, whose lives are interrupted by a war, and how that war took them on differing paths. Their story, and the study of it, consequently revealed a historically significant connection between two far-off cities which became a secret after 150 years.

James Sheldon turned out to be quite another challenge. He left no diary, although in the latter chapters of the book, his memoir speaks to us and his words are both historically vivid and touching. We are fortunate that while James' own thoughts about the events swirling around him in the early chapters are lost to history, the people who were near him provided recollections of these events with painstaking clarity. I would not have been able to tell the story of James Rhodes Sheldon without the contributions made to this book by my friends Mrs. James "Drusilla" Rhodes Sheldon of Corpus Christi, Texas, and Mr. Irving Sheldon of Saunderstown, Rhode Island.

My heartfelt thanks go out to Bob, Dru and Irv for helping to make this book possible.

Les Rolston 2009

A FROZEN BELL

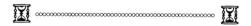

Two boys, ranging in age from nine to twelve, struggled
with the rope, the bucket and the ladder. The afternoon
was already getting dark and was cold enough that the
annual prank would work as it always had. Scrambling up the
roof of the little white schoolhouse was difficult enough without
having to worry about spilling the precious cargo of water.

Two of the lads, James Rhodes Sheldon and Elisha
Hunt Rhodes, lived next door to each other in nearly identical
houses on Broad Street in Pawtuxet Village. They were about the
same age and had a lot in common; both their fathers were sea
captains and their lives, like everyone else in the village, revolved
around the ocean. Most of the men worked on the ocean or dug
clams and quahaugs on the beach. The day was ruled by a natural
clock—the tides. If a mother asked the barber for the best time
to get her son's hair cut, he would say, "When the tide is out,"
meaning no men would be in the village and his shop would
be empty. If a man was out of work he would walk to the next
village seeking employment and "following the shore," became
the polite term for unemployment. [1]

Pawtuxet Village was not a booming port like Providence.
It wasn't elegant like Newport, or quaint like Westerly or Watch
Hill. The village was, as Rhode Island historian Henry A. L.
Brown describes it, "a bit seedy, full of hearty hard-working
New Englanders." [2] On May 2, 1859, a fire ripped through 28
buildings and destroyed most of the village. But neither the fire
nor the seasonal storms that battered the village could destroy
the spirit of the citizenry which prided themselves in being the
first to revolt against the British, long before the Boston Tea
Party or Paul Revere's ride.

Not to be confused with the city of Pawtucket ten miles north, which claims to be the birthplace of the Industrial Revolution, Pawtuxet was bustling with activity during the 1850s. Although the village spilled over onto both the Warwick and Providence banks of the river, it maintained an identity of its own. A typical stroll through Pawtuxet Village on a spring morning was usually eventful with its boats and docks; there was always something going on. Mr. Elisha Arnold always greeted James and Elisha with a smile when they walked into his General Store where customers could buy anything from dresses to drugs. If the boys' mothers needed to mail a letter, Mr. Arnold could take care of that too as he was also the postmaster. The boys often passed Dr. George Carr, one of Rhode Island's leading surgeons, on the street as he emerged from his large brick house which had once been a bank. Villagers needing a repair to their carriage or some other work of iron, would cross the bridge to visit Henry Johnson who was always at his anvil, as his furnace glowed orange-red.

Students such as Elisha and James spent the day in a white, one-room building near the cove. New England Yankees were famous for making good use of practically anything and nothing was discarded until they were certain another incarnation couldn't be found. The boards on the schoolhouse floor (a perfect example) were hewn from discarded molasses barrels from the West Indies. The boards were flattened, straightened and hammered onto the timbers of the building's floor. The finished product looked beautiful and seemed to be just what the school needed, but then, on the first hot day in June, a student couldn't walk to the blackboard as the teacher instructed. Seeping molasses stuck everyone's shoes to the floor, causing both the teacher and his students to roar with laughter. Throughout the spring the room was filled with the pungent smell of the syrup.

Every April, James, Elisha and other young boys would be on the bridge, elbow-to-elbow with old anglers trying to catch herring, or buckeyes, as they made their annual pilgrimage up the Pawtuxet River. The first man to catch a fish from the bridge in April was crowned "High Hook" for the year. People from near and far would travel by stagecoach to come in to the village and catch buckeyes for the day. They became known as "day tipplers," as many would wind up at the Carder Tavern or the Mitchell Tavern on the Post Road. Another popular drinking establishment was the Golden Ball Inn which was also a stagecoach stop. In the village itself was Charlie Gorton's Saloon where you could get a good steak and a beer. But if the beer tasted too good a man might find himself in Charlie's other establishment, the jailhouse by the bridge.[3]

At the end of the wharf on Aborn Street was one of the village's real characters, Sam Greene. Sam was a burly man who ran a wholesale fish business and wore a fur cap in the cold of winter and in the blistering heat of summer. James and Elisha never saw Sam without his cap. When the fur wore off he kept on wearing it.

During the early 1850s, Mr. Allen would periodically appear over the village in his hot-air balloon and everyone would follow his descent, creating quite a bit of excitement. Another daredevil caused a sensation when he walked across the Pawtuxet River on a high-wire and the story of his feat was heard a hundred miles away.

In the summer, you could swim or canoe on the river and in the cold of winter, there was ice skating on Arnold Pond on the other side of the woods. The bluffs that sloped down to the bay were great for sledding. And there was always one festival or another featuring parades, picnicking and, everyone's favorite new game, base, which was eventually called baseball.

The Slocum family ran the Pawtuxet Cove House — one of the few upscale establishments in the village. It was known as a clambake resort with Mr. Slocum always reigning as bakemaster. But if Pawtuxet could boast a native delicacy, it was Captain Eleazor Ralph's oyster stew. Captain Ralph never revealed his secret recipe but was known for his scrupulous inspections of his oysters, often personally dug. If the oyster passed his eye it would simmer for hours in a huge kettle of milk, cream and butter which came from the captain's own cows. The boys could often see the captain in the backroom of his shellfish store, stirring his stew with a giant wooden spoon. Another specialty of the captain was his traveling clambakes. He would prepare a barrel of clams, sausage, lobsters and corn, packed in seaweed and red-hot stones and placed upon his livery wagon. Once loaded and ready to roll, Captain Ralph's mule-driven wagon would make its way down Broad Street seven miles north to one of the many hotels in downtown Providence. The 90-minute journey was just enough time for the bake to be perfectly cooked! Once cracked open the barrels brought many a banquet or wedding to life with its lavish feast inside.

****

As the boys reached the ridge of the schoolhouse on Commercial Street they looked around quietly making sure they hadn't been spotted. Then slowly and carefully, and with the aid of many small hands, the heavy schoolbell was pushed and turned until it was completely upside down. Then the rope was applied. Every boy in the village knew how to tie a good knot, having been taught by their fishermen fathers. Once secured, the water was poured from the bucket into the bell. If the bucket was dropped or the water spilled, the trick would be ruined, so all eyes were on the pourer whose tongue was stuck in the corner of his mouth to help him concentrate. Within a few hours there would be ice and the upside-down bell would be frozen solid.

The next morning mothers throughout the village were fretting that the teacher, always a man in those days, must be sick as the morning bell failed to announce another school day. A few blocks away the teacher cursed and yanked on the bell rope, knowing the boys of Pawtuxet Village had made him the folly of another of their countless pranks. No one was ever injured by the freezing of the bell and no one was ever held accountable; since the Revolutionary War the villagers were the masters of keeping a secret.

James Sheldon and Elisha Rhodes carried with them their memories of growing up in the village. Pawtuxet was a great place to be a kid.

The Commercial Street Schoolhouse (then)
(Henry A.L. Brown Collection)

The school now serves as the second floor
of the Pawtuxet Volunteer Fire Station (now)

1

LITTLE FALLS

F ew places could have as much in common yet be so different as Pawtuxet, Rhode Island, and Thomasville, Georgia. But in the early 1850s, both were bustling with activity. Pawtuxet was home to several merchant vessels which often spent months on the seas. Thomasville typified the Old South with its sprawling plantations and elegant architecture. If you were traveling south from Pawtuxet, Thomasville was where the railroad ended—most of Florida was still undeveloped swampland.

The colony of Rhode Island was founded by Englishman Roger Williams whose nonconformist leanings brought him to America in 1631. Intelligent and opinionated, Williams decided the New World was the perfect canvas to paint his political ideology. He openly criticized the Massachusetts Bay Charter, which allowed the confiscation of Native American lands without compensation. He spoke out against the colony's policy toward church and state issues, and by 1635, Massachusetts' officials ordered him back to England. Williams left Massachusetts— but not for England. Instead, he traveled 50 miles to the south where he befriended and took up residence with local Indians in Rhode Island. Five years after emigrating from England, he and several of his followers established the settlement of Providence on Narragansett Bay. In this new colony, Williams founded the first Baptist church in America and arranged for the Indians to be paid for the title to their lands.

Rhode Island received a royal charter from England in 1644, becoming a haven for those seeking not merely freedom for their religion, but freedom for all religions.

In the tradition of Williams, the seafaring men of Pawtuxet, Rhode Island, were fiercely independent. Many of their fathers and grandfathers played a unique role in their fight with the British in the American Revolution. The H.M.S. *Gaspee*, had been sent by King George to enforce the Stamp Act, and it harassed unarmed vessels on Narragansett Bay for months until the colonial merchantmen could no longer bear her existence. On June 9, 1772, during an unusually low tide, the *Gaspee* ordered a small ship to stop as it sailed outside of Pawtuxet Cove. The lighter draught vessel, the sloop *Hannah*, defiantly ignored the order and raced toward a sand bar known only to local sailors.

The captain of the *Gaspee*, Lt. William Dudingston, took the bait and sailed in pursuit of the insolent Rhode Islanders. As the two ships crossed what is now known as "Gaspee" Point, the British heard a sudden rumble and scraping sound coming from her keel. She came to a grinding halt on the sandbar, powerless and suddenly very vulnerable. The silence of Narragansett Bay stilled the night as it does to this day, but there was anything but silence on the shore. The word of the King's hated menace being reduced to a small land-locked fort spread from Pawtuxet to Providence to Newport, and as in Paul Revere's famed ride three years later, local residents armed themselves, some boarding longboats. Before the night was over the crew of the *Gaspee* was overpowered and taken prisoner. Dudingston was severely wounded and as he was rowed ashore he watched his once mighty vessel burn to the waterline.

For Rhode Islanders the war for independence had begun. Among these freedom fighters was Christopher Sheldon, of whom young James Rhodes Sheldon would be a direct descendant. All involved swore they knew nothing of the attack on the *Gaspee* when the British investigated. As agreed, those involved took the events of June 9, 1772, to their graves.

Free-minded Rhode Island was the first of the thirteen original colonies to declare independence from the crown and the last to ratify the constitution and join the United States. Today the bronze "Independent Man" stares south to the ocean from atop the marble domed Rhode Island statehouse. To the south, directly in his midst, is the sandbar which boaters still avoid during a moon tide. The smallest state of a mere 1,050 square miles, Rhode Island remains a little different.

****

Rhode Island was as linked to the ocean as Georgia to its soil. The richness and variety of the land was a planter's dream. From peaches to peanuts, it grows in Georgia. In fact, with the exception of some tropical fruits, anything that grows in the continental United States can be grown in Georgia. Although rice was harvested in abundance along the coast, cotton was the crop in greatest demand after the invention of Eli Whitney's cotton gin, and it was being shipped to mills in the North and in Europe. Cotton was King and slavery its servant.

Georgia was the fourth state to enter the Union. Fifty times the size of Rhode Island and the largest state east of the Mississippi, Georgia was the last of the thirteen original colonies, founded in 1733, 125 years after the establishment of the Jamestown, Virginia settlement. Its founder, James Oglethorpe, had served in the European wars, witnessing both the battle of Blenheim and the siege of Belgrade. After leaving the military, he became a respected member of Parliament.

An English charter was granted for twenty-one years to a board of trustees for the land between the Savannah and Altamaha Rivers, and west to what was called the South Sea. The trustees named the area for King George II, who had signed the charter and chose Oglethorpe to be governor. With thirty-five families he sailed from England. In the spring of 1733, Oglethorpe founded a settlement on a bluff overlooking the Savannah River. This became the centerpiece of the new country, where religious freedom was guaranteed as long as you weren't Catholic. The purpose of the Georgia experiment was to give the poor an opportunity to start over, to provide a haven for the persecuted Protestants of Europe, and most importantly, to create a military presence between the Carolinas and Spanish Florida. Within a year a heavy influx of Salzburgers and Methodists prompted the settlement of other areas of Georgia. Both alcohol and slavery were prohibited.

When Spanish troops attacked Georgia in 1742, Oglethorpe's military experience paid dividends to both his colony and the British crown. Governor Oglethorpe and his small army of Georgians repulsed the Spanish, driving them off their lands.

After serving as Georgia's governor for twelve years, James Oglethorpe returned to England. Georgia was changing and its settlers were unhappy. As in Rhode Island, rum and slavery were hot commodities and Georgia laws prohibited the sale or trade of both. Settlers became discouraged, and at the end of eighteen years scarcely a thousand families had settled in Georgia. The prohibition of alcohol was eventually abolished and many argued slave labor was necessary for the colony's development and that negroes were better off in slavery than in their native Africa. In 1749, Georgia became a slave colony with strict laws prohibiting their mistreatment.

Georgia became a royal colony in 1752. Its people elected an assembly and the governor was appointed by the King. As in the other twelve colonies, its citizens could vote for government leaders, unless they were Roman Catholic. In the absence of Oglethorpe's idealism, Georgia soon boasted a population of 25,000 whites and roughly the same number of slaves. Its most common products were rice, lumber, indigo, and a fur trade carried on by the Indians. The cotton boom was just over the horizon.

At the time of the American Revolution, Georgia was predominantly rural. Organized schooling didn't exist and inland settlements were so cut off from the rest of the world that they seldom received mail. People rarely ventured far from their villages and had little or no contact with outsiders. There were few roads, and those that did travel did so via Indian trails in the woods. Farming was the primary occupation and there were few wealthy planters. Savannah was the only settlement that could call itself a city and was still mostly a collection of wood frame structures. Georgians, like Rhode Islanders, were quite content within their domain. But as their Northern counterparts understood, independence often required compromise. No single colony could singularly declare itself free of English rule and hope to survive; only through a confederacy could the colonies claim their true independence and not perish in the process.

Georgia fared terribly during the American Revolution as Loyalist and Revolutionary factions clashed bitterly. It was a colony as much at war with itself as it was with the British. After the war, Georgia was at odds with the federal government almost immediately. When the state entered into treaties with Indian tribes, the federal government deemed the agreements invalid. Deeply resentful, the first seeds of states' rights were planted in Georgia.

In the decades that followed, states throughout the South embraced the idea of autonomous rule. As early as 1847, fearing real or imagined Northern aggression, Georgia's Governor Crawford urged Southern states to enter into a confederacy. The issue of slavery would not go away and short term solutions such as the Compromise of 1850 only staved off the inevitable. It was impossible not to have a stand on the issue.

Perhaps Joseph Brown, who served as Georgia's governor fifteen years later, saw the quandary more clearly than most. An ardent secessionist, Brown believed that the abolition of slavery would eventually destroy the South. What makes this opinion interesting is that Brown, like many Southerners, was not a slave owner. Known as a latter-day Andrew Jackson for his flair and bold approach to issues, he was dubbed "Young Hickory" by many Georgians. From railroads to school systems, Joe Brown set out to bring Georgia to the forefront of 19th century America. Loved by the electorate, the thin, clean-shaven or at times long-bearded Brown, would hold center stage in Georgia politics like no one else during the coming conflict. "Self-willed and argumentative," as his peers described him, Brown would battle Richmond, as he had Washington, over the issues of states' rights during the Civil War.[1]

****

In 1829, Edward Remington and Simeon Smith of Pawtuxet Village, Rhode Island, ventured to Georgia near the Florida border where a settlement called Thomasville was being built. Although Thomas County was established in 1825, Thomasville was little more than an outpost in a pine wilderness when it was incorporated in 1831. Having made the journey alone, neither Edward or Simeon could have ever imagined how this decision would affect so many lives. Remington, 25, married Smith's 23-year-old daughter, Mary Arnold, on September 4, 1826, and in 1827 their first child, Francis Henry, was born in Rhode Island.

Simeon Smith made Thomasville his permanent residence in 1831, and he and Edward wasted little time turning this camping ground into a hatchling of a town. When Thomasville was chartered, Remington was appointed as one of its first commissioners. The city honored him by naming one of its first streets for him. To this day, the street and its name are intact, as is Smith Street, the other main thoroughfare.

The two men opened a general store of sorts and reaped the rewards of a growing population. Edward and Mary continued to have children. By 1846, Edward and Mary would be the proud parents of two boys and three girls. A decade later, Remington became a 55-year-old widower when Mary died at the age of 53.

Smith and Remington often returned to Pawtuxet and on their visits would regale their friends and family with tales of the blossoming little town that sat at the end of the railroad. Their curiosity piqued, Rhode Islanders began escaping the winter snows by visiting Thomasville. Many became fixtures of the social and business scene, sharing bonds between the distinctly different towns.

****

During the late 1830s and early 1840s, one of the most prominent of Pawtuxet's residents was Pardon Sheldon. Sheldon had been the master of the brig *Waltham*, then became the captain and part owner of the three-masted *Hanover*, named for the Massachusetts town where she was built in 1829. With Captain Sheldon at the helm, the 329-ton *Hanover* was routinely welcomed in Scandinavia and Russia where she was loaded with canvas and iron to be sold in the United States.

Pardon married Rebecca Aborn on December 11, 1825. Rebecca's family played a prominent role in the American Revolution. Her grandfather, Daniel Aborn, was captain of the elusive privateer *Chance*—a true thorn in the side of His Majesty's Navy. Aborn's luck eventually ran out and he was captured and imprisoned aboard the H.M.S. *Jersey*.

By 1842, Pardon and Rebecca were raising seven children, the youngest being 2-year-old James. Wanting to spend more time with his wife and growing family, Pardon sold his share in the *Hanover*, moved ashore, and was replaced as master of the *Hanover* by Captain Luther Martin. The ship's registration was surrendered in March of 1844 at Providence, the cause being "vessel lost."[2] Although no longer in command of his own vessel, the sea beckoned Pardon Sheldon after the sinking of the *Hanover*. In 1849, Pardon Sheldon, now the father of ten children, died; the circumstances of his death are not known. Five weeks after losing her husband, Rebecca Sheldon helplessly watched her son, Robert, succumb to tuberculosis just four days short of his 17th birthday. In the days between these family tragedies James Sheldon turned nine years old.

Rebecca had given birth twelve times over the course of her marriage to Pardon. Four months after they were married, Pardon

Jr., was born. The child died in its infancy. He would be followed by Israel in 1827, Louisa two years later, Patience in 1830, Robert in 1832 and Pardon in 1834. In 1836, baby Rebecca was born. She survived a mere fifteen months and was followed by another Rebecca a few months after her death. James and George were born a year apart in 1840 and 1841 and Mary, Huldah and little Frank rounded out the Sheldon clan during the years 1843 through 1847. They lived in a modest house on Broad Street directly across from, appropriately enough, Sheldon Street, which sloped gently down to the docks where the *Hanover* was berthed. A hundred yards or so south was the waterfall which the Narragansett Indians named "Pawtuxet" meaning "Little Falls."[3] It is here that the Pawtuxet River empties into the Atlantic Ocean.

Pawtuxet Falls at the time of the Civil War
(Henry A.L. Brown Collection)

*The homes of the Rhodes & Sheldon families as
they appeared at the time of the Civil War
(Henry A.L. Brown Collection)*

The Sheldon's next-door neighbors were the Rhodes family. Their oldest boy, Elisha, was born in 1842, and was a friend and schoolmate of James Rhodes Sheldon. The two boys had much in common and shared both the peaceful charm of Pawtuxet Village and the heat of the Commercial Street schoolhouse. Elisha's father, Captain Elisha Hunt Rhodes, Sr. was, like Pardon Sheldon, a sea captain, and could often be seen at the helm of the schooner *Worcester* sailing in and out of Narragansett Bay. In the autumn of 1858, young Elisha saw his father for the last time; just before Christmas, he would learn that the *Worcester* had been lost in the waters off the Bahamas. Captain Rhodes was 53 years old.

The Rhodes family was like most of the other families in the village of Pawtuxet—hard working and financially struggling. Elisha's mother declared in the 1860 census that she was 54 years old and owned real estate valued at $1000. Eliza's children living with her were: Emily, 21, James, 14 and Colville, 10. Her eldest child, Sarah, 25 years of age, was married to John Barton, a carpenter, and lived in Providence with their two young boys.

The death of his father forced Elisha to leave school and enter the job market. As the sole provider for his family, 18-year-old Elisha worked as a clerk in the office of Frederick Miller, a mill supplier in downtown Providence, not far from the home of his sister, Sarah, and her husband, John. Rather than make the long daily commute to Pawtuxet, Elisha moved in with his sister and returned home on weekends. His carefree childhood in the village had come to an end.

Rebecca Sheldon and five of her children lived next door. Also widowed, Rebecca claimed no real estate holdings in 1860 and claimed a personal estate of $1000–$2000 dollars less than a decade earlier. Rebecca, her 25-year-old daughter, helped her around the house and with the raising of George, Mary, Huldah and Frank, who ranged in age from 12 to 18. Rebecca's eldest, Israel, was a 28-year-old merchant, married to Alma Diana Carder, the daughter of Judge William L. Carder.

Israel's ambition to become a sea captain was put to rest when he was 17. With his father's blessing, he sailed to Russia as a merchant marine only to be shipwrecked and nearly drowned off the coast of Scotland. After a trek of several hundred miles, Israel and his shipmates reached the American embassy in Liverpool where they secured safe passage back to the States. Once home in Pawtuxet, he learned the jewelry trade, leaving his seafaring days behind. Israel and Alma doted on their 5-year-old son, William, and lived with her parents on the Post Road, about a half mile south of Pawtuxet Village. This house still stands and continues to be referred to as the Carder Tavern from its Colonial heyday.

****

Meanwhile, Thomasville evolved into an inviting place to settle and raise a family—there were few reminders of it having been an outpost. The town was flourishing by 1850 and Edward Remington's business was booming. A random listing of items he offered for sale were: "pianos, Negro goods, window and bed curtains, furniture, iron, plow points, crockery and glassware, bagging and bale rope, candle wicks and matches, soap, sugar boilers, clothing for all ages, such as 'Ladies Steel Extension Skirts from 8 to 36 hoops,' fans, jewelry, and hats."[4] Remington also offered groceries such as sugar, raisins and sardines. For those looking for a taste of alcohol—gin, whiskey and a selection of red wines were all available.

In the mid–1850s, on one of his recurring visits to Pawtuxet Village, Edward Remington met Patience, the daughter of his late friend Pardon Sheldon. They married on September 26, 1858, and left Pawtuxet to spend the rest of their lives in Georgia. At 28, she was 26 years younger than her husband, Edward. Thomasville had swelled to a population of nearly ten thousand and Remington had accomplished much during his two and a half decades there. Between his real estate holdings and personal assets he had a combined worth of seventy-thousand dollars.

There were other stores competing with Remington's and with the nearest bank being forty miles away, in Tallahassee, Thomasville soon had its own. There were hospitals, bookstores, photo studios, furniture stores and Johnson's Market, where Abel Johnson slaughtered livestock for his customers from sunrise to dusk. There were stores selling custom-made coffins. Lowry and Swift sold buggies and wagons and also offered a blacksmith service. An insurance agency opened. The Thomasville Book Store offered the latest best sellers and sheet music for popular tunes like "The Wreck of the San Francisco," "An Evening On The Water," and "Scenes of Childhood." Consumers willing to ride out to the nearby village of Dry Lake could buy one of Brown's Patent Washing Machines, while other stores sold doors or tailored clothing.[5]

As a result of slavery, Remington soon realized another opportunity. For slave owners, he advertised "100 pieces Georgia Plains and Kerseys, colored and white, 50 pieces Lindseys, 6 bales checked, striped, and white Isnaburgs; 200 very heavy colored negro Blankets, 100 white do., with a full and general assortment of Wool Hats, Shoes, & Co."[6]

Thomas County slaveholders provided housing for them that "compared favorably with that in other sections of the state," but their lot was still a hard one. An average of six or seven slaves usually lived in a single small cabin.[7]

The town ordinances of Thomasville mirrored the laws of the state's penal code and blacks were subjected to a different legal system than the whites. Slaves could not own property and could not even travel in each other's company without a white man accompanying them. There was a strict nine p.m. curfew, and gatherings of three or more blacks had to be supervised by whites. A black man, even if free, could not rent a horse and buggy. A slave had to have his master's permission to make a purchase of any kind or to sell any of his belongings. The sale of alcohol to slaves was so strictly forbidden that it was illegal for him to spend more than five minutes on any premises where liquor was sold. Historian William Warren Rogers noted, "It is difficult to generalize on the treatment of slaves. Individual masters and overseers might be cruel, benevolent, or both. The absence of any slave insurrections in [Thomas] county does not mean contentment on the part of the chattels, but perhaps it suggests there was no excessive mistreatment."[8]

Word of the thriving settlement attracted adventurers and entrepreneurs alike, and in the mid-1850s a man from Scotland decided to put roots there as well. Born in Edinburgh, Peter Alexander Selkirk McGlashan was in his late twenties when he first laid eyes on the booming little town near the Florida border. Peter McGlashan came from a long line of warriors and his father was a veteran of the battle of Waterloo. One of Edinburgh's prominent clans, the McGlashans were familiar with a brash American, William Walker, who lived there during Peter's youth. Walker left Edinburgh for Philadelphia and later, New Orleans, to pursue a career in journalism. But, during the California Gold Rush in the late 1840s, Walker headed west. Eighteen-year-old Peter McGlashan left Scotland with the same destination, traveling through Georgia on his trek to the west.

Nearly a decade later, world events again beckoned Walker. In 1855, he called for the overthrow of the Nicaraguan government and with less than sixty followers, including the young Scotsman Peter McGlashan, plotted a coup. Walker rallied dissidents to join in his cause and the government fell. The next year, Walker was president of Nicaragua and his takeover was blessed by President Franklin Pierce. To further strengthen his ties to the United States, President Walker abolished the anti-slavery laws of his country to show support for Southern states. His rise to power was short-lived, however, as he had made many enemies in other Central American countries. He soon sought exile in the United States, which was denied by President James Buchanan. Walker returned to Central America and was swiftly put on trial and executed. Throughout his rise and fall from power in Nicaragua, Peter McGlashan was with him.

McGlashan returned to the United States after Walker's death and began a business in Thomasville, making and repairing saddles and other equestrian gear. He married Anne Willis Seixas, the great grandniece of Nathanael Greene, completing another Rhode Island/Thomasville connection. With his height, dark complexion, black hair, hazel eyes and Scottish accent, McGlashan stood out among the men of Thomasville and within a short time earned the respect and admiration of many of the townspeople. A fatherless boy, James Sheldon, soon befriended the harness maker Peter McGlashan, also a newcomer to Thomasville.

Eighteen-year-old James Rhodes Sheldon traveled to Thomasville soon after his sister's wedding. Sheldon family lore contends that James' mother put him aboard a train to Boston with $12 in his pocket to find employment. On this train ride, the story tells us, James met a man who offered him a job in Georgia.

James Rhodes Sheldon

Although there is no evidence to support this version of how James ended up in Thomasville in 1858, Edward gave him a job as a clerk in his store. This was a different world to young James. Cotton and fruit trees dotted the landscape and no one knew what quahogs or stripers were.

In November of 1860, Abraham Lincoln was elected President of the United States. Although the victory of the anti-slavery candidate was hardly a mandate; war, or at least a rebellion of Southern states, appeared imminent. Only two days after the election, one of the first secession flags was raised in Savannah, Georgia. On it was a coiled snake stitched on a white background with the inscription, "Our Motto, Southern States, Equality of the States, Don't Tread on Me."

The debate over slavery raged as Lincoln insisted upon the containment of slavery, and as western territories became states, the federal government would not tolerate the institution of slavery within them. An indignant South thought that the citizens of these new states should decide the issue.

In Rhode Island the election of 1860 ushered in a new era both nationally and locally. William Sprague was only 29 years old when elected governor, making him the youngest governor of any state in the Union. Like his counterpart from Georgia, Joe Brown, Sprague was a dynamic presence. Flamboyant, and often described as "dashing," the "boy governor," as he often referred to himself, often used his military age as an asset as storm clouds gathered over the nation.[9] The youngest son of Amasa and Fanny Sprague, William grew up in a family of wealth and social prominence. Cotton picked by Southern slaves was shipped north to the A & W Sprague Manufacturing Company and woven into everything from women's finery to slave uniforms, known as negro cotton. The company flourished throughout William's childhood and he enjoyed the best of everything, including education. William and his brother, Amasa, were attending The Irving Institute in New York, when their world was changed forever by the murder of their father on New Years Eve of 1843. Three years later, young William began his career in the family's business. While he started at the lowliest of clerical positions, he was soon promoted to company bookkeeper, and by the time he was 26, he was a full partner in the business with his brother and a cousin. Under his energetic leadership, the A & W Sprague Company grew to be the largest calico printing textile mill in the world, but slavery was at the root of all this success—the source of his fortune was cotton.

In the early 1700s the slave trade had provided Rhode Island with a flourishing industry. Rhode Island, by geography, had few exports of its own beyond fish, cattle and lumber; but it got into the slave business as a direct result of Europe and Africa's demand for rum. The raw materials required to make rum were harvested in the West Indies by the slave population. Rhode Island ships would set out for Africa, loaded with rum to be traded for slaves, who were then traded by the Rhode Islanders in the West Indies for molasses and sugar. Back in Rhode Island, the rum would be distilled and the process would begin all over again. Essentially, the sailing vessels would leave Rhode Island ports full of rum and return with sugar and molasses, and in this unholy triangle the average Rhode Islander never saw a slave or knew of the state's involvement in the slave trade. But in the mid-1700s, Rhode Island merchants had become so adept at the triangle trade that it held a virtual monopoly over the slave importation industry.

As the 1850s drew to a close, William Sprague's devotion to his country and love of the Union never wavered. After his father's death, young William grew close to his Uncle William and became infected with his uncle's love of politics. In 1860, William sought and won the governorship of Rhode Island by a mere 2,000 votes. In Georgia, Governor Joe Brown fired a 100-gun salute in honor of the "boy governor."

But an unspoken relationship between mill owners of the North, "the Lords of the loom," and slaveholders in the South, "the Lords of the lash," put economics on a collision course with morality. Although they were as different as their constituents, both men were caught in the same trap.[10]

2

IT SEEMED AS THOUGH THE UNION ARMY MELTED AWAY

Prior to the election of 1860, Georgia's leanings had been mostly pro-Union, but with Lincoln's election all bets were off. In December, a convention of secession was held in South Carolina, and that state unanimously voted to secede from the Union. Other Southern states soon followed. Governor Joseph Brown was asked to advise the convention that would determine its fate. Rising above the fire of debate, Brown sought to take both Lincoln and emotion out of the issue.

Joseph Emerson Brown was born in 1821 in South Carolina and was the epitome of a self-made man. He came from a humble economic background and rarely hesitated to further his growing wealth by using his political power for his own business interests. Unlike William Sprague in Rhode Island, charisma was not Joe Brown's strong suit. He was not the friendliest of men and was neither an impassioned orator, nor of striking physical presence. But before Joe Brown would leave the political stage he would serve not only as governor, but as a circuit judge, state senator, chief justice of the Georgia Supreme Court, and United States senator. Brown's favored financial interest was the development of the railroad and he often mixed business with pleasure, riding up and down the Western & Atlantic's line. His personal wealth was not public record, but at the time of his death, some estimated his wealth at $12 million. After the 1860 election, he faced the biggest crisis of his political career as Georgia debated the idea of becoming an independent nation.

As the United States began to break apart, Brown was serving his fourth term as Georgia's governor.

As Georgia teetered on the brink of secession, its citizens held their own convention to determine the state's role in the national debate. On December 7, 1860, Governor Brown expressed his concerns about Georgia's future in his Open Letter to the delegates of the convention. Brown asked his constituents to consider if Lincoln's election was sufficient cause to justify Georgia and the other Southern states seceding from the Union. Although not a slave owner, Brown believed abolition in other sections of the Union would affect slavery in his own state, and worried that freeing slaves would ruin the employment market for whites.

Governor Brown was convinced the Federal government would soon abolish slavery in Washington and at the forts, dock yards and arsenals throughout the United States. He feared that the slave trade between the states would be abolished, thus prohibiting a slave owner in Georgia from taking his slaves into Alabama or South Carolina to sell them.

But Joe Brown understood that to sell his argument for secession, he must also convince the non-slaveholder that this was also in his best interest, asking, "what shall be done with these 4,500,000 negroes, when set free?"[1] Brown was convinced that nearly a quarter of the free black population would engage in crime or other forms of vice, landing them in government sponsored prisons and poor houses. As for the notion of sending the 4,500,000 freed slaves back to Africa, he assumed the North expected the Southern states to pay the quarter of a billion dollars this expedition was projected to cost. Brown was also quick to point out how inhumane leaving these people on a wild, naked sea coast would be. To make his point, he stated, "To such a proposition I might reply, send them to the moon."[2]

In a plea to Georgia's Southern neighbors, Brown said pointedly, "Let us all unite. If we cannot all see alike, let us have charity enough towards each other, to admit that all are equally patriotic in their efforts to advance the common cause...if we secede, the United States Government will attempt to coerce us back into the Union, and we shall have war."[3] Brown directed his closing comments toward Georgia's citizens, saying, "If we must fight, in the name of all that is sacred, let us fight our common enemy, and not fight each other."[4]

On January 19, 1861, in a vote of 208 to 89, Georgia declared itself independent from the United States. Seven other Southern states had already done so and talk of a confederacy was being heard. James Sheldon, 19, worked his brother-in-law's cash drawer and like thousands of other young men in Georgia, wondered what was going to happen next.

On April 15, President Lincoln's call for 75,000 volunteers following the attack on Ft. Sumter, resolved Virginia's secession debate—men throughout the South organized companies of militia expecting Northern retaliation. The Federal government deemed secession illegal and an armed invasion of Southern states by Northern troops suddenly seemed inevitable. Families, like the Rhodes and Sheldons, wrestled with their loyalties and the concept of civil war. Young James now faced the realization of living in a foreign country.

In Rhode Island, Sprague was one of the first governors to answer the president's call and swiftly went to work raising a regiment, using a portion of his personal fortune to do so. Sprague sought out some of Rhode Island's most honorable men to serve as officers; among them was Ambrose Burnside. Burnside, in his mid-thirties, was born in Indiana but had strong ties to Rhode Island through business. His story is colorful, to say the least. Unusually bright and extremely likable, he embarked on a military career when he was eighteen. Although struggling financially, his father was well-connected politically and managed to have Ambrose accepted at the United States Military Academy. On the first day of June 1843, Ambrose Everts Burnside began a proud, if often ill-starred, military life when he walked through the doors at West Point.

Burnside's career almost ended before it began. On his third day at West Point, he got into trouble and earned his first demerit. Garnering 200 demerits in any single term meant expulsion and young Ambrose received demerits for talking on guard duty, smoking, feigning illness, entertaining friends in his room, giving himself a day off for his birthday and leaving the barracks after taps. At the end of his first term, there were only four cadets with more demerits than Burnside and all four had been sent home. In spite of his shenanigans, Ambrose fared well in the classroom. He finished the year in the upper third of his freshman class while accruing more demerits than any other cadet, an astonishing 198!

General Ambrose Burnside

While managing to graduate in 1847, his tumultuous experience at the Academy ended with misspelling his name at the time of his commission. Although few could have guessed at the time, Lieutenant Ambrose "Everett" Burnside's rise to ultimate field command in the soon-to-be Union Army had begun.

Burnside served in the Mexican War without distinction. At war's end fate brought him to Newport, Rhode Island. The young officer was taken by the quiet duty, the charm of Narragansett Bay and the fall foliage. In 1853, he resigned his commission and served as major general in the Rhode Island State Militia. At the same time, Burnside immersed himself in his breech-loading rifle manufacturing business located in the seaside village of Bristol. But, as the railroad opened the road to the West, men like Burnside were drawn to the adventure. At the time of Sumter, Burnside was serving as treasurer of the Central Illinois Railroad.

Lincoln's call had come and Governor Sprague solicited the rifle maker of Bristol to help him answer that call. This was not the Burnside of West Point. Instead, he proved to be a brilliant organizer and wasted no time turning 2500 volunteers into soldiers while their wives and daughters stitched flags and uniforms. Providence was alive with the sounds of patriotic music, marching men, and galloping horses. Only days after Lincoln's call, Rhode Island troops began their fateful journey down to Washington and into history. Among them was Governor Sprague who was eager to see how his money was being spent. Thousands of flag-waving friends and family members lined the coast of Narragansett Bay to witness the departure of the steamer carrying the men of the 1st Rhode Island Regiment—cannon salutes boomed across the water.

In New York harbor, the 1st Rhode Island was transferred onto the steamer *Coatzacoalcos* which joined a small convoy bound for Washington. The voyage was pleasant and the sea was kind, but as the men stared blankly at the Virginia coast the reality of war began to sink in. There were no cheering crowds; just an unseen enemy watching the Rhode Island men chug by. A tugboat pulled alongside offering the latest war news; the United States government had destroyed the Norfolk Navy Yard before the Virginia rebels could seize it. At the same time, the Rhode Island men could see the mighty Fortress Monroe at the tip of the York-James peninsula, not knowing who was inside. As they passed within range of Monroe's big guns would they be forced to run the gauntlet should it be occupied by the enemy? Would Monroe fire upon the steamer or send boarding parties out to seize her? Raising the anxiety level yet another notch, the men of the 1st Rhode Island were issued ammunition for the first time.

The dawn of April 23 was sparkling and soldiers nervously lined the rails of the *Coatzacoalcos* to glimpse the man-made monster ahead of them, as Fortress Monroe loomed larger with every passing wave. Chaplain Augustus Woodbury was among those at the rail, and heard a man shout, "There, at last, are the stone walls of the fortress." The men strained their eyes to see. "There is the flag-staff. Thank God! There is the glorious old flag still flying from its head!"[5]

The voyage continued up the Chesapeake Bay. No one on board who stood at the rail that morning could have envisioned Fortress Monroe as one of the few United States government possessions on Southern soil that would never be seized by the Confederacy. Shortly after noon, under a heavy spring downpour, on that April Wednesday, the 1st disembarked at Annapolis, Maryland. The men made camp and began their march toward the capital early Thursday morning. The locals along the route jeered the bluecoats and warned that they would not see Rhode Island again. Rumors were rife that Confederate troops were in position to attack the Union column, but except for the occasional accident which often accompanied such marches, the day proved uneventful. The regiment was now within an hour's march of the railroad junction that led to Washington. The night was spent in moonlit bivouac, almost magical with its campfires, stars, music and plentiful rations.

On Friday, April 26, the men rose before three a.m. to begin their march to the trains. At ten o'clock that morning, Governor Sprague and his detachment of the 1st Rhode Island Infantry boarded a train headed for the seat of war. Two hours later, less than two weeks after Lincoln made his call for volunteers, the young governor personally offered these Rhode Island men, one of the first regiments to arrive in the capital, to the President. Rhode Island was in the war and when the news of the 1st's arrival in Washington reached home, hearts swelled.

****

On the same day, in Georgia, Governor Joseph Brown was digging in his heels, proclaiming that any debts owed to Northerners by Georgians need not be paid. Where this left Edward Remington and Simeon Smith is unknown, but these were honorable men and their business dealings with Northerners may have been negligible. In any case, this was a dreadful time for the transplanted Rhode Islanders, including Edward's wife, Patience, and her adolescent brother, James Sheldon. Events unfolded rapidly as Lincoln's naval blockade reached the Carolinas—both sides rushed to arms, only to find they were lacking in munitions. On May 3rd, seizing upon the stirring response to his first call to arms, Lincoln again called for volunteers, this time for a three-year term of service. Patriotism enveloped Northern states and Rhode Island was no exception to the excitement. At the same time, two young clerks were being drawn into a national nightmare. In Thomasville, Georgia, James Rhodes Sheldon worked as a clerk at Remington's store. In Providence, Rhode Island, his former schoolmate and next door neighbor worked as a clerk at Frederick Miller's mill supplies business. While men, young and old, trained outside their store windows, these two friends watched with interest.

****

After Elisha Rhodes began working at Miller's, he looked forward to the weekends when he would ride the omnibus down Broad Street to Pawtuxet. Saturday nights and Sundays united the Rhodes, and Elisha basked in the company of his family. But on this particular Saturday in early May, Elisha's short journey to the village filled him with apprehension, knowing that he would first have to fight a war with his mother before taking on the Confederacy. When he announced his intention to join the army, Eliza Ann Rhodes did not hesitate to tell her son that he wasn't going anywhere. She was adamant in her decision and reminded him that he was the family's sole provider. After an uneasy weekend, Elisha returned to Providence.

In the days that followed, Eliza couldn't help but watch as other boys from Pawtuxet left their families and headed for the training grounds in Providence. The following Sunday was as awkward as it was mysterious for the Rhodes family. Eliza was weepy, and her son kept a stony silence; Elisha avoided the situation by going to bed early. The icy atmosphere was broken as his bedroom door creaked open. Sobbing, the frightened widow poured out, "My son, other mothers must make sacrifices and why should not I?"[6] The following morning, Elisha, along with a friend, began his usual six-mile omnibus journey to Providence, not to Miller's but to the armory. Arriving early, he was immediately put to business. Elisha's bookkeeping experience at Miller's store drafted him into the company of newly appointed officers struggling to organize a regiment. To his amazement, he was elected 1st sergeant within a week of his enlistment and wrote in his diary, "Just what a 1st sergeant's duty might be I had no idea."[7] He was 19 years old.

Private Elisha Hunt Rhodes

Impressed with his obvious good character, the officers used his acquaintance with the other potential recruits to judge their qualifications. Elisha recalled that he conspired to have a neighborhood bully rejected due to "heart disease." [8] Even at this early stage of his career, Rhodes was in the right place at the right time, demonstrating the scope of his intellect and potential abilities. But more importantly, the 2nd Rhode Island Regiment was being organized and several fine men from around the state offered their service to command.

When Major John Slocum of the 1st Rhode Island returned home from Washington to oversee the training of the new volunteers, it became clear that he was the man to lead them. On the 18th of May, Sprague, although in Washington with the 1st Rhode Island, appointed him colonel.

Colonel John S. Slocum wasted little time preparing the volunteers of the 2nd for the ensuing conflict. He had spent his life as a soldier. As a young man he joined the Rhode Island State Militia and later fought with distinction in the Mexican War.

Colonel John Slocum

Like Burnside, Slocum found success in the manufacture of weaponry with a special talent for artillery. Although married barely three years, the 37-year-old Slocum answered his state's call without hesitation. The colonel carried an air of confidence with him, while at the same time was a warm and loving man. As Chaplain Woodbury wrote of him, "Those who knew him became strongly attached to him." [9]

Sullivan Ballou, of Smithfield, was another of Rhode Island's best and brightest young men who answered Sprague's call. Ballou was a successful attorney and had two young boys with his wife, Sarah. Slocum chose the devout Christian and patriot to be a major in the new regiment.

Major Sullivan Ballou

Having persuaded his mother to allow him to join the army, Elisha now had to overcome another obstacle. The doctor of the 2nd was not at all impressed by young Rhodes' physical presence and deemed him unfit for service without even examining him. Elisha begged to be inducted and the doctor, obviously tired, relented, but warned the recruit, "[You'll] be in a hospital in a week." [10]   Sergeant Rhodes of the 2nd Rhode Island was then thrust into the command of twenty-five troops who had to be led to the Cadet Armory in the center of Providence. Rhodes was thrilled and wrote that he "made the most of it." [11] Through a series of clerical errors, Rhodes rose to sergeant, fell to private and was then promoted to corporal, all in a week's time, but this mattered little to Elisha as he was at last a soldier in Sprague's fine new regiment. To celebrate, he returned to Pawtuxet Village in full uniform, impressing his village friends. There, he spent one last evening with his family before leaving for Washington.

A week and a half later, on June 19, the 2nd Rhode Island's orders came in. Before breaking camp in Providence, Frederick

Miller gave Elisha a Smith & Wesson revolver and holster. While marching to the wharf, Elisha recalled that his gear was "heavy" [12] and that he "could hardly stagger under the load," perhaps giving credence to the doctor's observation.

Unlike the departure of the 1st, the 2nd Rhode Island left home with little ceremony. For the most part, people stared rather than cheered. A lump of corned beef, mostly fat, was unceremoniously dumped into each passing haversack, and Elisha promptly threw his rations into the Providence River. The 2nd boarded the steamer *State of Maine* at Fox Point and was off to the nation's capital. In New York, on June 21, the 2nd boarded a train to Baltimore, where the prospect of violence became real. The 2nd was ordered to "march with your faces square to the front, and pay no attention to the mob, even if they throw stones, bricks, or other missiles; but if you are fired upon and any one of you is hit, your officers will order you to fire. Do not fire into any promiscuous crowds, but select any man whom you may see aiming at you, and be sure you drop him." [13] For the first time, the men were issued live ammunition.

The men stepped off the train and began their march through the dark streets to another train station across town. Angry crowds lined the streets and hurled obscenities at the Rhode Island soldiers, Elisha wrote "We said not a word and plodded on." [14] With a sigh of relief the men reached the waiting train and began the last leg of their trip. When the 2nd Rhode Island arrived at Lincoln's doorstep the next morning. Elisha was awed by what greeted him and remarked, "what a city! Mud, pigs, geese, Negroes, palaces, shanties everywhere." [15]

The 1st Rhode Island, most of whom would go home in a month, were thrilled by the arrival of the 2nd. Encamped together, the feeling was warm and the Rhode Islanders shared tales of their journey to the nation's capital. As the Rhode Island volunteers sat by their campfires, Augustus Woodbury surveyed the scene—many of them would never see home again. He would later recall, "The spirit of the 2nd Regiment was that of pure and conscientious patriotism, and it was this that gave it the good discipline and efficiency, which made it conspicuous in the subsequent scenes of the war." In camp, "they had had time to think and deliberate upon the matter, and they came to their decision with the dispassionate calmness of principle ...[They were preparing] to undertake the most dangerous and difficult enterprise of which man is capable."[16]

The men of the 2nd dubbed this open field "Camp Clark" in honor of Rhode Island's Episcopal bishop. By mid-July, Elisha wrote that it was beginning to look "warlike, and we shall probably have a chance to pay our Southern brethren a visit upon the sacred soil of Virginia very soon." [17] Lincoln's generals deemed the railroad junction at Manassas, Virginia, a vital target.

As Governors Joe Brown and William Sprague recruited officers for their states, Presidents Davis and Lincoln struggled to find military leadership for their nations, and each vied for the country's best soldiers and military minds. Unfortunately for Lincoln, most of the veterans of the Mexican War were Southerners, as were many West Point cadets who, foregoing graduation, left the Academy after Sumter.

Lincoln had a general in Winfield Scott, a formidable force in both the War of 1812 and the Mexican War. But Scott was a year younger than the Constitution and knew that it was time to hand the reins of the army to a younger man.

Lincoln's first choice was Robert E. Lee, the preeminent officer in the US Army, who led the Marine's assault on John Brown's "fort" at Harpers Ferry. Loyal to the United States but refusing to turn his back on his native state, Lee left Washington full of quieted emotion. Some who witnessed his departure claimed there were tears on his face. Lee crossed the river returning to Arlington, his home overlooking Washington. Two days later, Virginia Governor John Letcher appointed Lee military commander of Virginia forces.

Western Virginia was the Confederate Army's western flank on Washington, D.C., should Lincoln decide to send his army south. Leading the Confederate troops in northern

Virginia, was Pierre Beauregard, hero of Sumter. Beauregard, 41, was arguably the most talented artilleryman in either army, but he was now thrust into tactical command of thousands of ground troops. He organized his hastily trained soldiers into brigades and placed them behind the crossings of Bull Run, a steeply banked stream north and east of Manassas.

At the start of the war, both armies were made up of organized volunteer state militias. The command of the Department of the Ohio was entrusted to 35-year-old General George B. McClellan. McClellan was a gifted engineer and his love of this vocation would be his undoing. He gained national attention by taking credit for two of the minor early actions of the war: Rich Mountain and Carrick's Ford, both in western Virginia. McClellan believed he was God's chosen instrument for saving the Union—even telling his troops that he would look after them like a father over his children. He preferred to organize and design, and was more interested in building things than breaking them. Born to privilege, he was bold in stature and brilliant of mind—the barrel-chested young general was much like Governor Sprague—both were admired by men and adored by women; dashing figures, to use the vernacular of the day, they preferred the Napoleonic pose when having their image made.

The Confederate commander was Brigadier General R. S. Garnett. In the first weeks of the war, Garnett was Robert E. Lee's adjutant general. Lee dispatched Garnett, when Federal troops were rapidly massing on the Ohio River, to prevent the western Virginia region from being overrun. He entrenched on the slopes of Laurel Hill and Rich Mountain.

McClellan sent Brigadier General William Rosecrans with 3000 men to attack Garnett's forces—they met at Rich Mountain on July 11, 1861. Rosecrans prevailed and pursued the Southern troops. McClellan came east, the Federal troops were divided and the chase was on—McClellan moved at a dogged pace but Rosecrans pressed his command with vigor. The Southern army was scattered, about 500 prisoners were taken and General Garnett was killed at Carrick's Ford on the Cheat River. It was the first defeat for the South.

Ironically, this small affair would bring Robert E. Lee, who had dodged the spotlight, onto center stage. He was ordered to western Virginia to take command of the army in the region. His first problem was to settle disputes between former Virginia governor, now brigadier general, Henry Wise, and Brigadier General John B. Floyd. Lee arrived with reinforcements enough to assemble an army of 16,000 for the remnants of the failed Southern commands. He was ultimately unsuccessful and Federal forces kept their grip on the region—leading to statehood for West Virginia.

McClellan was the antithesis of the aged Scott—the North, desperately in need of a leader, saw the young general as their best hope for the future. So did Lincoln.

But in mid-July 1861, Irvin McDowell, was in command of the Army of Northeastern Virginia. Although he had never led troops in the field, McDowell was a favorite of General Scott—he was a West Point graduate and studied tactics in France.

On the afternoon of Tuesday, July 16, the 2nd Rhode Island formed on Pennsylvania Avenue. They joined the 71st New York, the 2nd New Hampshire and the 1st Rhode Island, becoming the 2nd Brigade of the 2nd Division under the command of Colonel Burnside. Colonel Slocum used his Rhode Island connection to secure for his regiment the honor of leading Burnside's Brigade across Long Bridge into the uncertainty of Virginia.

A hot, disorganized march of several days brought McDowell's army, 35,000 strong, near Manassas where 22,000 Confederates waited. Elisha recalled that the men of the 2nd were in a lighthearted mood, picking berries and swapping jokes as they marched. Undisciplined as raw volunteers are, many consumed the rations they had stuffed into their haversacks on the first day of their march before reaching Manassas. This worried the general, as did the upcoming expiration of the 90-day volunteers. He reported, "I am somewhat embarrassed by the inability of the troops to take care enough of their rations to make them last the time they should… In a few days I shall lose many thousands of the best of this force."[18]

On this day near Bull Run in northern Virginia, the spotlight was on McDowell and he knew it. He knew he held a numerical advantage and he would need it to execute a crippling first strike to open the road to Richmond. Beauregard commanded 7 brigades, 29 guns and 1400 cavalrymen, for a total of 21,900 men. What he didn't know was that while he was waking his army on this Sunday morning, 8,500 Confederate troops, under the command of General Joseph Johnston, were arriving by train from Harpers Ferry, raising the number to 30,400, taking the Union's advantage off the board.

The day before the first major battle of the young war, General Irvin McDowell was determined to make sure his orders were followed precisely. He told his commanders, "The enemy has planted a battery on the Warrenton turnpike to defend the passage of Bull Run, has mined the stone bridge, and made a heavy abattis on the right bank to oppose our advance in that direction… It is intended to turn the position, force the enemy from the road, that it may be reopened, and, if possible, destroy the railroad leading from Manassas to the valley of Virginia, where the enemy has a large force."[19]

The orders were clear, and detailed the expected movements of the various divisions of the Army of the Potomac. The last portion of McDowell's order would prove prophetic as he said, "These movements may lead to the gravest results, and commanders of divisions and brigades should bear in mind the immense consequences involved. There must be no failure, and every effort must be made to prevent straggling."[20]

At about 2:30 a.m. on July 21, McDowell began the final advance with the 2nd Rhode Island among the leading regiments. Facing McDowell would be his West Point classmate, Pierre Beauregard. When they reached the ford at Sudley Springs, part of Burnside's Brigade had been slow in crossing and stopped to drink from the cool waters. As they quenched their thirst, a large cloud of dust from the direction of Manassas revealed the approach of a significant force. For the first time, anxiety cast a pall over McDowell's army as Burnside's Brigade resumed its march. Corporal Elisha Rhodes and the 2nd Rhode Island continued on for about a mile through thick woods until reaching a point where both sides of the road were open. After another mile, they encountered large rolling fields extending down to the Warrenton Turnpike, which crossed through the valley of the Bull Run Stream. It was here that the Union attack opened—beginning with artillery and followed by infantry. the Confedates responded in kind. "The leading brigade (Burnside's) had to sustain this shock for a short time without support, and did it well," according to McDowell.[21]

Elisha Hunt Rhodes

At 5:15 a.m. on July 21, McDowell's artillery opened the first major battle of the American Civil War. For several hours, Union gunners pounded Confederate positions as Slocum's 2nd Rhode Island marched toward the sound of the cannonade. General Burnside's Brigade halted for water at about 9:30 a.m., and after a short rest, advanced, while Colonel Slocum's 2nd

Rhode Island was ordered to deploy skirmishers on both of its flanks and in its front. Soon they confronted Beauregard's forces and Burnside's Brigade found itself locked in combat. Elisha and the 2nd Rhode Island Volunteers were immediately sent forward with a battery of artillery, while the rest of the brigade formed in a field to the right of the road.

By late morning it was growing warm and Colonel Slocum led his men out of the shade of the woods and across an open field. From the left, a sudden cluster of musketry split the air and the buzz and whir of minie balls swarmed over the heads of the Rhode Islanders. Instinctively, Corporal Rhodes and his comrades hit the ground.

Slocum ordered his men to their feet and the 2nd nervously continued their march across the field. A soldier near Rhodes had been so shaken by the gunfire that as he was climbing a wooden fence, he fell, breaking his bayonet. All who witnessed his fall couldn't help but laugh. As they hurdled the fence, another Confederate volley was thrown into their ranks. Shells burst around them and the 1st Rhode Island's battery was rushed forward, offering a furious reply. Chaos ensued as the scope of the young battle widened. Uniforms were not yet standardized, and unable to distinguish friend from foe, men on both sides fell victim to friendly fire. The ominous sound of minie balls in flight filled the smoky air, occasionally punctuated by dull thuds as they claimed a target. There was nothing funny now; all hell was loosed upon the woods and fields north of Manassas Junction. Men were falling as terrified horses, some on three legs, were running wild. Broken caissons and gun carriages lay on both sides, littered with the mangled bodies of their operators.

The 2nd Rhode Island was in dire trouble. Burnside tried vainly to push the entangled 71st New York and 2nd New Hampshire to their aid. The 2nd held and the Confederate defense began to weaken. General McDowell liked what he saw. "We passed Bull Run. Engaged the enemy, who, it seems, had just been re-enforced by General Johnston. We drove them for several hours, and finally routed them."[22]

Slocum inspired his men with his audacity and Burnside desperately organized his brigade. Governor William Sprague wanted to be in the fight and wouldn't take no for an answer, even after having his horse shot from under him. Seeing Confederate regiments approaching from the base of the hill on which the 2nd was positioned, Slocum ordered his men into the line of battle. The 71st New York and 2nd New Hampshire followed suit while the 1st Rhode Island was put into reserve in the nearby woods, but the woods proved to be no shelter—Confederate artillery shells tore through it.

The 2nd Rhode Island was hotly engaged with not one, but three regiments made up of Alabamians, Georgians and South Carolinians. Confederate artillery pounded their position on a hill where a small house owned by a Mr. Matthews served as the only landmark. The Southerners pushed forward up the slope, hoping to break the Rhode Islanders' line by their sheer numbers. But Slocum's men were up to the challenge and frantically fired and reloaded. In his haste, Elisha's gun got jammed and he smashed it against a tree. He grabbed the gun of a fallen comrade and rejoined the fight.

The Confederates fell back, reorganized, and charged again. The New Yorkers and the New Hampshire men were still trying to get out of each other's way, leaving the 2nd Rhode Island to fend for itself. For half an hour, the 2nd held the field alone until the 1st Rhode Island charged out the woods with a roar of musketry. The 71st New York and 2nd New Hampshire were finally coming into the fight and began to mix it up in earnest. Confederate forces continued to grow in numbers but Burnside's Brigade held. Elisha stayed close to Slocum. Surveying his position, Slocum decided to advance his regiment closer to the crest of the hill. Satisfied with what he saw, he turned to wave the 2nd on and began climbing a wooden fence. Elisha watched in horror as a minie ball shattered his colonel's ankle and another tore through his skull. Slocum fell back, motionless—Corporal Rhodes and others rushed to his aid. In shock and unable to speak, it appeared he wanted no one to touch him but seemed to recognize those around him as Elisha wiped blood from his face. He was carried to the Matthew's house which had been transformed into a hospital by Dr. James Rivers.

The 2nd Rhode Island had a quick baptism by fire. Burnside recalled, "The Second Rhode Island Regiment of Volunteers had steadily borne the enemy's attack, and had bravely stood its ground, even compelling him to give way... Major Ballou was very severely injured by a cannon ball, that killed his horse and crushed one of his legs. The regiment, under command of Lieutenant-Colonel Wheaton, continued gallantly to hold its position."[23]

The battle raged on and Rhode Island men fell in increasing numbers. The sun beat down mercilessly and the ammunition of the 2nd dwindled to a precious few rounds. Burnside pleaded for reinforcements and at about three p.m., Colonel William Tecumseh Sherman led his brigade to relieve Burnside's. The 2nd Rhode Island Regiment, tired, thirsty and badly hurt, fell to the rear and the relative safety of the shady woods. They had fought superbly, passing their first great test. But the cost was high. Colonel Slocum was killed and Major Sullivan Ballou was severely wounded and in the hands of the enemy.

Reported General McDowell, "The enemy was evidently disheartened and broken... But we had then been fighting since 10:30 o'clock in the morning, and it was after 3 o'clock in the afternoon. The men had been up since 2 o'clock in the morning... the longest distance gone over was not more than 9 1/2 miles; and though they had three days' provisions served out to them the day before, many, no doubt, either did not get them, or threw them away on the march or during the battle, and were therefore without food."[24]

In all, the 2nd Rhode Island had lost 104, or about 10% of its men who had been killed, wounded or taken prisoner. As the men sat eating and drinking in the coolness of the woods, the men consoled themselves by knowing their colonel would have been proud of them.

By three in the afternoon the sounds of battle began to subside and as stragglers came off the field, they relayed reports of the enemy being in retreat. But on this day of shifting fates, yet another name would enter the history books. Thomas Jonathan Jackson held his brigade of Virginians in reserve while Beauregard's army was collapsing all around him. Jackson's men stood firm waiting for their orders. The Virginians fixed bayonets, and on his command, drove into the Union center. This sudden counterattack threw McDowell's army into confusion and then panic as their escape was blocked by their panic stricken comrades. In the midst of victory, the Army of Northeastern Virginia was being crushed under its own weight.

Resting in the woods, the men of the 2nd Rhode Island began to hear gunfire intensifying in the distance. Weary from their efforts earlier in the day, Elisha and his brothers-in-arms believed that the road to Richmond would be open to McDowell's army the following morning and Beauregard's army would surely be destroyed.

Suddenly, a shell crashed through the trees and the 2nd Rhode Island scurried for cover. There was little ammunition left, but the men grabbed their equipment and nervously prepared to defend themselves. Men came flying into the woods, many without weapons. The 2nd suddenly realized they were not the enemy, but fleeing Union men insisting the battle had been lost. Officers tried to stop the retreat, but even at gunpoint these soldiers ran. Within minutes the Army of the Potomac was in full rout. As Chaplain Woodbury put it, "It seemed as though the Union Army melted away." [25]

Lt. Colonel Frank Wheaton, now in command of the 2nd, was ordered to serve as the rear guard until the bulk of the army had escaped. Amid total pandemonium, civilians and soldiers, even the wounded, fought with each other in a run for their lives. Broken gun carriages and dead horses clogged the roads. Wounded men sat everywhere, too injured to save themselves.

The 2nd Rhode Island had just replenished its ammunition when to their dismay, they were ordered to protect the retreat.

They remained in this rear guard position for fifteen minutes, then a general retreat was ordered. But just as Burnside's retreating brigade approached a bridge which offered a safe escape, the emboldened Confederates pressed the issue. General Burnside remembered the desperate moment, saying, "the enemy opened fire upon the retreating mass of men. Upon the bridge crossing Cub Run a shot took effect upon the horses of a team that was crossing. The wagon was overturned directly in the center of the bridge, and the passage was completely obstructed. The enemy continued to play his artillery upon the train, carriages,

Lt. Colonel Frank Wheaton

ambulances, and artillery wagons that filled the road, and these were reduced to ruin. The artillery could not possibly pass, and five pieces of the Rhode Island Battery, which had been safely brought off the field, were here lost... The infantry, as the files reached the bridge, were furiously pelted with a shower of grape and other shot, and several persons were here killed or dangerously wounded." [26]

The 2nd was the last to leave the field—sparring with Confederate artillery. The Rhode Island losses continued until the enemy gave up the chase. By nine p.m., Burnside's Brigade was back in the relative safety of Centreville and prepared to bivouac. McDowell, broken and distraught, could only imagine further disaster and two hours later, ordered his men to resume the retreat to Washington. The responsibility of leading the column once again fell to Burnside's Brigade.

By sundown, McDowell's army was in serious trouble as most of his men had assembled behind a ridge near Centreville.

The general weighed the pros and cons of making a stand at that position. Much of his artillery had been tangled in the massive traffic jam or had become separated from its ammunition trains and most of his men were without rations. Worse, after sending his staff officers to investigate, McDowell learned that many of his men were already on the road to the rear. Confusion abounded as his supply trains, "hurriedly gotten together, with horses, wagons, drivers, and wagon-masters all new and unused to each other, moved with difficulty and disorder."[27]

A distraught Wheaton wrote in his report a few days after the battle, "It is my mournful duty to record as amongst the first killed, as he was first in the fight, our gallant colonel, John S. Slocum, who was three times wounded, and left in a dying condition. Major Sullivan Ballou, while bravely assisting in changing the position of our center, was struck from his horse by a ball from a rifled cannon, and also left unconscious and dying."[28] In a follow-up report Burnside felt compelled to commend Frank Wheaton, saying, "Of the two Rhode Island regiments I have already spoken more fully, but cannot close this without again attesting to the admirable conduct of Lieutenant-Colonel Wheaton." In closing, Burnside lauded the Rhode Islanders, saying, "No troops could have behaved better under fire."[29] The colonelcy of the 2nd Rhode Island now belonged to Frank Wheaton.

The 1st Rhode Island, in its first and only battle, did itself proud as well. But it was now evident to the Union high command that their army was not ready. "Such a rout I never witnessed before. No efforts could induce a single regiment to form after the retreat was commenced," said General Sam Heintzelman, the commander of another division. "Raw troops cannot be expected to stand long against an unseen enemy."[30]

By mid-morning of the 22nd, the 2nd Rhode Island was back in its old camp and the reality of the disaster quickly sank in; even the most dedicated of the regiment were disheartened. Elisha wrote of the retreat, "I suffered untold horrors from thirst and fatigue but struggled on, clinging to my gun and cartridge box. Many times I sat down in the mud determined to go no further, and willing to die to end my misery."[31] The survivors sought out friends who were missing; perhaps lost and resting in their solitary retreat. All of the wounded who were being treated at Matthew's house were now in enemy hands and being transported to Libby Prison in Richmond.

Major Ballou had lingered a couple of days as a prisoner before succumbing to his wounds. It was rumored that his remains were mutilated by a group of Confederates; the final humiliation of the events of July 21, 1861.

****

The following day, as newspapers from Rhode Island to Georgia had a field day describing "The Great Skedaddle," James Sheldon in Thomasville and his brothers Israel, then 34, and George, 19, in Pawtuxet, awaited their fates. Lincoln summoned George Brinton McClellan to the White House while the Confederate Congress declared a day of thanksgiving.

On the 25th, the 1st Rhode Island headed home to be disbanded, leaving the men of the 2nd with an eerie feeling of loneliness. They made the best of this sad situation by moving into the 1st's now abandoned Camp Sprague, and the quality of their daily life took a turn for the better. Two days later, General McDowell was relieved of his position and McClellan assumed command of the force he soon renamed the Army of the Potomac. Both sides prepared for a much different kind of conflict. Some Southern generals, including Jackson, feared that their failure to seize Washington following the victory at Manassas would prove to be the Confederacy's death knell. The United States would take the war seriously now.

George McClellan was born in Philadelphia on December 3, 1826. In 1841, he entered the University of Pennsylvania but the following year enrolled at West Point. In 1846, he graduated second in the largest class that had ever left the Academy, placing first in his class in engineering. In June, he was commissioned second lieutenant and sent to Mexico three months later. He distinguished himself under General Scott in the battles of Contreras, Churubusco, Molino del Rey, and Chapultepec, and was promoted to captain for gallantry in action. At the close of the Mexican War, he was assigned to command the engineer corps and returned to West Point as an assistant instructor of practical engineering. He directed the construction of Ft. Delaware in 1851 and in 1855 was sent to observe the war in the Crimea.

Two years later, McClellan resigned his commission and entered the rapidly growing railroad boom. By the time the Civil War broke out he'd become quite successful but, guided by his strong sense of patriotism, he left his business ventures behind to volunteer with the Ohio militia where he was commissioned major general. He had barely served two weeks when General Winfield Scott placed him in command of the Department of the Ohio.

****

Following the battle at Manassas, both armies faced the reality of being unskilled in the art of war. Slugfests were costly in manpower and ineffective in strategy. Davis, knowing he could only win by an early knockout, and Lincoln, needing a victory to boost his sagging popularity, were both eager to get on with the fight. Generals Johnston and McClellan thought otherwise and neither man would be pushed into launching another campaign with inexperienced troops. The relationships between the presidents and their generals began to sour and would never recover from their mutual mistrust. Washington and Richmond entered a time of uneasy quiet.

August would not be without incident, however. At Wilson's Creek, Missouri, the Confederates defeated Union Brigadier General Nathaniel Lyon and his 5,400 troops. Lyon lost his life and the Lincoln administration sustained yet another public relations disaster.

On the 16th of August, Lincoln reciprocated Georgia Governor Joe Brown's commercial embargo between the North and South, putting the final squash on Edward Remington's financial relationship with his Rhode Island friends. But the worst was still to come for Lincoln. Munson's Hill, with its heavy artillery, glared at Washington from Alexandria. On the 28th, Union troops finally attacked what turned out to be a deserted fort. The big guns were nothing more than mere trimmed tree trunks painted black, known as "Quaker guns."[32]

October brought with it the pleasures of persimmons and chestnuts. The 4th Rhode Island had arrived, splendid in dress, and the men of Camp Sprague were somewhat appalled by the new uniforms after having just been humbled by defeat. Elisha, at 19, was already a seasoned veteran of the new war and complained that life in Camp Clark was dull.

By mid-month, the 2nd had come up with a scheme they called the "California Oven,"[33] created by lighting a fire in the tent and letting the smoke escape through a hole in the top. Boredom was now the enemy. Even a visit by President Lincoln failed to inspire the men as word spread through the camp of his turkey feast with the division's officers, while each enlisted man was issued a bowl of rice.

On October 21, exactly three months to the day after Manassas, the Union Army would receive its most stinging defeat. Believing Confederate troops were evacuating the heights on the Potomac near Leesburg, Virginia, Lincoln ordered his friend, Colonel Edward Baker, to "make a slight demonstration"[34] against them. The Confederates returned, and in force. Baker was killed and bodies of Union soldiers, who drowned in their attempt to escape, floated into the nation's capital days later. The rains poured down on Camp Sprague and the men shivered in their tents. Bored, demoralized men sat by their California Ovens reading the news of the defeat at Ball's Bluff. "Stay at home heroes,"[35] Elisha thought to himself about the press.

Winfield Scott had seen enough. He had retained the title of General-in-Chief but the defeats and the impudent young General McClellan were more than the aged warrior could bear. Suffering from chronic diarrhea and obesity, Scott decided to retire. On November 1, George McClellan became the second most powerful man in the United States and controlled all its armies, but even he was saddened to see Scott's end. In a pouring rain, McClellan paid his respects to Scott wishing him farewell in the early morning hours at a Washington train station. Three days later, Thomas "Stonewall"[36] Jackson was assigned to the Shenandoah Valley. His reputation, even at this early stage of the war, put fear into the raw Union recruits—the Valley pointed like a dagger at the heart of their capital.

****

On the 5th, Elisha was summoned out of his tent by Colonel Wheaton and asked if he would like to clerk for division commander, Don Carlos Buell. Rhodes agreed, but a week later Buell was replaced by Erasmus Keyes.

Keyes' office was in downtown Washington and Elisha said good-bye to Camp Sprague to begin a more cosmopolitan existence on Pennsylvania Avenue. He worked long hours and shared sleeping quarters with the other clerks. Elisha liked working for General Keyes who was easygoing, and by having his daughter Nellie with him, the general created a family atmosphere at the office. "One day is much like another,"[37] Elisha wrote as restaurant meals and smoking breaks replaced drills and dress parades. Even though it was still under construction, he found the Washington Monument impressive.

November of 1861 brought more crisis to the Union and war with England loomed large. The British steamer *Trent* was snared by Lincoln's naval blockade and to the United States' delight, two Confederate agents were found on board. For weeks, the fate of the two agents held the world's attention. Would they be imprisoned, executed or set free? Davis and Lincoln anxiously watched the Royal Navy as Christmas approached. Suspected of being spies, Mason and Slidell were detained in Boston as Europe waited for war to begin between the United States and Great Britain.

By Christmas, Elisha felt at home in the capital. In addition to his salary of thirteen dollars a month, he earned 65 cents a day for meals and for performing extra duty. He was even given a horse. The world was just beginning to open up to Corporal Rhodes. He enjoyed the company of the beautiful young women of Washington, and was often free to roam the city—relaxing in the evening alone, writing in his diary.

Elisha was no longer the boy of Pawtuxet, but sometimes longed for home and his mother, Eliza. The Christmas season had brought with it, as in all wars, fabricated tales of sick mothers at home, but Elisha's plea was uniquely innocent compared to most.

On December 30, Elisha strode into General Keyes' office and suddenly announced, "General, I want to go home. I want to see my mother." Keyes was amused by his directness and asked how long it had been since Rhodes had been home. Elisha had not been home since before Bull Run. Keyes then asked the key question, "Is she sick?" Corporal Rhodes answered "No, I hope not." The sincerity of his answer obviously touched the general and Elisha Hunt Rhodes was granted leave. He began to prepare for his journey home to Pawtuxet Village.[38]

The year of 1861 was gone, and Elisha Rhodes had seen a lifetime and many lives pass through it. On New Year's Day, Mason and Slidell were released from their jail cells in Boston, averting a war with England. In Thomasville, Georgia, talk of the Civil War grew louder. Listening closely was Elisha's former schoolmate, James Rhodes Sheldon.

3

WE ARE LIVING AS FINE
AS YOU EVER SAW

In Thomasville, Georgia, and throughout the South, the
effects of Lincoln's nine-month naval blockade were
becoming more evident every day—basic commodities such
as salt were in short supply. But the young Confederate States
of America, bolstered by its stunning victories at Manassas,
Wilson's Creek and Ball's Bluff, felt a boldness that flirted with
audacity. Fighting on its own turf and being led by military men
rather than politicians, the South seemed to hold the advantage
over the North.

Southern confidence was misguided—the Union dwarfed
the Confederacy in both men and machines. With a population
of over 22 million, it outnumbered the South by a margin of over
two to one. They also reaped the harvest of both an agrarian and
industrial economy. But in January of 1862, neither Lincoln nor
his war was popular in the remaining United States. Lincoln
desperately needed a victory. The Ball's Bluff operation was
intended to stave off public opinion until military operations
resumed in the spring. With its failure, Lincoln faced a long
winter of inactivity. To make matters worse General George
McClellan began the new year battling typhoid fever.

Meanwhile, Elisha, thrilled by the thought of seeing
Pawtuxet again, spent New Year's Day in high spirits making
the social rounds with his boss, General Keyes. Keyes relaxed
in the company of his clerks and his humor often poked fun at
other generals. He sometimes joked that any clerk who repeated

his good-natured jibes about other generals would be sent back to the front.

General Erasmus Keyes

The following morning, Elisha's furlough papers still hadn't been delivered to Keyes' office. Anxious to begin his leave, Rhodes stormed over to McClellan's headquarters and asked for the documents. He could see his furlough on the clerk's desk, but he was treated rudely and sent away. When General Keyes heard what had happened, he personally visited headquarters and angrily demanded the papers. Elisha was on a train that evening bound for Providence and home.

Throughout the first week of January, "Stonewall Jackson" built upon the legend born at Manassas a few months earlier. Reports of his movements in western Virginia and Maryland had an unsettling effect on the Army of the Potomac and rattled the nerves of President Lincoln. On the 6th, Lincoln met with McClellan, who was somewhat recovered, to discuss the state of the army.

With Washington facing imminent peril, another man from Pawtuxet Village decided it was time to offer his services to his country. On January 9, James Sheldon's older brother, Israel, made the six-mile journey up Broad Street to Providence just as Elisha Rhodes had done. Elisha was on furlough in Pawtuxet at that time, and perhaps influenced Israel's decision to enlist. At 34, Israel, well respected in his community, was older than most volunteers but maturity was an asset recruiters were looking for. Israel volunteered and returned home to Pawtuxet to wait for an assignment. Just three days later, he was mustered into the 1st Rhode Island Light Artillery, Battery E, commanded by Captain George Randolph.

Captain George Randolph

Randolph's ancestors were among the first settlers of the colony of Virginia. His grandfather was President William Henry Harrison's nephew and President Benjamin Harrison's third cousin. One of seven children, George Randolph was born in Quincy, Illinois, on March 29, 1840. His parents moved to Rhode Island in 1846 and their children attended public schools in Providence. Before the war, teenage George worked as a clerk in the E. C. Thayer Shoe and Leather business. Two months after the attack on Ft. Sumter, George enlisted into Battery A, 1st Rhode Island Light Artillery as a sergeant. He was wounded in both legs above the ankles at the Battle of Bull Run, but returned a month later and was commissioned 2nd lieutenant. He was promoted to captain in September of 1861 and the following month was transferred and put in command of Battery E, later known as Randolph's Battery.

The battery was going through significant changes in January of 1862. Lieutenant Walter Bartlett was promoted captain on January 26 and put in charge of Battery B. To fill this vacancy, Israel Sheldon, a man who had never fired a cannon, was commissioned lieutenant. Also promoted was Lieutenant John Perry of Coventry who would now serve as the battery's chaplain, although Perry was not devoutly religious. "He was not a perfect chaplain and so far as I ever learned never preached to the Battery after his promotion. He had his good traits," remembered another officer in Randolph's Battery. [1]

When Israel Sheldon enlisted, Randolph's Battery was encamped a few miles southwest of Alexandria, Virginia, and Israel rushed to join it. The battery had been organized on September 23, 1861 in Providence and less than two weeks later was stationed with the 2nd Rhode Island Infantry at a new camp, Camp Sprague, defending the nation's capital.

George Sheldon accompanied his older brother to New York where Israel quickly purchased a sword and sash with $25 an uncle had loaned him. They visited friends in Brooklyn during the afternoon and said their final good-byes at a New Jersey train station. Lieutenant Sheldon arrived in the capital early on the 31st. He lunched at a saloon and spent some time sightseeing before taking the ferry to Alexandria where he paid a man $5 for a carriage ride to his new home at Camp Lyon, named for the fallen general of Wilson's Creek. He was greeted by Lieutenants William Arnold of Providence and Pardon Sheldon Jastram, who graciously welcomed him to their headquarters. The next morning he met the battery's captain, George Randolph, who Israel described as "a perfect gentleman."[2] After breakfast Lt. Arnold took Israel on a tour of the camp and gave him a basic rundown of what his duties would be. There was little to do in camp and he and Lt. Jastram ordered horses for February 2. They had a grand day out socializing through the other camps, ending the day as the dinner guests at Battery C, feasting on roast turkey. A soldier's life agreed with 2nd Lt. Sheldon.

****

General Burnside, who had shone so brightly despite the outcome at Bull Run, longed for another crack at the Confederate Army. During the fall of 1861, he came up with a grand scheme. With the Shenandoah too dangerous a path to Richmond, and Johnston well dug in at Manassas, Burnside conspired to bypass the Confederate capital and strike south of Virginia. His time spent on the Rhode Island coast before the war convinced him that this operation could be carried out by an amphibious landing in the Carolinas. He pitched his plan to McClellan and gradually gained his interest. While McClellan pondered the opportunity, Burnside personally sought out and inspected vessels that could be used in his expedition.

By Christmas nearly everything was in place for this highly classified mission; there were enough ships to transport almost 10,000 troops to the Carolina shore. In the first week of the new year, McClellan, still weak from the fever, gave his blessing. Burnside's orders were signed and he was appointed commander of the Department of North Carolina. On January 6, one hundred vessels of all types struggled out of each other's way as the flotilla clumsily hugged the Chesapeake coast on its way to Fortress Monroe. In the darkness of Saturday, January 11, Burnside's armada left the safety of Monroe in heavy seas and headed south out into the open ocean. With them they carried the Union's rising star, the general who survived West Point by a handful of demerits.

On this same Saturday, Elisha Rhodes was dutifully making his way back to Washington. He spent Sunday with his regiment, delivering messages from loved ones and regaling his friends with stories of home. While Elisha held court in camp, President Lincoln did likewise at the White House.

Lincoln was determined to get the Army of the Potomac moving and had assembled several members of his cabinet as well as Generals McDowell and Franklin. McDowell basked in the light of the moment, asserting himself as a true military mind. A hush fell over the group as General George Brinton McClellan, still suffering the lingering effects of typhoid, suddenly appeared. He wrote to his wife that his surprise appearance had the effect of a "shell in a powder magazine" and that all present looked "ashamed." The President closed the meeting and asked everyone, including McClellan, to return the following day for further discussions.[3]

Up to this point, McClellan had failed to befriend Lincoln's cabinet, but on Monday, January 13, he totally alienated himself from it. When they challenged him to divulge his plan for a spring offensive, some hinted that perhaps he didn't even have one. The general was furious and coolly told the president that yes, he had a plan, but he felt some cabinet members were incapable of grasping it. He then took his contempt a step further, stating that some in the room couldn't be trusted with such sensitive information. McClellan's relationship with Lincoln's cabinet died in that moment but the general still had the desperate president's support. About noon of the same day, Burnside's fleet crossed the bar near Roanoke Island, North Carolina.

****

On Tuesday, Washington was blanketed with snow which melted as soon as it hit the ground, creating more of what the capital already had too much of—mud. A gloomy Elisha went back to work at General Keyes' headquarters. By the weekend, news of a Northern victory at a place called Logan's Crossroads in Kentucky cheered the men of the Army of the Potomac.

****

As the first month of 1862 came to a close, Lincoln and Davis moved their chess pieces. Davis ordered Beauregard to the growing crisis in the west, leaving Joe Johnston in command of the Confederate Army in Virginia. Burnside massed his transports and cargo of ten thousand men on the waters inside Cape Hatteras.

****

On the 30th of January, a strange machine made of iron waddled out of New York Harbor for a shakedown cruise, disproving skeptics who believed the U.S.S. *Monitor* would not float. A bored Elisha Rhodes had boats on his mind too. There was so much water and mud in the streets of Washington that he amused himself by thinking of opening a steamboat line as a business. His disenchantment with Washington and an eagerness to fight grew with each passing day. "If I was owner of this town I would sell it very cheap,"[4] he joked to his friends. Lincoln, also in a foul mood, closed the month by issuing Special Order #1 and there was no question as for whom it was directed; seize Manassas on or before Washington's Birthday was the message to McClellan.

Burnside wasn't the only bulldog in Lincoln's kennel of generals. Ulysses Simpson Grant gained national attention as February 1862 began. His military background prior to the war had been lackluster, even by Burnside's low standards. He struggled at West Point but fought in the Mexican War with some distinction. After the war, he served in the west where his career fell apart. Rumored to be an alcoholic he was finally threatened with a court marshall for negligent service and resigned. He returned to civilian life and failed miserably in several business ventures, but then saw Lincoln's call for volunteers as a shot at redemption. Offering his services to Illinois, the former captain was appointed brigadier general. On February 2, he began his campaign on the Tennessee River. As Grant began amphibious operations, McClellan watched with growing interest.

Within two days, Grant had landed his troops on the banks of the river near Ft. Henry. Forty-eight hours later, 3,000 Confederates evacuated the fort, fleeing eastward to Ft. Donelson, leaving only a token artillery force at Ft. Henry which three U.S. Navy ironclads and two gunboats quickly battered into submission. Within three hours Grant seized Ft. Henry and delivered a crucial, if under appreciated, victory to the North. Fort Henry was the first step in providing the Union navy with unmolested passage on the rivers that served as the South's life blood. The Army of the Potomac remained mired in the Washington mud.

Ulysses Grant was just getting warmed up—the day after Ft. Henry fell he gazed through his binoculars at Ft. Donelson from the Cumberland River. With a gunboat fleet bearing down on Ft. Donelson and a defeat the day before at Bowling Green, Kentucky, Davis rushed Confederate reinforcements to the fort. Burnside's troops began landing on Roanoke Island and suddenly the Confederacy was reeling in the South and West. Worse still, many Southern volunteers were going home. Jackson moved south in the Shenandoah as Union troops reoccupied Romney. Hope appeared to be fading fast for Jefferson Davis and his young nation.

Then nature played its hand against both sides. The worst rainy season in two decades swamped Washington and northern Virginia—it rained for the next two months.

****

On February 8, at Roanoke Island, North Carolina, Burnside's 7,500 men trapped 2,000 Confederates and captured nearly all of them. Burnside now had a solid base of operations to conduct war on the North Carolina mainland. Lincoln was thrilled but his attention was focused on his son, Willie, who had suddenly taken ill.

As if competing with Grant, Burnside charged ahead, capturing Elizabeth City and spreading fortifications along the North Carolina coast. On February 14th, news of Burnside's thrilling victories reached Washington—Elisha and the 2nd Rhode Island felt pride for their former brigadier general. On the same day, the U.S. Navy sent to Ft. Donelson, four ironclads and two gunboats which opened up on the fort with a fury. Insisting on the surrender of the 15,000 Confederate troops holed up inside the fort, he demanded, "No terms except unconditional and immediate surrender can be accepted. I propose to move immediately upon your works."[5] Grant was now a national hero and promoted to major general. Four days later, Grant set his sights on Nashville, the capital of Tennessee. The state's leaders immediately moved the seat of government south to Memphis. Grant's trophies included 13,300 prisoners, 20,000 stands of small arms, 60 pieces of artillery, tons of ammunition, thousands of livestock, wagons, and stockpiles of commissary and quartermaster's stores. The real prize was the opening of the Cumberland River which allowed free passage of Union gunboats and transports as well as the breaking of the South's line of defense.

****

As good as this news was, morale continued to suffer in the ranks of the Army of the Potomac. Aside from a snowstorm that Israel wrote about on the 15th, the weather took a brief turn for the better and McClellan ordered that his men be allowed to go sightseeing in the capital. His generous attempt to boost the men's spirits failed when Willie Lincoln died on February 20, at age twelve. The entire city went into mourning—the President was devastated by the loss.

Elisha left the dreary city for his regimental camp to celebrate Washington's birthday. The sky cleared and the afternoon was filled with festivities—sack races, bonfires and gun salutes. Rhode Island clam chowder flowed. Israel was thrilled to receive a box from home containing snacks and articles, including socks he had forgotten to pack before his departure from Pawtuxet. But a sadness hung over the day in spite of the celebration. Lincoln's ultimatum to McClellan, General Order #1, came and went—Jefferson Davis was officially sworn in as president of the Confederate States of America.

The mild weather on Washington's birthday gave hope to the men in McClellan's army that perhaps they'd at last be moving. Then, two days later, Washington was lashed by the worst storm of the season. The sheer force of the wind shattered a window in Keyes' office. The general dryly joked that at last there was fresh air in the building.

On the same day, Israel Sheldon got his first taste of warfare. At one p.m., Randolph's Battery received marching orders. Within half an hour, Israel had the battery loaded with provisions and was ready to roll. They moved seven miles in the direction of the enemy and stopped at the top of a hill. "After waiting about an hour or so without seeing the enemy, [we] started for camp again, being called out on a false alarm."[6] As it turned out, there had been a brief but deadly skirmish between the picket lines, leaving one Union soldier dead and two more wounded. Israel recalled, "On our way back an officer overtook us and requested the captain (George Randolph) to send two pieces back in order to attack a house on the other side in the morning. I came back in charge of the remainder."[7]

Israel Sheldon was in the war.

As the month of February ended, Union troops swept into Nashville—Captain Randolph went to Washington in search of fresh horses—Lincoln pleaded with McClellan to get moving, and Davis warned Johnston to be ready to retreat.

March began with yet another snowstorm covering the Army of the Potomac. Israel received a letter from his sister, Mary, on the 2nd which included a copy of a letter his mother had received from James in Thomasville, Georgia. Israel wrote back to his sister as there was little else to do. "It snowed nearly all day,"[8] he wrote. Between the weather, a sick general, and a grief-stricken president, it appeared the army wouldn't be going anywhere soon. Lincoln issued the second and third of his General Orders. The second ordered that Washington remain adequately defended regardless of whatever George McClellan's plans were. The third order relieved McClellan as general-in-chief, leaving him in command of only the Army of the Potomac. Both orders exacerbated the already poisoned relationship between president and general.

But President Davis had his own set of philosophical and military problems—he summoned Robert E. Lee to serve as his advisor. As the war's duration stretched from weeks into months, the young nation would be forced to compromise states' rights, the very heart of its existence.

In the North, the ranks were filled, and factories and mills cranked out everything from coats to cannons. Many Southerners wrongly assumed that the schools and industries in the North were closed as were their own. More importantly, President Davis faced a crisis in troop strength and could see his resources being tapped out daily. Belying its opposition to a strong central government, Richmond became just that. In the spring of 1862, congress approved a plan to bring all able bodied young men between 18 and 35 into the army. The Confederate military draft would begin in April.

Although resented by many, the Conscription Act was effective in an unexpected way. Young men facing the looming prospect of being drafted might as well volunteer and receive the fifty dollar enlistment bonus—the equivalent of four months' salary. Thousands of men throughout the South joined the army in March. The term of service was three years or the duration of the war.

Governor Brown called on the men of Georgia to enlist rather than be conscripted. But many men in south Georgia were not so eager to rush to arms. In spite of the Federal Navy's blockade of Southern ports, the young war still seemed distant from Thomasville as newspapers brought word of events at foreign sounding places such as Manassas and Ball's Bluff. From Georgia, the war in the east appeared to be going well for the South. The Confederacy's recognition by England and France appeared imminent, certain to bring Lincoln to the bargaining table.

Cicero Holt Young was one of Thomasville's most popular figures. At 38, he had found success in Montezuma, Georgia, operating a warehouse and a hotel. In Thomasville, he was the proprietor of Young's Tavern, an eating and drinking establishment that was often the hub of the town's social and political activities. While Cicero poured beer and whiskey, Annie, his wife of eight years, served diners; the talk was almost always about the war. Cicero Young argued his case for forming a local militia of Thomasville men, filling his audience with patriotic sentiment and dreams of glory on the battlefield. Among these patrons were 21-year-old James Rhodes Sheldon and his young friend, John T. Chastain.

Chastain's father was one of the early settlers of the wilderness that became southern Georgia. He befriended local Native Americans and once peacefully settled a dispute over a stolen horse with them. After agreeing to drop all charges against the admitted thieves, Chastain and his small party were ambushed by this tribe as they returned to Thomasville with their rescued horses. Two of John Chastain's comrades were murdered but he escaped with only the loss of a finger. An irate mob demanding the lynching of the Native Americans greeted him when he finally returned to town. But Chastain insisted that justice must prevail and the crime was reported to the governor. The governor demanded the appearance of the tribe at Tallahassee where John Chastain identified five of the band who had attacked his party. Of the five men put on trial, one died in captivity and another escaped. The three others were hanged in Thomasville; the first death penalty ever carried out in Thomas County.

John Chastain, Sr. was a carpenter by trade and built some of the first houses in Thomasville. Later in life, he and his wife moved about nine miles north, where he farmed until his death in 1851—John T. Chastain was 10 years old.

After attending the Thomasville schools, young John took a course at the Fletcher Institute and learned to set type in the office of *The Southern Enterprise*, a regional newspaper. There, at the tender age of 13, he inked the type to print the first newspaper issued in Thomas County, T*he Thomasville Watchman*.[9]

****

Cicero Young suddenly found himself as the organizer of the "Rangers"[10] and the men elected him to be their captain. The Thomasville volunteers agreed to meet at the new courthouse on Tuesday, March 4, where they lined up on the building's steps to answer Governor Brown's call. Peter McGlashan, the saddle maker with a Scottish accent was elected to be Young's lieutenant.

The population of Thomasville was 2,500 in 1862. Thomasville and the surrounding county had organized companies throughout 1861, and by March 4, 1862, able-bodied young men were in short supply, but the "Rangers" still drew 103 volunteers. Any Thomasville man who had not volunteered faced the scorn of his fellow citizens. The ladies of the town stopped going to church to avoid speaking to these men; some even went so far as to mockingly talk about forming their own town militia to protect these cowards should Thomasville be invaded. For the most part, patriotism held sway over the population and throughout the South, men signing up for battles and bonuses was a familiar scene.

Israel Sheldon was given time off during the first week of March and he made the most of it. He wrote letters to his family and visited friends in Alexandria. He took a steamboat to Washington where he visited the camp of the 2nd Rhode Island and his old Pawtuxet friend Elisha Rhodes. Israel returned to Camp Lyon by horseback and feeling homesick wrote a letter to his sister, Rebecca. On the 10th, Israel's friend Lt. Pardon Jastram went into Washington and returned with the exciting news that the Army of the Potomac was moving and that the "roads were full of troops." [11] It was fine weather for a campaign, thought Lt. Sheldon.

General McClellan no longer impressed Lincoln, but he still inspired the men of the Army of the Potomac. An officer in Randolph's Battery said of the general, "At a report of a skirmish along the lines the 'Young Napoleon' would go dashing through the streets followed by a most brilliant staff, the observed of all observers. Mac was certainly a handsome and striking officer in those days and we felt that he would surely lead to victory." [12]

****

Six days after James Sheldon's Thomas County "Rangers" were formed, the Army of the Potomac finally starting moving south, stirring patriotism in all who witnessed this grand procession. Elisha was relieved of his duties at Keyes' headquarters and returned to the 2nd Rhode Island to learn that he had been promoted to sergeant major. On the morning of the 10th, the big day had come and with overstuffed knapsacks, the men of the 2nd retraced their steps of the previous July. No one knew for certain where they were going, but all were eager to fight. Rumors spread through the ranks as the men marched; Johnston was retreating to Richmond, the Union had won a big victory at some place called Pea Ridge, and, the strangest rumor of all noted that some new type of warship was tearing up the United States Navy off Fortress Monroe.

The 2nd Rhode Island marched about eight miles into Virginia and once again the weather set them back. Elisha wrote, "We are having a hard time sleeping out of doors. Last night it rained, and we suffered much from the wet and cold." [13] It was during this expedition that Private George Wilcox was killed after tampering with a live shell he had found along the march. But the rainy weather was as contentious as the Confederates and within days the regiment was back in Washington, cooking rations and gearing up for another attempt to get into the war. On the 11th, Israel's battery left Washington and marched to Manassas where it was designated as part of the reserve, much to the disappointment of the men. Preparing to abandon his base at Manassas, General Johnston burned his supplies which included a million pounds of bacon, creating a terrific spectacle. Three days later, the battery received orders to march again—this time for Alexandria.

****

In southern Georgia, nine more companies of volunteers were being raised in Thomasville's neighboring counties. On March 17, these companies began converging on the little town of Guyton near the Ogeechee River, 200 miles northeast of Thomasville and 25 miles from Savannah. The Atlantic & Gulf Railroad connected Thomasville to Savannah and the "Rangers" rode the train to Camp Davis. Four days after arriving in his first camp, 1st Lieutenant McCall wrote a letter to his father, saying, "I think we'll be stationed at the Alapaha Bridge on the Gulf road after we drill here for a few weeks. We have not had anything to do yet." In a letter to his sister, McCall wrote, "I did not tell you about our trip down here, we had a fine trip, there was about six thousand men a part of the way, in Valdosta there was some speaking and then some young ladies sang songs for us that beat anything I ever heard about." Camp Davis was a paradise providing, "[a] plentiful growth of oak and pine with the prospect of an abundant supply of wood and water. Convenient to the whole is an open field large enough for 5,000 men to drill on." The place was teeming with men; nearly a whole division of volunteers. The companies were grouped together forming the regiments of the 47th, 48th, 49th, 51st and 54th Georgia Infantries.[14]

But some of the men were worried that their families' spring plantings would fail as a result of their absence. Washington Waters (of the 50th's "Satilla Rangers" Company A), was one of these men and he risked serious punishment when he deserted his regiment, walked home and planted a crop for his family. His labor finished, he then hiked all the way back and rejoined his regiment.

****

For soldiers like schoolmates James and Elisha, the day began at five a.m. in the summer and six a.m. in the winter, when they were awakened by reveille. After roll call, the men ate breakfast and prepared for their first of as many as five drill sessions. During these drills the men learned to shoot rifles or whatever weapons had been assigned to them; maneuvers featuring line drill were equally important. Drill sessions lasted about two hours and no one ever enjoyed them. One soldier described his days, saying, "The first thing in the morning is drill. Then drill, then drill again. Then drill, drill, a little more drill. Then drill, and lastly drill."[15]

When not drilling, the men, in various details, gathered wood, collected water, cleaned their camp, built trenches, roads and latrines, and most importantly, took care of their weapons. Guns were broken down, cleaned, put together and cleaned again. The most anticipated part of the soldier's day was meal time. Early in the war, rations were mandated as at least 20 ounces of fresh or salt beef, or 12 ounces of salt pork, more than a pound of flour, and beans. Vinegar, sugar and salt were also issued. The most sought after commodity by the men of both armies was coffee, and when it wasn't available, they created substitutes from peanuts, potatoes, peas, and chicory. Soldiers with cash could visit the sutler to purchase such luxuries as tobacco, sweets, and newspapers from home. The sutler's prices were always high and the quality of his goods often suspect.

The chief nemesis of men in camp was boredom. Most men spent their free time writing letters and playing a variety of games, many of which were invented in camp. A game called Base featuring a round bat and ball was the newest craze. Boxing matches were also a popular pastime while some men preferred tamer pursuits such as card games. Some sought darker forms of entertainment and cockfighting, gambling and alcohol abuse were rampant in many regiments. Regiments encamped in and around cities suffered from outbreaks of venereal disease. Fortunately for the men of the 2nd Rhode Island and 50th Georgia, these problems were rare, but they still found camp life difficult, having never been so far and so long away from their homes. Due to a shortage of rifles many of the men of the 50th spent their days doing "most nothing but lying about camp, we have not drilled much yet and have not had any guard [duty] on account of bad health."[16]

On the morning of March 17, James Sheldon arrived at camp in Georgia and Israel's battery received orders to break camp and march to the wharf at Alexandria. "Our teams stuck in the mud and several barrels of pork and other things were left by the road side. We never saw those supplies again, although we sought them in tears. We had a most interesting time wallowing through the mud but we finally arrived and loaded ourselves upon the boats."[17] The battery was put on the barge *St. Nicholas* and the horses were put on three different vessels. By the time Randolph's Battery was ready to embark, it was late in the evening and many of the men were sleeping on the wharf. Israel relaxed, quietly entertaining himself with a letter from home. The next morning, the fleet, described by Israel as "consisting of about 30 crafts of different kinds set sail about 11 A.M."[18] The fleet ran aground later that evening having barely left Alexandria. General McClellan, following Burnside's lead, asked the navy to garner the services of just about anything that could float and then persuaded Lincoln to approve the largest amphibious campaign in history. It included 113 steamers, 188 schooners and 88 barges prepared to carry over 150,000 men and their equipment, 44 batteries of artillery, over a thousand wagons and 15,000 animals to Fortress Monroe. Lincoln was relieved to see the Army of the Potomac finally moving. But General Order #2, which required McClellan to maintain an adequate defense of Washington, was about to rear its ugly head. The 2nd Rhode Island watched as thousands of troops marched out of Washington while they packed their gear and anxiously awaited orders.

Randolph's Battery was still having problems getting moving. Two days after being grounded they were once again heading down the Chesapeake only to run into a severe gale which forced their damaged vessel to seek safe harbor. They wouldn't move again for several days. Out of boredom, Captain Randolph, Israel and other officers went ashore and bought some chickens, eggs and butter for their meals. By March 23, Captain Randolph took the matter of his crippled boat into his own hands. Putting military diplomacy aside, he took some of his men, carrying weapons, to two nearby tug boats and pressed the captains into providing a tow for his stranded battery. By nine o'clock the next morning his men were disembarking at Fortress Monroe. Israel caught a glimpse of the celebrated Monitor. Randolph's Battery then marched five miles north to the town of Hampton, still smoldering in ruins after being evacuated by the Confederates, and set up camp nearby. Richmond was only 75 miles away.

On the 21st, Elisha Rhodes celebrated his twentieth birthday. His enthusiasm for military life was never higher and he wrote in his journal, "Sleeping on the ground is fun, and a bed of pine boughs better than one of feathers."[19] As Elisha enjoyed his day at Camp Brightwood, hundreds of miles south, the Thomas County "Rangers" waited in line to be examined by Confederate doctors. Two days later, a Sunday, Peter McGlashan, Cicero Young, John Chastain, Francis Kearse, James Sheldon, and a six-foot-two-and-a-half 16-year-old, "Gussie" Brack, were mustered into the military service of the Confederate States of America.

Stripped of its individualism, the Thomas County "Rangers" was simply dubbed Company E. A soldier wrote to his father, "We have not had anything to do yet. We have got our tents and cooking utensils [and] we get plenty to eat such as bacon, coffee, flour and corn meal. We are living as fine as you ever saw."[20] The 50th Georgia Infantry was born.

Peter McGlashan
(Thomas County Historical Society)

While regimental elections were being held that afternoon, William Manning, 45, was commissioned colonel of the new regiment. A father of six and former justice of the peace of Coffee County, he and his wife, Virginia, were living near Valdosta when the war began. From 1846 to 1852, he had served as the colonel of the 58th Regiment of the Georgia Militia.

Manning was born into a military family in 1817, and by 1862, owned hundreds of acres and scores of slaves in Coffee and Lowndes Counties. Although he suffered from chronic hepatitis, he had served six years as a colonel in the Georgia militia and felt compelled to offer his services to the Confederacy.

While not a native Georgian, 25-year-old Francis Kearse was as dynamic as he was charismatic and was elected lieutenant colonel. Cicero Young remained captain of the "Rangers" and Peter McGlashan would serve as his 1st lieutenant.

The men of the 50th were given little time to become acclimated to army life. Unlike the spring of a year earlier, the two armies would no longer be sizing each other up; they would instead be throwing haymakers. Burnside was spreading his web through North Carolina and Grant was tearing up the Confederacy's major rivers. Savannah was likely to be a tempting target for the North and it would be the duty of the men in Guyton to defend it. Lincoln was looking for an early knockout in Richmond and the first battle of ironclad warships frightened the world's navies. The Army of the Potomac was invading Virginia while the worst rainy season in twenty years pummeled everyone and everything stayed perpetually damp. Sickness permeated the camps, North and South. Over 100 men of the 50th (a tenth of its roster), would die or be discharged due to disease before the regiment left Georgia soil.

Private James Sheldon was among the thousands that fell ill with measles, pneumonia, diphtheria or other illnesses contracted in the camps outside of Savannah. Hospitals overflowed and scores of private homes in Savannah became makeshift hospitals. Among these was the home of Hiram Roberts, at 228 W. Liberty St. The 56-year-old Roberts, a successful lawyer, also served on the board of directors of the Atlantic & Gulf Railroad. He shared his home with his wife, Mary, and their nine children. Their oldest daughter, Louisa, was 20 years old and as a member of St. John's Church, did her part in caring for the sick soldiers.

During the week of March 17, *The Augusta Constitutionalist* described the plight of Savannah's overflowing hospitals:

> "Among the several beneficent institutions established in Savannah for the relief and care of sick and wounded soldiers, this charitable enterprise commends itself with peculiar force to the liberal and patriotic. Foreseeing the necessity

for enlarged facilities for the care of the sick, Hiram Roberts, Esq., tendered the use of his elegant private residence, as a free hospital, and through the liberality of a few citizens of that city, a fund was raised to set the enterprise on foot. As the doors are open alike to any of the troops stationed at that city, who may require medical aid, it is but just that other citizens of Savannah should have the privilege of contributing to its support...the Hospital is under the immediate supervision and care of the ladies of St. John's Church...These ladies daily detail two of their number for Hospital duty, who give their personal attention to the sick soldiers; and are their nurses."[21]

James' brother-in-law, Edward Remington, with extensive business dealings in Savannah, knew Roberts.

Hiram Roberts

On Sunday, March 23, eight months after the fight at Manassas, the remains of Colonel Slocum and Major Ballou were delivered in a solemn ceremony to the 2nd Rhode Island. Elisha promised himself that the 2nd would carry their revenge to the enemy. As the Rhode Islanders mourned their fallen officers there was fighting in the Shenandoah Valley. After marching a total of 35 miles in two days and ending up in Kernstown, "Stonewall" Jackson's Army of the Valley was worn out. He decided to go into bivoac, but after learning that four Union regiments were in the area, reversed this order and poised his men for battle. But Jackson's information was incomplete. It was true that four Union regiments were in place as reported but what he didn't know was that the main Union force was still in the area and able to reach the field. Jackson threw his 4,000 troops into action around one p.m. Sunday afternoon and by mid-afternoon had nearly 10,000 angry Union troops to contend with. He was forced to withdraw—even in defeat, Jackson won the day—Lincoln and his cabinet were convinced that the great "Stonewall" would never have attacked with inferior numbers and had held back his main force, hoping to trap the Union force should it counterattack. Washington was in greater danger than previously believed and McClellan would have to do without McDowell's Corps, held back to protect Washington, as he had counted on. Lincoln's General Order #2 came into play.

Three days later, at four in the morning, the 2nd Rhode Island and Sergeant Elisha Rhodes got the call they had been waiting for. Colonel Frank Wheaton marched the 2nd down to the Alexandria wharf to board the steamer *John Brooks*. The days spent in camp in Washington would soon fade into memory. The ship was crowded and the men joked that it was "decidedly inferior to a first-class hotel," [22] but at least they were finally on the move. Their departure was much like the one they'd experienced when they left Narragansett Bay almost a year earlier. The weather was warm, flags flapped in the wind and patriotic music wafted in the sea air. The flagship, *Daniel Webster*, carrying General Keyes, could be seen leading the fleet toward the open waters of the Chesapeake. Early the following morning, Friday the 28th, the men of the 2nd caught a glimpse of the *Monitor* as the *John Brooks* arrived at Fortress Monroe without fanfare. The business of war was at hand.

With Jackson in the Valley and McClellan on the York/James Peninsula both presidents panicked. While Lincoln feared for the survival of the capital, McClellan's grand amphibious campaign forced Davis to call Joe Johnston out of northern Virginia to bolster the 15,000-man force at Yorktown.

From the moment McClellan's ships left Alexandria, the fate of the Confederacy was left in the hands of General John Magruder. From the dashing Sprague of Rhode Island to the quietly elegant Lee of Virginia, the war was ripe with colorful characters. But there was no one so flamboyant and audacious as the general who thought himself a prince. In his early fifties, Magruder had already enjoyed a successful military career. He served in the Seminole and Mexican Wars where he won two brevets. During the 1850s, he was awarded one of the most coveted of commands, Ft. Adams in Newport, Rhode Island.

Magruder loved Newport with its breathtaking vistas and social life. He became the darling of the city's elite, and entertained guests regularly at the fort. His lavish dinners provided an opportunity to indulge in his true passion, the stage. The soldier/thespian never missed an opportunity to perform and enjoyed being called "Prince John" by his friends. But he thought his name still lacked that certain something which would be more fitting for an actor, and by the time of the Civil War, he had reinvented himself as John "Bankhead" Magruder.[23]

Magruder resigned his commission in the United States Army when Ft. Sumter was attacked. He offered his services to the Confederacy and was assigned to the York/James Peninsula assuming nothing much would happen there. On June 10, 1861, Magruder got into a skirmish with Union troops out of Fortress Monroe, near Big Bethel Church, just outside of Hampton. The Union troops withdrew and Magruder convinced himself that he had won the first land battle of the war. It was five weeks before the Union Army would cross the stream at Bull Run.

Now, at the end of March 1862, Magruder's 15,000 troops were dug in along the Warwick River near Yorktown waiting for McClellan's 100,000 man force to approach. From a military standpoint his situation was dire, but from a theatrical standpoint he had the audience of his dreams. The stage was set and "Prince John" was about to give the performance of his life.

****

Colonel Frank Wheaton and his 2nd Rhode Island Infantry left Fortress Monroe as quickly as they had arrived. Early in the morning they struck the Yorktown Road, marching for three miles before setting up camp between Hampton and Newport News Point. Sergeant Rhodes knew that Randolph's Battery was camped nearby and that his Pawtuxet friend, 2nd Lt. Israel Sheldon, was there. But Elisha, tired and with no supper available, decided to become acclimated to his new camp instead of visiting. The 2nd went into bivouac under a spring sky at Camp W. F. Smith. The following morning brought heavy rain as tents and commissary stores arrived. The spirit of the regiment was high and Elisha enjoyed his new settings, feasting on steak and sweet potatoes. John Magruder and the Confederates were a mere 15 miles north on the Warwick River at Yorktown.

****

On April Fool's Day, McClellan left Washington to join his command on the peninsula. He was in a foul mood. The day before, Lincoln had assigned one of the divisions originally earmarked for McClellan's campaign to the mountains of north and western Virginia—the loss of these ten thousand men was only the beginning of the general's woes. Two days later, discovering that McClellan had left fewer than 20,000 troops to defend Washington, Lincoln countermanded McDowell's orders to march overland to Richmond to meet McClellan. Lincoln and McClellan were furious with each other. The president saw Washington defended by clerks and otherwise non-battle tested soldiers and felt betrayed by McClellan. McClellan, on the other hand, felt Lincoln had broken his commitment of 150,000 troops to the Peninsula Campaign. Facing 15,000 Confederates,

McClellan would have to make the most of his 100,000 troops, and irritating him further was Lincoln's order that the Army of the Potomac was to move forward "at once."[24]

On the 3rd, while writing a letter to Alma, Israel watched as McClellan set up his headquarters in the same field as Randolph's Battery. The battery marched through the night to Bethel where it bivouacked about suppertime on the 4th. First Lieutenant John McCall of James Sheldon's 50th Georgia also wrote a letter that day, telling his father about life at Camp Davis. "We have a right smart of sickness in camps though the boys are all mending and I think the worst is over." Eager to get into the fight he continued, "We have to leave here tomorrow between seven and ten o'clock for Goldsboro, North Carolina. We have built very good log houses to leave the sick though there is but few of our men that is sick enough to leave [behind]."[25]

****

Meanwhile, "Prince John's" opening act began with theatrical flourish and the Warwick River was his stage. Magruder stretched out his few artillery pieces for miles along the river; ordering them to keep up a sporadic and random fire aimed mostly at nothing. He ordered regimental bands to play throughout the night creating the sonic illusion of arriving reinforcements. By day, he had the same regiments and brigades march in and out of the woods along the Warwick's banks, flags fluttering in the spring air and bayonets gleaming. Magruder's men joked that they were tired from marching to nowhere.

Suspicious of Washington, McClellan sought the services of a private investigator to determine what kind of enemy he was up against. He chose a native Scotsman, Allen Pinkerton, a.k.a. E. J. Allen. Pinkerton was determined to remain gainfully employed by the general and if McClellan was wary of Magruder's numbers, his detective would feed his fears. Between Pinkerton's opportunism and Magruder's theatrics, McClellan was beside himself with anxiety. Making his situation worse,

McClellan was faced with the realization that his maps were wrong. The Warwick River at Yorktown did not run parallel with the York and James Rivers as he had thought, but ran east to west, nearly bisecting the peninsula and creating the need to ford it before taking the town. Before the first week of April was out, Magruder's demonstration had convinced McClellan that he was facing a force of perhaps 100,000 men. Lincoln urged him to attack at once and the general wrote his wife, Ellen, saying he was tempted to tell the president to come do it himself.

McClellan, the general, drew upon his skills as an engineer and announced his plans for a siege of Yorktown. In keeping with Little Mac's grand style this would be no run-of-the-mill siege operation. McClellan spent the following weeks organizing an unprecedented array of firepower, including two 200-pounder Parrott guns, weighing nearly 16,000 pounds each, twelve 100-pounders, scores of lighter Parrotts and siege guns, along with several 10-ton mortars whose ordnance weighed an astounding 220 pounds. With each salvo McClellan could land nearly four tons of iron on Magruder's men across the Warwick River. Yet, as these pieces came on line McClellan waited, desiring the full effect of all his guns. And as he waited, Confederate reinforcements of Joe Johnston poured into Yorktown. Sergeant-Major Rhodes heard sporadic firing along the river.

On the 5th, Randolph's Battery arrived at the Warwick River—at four p.m. and 2nd Lt. Israel Sheldon saw serious action for the first time. Ordered to relieve another battery Israel recalled, "I was sent to the rear in charge of the caissons. In about one-half hour, one of my drivers came with the report that two horses on duty were killed. We continued firing until dark, then retired. We lost seven horses but not a man was injured. Soon the firing commenced and Captain [Randolph] sent for one of the caissons. I went with it and stayed until the firing ceased."[26] Elisha heard the firing, not knowing it was the work of his old Pawtuxet neighbor.

The next few days were lazy for Randolph's Battery. Except for the random shell fired at them from an equally bored enemy not much happened. The men wrote letters and tended to camp chores. A terrific rainstorm once again drenched the Peninsula, and the battery struggled to stay dry and warm. On the 11th some of Magruder's starving men crossed the river in an attempt to rustle some of the battery's cattle, but were quickly fired upon, forcing them back to the northern side.

****

War news was everywhere. At Pittsburgh Landing, Tennessee, Grant was fiercely attacked by one of the Confederacy's best and brightest generals, Albert Sidney Johnston, on April 7. The battle went poorly for Grant who was late arriving from upriver, but Johnston was killed and the Confederate command fell to Pierre Beauregard. The following day the Confederate attack fell apart and was repulsed with great loss. What promised to be a great victory for the South turned into a draw as total casualties approached 25,000. Beauregard retreated south to Corinth, Mississippi, giving Grant cause to claim victory. The news stunned both armies at Yorktown, Virginia.

At Camp Davis, Georgia, James Sheldon and the men of the 50th continued to wait. One soldier wrote, "I don't know how long we will stay here or where we will go, I think now that we will stay here long—this is a very pretty and healthy looking place."[27] But in spite of the aesthetic appearance of their environment, measles, diphtheria and pneumonia continued to sweep through the camp. Said Lt. John McCall, "I have no good news to write you. There is a good deal of sickness in camp. I reckon you have heard of the death of Mr. Alderman, Daniel Alderman's brother. He died on Sunday last about one o'clock and William Studstill is very low. I don't think he can live more than three hours longer, the rest is getting along very well."[28] William Alderman, 38, died of diphtheria, and Studstill, 19, died ten days later. The war grew closer to the 50th Georgia when Ft. Pulaski on the Savannah coastline surrendered. On April 9, Lincoln telegraphed McClellan in a desperate tone pleading, "You must act!"[29]

By mid-April, Magruder's troops had swelled to 30,000 with McClellan still holding a better than three to one advantage. Magruder could not believe that McClellan hadn't simply overrun him. As their numbers increased, the Confederates' confidence grew and sometimes bordered on brashness. Pickets of the 2nd Rhode Island couldn't ignore the badgering of their enemy counterparts across the Warwick, who one day hooted and flashed canteens and knapsacks that carried the lettering "2nd RI" on them—souvenirs of the Battle of Manassas. As antagonistic as this encounter was, fraternization with the enemy across the river became more and more common. Pickets became familiar with their opposition and newspapers, coffee and tobacco were often traded. Men sometimes made miniature rafts for just such a purpose and some pickets took turns sharing a favorite swimming hole. Officers soon went to work to put an end to such pleasantries.

Governor William Sprague visited Israel's camp on the 13th.

On the 16th, the first of the Confederacy's conscription acts became law, calling into service all white males between the ages of 18 and 35. Within two years, these ages would be expanded from 17 to 50. On the same day, McClellan sent four companies of Vermonters across the Warwick near the Confederate center to probe Magruder's strength in the area. The "Green Mountain Boys" waded across the water, seizing an abandoned fort before being driven back with great loss. Lieutenant Sheldon's battery had kept up a steady fire in support of the Vermonters and Magruder's artillerists responded in kind—with three shots passing very close to Israel's head.

To McClellan's great relief, Lincoln finally released McDowell's Corps from northern Virginia on April 18 and sent it marching to make a junction with McClellan outside of Richmond. Jackson's whereabouts were still uncertain, but Lincoln saw his window of opportunity beginning to open in Virginia. In New Orleans, David Farragut's fleet began bombarding the forts on the approaches to the city with nearly 3,000 projectiles. Seeing that his intensive fire had failed to deliver extensive damage to the enemy batteries, Farragut decided to run the forts and sailed past under a torrential fire into the city, opening the way for Ben Butler to capture it. Lincoln was jubilant.

At Camp Davis in Guyton, Georgia, Colonel Manning of the 50th was consumed with the organization of raw recruits. His biggest concern was the hundreds of pounds of spoiled beef sent to feed his men. Manning coyly responded to the high command that "the last mentioned beef be taken out of the barrels and smoked, and then issued as rations. We recommend that in future so far as practicable purchases be made of beef carefully put up & well cured."[30] Manning was not taking any chances and discarded the meat rather than feed it to his troops. In May he wrote in his report, "This regiment is still unable to turn out a very large number of effective men owing to the prevalence of Measles, Mumps and the effects of vaccination. Quite a large number too who have had Measles - Pneumonia, Rheumatism and other diseases incident to camp and new regiments are yet invalids and unfit for duty."[31]

The Union firing along the Warwick intensified nightly; so much so that Sergeant Major Rhodes had trouble sleeping. On the 23rd, Rhodes got his first taste of action on the peninsula. While on picket duty some members of the 2nd got into a firefight and the enemy drove them into their camp. Hearing the firing, the 2nd sprung into action. Rhodes was delighted, saying, "We never get lonesome now, for something exciting is going on all the time."[32] Israel and Captain George Randolph spent the rainy day ill; the lieutenant with an eye infection and the captain with a fever. President Davis spent an anxious day, having received word that McDowell was on the move.

As April closed, the men of the Army of the Potomac were cheered by news of victories at New Orleans and Ft. Macon, North Carolina. McClellan's siege operations were in full swing and the magnificent cannonade reminded Elisha of the 4th of July. Union artillery pounded Magruder's men mercilessly and as May dawned, McClellan launched into his main event. His 13-

inch mortars were finally in place and with a deafening roar, he began the final dismantling of Magruder's Army of the Peninsula. Strangely, Magruder's artillery replied with a fury. For weeks, the Southern men had suffered untold hardships while living in cold, water-filled trenches fighting off leeches, mosquitoes and ticks. Sickness and hunger permeated the ranks. Magruder issued strict orders prohibiting fires which would provide tempting targets for Union gunners. While under almost incessant artillery fire, many a Confederate soldier wondered where his own artillery was. But in the early hours of May 4, these dispirited men were heartened to hear that their batteries were giving the enemy a taste of iron. The scene was a pyrotechnic marvel. Israel remarked that there was "heavy firing from the Rebels all day and night,"[33] but few on either side realized the Confederates were actually firing their ammunition to avoid letting it fall into enemy hands. The evacuation of Yorktown had begun.

At dawn, the Army of the Potomac gazed across the river to see nothing but empty smoking ruins left behind by Magruder. "News this morning is that our flag flies over the enemy's breastworks,"[34] Israel Sheldon wrote. Randolph's Battery packed a day's rations and marched through Yorktown, setting up camp three miles west of town. McClellan's army crossed the Warwick River finding only the debris left behind by a hastily departed host. Mounds of spent oyster shells and a curious number of sardine cans littered the trenches. The Confederates left anything they couldn't carry—tents were slashed and food stores were doused in turpentine or other toxic fluids.

After weeks of inactivity McClellan suddenly ordered his army forward to Williamsburg. McClellan telegraphed Lincoln, "The success is brilliant."[35]

He pushed the Army of the Potomac forward as Magruder's Army of the Peninsula fell back along the Yorktown and Lee's Mill Roads toward the defenses of Williamsburg ten miles to the northwest. Except for rear guard action featuring some of Magruder's cavalry near the "half-way house," [36] known as such for being the midpoint between the two towns, the road appeared open to McClellan's pursuers. The general chose not to join in the chase personally and instead decided to oversee the arrival at Yorktown of one of McDowell's divisions, commanded by William Franklin.

It had rained all the previous night, turning the roads into rivers of mud and overflowing swamps. The 2nd Rhode Island Infantry and Randolph's Battery were leading elements in the mud-race. The battery repeatedly sought solid ground to fire upon the retreating enemy. Israel Sheldon learned first hand of the depth and difficulty of the mud. Another lieutenant in his battery wrote, "In the approach to Williamsburg, Lieutenant I. R. Sheldon attempted to take a battery wagon and caisson. The mud in the road seemed to be deep and he pulled obliquely into a wheat field to obtain better footing. He led on through the field three hundred yards perhaps, the horses sinking deeper at every step until they went down the length of their legs. He had them unharnessed and led forward until he found the remainder of the battery on the campus of William and Mary. Captain Randolph was not pleased and ordered Lieutenant John Bucklyn to go early in the morning for the carriages. Taking two pair of horses from the left section and part of the cannoneers of the left he looked for the carriages, finding them in a field east of the road. Finding it impossible to obtain standing ground for the horses in the field, two picket ropes were tied together and the horses were placed on the road 400 feet from the carriages. At first trial the horses took the carriages out of the slough and almost into the road. The sticky clay mud where the horses were pulling was not less than one foot in depth."[37] This was not the war Israel had envisioned back home in Pawtuxet.

By late afternoon the 2nd Rhode Island found themselves in front of an imposing earthen fort about a mile in front of Williamsburg. Another Union regiment made the mistake of closing within range of the fort's guns and got pinned down under their pounding. Elisha could see the Confederate gunners moving about their batteries and the men of 2nd Rhode Island began pouring a fire of their own into Ft. Magruder. The 2nd's decisive action took the Confederate gunners' focus away from the trapped Union regiment long enough for it to move to a safer position.

Colonel Wheaton ordered his regiment to cease fire and from dusk until about midnight it withstood a battering from Ft. Magruder's guns. Lying in the cold mud for hours without returning a single round deflated the morale of the men but concealed their position. All around them a battle was being waged with terrific loss of life on both sides; this was perhaps the longest night of the war for the men of the 2nd. Although Israel's cannons arrived too late to take part in the battle, the bulk of the 1st Rhode Island Light Artillery had positioned itself directly in front of the fort and seriously damaged the interior, inflicting untold casualties. By dawn, Ft. Magruder was a shambles, a mere remnant of a mighty stronghold. Elisha could hear the rattle and clank of Magruder's wagon and artillery train pushing itself off through the Virginia mud—heading north once again. As the sun began to cast its first rays on the scene Elisha and a friend, Major Nelson Viall of Providence, could no longer suffer their bed of mud. Seeing no activity inside the fort the two young soldiers crawled on their stomachs to reach one of its embrasures.

Inside the fort the scene was ghastly. Dead men and horses, broken equipment and burning supplies littered the fort. Elisha and Viall stood in stony silence, but the solemn moment was abruptly broken as the 10th Massachusetts charged into the fort.

Remnants of Fort Magruder (today)
(to the right of this site is the swimming pool of a hotel)

It was war at its most horrible, yet absurd, as the Union soldiers looked around the fort and assumed it had been captured by two young men from Rhode Island. When McClellan's forces occupied the town on May 6, Magruder fell back through Williamsburg and beyond, but the Union victory at Williamsburg had been costly with 456 dead, 1410 wounded, and 373 men missing. Retreating in great haste, Magruder's reports were inconclusive. He claimed 288 killed and 975 wounded, but he left many of his severely wounded either on the field or in Williamsburg without taking an accurate account. For the next six days Confederate wounded busied the already overburdened Union surgeons. McClellan's men buried 800 Confederate corpses.

Randolph's Battery did not arrive at Ft. Magruder in time to get into the fight but witnessed the carnage as the men marched to Williamsburg the next day. "I saw hundreds of dead and wounded lying around," [38] Israel wrote. Another officer in the Israel's battery recalled, "The slaughter in front of the forts of Williamsburg was fearful. The road and fields ran with blood.

The enemy knew the range and from his well constructed works sent his shot with telling effect. Not until towards night did his fire slacken or courage seem to waver."[39]

The scene in the town on the morning of May 6 was chaotic. "Everything told of a hurried flight, many wounded left in the houses, guns abandoned by the way and camp equipage abandoned told the story. The inhabitants seemed to think it most unaccountable that Yankees should drive Virginia troops. They said we had not whipped their friends but occupied only what they had abandoned."[40]

The men of the Army of the Potomac were eager to push on to Richmond believing they had the momentum and the enemy was on the run. But McClellan insisted on waiting until his army reunited and supplies arrived before resuming the pursuit. An aggressive new figure appeared on the scene out west, Philip Sheridan, and his presence cast doubt upon McClellan's leadership. "[General] Sheridan would have borrowed supplies from the enemy and done it quickly," wrote a man in Randolph's Battery.[41]

It was a fateful decision by McClellan. Indeed, the Army of the Potomac had inched closer to Richmond but Magruder's Army of the Peninsula had escaped. Worse still for McClellan, Johnston and his army merged with Magruder's. An officer in Randolph's Battery told of the lost opportunity. "We waited here some days and learned too late that the wagon train of the enemy was but a few miles from us parked in a lot where the mud was so deep that teams could not be moved. Prisoners some days later told us that they expected to lose all their wagons and some of their guns."[42] Joe Johnston, only slightly more competent than Magruder, took command of all Confederate forces on the peninsula and began reporting directly to President Davis.

The Army of the Potomac's brief stay in Williamsburg gave Israel Sheldon a lesson in human nature. "The [William & Mary] college building was used as a hospital and filled with sick and wounded, friend and foe. On our first entrance the people were much afraid and were very polite. They soon learned that we would not disturb them and became loud and disagreeable."[43]

But the big question still remained for President Lincoln. Where was Jackson? More than an annoyance, he was an outright danger and a very real threat to the Union government's survival. It was becoming clear that the Jackson problem would have to be solved before the bulk of McDowell's Corps could be released to McClellan.

The answer came on May 8, when Jackson's 10,000 man "foot cavalry"[44] was spotted just west of the Shenandoah Valley near a mountain town ironically named McDowell. Union General John Fremont's 6,000 troops felt relatively secure at McDowell, but before the day was out these men were badly cut up and fleeing for western Virginia. Jackson gave hot pursuit before returning to the Valley. The Valley Campaign had begun—to this day it is argued as perhaps the most ingenious in the history of warfare.

Jackson moved north.

With Johnston making a fighting retreat to Richmond, Norfolk and its navy yard were left defenseless and on the day after the Battle of McDowell, it was evacuated and burned by the Confederacy. The famous C.S.S. *Virginia (Merrimac)* was blown up in an explosion that was heard for miles. It seemed that the fates of Richmond and Washington were changing almost hourly, creating the possibility of both capitals falling to their enemies.

President Lincoln toured the southern Peninsula, pleased by what he saw, while Davis wrote an impassioned letter to his top general. Johnston had felt mistreated and overlooked by Davis after Ft. Sumter, but now the future of the nation devolved on him. Acutely aware of Johnston's feelings, the president chose his words carefully, saying, "I have been much relieved by the successes you have gained, and I hope for you the brilliant result which the drooping cause of our country now so imperatively claims."[45] This plea almost echoes Lincoln's urgings to McClellan of only weeks earlier.

With both armies now constantly on the march, the relative comforts of camp life dissolved into memory and by mid-month, Sergeant Major Rhodes was no longer dining on steak and sweet potatoes. The men of the 2nd had to forage or go hungry. Basic staples such as salt or bread were scarce or non-existent. Rhodes wrote that he was "most starved."[46] On May 15, Randolph's Battery marched all day in the rain to Cumberland Landing, about one mile south of White House Landing. Along the march, Israel received a letter from his sister, Mary, with the latest news from Pawtuxet. McClellan set up his base of operations at White House Landing, a Lee family place inherited from George Washington. The plantation stood where the Pamunkey flows into the York River, a mere 24 miles from Richmond. Nearby were the camps of the 2nd Rhode Island Infantry and Randolph's Battery. The sight of the general on his magnificent horse, Daniel Webster, cheered the weary army.

Not to be outdone by the army, the United States Navy attempted to sail up the James River into Richmond. The absence of the C.S.S. *Virginia* appeared to make this a feasible battle plan until the fleet, which featured the famous *Monitor* and McClellan's experimental ironclad flagship *Galena*, hit the shallow waters beneath Drewry's Bluff and the guns of Ft. Darling, manned by the crews of the scuttled *Jamestown*, the *Patrick Henry* and the destroyed C.S.S. *Virginia*. The Confederates had scuttled the *Jamestown* and several other old vessels beneath the bluff and dumped various forms of debris there for just such an occasion. The Union Navy had made two critical miscalculations: the steepness of the bluff itself and the shallowness of the water beneath it. The *Galena's* guns could not be elevated enough to put up fire on the fort and the *Monitor* risked running aground and being captured. After taking a brutal beating, the *Galena* limped away and the impotent *Monitor* followed suit. A contemptuous Confederate gunner yelled at the retreating ironclad, "Tell the captain that is not the way to Richmond!"[47]

McClellan continued his march and within days was only nine miles from the capital. McDowell was making progress as well and by the 17th, had reached the Rappahannock River near Fredericksburg. Lincoln now ordered him to march to meet McClellan and form a consolidated front. McClellan wanted McDowell sent via Fortress Monroe, but Lincoln saw McDowell's Corps as a means of keeping Jackson in check as it slithered south to Richmond. McClellan now realized he would have to swing his army to the north to meet McDowell. As McDowell moved south, Jackson's fleet-footed Army of the Valley raced north, and the Union force fell back in fear. Once again Lincoln worried about Washington's safety, but this time he was determined to do something about it.

On May 20, Elisha was at Gaines's Mill, a family-owned establishment where he found some cornmeal to panfry Rhode Island Johnnycakes. He also talked with some of the locals, getting their obvious bias on the war, but also learning that they were surprised the Northern soldiers were not destroying their property. Israel's battery moved three miles ahead to the Chickahominy River, firing on Rebel positions as they waited for the Army of the Potomac to catch up. A brief and much needed rest followed for the Rhode Islanders.

Two weeks after his victory at McDowell, Jackson suddenly appeared again, this time farther north than anyone could have expected. With 16,000 men, Stonewall routed a small force of 800 Union men who were keeping the way open for General Nathaniel Banks' army which was making its way back to Washington. Banks' 8,000 men found themselves on the wrong side of Jackson, who, knowing Banks was moving north, hoped to cut him off at Winchester, opening the way to Washington.

On the evening of May 23rd, the 2nd Rhode Island came under artillery fire near a place called Ellison's Mill. As Union batteries were rushed into position and began returning fire, a Confederate projectile landed only a few feet from Sgt. Major Rhodes who froze in fear. He later confessed, "I thought my time had come."[48] After a few seconds, he sighed with great relief discovering it was not a shell but solid shot. The enemy ceased firing and dispersed; the 2nd pushed on.

The next day the men of the 2nd Rhode Island spent some time tearing up the Richmond & Fredericksburg Railroad line, twisting and bending track. Crossing the Chickahominy River, some of the men climbed a hill and saw Richmond in the distance. Gunfire could be heard and hours later, as they marched into the run-down Richmond suburb of Mechanicsville, the Rhode Island men couldn't get over how much the buildings had been shot up. The prize was now in their midst and from a hilltop, Elisha could see the steeples of Richmond churches. In the outskirts of Richmond they found an unexpected treat. "Strawberries and peas are ripe, and we get a few occasionally," Elisha happily wrote in his diary.[49]

With the capture of Richmond close at hand but Washington still in jeopardy, Lincoln lost all patience with McClellan. He was irate because Jackson's Army of the Valley seemed to operate without any concern about the Union Army. The President once again called McDowell's Corps, or at least 20,000 men of it, away from Richmond, telling McDowell, "Your objective will be to capture the forces of Jackson and Ewell."[50] This fueled McClellan's feelings of betrayal by the White House.

Sunday, the 25th, found Jackson once again failing to observe the Sabbath as his army smashed into the retreating Federals near Winchester. General Banks put up a valiant fight but ultimately was no match for Jackson's razor-sharp Army of the Valley. Jackson suffered 68 killed, 243 wounded, and 3 missing. Banks managed to untangle his army from "Stonewall's" grasp and stumbled toward Harper's Ferry, by latitude north of Washington. Of his 8,000 men Banks counted slightly over 300 killed or wounded, but 1,700 men, nearly a quarter of his army, had either deserted or fallen into Jackson's hands along with many of his wagon trains and supplies.

Once again, Jackson disappeared into the Valley. Panic stricken, Lincoln wired McClellan, "I think the time is near when you must either attack Richmond or give up the job and come to the defense of Washington." Meanwhile, Secretary of War Stanton called on the states to send any and all available men to come to the defense of Washington. Realizing he was stuck with McClellan, Lincoln appealed to his general in a more conciliatory tone the next day, asking, "Can you get near enough to throw shells into the city?"[51]

4

WHY NOT?

At the stroke of midnight on May 25, the telegraph in the office of Rhode Island Governor William Sprague clicked off two simple sentences: "INTELLIGENCE FROM VARIOUS QUARTERS, LEAVES NO DOUBT THAT THE ENEMY, IN GREAT FORCE IS ADVANCING ON WASHINGTON. YOU WILL PLEASE ORGANIZE AND FORWARD IMMEDIATELY ALL THE MILITIA AND VOLUNTEER FORCE IN YOUR STATE."[1]

This plea came from Secretary of War Stanton. Before the young governor could grasp the seriousness of the situation, a second message was received from Stanton squelching any debate over the direness of Washington's plight: "SEND ALL THE TROOPS FORWARD THAT YOU CAN IMMEDIATELY. BANKS IS COMPLETELY ROUTED."[2]

As he had a year earlier, Sprague acted without hesitation and within an hour issued the following order: "Citizens of the State capable of bearing arms will at once report themselves to the nearest military organization. The commandants of the chartered and volunteer military companies will at once organize their companies and the men so reporting, into companies of eighty-three men, rank and file, and report to their headquarters, where they will be armed, equipped and moved under the direction of the Commander-in-Chief, to Washington, to protect the National Capital from the advance of the rebels, who are now rapidly approaching."[3]

Once again, Rhode Island responded. Sprague was in a fighting mood and he made it clear that nothing would stand between his two new regiments and Washington, saying, "Rhode Island troops will move through Baltimore, and if their progress is impeded by the rebel mob of that city, they will mete out to it the punishment it has long merited."[4] In that spirit, the 9th and 10th Rhode Island Infantry Regiments were born.

On May 26 Rebecca Sheldon watched the third of her four sons march off to the war. George Frederick Sheldon, 20 years old, made the same six-mile trek to Providence as brother Israel and neighbor Elisha had done before him. The alacrity in which the new regiments were organized, equipped and deployed was mind-boggling, even in light of the White House's desperate call. This was due partially to good timing and a stroke of luck. Only two days before, when Sprague called for troops, a group of volunteers offered their services to the state to meet any emergency that should arise. They dubbed themselves "The First Regiment Rhode Island National Guards."[5] In command of this regiment of 736 men was Captain Zenas Bliss of the United States Army. Bliss wasted no time preparing his men for active service and all companies of the regiment were ordered to report to their respective armories by nine a.m. on the 26th. At two p.m., the volunteers convened on Exchange Place in Providence for assignment. By seven p.m. that evening, less than 24 hours after Stanton's telegraph, the regiment was outfitted and ready to march. Assisting Bliss was the immensely popular Providence native, Lt. Colonel James Shaw, Jr. The 32-year-old Shaw was the favorite to lead the regiment, but he deferred to the experienced Bliss. The regiment's designation officially became the 10th Rhode Island Infantry. George Sheldon was now Private Sheldon, Company H, commanded by Captain Christopher Duckworth of Pawtucket.

"We left Providence on the 27th, at 5:20 p.m., and were received everywhere on the route with great enthusiasm," a member of the 10th wrote.[6] The men boarded a steamer at Groton, Connecticut, that evening but first had to withstand a heavy downpour while waiting on the wharf for two hours. At last aboard, they were soaked, hungry, and anticipating their government rations. When they left Rhode Island, the men of the 10th were stocked with fresh sandwiches and sponge cakes, and assumed Lincoln would provide similar fare. It was not to be. A soldier on the boat remembered being issued, "A greasy mass, which might be meat or bone."[7] Out of sight of the officers, the men discreetly fed the fish.

Arriving at Philadelphia the men of the 10th were greeted with a feast and their haversacks were filled by the Cooper Volunteer Relief Association. Later, the 10th passed through Baltimore filled with apprehension. For the first time ammunition was distributed and the reality of killing fellow Americans was ever present. But aside from occasional jeering, the trek through Baltimore passed without incident.

The march to Washington was oppressively hot. One soldier stored a few fresh eggs in his haversack and was surprised and delighted to find them "handsomely baked"[8] when he rested on the outskirts of the capital. Another soldier recalled, "Arriving at Washington at six o'clock p.m. of the 29th, we were quartered for the night in the barracks near the depot, and the next day marched to Tennallytown, about six miles northwest of the city. As we passed along Pennsylvania Avenue, by the White House, the regiment was received with loud plaudits. Lt. Colonel Shaw was in command."[9] One member of the 10th recalled that the regiment was "much disappointed in the general appearance of the city."[10]

A two-hour march took George and his comrades to the outskirts of a small village south of Washington. The scene was almost comical. In Governor Sprague's haste to answer Secretary of War Stanton's call, no one had thought about tents. One soldier recalled that the 10th's arrival at their first camp was filled with rain as well as lightning and that few of these men had ever set up a camp. Most had never pitched a tent or even stood under one. But during the night, tents arrived and things changed for the better. The soldier wrote, "The morning dawned, and the sun, as if to welcome us, touched up the wall of our canvas city with golden hues, while the birds, never happier, warbled their morning songs from the tree tops above us."[11]

The 10th Rhode Island encamped at Tennallytown on a gentle slope dotted with beautiful oaks. They christened "Camp Frieze"[12] in honor of their state's quartermaster general. George and the other men were mustered into the service of the United States for a term of three months. As they stood in the open air taking their oaths, more than one soldier wondered if it rained like this all the time in Virginia.

Camp Frieze was laid out in rows of tents, and the spaces between them were named for streets in Providence, such as "Atwood" and "Benefit." A typical day consisted of: reveille 4:30, police call and breakfast 6:30, sick call 7:00, adjutants call 8:45, guard mounting 9:00, orderly call noon, lunch 1:00, supper 6:30, form under arms sunset, tattoo 9:00, and taps at 9:30. The men enjoyed their new surroundings, complained little, and for the most part they liked their officers. They even found a secluded place to bathe. The two gripes they did have, regarding uniforms and rations, were legitimate. No one's uniform fit properly and pants were too long, too short, too tight, or falling down.

The food situation was even worse. A soldier described one evening meal "Four bones, gross weight 2 ½ pounds, and some meat, gross weight the same minus the two." The most common ration was salted meat, usually pork. The men joked about their pork intake and many a conversation was sprinkled with oinks and squeals. "They gave us rations of salt meat and pork which would almost motion to us when to come to dinner,"[13] a soldier joked. Of course there was hardtack, a rock-hard biscuit made of flour and water. The general opinion of this staple of army life was that it was "notoriously poor eating,"[14] and the men made a pact that anyone receiving food from home would share it equally with his friends.

General Burnside paid Camp Frieze a visit in early June and buoyed the regiment's spirit. An order allowing the men to go sightseeing in Washington boosted morale. Companies routinely patrolled the Virginia countryside searching for enemy supplies. While searching a barn, a small Confederate field howitzer about two feet in length was found and taken back to camp. (Today the cannon is on display at the Rhode Island Historical Society Museum in Providence.)

****

As May ended, so did Davis' patience with Joe Johnston. As Lincoln had doubted McClellan weeks before, Davis now wondered if Johnston had a plan at all.

Lincoln and his cabinet realized they had been swept into Jackson's net. "Stonewall" was obviously racing to Richmond having kept Banks and Fremont at bay. Lincoln telegraphed an order to McDowell to catch Jackson, saying, "[this is] for you a question of legs. Put in all the speed you can."[15] Johnston believed that McDowell's intention was to join up with McClellan north of Richmond. In Johnston's mind, McClellan was now forced to leave one of his five corps on the south side of the Chickahominy, delaying his final assault on Richmond. As the rains fell on Private George Sheldon at Tenallytown, Joe Johnston saw his moment. The Army of the Potomac was temporarily divided. The Confederate general watched McClellan's movements closely during the closing days of May. "We must get ready for this," he confided to his staff. Johnston decided to attack.[16]

Elisha and the 2nd Rhode Island spent the last days of the month near Atlee's Station inspecting the damage Union cavalry had incurred upon the Rebel railroad tracks a few days earlier. Finding the enemy had repaired the tracks, the Rhode Islanders decided upon another scheme. They greeted the next train with a blast of artillery, getting the attention of all aboard, who were sent fleeing for the woods. Elisha and the other men promptly loaded the empty train with explosives and blew it up. The next morning, they were chased back to their camp at Four Corners, Virginia, by angry Confederates who were fleeing from a bigger fight four miles away.

James Sheldon and his fellow Georgians were growing stronger with each passing day. The illnesses that had ripped through Camp Davis seemed to have left the men in a hearty physical state. Lt. McCall wrote to his sister on May 29, saying, "I am now in better health than I ever was in my life before and hope this will find you enjoying the same blessing." Regarding the 50th's activity, he explained "[We are] about six or eight miles from camp. Right up the river cutting a live oak to blockade the river. There is 100 men here at work to our regiment, we are getting the river pretty well blockaded though it will take some time yet to get it completed." [17]

On May 30, 2nd Lt. Israel Sheldon made a simple entry into his diary, writing, "Heavy thunder storms lasting 8 hours." [18]

The Battle of Seven Pines, or Fair Oaks, was supposed to begin early on the morning of Saturday, May 31. The Union corps isolated on the Richmond side of the Chickahominy was of Elisha's former boss, General Erasmus Keyes. As the waters rose, so did Johnston's optimism for a quick decisive blow. The initial stage of the attack was entrusted to General James Longstreet and of the nearly 52,000 Confederate troops available for duty at Seven Pines, two-thirds would be under his command. The remaining third would guard against the rest of McClellan's army across the river should it attempt a counterstroke against Richmond. At least that was the plan. Longstreet was hearing impaired. To compensate, he sometimes appeared detached when in group conversation and gave curt replies after being spoken to at length. Before the Battle of Seven Pines, he was given his orders verbally.

There were three main roads heading east out of Richmond; the Nine Mile, the Williamsburg and the Charles City. The Nine Mile and Williamsburg converged near the Union position by a train station called Fair Oaks near Seven Pines, named for a stand of trees that served as a landmark. The orders of the day were simple. General Daniel Harvey Hill, Jackson's brother-in-law, would send three of his brigades down the Williamsburg Road as Longstreet marched to converge with him at Fair Oaks.

Since Longstreet was already encamped on the Nine Mile Road, little organization was required. He only needed to get there on time. But by mid-morning, Longstreet was causing a traffic jam, blocking Hill's advance on the Williamsburg road. Four divisions were to converge on the enemy along three roads per Johnston's plan, but with three of the four now bogged down on the same road, the element of an early surprise attack was lost. Hill's attack finally began at one o'clock in the afternoon.

The result was a murderous mud-wrestle—man, beast, and machines were swallowed in the ankle to waist deep mud. One Confederate colonel was swallowed up whole by the mud while leading his men across an innocent looking puddle. The confusion of the day continued into the next, and both sides fought with valor in spite of the elements.

The 2nd Rhode Island was held out of the fight, but Elisha witnessed the suffering of his comrades. Israel Sheldon and his battery were pushed forward, watching as "the enemy attacked [Union general] Casey's Division and after struggling entirely repulsed them (the enemy) 9 times. The loss was heavy on both sides. The enemy occupying the ground at Casey's Camp. Our battery [was] behind the breastwork ready to receive the enemy should they make their appearance out of the woods... [We] loaded our pieces and were ready to receive them but they did not come. McClellan made his appearance where we were at the breastwork."[19]

General Joe Johnston had been avoiding President Davis who had come in from Richmond to observe the situation. The general had positioned himself not far from Fair Oaks Station, exposed to Union artillery fire. Having been wounded in previous wars, he made light of his endangerment to the younger officers around him, when suddenly he was struck in the right shoulder by a minie ball as a shell exploded a few feet away, knocking him from his mount. Regaining consciousness minutes later, he inquired as to the whereabouts of his prized sword and pistols that his father had carried in the Revolution. Although his prized possessions were recovered, Johnston had lost command of the Confederate Army in Virginia. His recovery would take six months.

The battle was a draw. Forty-thousand men of each side opposed the other, and each lost five to six thousand. When the carnage ended, neither army had gained ground. But Johnston was gone and for the first time McClellan was challenged by his "children."[20] When McClellan declared, "I will be with you in this battle and share the dangers with you!" even the ever-loyal Sgt. Major Rhodes asked sarcastically, "Why not?"[21]

****

Davis turned to his military advisor and aide, Robert Edward Lee, to save Richmond. Accepting the position, Lee officially designated his command the Army of Northern Virginia, leaving no mystery as to where he intended to fight. The news, that "Old Granny"[22] Lee, as many disparaged him, had taken command disappointed the average Confederate foot soldier. But Lee had something going for him which other Southern generals did not. He knew and understood both McClellan and Lincoln. He knew Lincoln would want a swift decisive close to the campaign while McClellan would instead be cautious.

****

On June 2, 1862, while "Stonewall" Jackson and his foot cavalry were slithering south out of the Shenandoah Valley, Lee was getting his feet wet, both literally and figuratively. George Brinton McClellan could hear the church bells of Richmond—victory was within his grasp. Private James Rhodes Sheldon celebrated his 22nd birthday at Camp Davis in Guyton, Georgia.

The 2nd Rhode Island was left in a dreadful position after Seven Pines. Even though the 2nd had been held out of the battle, much of the regiment was sick. Mosquitoes and ticks were a nuisance and the constant dampness fomented malaria that would revisit many of these men decades after the war ended. Food was scarce and enemy artillery fire was incessant—Elisha wrote that the shells sounded like "steam whistles." [23] The stench of unburied dead in fields and swamps, decomposing in the humidity, permeated everything. The Rhode Island men were without tents, and blankets and uniforms stayed perpetually damp. It was Elisha's first anniversary as a soldier, and the memory of sailing out of sparkling Narragansett Bay amid the throngs of well-wishers had long faded. He sat in the heavy rain as the Chickahominy River once again blew its banks. "May God help us," he wrote. [24]

****

By the end of the first week of June, Ulysses Grant had claimed Memphis and set his sights on the biggest prize of all, Vicksburg. Paralleling Grant's move south was Jackson's stealthy movement as he pushed his small army of 13,000 barefoot and hungry men toward Port Republic. Lincoln was determined to keep the elusive Jackson from joining Lee at Richmond and ordered the armies of Fremont, Shields and McDowell, a total of 50,000 men, to capture or destroy Jackson. On June 8, they spotted Jackson's army resting on the west bank of the south fork of the Shenandoah River near Cross Keys. Jackson was distracted by the death of his most trusted officer, Turner Ashby—killed in a rearguard action at Harrisonburg on June 6. He stated that he never knew a "superior"[25] officer to Ashby and took this loss very hard.

Ashby had done his duty faithfully, and Fremont reached the North River Bridge only to find it in smoldering ruins. Unable to link up with Shields on the opposite bank of the Shenandoah River, Fremont could only watch with horror as Shields forces were taken apart by Jackson.

Lincoln's pursuit of Jackson ended in disaster forcing the President to call his broken armies back to Washington. As Jackson's army began making its way to Richmond, General McDowell was ordered not to reinforce McClellan after all, but instead to come to the defense of Washington. As the battles of Cross Keys and Port Republic had raged, Elisha Rhodes, outside of Richmond, watched the Army of the Potomac's observation balloon drift into the skies, as if taking with it any remaining hope for McClellan's Peninsula Campaign.

On June 12, another Confederate found a way to use McClellan's paranoia as an advantage. James Ewell Brown Stuart, barely into his thirties, was ordered to explore McClellan's strength along the Chickahominy. Finding little resistance and shocking Union camps with his sudden intrusions, he started taking prisoners and capturing their stores and supplies. With no official order to do so, ""Jeb""[26] Stuart took 1,000 of his cavalrymen for a stunning 150-mile ride around McClellan's army and immediately became the new darling of Southern newspapers. The reports of Stuart raising havoc, coupled with uncertainty of Jackson's whereabouts, had McClellan beside himself with worry. Three days after Stuart began his ride, his band of cavaliers returned to Richmond, leaving both Lincoln and McClellan completely unnerved.

****

The next day, 2nd Lt. Israel Sheldon's battery moved closer to the front and "went into position behind a light breastwork."[27] Hearing constant skirmishing throughout the day, Israel feared an attack was coming and sent his caissons to the safety of the woods in the rear. Typically a battery consisted of three sections of two cannons each—Lieutenant Sheldon commanded one section.

The morale of the 2nd Rhode Island was not good. The men were hungry—much of their gear had been sent to the relative safety of the rear. The air reeked of death. Some of the men began fraternizing with Confederates while on picket duty, making small talk and exchanging newspapers. This jungle existence brought the starving men to new depths—a year earlier, none would have considered eating frogs and snakes but many of the Rhode Island men now found them a delicacy.

Day and night, Lt. Israel Sheldon listened to increasing firing in the distance, and kept awake from the sound of the intense picket sparring, he was convinced an attack was imminent. The horses of the battery were " hitched up all night," [28] he wrote on Wednesday, June 18. For the next three days, Randolph's Battery listened and waited. Jackson's army was out of the Valley on its way to Richmond. Lee feared a siege knowing Richmond would not prevail—Lincoln asked McClellan when he would attack.

On June 20, Private George Sheldon and the 10th Rhode Island finally got word that they were at last going into action. Camp Frieze buzzed with a mixture of excitement and anxiety and it was rumored that the 10th was to be hurried to the peninsula to join McClellan in a final grand assault upon the city. The men nervously talked away the hours—but few actually spoke of the prospect of fighting. Colonel Bliss was ordered to have his men armed and ready to march at a moment's notice. But for now George Sheldon had to wait.

While the 10th waited near Washington, the 2nd Rhode Island made a dramatic move, crossing the Chickahominy River over a wooden bridge that spanned nearly a mile. This march would end near a run-down little town called Mechanicsville, closer to Richmond.

On the 23rd, it was Israel Sheldon's turn for a bit of excitement as a nasty skirmish broke out directly in front of his battery. His section fired off three rounds driving the enemy back in retreat. The following day they rested and to his delight, Israel received a handful of letters. The most important letter of all, of course, was from Alma. Mother, Rebecca, and sisters Mary and Louise, also wrote telling of daily occurrences in Pawtuxet. A fifth letter was from Private George Sheldon, 10th Rhode Island Infantry, Camp Frieze, Washington. While losing himself in thoughts of family and Pawtuxet, the sounds of battle grew in the distance—by morning a major battle was raging. "This morning had a severe fight. The 20th Indiana losing heavily. Firing kept up during the night," wrote Israel. [29]

The first of the Seven Days' Battles, Mechanicsville, had begun. The 2nd Rhode Island was right in the thick of it. On the morning of June 25, their brigade advanced toward the sound of the fight, taking them across the previous month's battlefield of Seven Pines. The scene was ghastly. Bloated, rotting corpses of the unburied dead were strewn about the field. After noon, the 2nd pressed on until Confederate artillery fire started tearing up their ranks. Elisha stated that the Rebel fire of "shell and canister came thick and fast, and several were killed and others wounded." [30] Elisha and the others immediately began digging makeshift trenches for protection, unearthing decayed human remains as they worked. These trenches flooded with water but provided some shelter from the firestorm. The Confederate barrage waned then began again. As darkness set in, the battle intensified and minie balls buzzed like bees above the trenches. Suddenly, the Confederate infantry attacked with its Rebel Yell, three times charging at the 2nd Rhode Island. But the Rhode Islanders held and at daylight they were relieved—sent to the rear where another attack was feared but didn't materialize. The 2nd Rhode Island performed brilliantly but at a cost of thirty men, killed or wounded.

As the fight at Mechanicsville raged, reveille blared through Camp Frieze, waking Private George Sheldon at two a.m. on the morning of the 26th. The 10th Rhode Island broke camp and began marching toward Washington, crossing the Potomac over the Long Bridge about ten that same morning. As George Sheldon marched in lockstep, the old wooden structure shook as the Virginia sun beat down upon the men. Reaching Fairfax Seminary, a few miles west of Alexandria, the 10th halted and made camp. By morning, Lincoln received confirmation that Jackson was in Richmond and posed no threat to Washington. For the men of the 10th there was no enemy to fight.

At Mechanicsville, Lee's battle plan had gone awry. A weary Jackson had arrived but contributed little. Only a portion of the brigades Lee had intended to use got into action. It was a clear victory for McClellan but the general didn't like seeing his army getting its nose bloodied. He decided to change his base of operations to the James River and regroup his army. But his men knew better—the Army of the Potomac had simply been on the Peninsula too long. They were starving, unsheltered and tired. "Well, the Grand Army is on the retreat,"[31] Elisha Rhodes wrote. In the first battle outside Richmond, McClellan had been victorious, but his Peninsula Campaign was essentially over.

If McClellan was finished, Lee was just getting started. Near Dr. Gaines' Mill, Lee threw 57,000 men against the corps of Fitz-John Porter. A 40 years old from New Hampshire, Porter was there to keep pressure on Richmond while the bulk of McClellan's army slipped away from the city, heading toward Harrison's Landing on the James River. But Lee, believing he understood McClellan's intentions, left Richmond undefended and struck at Porter who'd been ordered to hold until the last man if necessary.

The bulk of Porter's men were dug in on a slope behind a deep ravine containing Boatswain's Swamp—their artillery masked by the landscape. The swamp, surrounded by slippery slopes, was steaming with humidity and teeming with insects. Israel could hear heavy cannonading all day and what sounded like "severe fighting."[32] Many Confederate soldiers went into Boatswain's Swamp and saw their entire regiment torn apart. Men got lost as black smoke hung thickly in the air and hand-to-hand combat by wild-eyed men filled the swamp. Many who were there claimed that Gaines' Mill was the scariest fight they had been in to date. When it was over the Union counted 7,000 casualties compared to 9,000 Confederates killed, wounded or missing. McClellan continued moving to the James River. Israel wrote that his battery "packed up at one a.m. and started for the rear with the whole army."[33]

Lee, certain that McClellan was retreating to the James, hit him again on the 29th at Savage's Station. But once again, the Confederate attack was disorganized and Jackson failed to make a strong showing. Although Lee was stalled, McClellan insisted on continuing his march despite the protest of one of his generals. Worse, the morale of the Army of the Potomac plummeted after a field hospital at Savage's Station was abandoned. As a result, 2,500 sick and wounded soldiers fell into Confederate hands. McClellan ordered his mountains of supplies burned before his ragged army continued its retreat. Israel Sheldon's battery "kept moving about all day,"[34] while a disillusioned Sgt. Major Elisha Rhodes wrote, "no one will know how much the army has suffered. No sleep, scant food, and almost tired to death…"[35] One bright spot for Rhodes that day, was his capture of a Rebel who was carrying a beautiful Colt revolver. Elisha had it shipped home to Pawtuxet, but there was little else to feel good about.

On the last day of June, the two armies clashed again, this time at White Oak Swamp. Organizational failures plagued any chance of catching McClellan as he steadily slipped away. Lee never succeeded in launching a consolidated attack and was stymied, losing over 3,000 men. McClellan's army creaked and cranked its way to the James.

After an all-night march, the Army of the Potomac reached an elevated field not far from the James. The length of this field, known as Malvern Hill, belies its slope and McClellan the engineer loved what he saw—an artillerist's dream, a perfect killing field. After throwing away two field victories, McClellan was finally ready to fight.

McClellan inspected the formation of his artillery and was delighted—250 field pieces capable of sweeping the field in all directions—pulled back slightly behind the crest of the hill. Berdan's Sharpshooters were ready and 200-pound balls were ready to be launched from gunboats on a bend in the James River. Finally there was the field itself—a Confederate charge would have to cover the equivalent of ten football fields—under fire the moment they stepped out from the edge of the woods.

As the first regiments of the Army of Northern Virginia reached Malvern Hill, an unspoken fear gripped the men. Lee's only hope of defeating McClellan at Malvern Hill was to simply overwhelm him by sheer numbers. If successful, a massive coordinated attack would push the Army of the Potomac off Malvern Hill and drive it into the James. But everything would have to go perfectly if Lee was to succeed.

Lee and his staff were worn out, and the general wasn't feeling well. The fatigue of Jackson's Valley Campaign took its toll on "Stonewall" and it showed in his performances of the Seven Days. Longstreet and A. P. Hill had seen their divisions suffer terribly and badly needed rest. That left Generals Daniel Harvey Hill, the unspectacular Benjamin Huger, and "Prince John" Magruder to carry the fight to McClellan.

Lee met with his generals and discussed what had to be done. Who would lead? Which roads led to the battlefield? When would the attack commence? Lee surveyed the room. D.H. Hill expressed his fears that the attack would fail. His friend Longstreet needled him, saying, "Don't get scared, now that we've got him licked!"[36] Lee put the bulk of responsibility for leading the attack on Magruder and Jackson. While Jackson was not in peak form, his troops were relatively well rested. Lee didn't know that "Prince John" was not well. Stomach problems not only made him feel ill, but robbed him of sleep, and the medications his doctor had given him made him nervous and excitable. As the meeting ended, Lee gave each of them directions and names of roads and landmarks to guide them to the approach to Malvern Hill. Lee had the only available map of the area but Magruder, in his compromised condition, never looked at it. He had guides who knew the area and that was all he needed. Lee instructed that after the divisions of Magruder and Jackson were in place, a general advance would begin. Within all of this was a key element: Confederate artillery to the left and right of the army's right rear would pound away at McClellan's lines until they started to break. At that moment, General Lewis Armistead was to advance his men out of the woods "with a cheer,"[37] to signal the general advance of the infantry.

On the morning of July 1, Magruder and his division got lost on the way to Malvern Hill. Longstreet rode out to find the general and reverse his march on a road already jammed with thousands of men and hundreds of horses pulling artillery and supplies. About one p.m., the crest of Malvern Hill erupted in what was one of the greatest artillery barrages of the war.

Confederate guns were in short supply and the Union gunners had a field day destroying one Rebel battery after another. Magruder finally arrived at Malvern Hill about four o' clock. Union skirmishers, daring to leave their positions, approached the edge of the woods hoping to pick off unsuspecting targets. Confederate skirmishers rushed out of the woods pushing the enemy back. When Magruder saw Union soldiers being driven back, he assumed that he had arrived precisely at the moment of the general advance and sent his division out of the woods. Other units followed. A consolidated attack on the hill never happened, and brigades and regiments offered themselves up piecemeal to the Union guns.

D. H. Hill, seeing his men annihilated never forgave Lee. "It was not war, it was murder,"[38] he said angrily. Almost all of the Confederate casualties were from artillery, a rarity in the war, but the Confederates inflicted serious damage as well. Israel Sheldon wrote that his battery, "was ordered in to engage the enemy... [a man] was killed instantly while at his post."[39] In the evening the firing died away and men on both sides sought out their wounded or dead comrades in the darkness. It began to rain, lightly at first and then heavily. One of Jackson's staff wrote of the scene, "Night, dark and dismal, settled upon the battlefield of Malvern Hill, its thousands of dead and wounded. The rain began to fall on the cruel scene and beat out the torches of brave fellows hunting out their wounded companions in the dark. The howling of the storm, the cry of the wounded and groans of the dying, the glare of the torch upon the faces of the dead or into the shining eyes of the speechless wounded, looking up in hope of relief, the ground slippery with a mixture of mud and blood, all in the dark, hopeless, starless night; surely it was a gruesome picture of war in its most horrid shape."[40]

After the battle, Jackson ordered some of his pickets to move forward at first light to protect against a possible counterattack by McClellan. But the general confided to his staff, that the Army of the Potomac would be gone by morning and true to form, McClellan proved him right. Second Lt. Israel

Sheldon wrote, "We were ordered about 12 o'clock tonight to move very quickly which we did, as did the whole army to Harrison's Landing."[41] Sgt. Major Elisha Rhodes described the battle, saying, "O the horrors of this days work, but at last we have stopped the Rebel advance, and instead of following us they are fleeing to Richmond. Our regiment supported the Batteries of our camps and did not suffer much, but saw the whole grand fight."[42]

The morning of July 2 concealed the slope of Malvern Hill with heavy fog. As the sun began to burn away, the curtain of mist gradually rose, revealing what a Union soldier described as an "appalling spectacle…enough [Confederate soldiers] were alive and moving to give the field a singular crawling effect."[43] Some of the dead and wounded would lay in the scorching July sun for up to four days. Union losses were 3,200 and the Confederate numbers were even worse. Nearly 5,500 of Lee's men were lost at Malvern Hill. A week of continuous fighting was over and the Seven Days' Battles took with them 20,000 Confederates and 16,000 Union men killed, wounded or missing.

****

While the events of the war were swirling around Richmond, Private George Sheldon and the 10th Rhode Island remained at the ready in their camp near Fairfax Seminary. On June 30, the regiment was ordered to march to Alexandria. From Alexandria, the men were transported by ship to Washington. That evening George Sheldon and his regiment found themselves back at Tennallytown and slept in an open field without shelter or even blankets. In the morning they were given a new assignment. The regiment was divided by company and assigned to several earthen forts that ringed the downtown area for eight miles, from Chain Bridge on the Potomac to the several main roads leading into the capital. Assigned to Ft. Cameron, this would be home to George Sheldon for the next two months.

On the third of July, a Confederate battery found a bluff overlooking Harrison's Landing and seized the opportunity to add a final insult to the weary, defeated Army of the Potomac. After firing off a few rounds, Israel Sheldon said his battery was "ordered out to return their fire, after a few minutes [we] silenced their pieces."[44]

July 4th was a holiday revered by the men of both armies. Israel began the day with a letter from Alma. Later, his Battery "moved back and encamped about a mile from the landing."[45] McClellan reviewed a portion of his army, and in Washington, the 10th Rhode Island celebrated the 4th of July by raising a flag stitched by the women of Providence. Sgt. Major Rhodes had an eventful day. "As I was going to the spring I met General McClellan who said good morning pleasantly and told our party that as soon as our forts are finished we should get some rest. He took a drink of water from a canteen and lighted a cigar from one of the men's pipes. Rest is what we want now, I could sleep for a week. We expect to have something to eat before long."[46] On July 6, Israel wrote that Randolph's Battery had "been lying still in camp all day."[47] The next two days were "the warmest by far of the season," he said.[48] The Army of Northern Virginia was also battle weary and hungry. Lee met with Davis and agreed that the men needed rest. Both armies licked their wounds.

Lincoln had read enough telegraphs and sat through more cabinet briefings than he could bear. On July 8, he arrived at Harrison's Landing to see for himself what was going on with his army. Second Lt. Israel Sheldon described the event, saying, "This [evening] about 6 o'clock President Lincoln made us a call. We were ordered to the front of our Camp [and] fired a Salute of 21 guns while he and his party were passing."[49] Lincoln met with George McClellan face-to-face. For Elisha, seeing McClellan was an everyday event—he saw Lincoln too. The Army of the Potomac was loyal to its commander, but morale was at an all time low. Elisha wrote, "How I should like to see my home. We hope to get some money some day."[50]

Compared to the intensity of the Seven Days', the balance of July seemed uneventful. Boredom of camp life replaced the excitement of battle, and the men of both armies filled their days by improving their quarters, writing letters, and visiting friends. Both Elisha and Israel enjoyed the lull in the fighting and the beauty of Harrison's Landing. Israel had dinner guests on several occasions. On Sunday, July 27, Elisha was visited by some Rhode Island artillery boys, and treated himself to some new shaving gear and a good cigar. The weather was spectacular and bands played as officers inspected the troops, boosting the morale of the army as it began to rebuild its confidence.

****

On July 17, 1862, Private James Sheldon's 50th Georgia received the orders they'd been waiting for. Colonel Manning was taking his regiment to join General Lee's forces near Richmond. As part of Drayton's Brigade, James and the other men marched to downtown Savannah and boarded a train to Charleston, South Carolina, where they were delayed for twenty-four hours. Resuming their journey, the regiment spent another two days inside and on the roof of boxcars, until they reached Richmond on the 20th and immediately began building a camp.

But James' stay in Richmond was short. After a few days, the 50th was ordered to Malvern Hill, using spades to dig strong entrenchments. With the Army of the Potomac massed only ten miles south at Harrison's Landing, the Confederate force at Malvern Hill remained on constant alert. For the next several weeks, James, Peter McGlashan, John Chastain and Gussie Brack passed their days on picket duty or doing camp chores.

The organization of the Union Army was rapidly changing and on the 27th, Israel Sheldon turned over his section's guns to a New Jersey battery. The next day, he and his men marched down to the wharf where they received six new light 12-pounders.

On the next to the last day of July, McClellan was ordered to send his sick and wounded men back to Washington. The

Peninsula Campaign was officially over. As McClellan began moving his sick and wounded, Confederates made an attack on Harrison's Landing which proved more disheartening than damaging to McClellan's men. "The enemy fired a number of shells from the other side of the river all night," wrote Israel. [51] Colonel Wheaton of the 2nd Rhode Island requested a promotion for Elisha. His spirits soared.

****

The fighting of the Seven Days overshadowed another significant event. On June 26, Major General John Pope, a Kentucky native and 1842 West Point graduate, was given command of the newly formed Union Army of Virginia. An engineer by trade, Pope earned two brevets in the Mexican War showing great promise as an officer. Pope's swagger was bigger than his talent and he instantly insulted his new army.

Pope was appointed brigadier general of volunteers after the attack on Ft. Sumter—proving his potential in a campaign along the Mississippi River. He was promoted to the rank of major general and given command of the new Army of Virginia, assembling the forces under Banks, Fremont and McDowell into one command. Pope's assignment was to protect Washington and neutralize "Stonewall" Jackson's Army of the Valley. But the bombastic general immediately drew the ire of both the Army of the Potomac and Robert E. Lee when he unfavorably compared the army to his former commands in the West and threatened to pillage the bounty of Virginia. But with McClellan's Peninsula Campaign in ruins, Pope appeared to be the Union's next best hope for success in Virginia.

Lee wanted Pope's carnage stopped—Jackson wanted to drive northward, and his lightning quick troops were the South's tool to suppress Pope and end the war on northern Virginia soil. On the morning of July 31, the camp of the 2nd Rhode Island came under attack; at least that was Elisha Rhodes' initial thought when a shell burst close by. A Confederate battery had attacked the Union fleet at Harrison's Landing and a few errant rounds flew into the camps. The heavy gunboats returned fire and a hot cannonade ensued which Elisha referred to as "music."[52] The Confederate guns were silenced and the next morning, the 2nd Rhode Island thought they were joining General John Pope's march. Beginning their march at 7 a.m., Elisha and the men were issued two days' rations, but instead of marching in the direction of Washington, they headed along the James toward Richmond. The march was hot and strenuous, and there was little contact with the enemy. The purpose of this operation was to be noticed by Confederate pickets and create the diversion of an attack on Richmond, thereby freeing up Pope from Confederate attention. Twenty-seven hours after beginning the march, Elisha and the rest of his sleepless, exhausted regiment tumbled back into their camp. After getting some much-needed rest, Elisha rode down to the James River for an evening bath.

On Saturday, August 2, Pope began moving his Army of Virginia south while McClellan's Army of the Potomac was being sent by water toward Fredericksburg. McClellan was instructed to go to Washington to defend the capital. He was livid, but there was nothing he could do.

Sunday was oppressively hot and many men of the Army of the Potomac were sick. Elisha was issued six days' rations and told to be ready to march in the morning to an undisclosed destination. Israel Sheldon and Randolph's Battery received similar orders, but they were promptly countermanded. Confusion filled the ranks.

A week later, Pope had made unmolested progress to the area of Brandy Station and intended to continue on to Gordonsville where the Virginia Central and the Orange & Alexandria Railroads intersected. Lee, embittered by Pope's policy that his men would subsist on the fruits of Virginia, decided it was time for the new general to meet "Stonewall" Jackson.

Jackson was in large force just to the south of Pope's advancing army on August 9. His scouts informed him that the Union army was divided into three corps and the one led by Nathaniel Banks was in advance. Jackson had his opportunity to once again defeat a large, but isolated, part of an army. But this time, Banks got word of Jackson's presence and didn't hesitate to seize the initiative. At a place called Cedar Mountain, his corps slammed into Jackson and fought furiously, driving him back. But, in his eagerness to strike first, Banks failed to organize his attack and found himself being flanked by A. P. Hill's division. Banks fell back, losing over 2,000 men, while Confederate losses were a little over half that number. On the same day, McClellan began his march to Washington, so on the 13th Lee ordered all of the Army of Northern Virginia north to Gordonsville. The campaign that would bring the eastern war back to the Manassas battlefields had begun.

Five days later, Pope, anxious about the large numbers of Confederate troops massing before him, crossed to the north side of the Rappahannock, wishing McClellan would hurry. Skirmishing along the river intensified.

On August 16, James Sheldon and the 50th Georgia camped about six miles from Gordonsville, Virginia. William Fleming, a lieutenant in the regiment, took a few minutes to write a letter to his family back home. "I am once in sight of the mountains of this State—a spur of the Blue Ridge being over a few miles distant and in full view. Our army is swelling to a considerable size on the line of the Rapidan though if reports be true the enemy are in greatly superior force. General Jackson has issued an order to the troops to fight against any odds and be victorious at any cost. This is the ring of the right metal. If we will only carry out the order, placing a firm reliance in the God of battles, we must be victorious. There is no telling how long the terrible conflict will be postponed, but come it must and that soon. The rapid movement of troops from one point to another augurs a battle near at hand. It is thought that we will attack the enemy notwithstanding our inferiority in numbers... In my opinion the advantages are greatly in favor of the attacking party ... We left all our baggage in Richmond to be brought around in wagons so that we are here with nothing but what we could carry on our backs. I have my overcoat and a small single blanket."[53]

The men of the 50th Georgia were about to get their first taste of battle. Their anxiety grew as each day passed. Many of the men, including 16-year-old Bill Johnson and 50-year-old George Evans, sought the company of their chaplain, William Curry.

On August 14, the *Augusta Constitutionalist* reported "There are four Hospitals in the city of Savannah, viz: The Georgia, the St. Johns, the Medical College, and General Hospital or Barracks... Guyton Hospital, located at Whitesville, No. 3, Central Railroad, is now a very important point, being (together with Springfield, where a convalescent camp is located) the headquarters of the sick from every point."[54] James Sheldon of the 50th Georgia, now in good health, had stayed several weeks at Savannah under the care of volunteer nurses, including Louisa Caruthers Roberts.

During the third week of August, both Elisha and Israel passed through Williamsburg and Yorktown witnessing firsthand the condition of the towns and countless freshly dug graves. "We are moving in the wrong direction it seems to me,"[55] thought Rhodes at Yorktown. The end of the war seemed no closer than when he arrived there the previous spring. On the morning of the 20th, Israel Sheldon marched to Yorktown's wharf. Randolph's Battery boarded three schooners which sailed away from the wharf and spent the night anchored in the river. At four in the afternoon of the 23rd Israel and his battery were back in Alexandria. They promptly boarded a train headed to meet Pope's army near Manassas. The 2nd Rhode Island was ordered held at Yorktown until Friday the 29th.

On the eve of the third great campaign in Virginia, Private George Sheldon, still outside of Washington at Ft. Cameron, received new orders. The 10th Rhode Island was being relieved by two New York regiments and would be going home. George began the long march through Baltimore, Harrisburg and Easton, Pennsylvania, until finally reaching Elizabethport, New Jersey, where the regiment boarded the steamer *Bay State*. George arrived at Pawtuxet Village, Rhode Island, on August 25.

On the morning of the 28th, the 10th Rhode Island was welcomed with full military honors at a ceremony at Exchange Place in Providence. One observer noted, "No regiment ever left the State more promptly in response to the Governor's call, and no regiment hastened to the rescue of the Capital under a more solemn sense of duty."[56] Colonel Bliss had left the regiment a month earlier to take command of another regiment, and upon its return home, it was fitting that the popular James Shaw was at last its colonel.

Lieutenant Colonel James Shaw

Colonel Zenas Bliss

In his final report, Shaw told Governor William Sprague, "Of the character and conduct of the Regiment, I cannot speak in too high terms of praise. It was all that could be asked. The guard-house was almost a useless institution. We were permitted to perform but a humble part in the great struggle for all that we hold most dear, but I hope that this part was well done, and that it will meet your approval, and the approval of the citizens of our honored State."[57] The term of service for the men of the 10th Rhode Island had expired and the regiment disbanded.

On the first day of September, Israel was somewhere in northern Virginia. Brother James was not far from him but on the side of the Confederacy. In Pawtuxet, Rhode Island, Rebecca Sheldon saw one of her boys come home.

5

WHERE IS YOU? WHERE IS YOU?

As the Union army lumbered back to Manassas, the 50th Georgia and Private James Sheldon were about to emerge in Richmond. Upon their arrival, William Manning's 50th was brigaded with the 51st Georgia, the 3rd and 15th South Carolina and the Phillips Legion. The brigade was commanded by Brigadier General Thomas Drayton, a 54-year-old South Carolina plantation owner and passionate secessionist.

General Thomas Drayton

At mid-month, Drayton's Brigade, now officially part of the Army of Northern Virginia, was rushed north to join Lee and Jackson's forces near Manassas. Colonel Manning, finally getting his men to the seat of war, was falling ill due to chronic hepatitis and the command of the regiment often fell upon Lt. Colonel Frank Kearse. James Sheldon and the other men of the 50th Georgia stopped at Gordonsville and made camp. For the first two days they were without food—a miserable experience for country boys with big appetites. Rations arrived on the third day and their week-long encampment turned more pleasant. A peculiar smell filled the northern Virginia air and some of the men explained that the minty fragrance was that of pennyroyal. For many, the scent would linger in their memories for years.

On about the 20th of August, Drayton's Brigade was ordered to march in the direction of Washington with Longstreet's command—the right wing of Lee's army. The men were told to leave their haversacks in camp, indicating that they had to get somewhere in a hurry. James endured a grinding twenty-four hour march, and along the route the fragrance of pennyroyal was replaced by the stench of dead horses. With Colonel Manning at the head of the column, they marched through the beautiful countryside of Culpeper County until they reached the Rappahannock River on the 23rd. Shells from Pope's artillery fell in among the men.

A violent thunderstorm eclipsed the sound of the shelling and eventually the guns fell silent. On the morning of August 25, James was marching again, planning to join forces with Jackson who was working around Pope's right flank. That evening, the 50th camped near Warrenton where the regiment again came under artillery attack but managed to get through the night without any casualties. The brigade hit the road the next morning, marching through the town of Salem late in the day. After breaking for a quick dinner, they continued down a hill through Thoroughfare Gap, where James caught his first glimpse of General Lee on his famous horse, Traveller. The roaring sound of musketry in the distance was another first for the regiment. The 50th reached the scene of the action too late to take part in the fighting. They made camp, and slept among the bodies of dead Union soldiers.

Throughout the next day and night, Drayton's Brigade marched hard until reaching the Manassas area about eleven a.m. of the 28th. Exhausted and thirsty, James filled his canteen from a muddy puddle. Some of the men were detailed to picket duty and as darkness draped the fields north of Manassas, the men of the 50th bivouacked in a pine grove.

Randolph's Battery was also marching that day. During the morning hours, Lt. Israel Sheldon and his right section, "passed through Manassas and reached Centreville about 8 P.M." [1]

On August 28, the area north of Manassas erupted in fury. Jackson hoped to draw Pope's army out into the open—he ordered an attack on a Federal column that was marching on the Warrenton Turnpike. After fighting for several hours with neither side gaining an advantage, Pope believed that he finally had Jackson cornered. Throwing the bulk of his army against him the next day, Pope repeatedly attacked Jackson's position dug in along an unfinished railroad cut.

James Sheldon and the 50th Georgia went into battle hungry. Their rations were long gone and they had to get by on green corn and apples. The regiment spent the day covertly moving from one position to the next without coming under fire. But one officer earned the men's scorn when his loud talking gave away the regiment's position, sparking a barrage of Union shelling. An unlucky soldier was struck on the hand by a piece of shell, and required the amputation of three fingers. By nightfall, the fighting subsided and James was delighted by the delivery of hot rations and fresh bread. With no butter available, the men spread tallow over their bread as a substitute.

The 50th held this position near the front lines until the afternoon of the 29th, when it marched at the double-quick about a mile toward the sound of heavy firing. Believing he was being flanked, General Drayton halted his brigade and prepared his men for defense. The report of the flanking movement turned out to be false and the 50th spent the night on picket duty.

The day's fighting had been bloody with heavy casualties on both sides—Jackson had held. On the 30th, unaware of the presence of Longstreet Corps, Pope resumed his attacks on Jackson. Massed Confederate artillery blew back the Union 5th Corps and in a stirring moment, Longstreet's 28,000 men counterattacked. In what was the largest coordinated attack of the war, Pope's left flank was crushed. The 50th Georgia was held out of the fighting until after dark. Poised to enter the fray, with Pope in retreat, the order was rescinded. Pope's army was driven back to Centreville where it regrouped, averting a disaster. The next day, on August 31, Jeb Stuart reported the condition of Pope's army to Lee, who ordered a pursuit, hoping to turn the Union right flank.

The Battle of 2nd Manassas is as difficult to understand today as it was the day it happened. Union generals blamed one another for the failure. Some even claimed that McClellan deliberately held back to sabotage Pope's campaign. Israel Sheldon was in the thick of it, and recalled, "the battle of Bull Run commenced—we were ordered up—took a position and commenced firing. In this action we lost one man. A severe fight." [2]

Captain George Randolph's battery was quickly earning a reputation as one of the better light artillery units. The battery reported to General Hooker, near Catlett's Station, on the 27th. It was immediately ordered to move along the road to the left of the railroad toward Bristoe Station. Randolph informed Lieutenant Israel Sheldon that the enemy had been seen on the right of the railroad. But shortly after beginning their march Confederate batteries were spotted atop some prominent hills to their front and right. The captain wasted little time in getting his battery into action. Israel went to work targeting an enemy battery about 1,000 yards in his front and opened fire with solid shot from his two Napoleon guns. After firing a few rounds the enemy withdrew. After repositioning himself on a range of hills across Broad Run, he fired again. Randolph described his battery's involvement in the fighting at 2nd Manassas, saying, "I threw a few shots into his cavalry as it retired supporting the battery. After changing position to a more commanding hill, a little to the front and right, I engaged two batteries placed on the hills opposite. His fire was severe from two different points, but a well-directed fire of shell and solid shot compelled him to retire hastily." [3] Israel Sheldon's battery had fired a total of about 150 rounds, mostly of solid shot. Two of Randolph's men were killed.

Lieut. Israel R. Sheldon.

Lieutenant Israel Sheldon
(History of Battery E by George Lewis)

A disheartened Israel recalled, "About 4 pm severe fighting on our left. The enemy finally drove our troops when the whole army began a retreat about sundown." [4] A man in brother James' 50th Georgia wrote, "We could hear the enemy wagons retreating." [5]

Approximately 100,000 men fought at 2nd Manassas and the casualty numbers were mind-numbing; 1,153 Confederates were killed, 7,812 wounded and 109 reported either captured or otherwise missing. The Union numbers were nearly identical except for the staggering total of 4,263 men that had fallen into Confederate hands.

Sergeant Major Elisha Rhodes landed at Alexandria on the last day of August. He'd heard that a great battle had been fought at Manassas and General Pope's defeated army was retreating to Washington. While at Alexandria, Elisha enjoyed a day of days. He and a Pawtuxet friend managed to purchase a quart of fresh milk, a luxury in wartime Virginia. Sharing the same cup they were interrupted by Colonel Wheaton who put out his hand to "Lieutenant" Rhodes. "Well, I am proud, and I think I have a right to be,"[6] Elisha wrote in his diary.

September 1 brought with it the finale of 2nd Manassas as Jackson struck Pope's retreating army. Israel's battery was once again heavily engaged. General Phil Kearny ordered Captain Randolph to take his six guns to a knoll directly in the rear of General Birney's line. Once in position, Randolph's Battery began firing solid shot into the woods occupied by the enemy. This position immediately proved difficult as Randolph explained, "My position was such that I could not fire with much accuracy or effect for fear of injuring our own line of infantry, over which I was firing. What the effect of my firing was I am unable to say."[7]

Lieutenant Israel Sheldon described the action at Chantilly, saying, "we took our position about sunset [and] fired solid shot entirely… Our division general [Philip] Kearny was killed soon after leaving our battery. His loss is very great not only to his division but to the whole army and to the cause in which we are engaged. General [Isaac] Stevens was also killed at this battle."[8] Randolph's Battery's only casualty in this heated contest was a horse, as the Rhode Islanders fired about 100 rounds, mostly of solid shot. The captain recalled later, "I withdrew my battery after dark, and after remaining in my first position several hours marched to Fairfax Court House, where I joined the division on the morning of the 2nd."[9]

In a driving rain, the 2nd Rhode Island marched through Fairfax Court House and Germantown. Elisha Rhodes could hear the roar of artillery mixed with thunder, and the sky flashed with the powers of both man and nature. "I never in all my life ever heard such thunder or saw such lightning,"[10] he thought. The fight never quite reached the 2nd, but the night did not come without its horrors as Elisha and the other men tried to sleep with the dead and dying strewn among them. This Union defeat was the Battle of Chantilly.

As darkness brought the fight to an end, Israel Sheldon marched through the night toward the safety of Washington. The next day, Israel followed Elisha's trail, passing through Fairfax Court House where he heard that General McClellan had been put in charge of Washington's defenses. At noon, Randolph's Battery rested for about an hour before resuming its trek to Alexandria. The 2nd Rhode Island, weary and hungry, entered Washington around midnight on the 3rd. Seeing the capital filled Elisha with dismay at how futile the Union's efforts had been. Twelve hours later, Israel's battery fell back into its old camp. Confederate losses during the 2nd Manassas Campaign numbered nearly 10,000 killed, wounded or missing, while Union casualties were reported at over 16,000.

****

It was as if nothing had changed—Pope was gone and McClellan was back. Confederate forces gathered near Chantilly and optimism bloomed in Virginia. The Deep South remained imperiled but Richmond, the capital of the new nation, was secure. Washington, on the other hand, seemed a viable conquest. Lee's Army of Northern Virginia crossed the Potomac River. As the Army of the Potomac evacuated Frederick, Maryland, Jackson swept in. The Confederate Army, having escaped destruction only a month before, was now north of Washington and posing a threat to a divided Baltimore. Lee appealed to the citizenry to support his army, saying, "We know no enemies among you." [11] McClellan, cautious as always, moved his army north.

On September 9, Lee issued special order #191. In it, Jackson was sent to capture Harper's Ferry, and Longstreet's command, which included Private James Sheldon and the 50th Georgia Infantry, was sent to Hagerstown, Maryland. McClellan plodded on, receiving reports that Lee had fallen back from Frederick. Before the 10th ended, sporadic skirmishing was breaking out near Frederick and Boonsboro. While Israel Sheldon and his battery were sent near the Fairfax Seminary, Elisha and the 2nd Rhode Island encamped at Poolesville, only nine miles from the freshly emboldened Confederates.

The next day, the Confederate Army seized Hagerstown as McClellan continued his chase. Pennsylvania was in a panic and the governor put out an urgent plea for 50,000 volunteers. On the 12th McClellan was still uncertain of the Army of Northern Virginia's position. Jackson pressed on to Harper's Ferry while Union forces reoccupied Frederick.

Saturday, two Union soldiers found a few cigars wrapped around a copy of special order #191. It spelled out the complete detailed orders of Lee's Maryland campaign. McClellan was suspicious of the document and plodded on. By nightfall, Lee's scouts had informed him of the "Lost Order," [12] and the "Grey Fox" swiftly changed his game plan.

On Sunday, September 14, the left wing of the Army of the Potomac marched through the Maryland mountains to reinforce the Union's hold on Harper's Ferry. There were few passable gaps between the Elk Ridge and South Mountain, and both armies approached cautiously.

James' 50th Georgia, led by its popular lieutenant colonel, Frank Kearse, marched through the little town of Boonsboro around noon. Upon the 50th's arrival, Kearse learned of a terrible fight about six miles south at a little known pass known as Fox's Gap. James Sheldon and his "Thomas County Rangers" quick marched with the rest of the 50th in a grueling uphill demonstration.

Reaching the field of battle, the 50th Georgia was part of a hinge in a left wheel charge that would sweep the enemy in their front off the road, across the fields and down the mountain. But the wheel broke, and within minutes, scores of men had been cut down and the survivors listened as firing intensified back at the gap where Drayton, Kearse, Manning (who was briefly back in command) and Private James Sheldon were getting their first real taste of war. Drayton cooly ordered the 50th and 51st to position themselves on the Old Sharpsburg Road, while ordering the rest of the brigade into a field to the south. Things went badly immediately. On their left, Union men, concealed by wooden fences opened fire upon the 50th—900 men strong the 17th Michigan moved in behind the 50th.

William Fleming, a 27-year-old lieutenant in the 50th, described the awful scene, "We were taken at once to a point to charge a battery of the enemy. While forming in line of battle, so as to be in position to make the assault, we were exposed to a much dreadful rifle and musket fire. [We] were under the hottest fire. Our position was in a narrow road between an embankment eight feet in front as we were faced, and a stone wall on an embankment about four feet high in the rear. The embankment in front of us gradually declined on the left, until it gave us no protection at all from the balls of the enemy. It was painful to see men shot down while taking their positions." [13]

James and his regiment kept one eye on the enemy and the other on their commanding officers. This was a bad position and the Georgians knew it. Lieutenant Fleming bitterly recalled, "The enemy were posted behind a fence and trees, not over sixty or seventy yards from us, pouring their deadly volleys into us in comparative security. Some of the bolder of the enemy would come out into the road and fire down it. Our boys acted nobly, loading and firing as fast as they could; but am afraid, though, they aimed when the enemy was concealed – very few of their bullets struck a Yankee. We had been exposed to this fire about twenty minutes, when a Yankee regiment made its appearance in our rear about 80 yards distant. The command was given them to charge, and they came towards us at the charge bayonet about 20 or 30 yards when they stopped. I directed my men to fire at them, which the few that were left did, with some effect. About this time there was a general move out of the lane, and we followed... I asked Colonel Manning, who was not far from me, why we were left in such a place – that I thought we should either advance on the enemy or return. He said he could not understand it." [14]

The remaining men of Drayton's Brigade tried to come to the support of the 50th and 51st, but were beaten back under heavy fire. At about eight o' clock, under the cover of darkness, the Georgian survivors of Fox's Gap ran for their lives. The 50th suffered losses of 34 wounded, 29 dead, and 21 missing, 14 of whom were known to have been taken prisoner. As Elisha and Israel had done before him, James now also witnessed the horrors from the other side of this war.

On the 15th, Jackson captured Harper's Ferry and a grand total of 12,000 Union troops. At the same time, Lee's Army of Northern Virginia was moving away from McClellan. But news of Jackson's stunning victory swayed Lee to hold at the little town of Sharpsburg, which has a creek running near it that the locals call Antietam. Lee began forming his line along Antietam Creek and the following day, after a punishing march, Jackson arrived.

While Private James Sheldon and the 50th Georgia retreated, Lieutenant Elisha Rhodes and the 2nd Rhode Island were marching toward Sharpsburg. Lieutenant Israel Sheldon read the accounts of the recent fighting, along with letters from Alma. The three old friends from Pawtuxet were experiencing the war in their own unique ways. James retreated, Israel rested and Elisha was in hot pursuit of the enemy, nine miles from Harpers Ferry where he passed a field littered with unburied dead.

McClellan caught up with Lee on the evening of the 16th. Lee worried about his troop strength and wondered if McClellan had become more aggressive since his reinstatement. Although outnumbered at least five to three, maybe even two to one, he decided to make a stand. Private James Sheldon arrived at Sharpsburg with the 50th Georgia on the 15th. Still staggering from the beating at South Mountain, they were positioned on a bluff overlooking a stone bridge just a mile south of the town. James watched anxiously as thousands of men in blue gathered on the opposite side of the bridge. As darkness fell, sporadic gunfire stirred the quiet town. The morning promised a fight—a bad one.

Throughout the evening of the 16th McClellan had intensified his artillery barrage and the men of the 50th Georgia again suffered terribly. Artillerymen on the bluff tried to sleep beneath their batteries, seeking shelter from the pounding. Slightly after midnight, nature added to the misery as a light drizzle turned into a steady downpour. Three hours later, light skirmishing broke out.

At first light on September 17th, Union artillery opened up on the Confederates across Antietam Creek, specifically targeting men above the stone bridge. An unexploded shell landed near a South Carolina soldier who was cooking breakfast and the missile rolled directly into his campfire then exploded, mutilating his leg. He was carried to the rear—America's bloodiest day had begun. McClellan's artillery fire pounded relentlessly, and Private James Sheldon sought cover as the earth shook.

McClellan attacked Jackson just north of Sharpsburg in a forest known as the West Woods. To the south was a church of the humble Dunkard faith; this building would serve as a landmark during the battle. McClellan also attacked the center of Lee's line by crossing Middle Bridge, where he ran into Confederate regiments that were entrenched in a road sunken by decades of wagon traffic. But it was crucial that he control the stone bridge on the lower Antietam Creek and secure the high ground on its opposite bank. He assigned General Ambrose Burnside to take the bridge.

Burnside had trouble organizing his assault. Drayton's Georgians fired sporadically at the Union men gathering below them on the opposite side of the stone bridge. By late morning, the 2nd Maryland, 2nd Maine and 6th New Hampshire attempted to secure the bridge, taking a serious beating from Private James Sheldon and the other Georgians above them. The 50th Georgia, once again commanded by Lt. Colonel Frank Kearse and reduced to slightly over 200 men, was forced to spread out in a defensive position nearly one-quarter of a mile long, weakening its effectiveness.

As this was happening, 2nd Lieutenant Elisha Rhodes and the 2nd Rhode Island arrived on the battlefield. Placed in reserve, the men sought high ground where they watched the battle "almost at our feet,"[15] as Rhodes recalled later.

The men of a Connecticut regiment tried to ford the creek, only to discover it was nearly shoulder-deep. The Georgians opened fire upon them as they helplessly carried their rifles and cartridge boxes over their heads. The bridge crossing proved to be an act of suicidal futility, so Union regiments began looking for other fords to get behind Drayton's Georgians. With bayonets fixed, the 6th New Hampshire and 2nd Maryland made their assault until a scathing small arms fire poured down on them from the Confederates who held the heights. The Georgians, already low on artillery, began scrounging for anything they could load into their cannons.

Burnside was growing impatient nonetheless and he ordered 30-year-old Union Colonel Edward Ferrero to take the bridge. Ferrero, a Spaniard, owner of a New York dance school and a renowned teetotaler, prohibited alcohol use by his men. Burnside pressured him to take the bridge with his battle-seasoned 51st New York and 51st Pennsylvania. But the Pennsylvanians knew what they were facing and demanded their right to whiskey should they successfully take the bridge. Reluctantly, Ferrero gave in. The men of the 51st cheered, and although exhausted, began making their way to the bridge.

The 51st Pennsylvania and 51st New York closed in on the mouth of the bridge, climbing rail fences while under thick rifle fire from the Georgians above and across the creek. The 35th Massachusetts and 48th Pennsylvania were also ordered to begin heading for the bridge. By sheer numbers, will, and the promise of whiskey—the tide at Lower Antietam Bridge was about to turn.

The 9th New York waded into the Antietam's cold waters but there was no safety in the creek and bullets rained down on them. James Sheldon and the 50th Georgia poured a steady rifle fire on the New Yorkers, hitting two of them as they forded the creek. As the 51st Pennsylvania and 51st New York fought their

*Antietam Bridge as it looked to James Sheldon
and the 50th Georgia during the Civil War*

way across the bridge, hundreds of Union troops began scaling
the slopes toward the Georgians' position. Badly outnumbered,
James Sheldon and his brigade left the bridge to the enemy. It
was mid-afternoon. For the second time in a week, the men of
the 50th Georgia were forced to carry their wounded as they ran
for safety. An hour later they rested against a stone wall near a
cornfield and checked their ammunition. There was none. The
men fixed bayonets but an attack never came. Late in the morning
the 15th and 17th Georgia, supported by five companies of the 11th
Georgia Regiment, came onto the field to help defend the bridge.
The sight of these reserve troops cheered James and the other
men of the 50th, but their celebration was short lived. The 2nd and
20th Georgia repulsed five separate assaults. Suddenly, there was
a commotion to James' right. Confederate General A. P. Hill's
division had arrived after a grueling march from Harper's Ferry,
and the timing could not have been more critical. Hill's men
quickly formed a junction with James' division and several of
his batteries began firing on the enemy, who were stopped cold.
In three days of fierce fighting, James Sheldon's 50th Georgia
suffered 29 men killed and 97 wounded. One company captain
suffered a most gruesome wound, having been shot in the face.

Union Colonel Ferrero ordered two barrels of whiskey for his Pennsylvanians and paid for it out of his own pocket. But he'd lost 120 of his 335 men.

In what amounted to a draw, the Battle of Sharpsburg brought the war to a new plateau of casualties. Lee and McClellan lost a combined 25,000 men. The next morning, Lieutenant Rhodes surveyed the field, observing, "I have never in my soldier life seen such a sight. The dead and wounded covered the ground. In one spot a Rebel officer and twenty men lay near the wreck of a battery." [16]

Lee began a weary trek to the safety of Virginia. McClellan, with 24,000 men still in reserve and another 12,000 new volunteers, did little except order some cavalry expeditions. The 2nd Rhode Island took part in a light skirmish, but by the 19th, except for the burying of the dead, the affair was essentiality over. On September 19th, Israel Sheldon read the news about the battle at Sharpsburg and "the rebels" [17] evacuating Harper's Ferry. He also caught up with the goings-on at home with a letter from Alma.

But Lincoln saw the opportunity to claim victory. Five days after the Battle of Sharpsburg, the President offered a preview of his Emancipation Proclamation. Lincoln's sudden political boldness contrasted sharply with McClellan's timidity.

Elisha Rhodes and the 2nd Rhode Island spent the remainder of September in Maryland camped near the little town of Downsville. The men were in dire need of rest. They were, as Elisha described it, "weary and used up." [18] There was a shortage of food and clothing but the 2nd enjoyed the quiet days and late summer moonlit nights. A few of his men discovered a beehive and Elisha enjoyed a feast of honey. Eventually, some of the locals were willing to sell food to them. The hiatus was marred briefly by a death in camp; the soldier was buried during an emotionless military ceremony. Everything went on as usual in camp as if nothing had happened, for "death is so common that little sentiment is wasted. It is not like death at home," [19] Elisha commented.

On September 30, Lincoln visited Elisha's 6th Corps on his way to Harper's Ferry to confer with McClellan. The shabbily outfitted 2nd Rhode Island did its best to give a proud impression.

On the first day of October, Lincoln met with McClellan to express his disappointment in his general. But if Lincoln had any intention of replacing McClellan, he kept it to himself. McClellan again made his argument for a cautious campaign. At a dress parade honoring the President, Lincoln sarcastically quipped to an aid that the Army of the Potomac was McClellan's "bodyguard."[20] As Lincoln departed for Washington, a costly battle was fought at Corinth, Mississippi, with both sides unable to claim victory.

October opened with a grim day for James and the Thomas County Rangers. Cicero Young, their charismatic captain and friend, succumbed to typhoid fever and was buried in Winchester, Virginia. Captain Young's body was never returned to Georgia.

****

While Lincoln and McClellan were discussing the war, Lieutenant Israel Sheldon took his section out for a spectacular review by corps commander Heintzelman. Captain Randolph served as chief of artillery and a total of six batteries participated in this event, which was also intended to keep the men sharp. Two days later, anxious to get back into action, Israel took his section out to drill for the first time in weeks.

On his return to Washington, Lincoln considered the results of his meeting with McClellan. He sent a stern message to his general, saying, "The President directs that you cross the Potomac and give battle to the enemy or drive him south." Concerned that another winter of idleness and bad weather loomed not far off, Lincoln added, "Your army must move now while the roads are good."[21]

Israel Sheldon's desire to get back into the fight was quenched at four p.m. on October 10, when Randolph's Battery was given orders to prepare to march at eight o' clock the next morning. The entire brigade was to join Stoneman's Brigade at Poolesville, Maryland. At dawn his battery joined the march and moved out toward Poolesville passing through Georgetown. About four p.m., Randolph's Battery reached Rockville, Maryland, where the men cooked rations and bivouacked for the night.

Lieutenant Sheldon and his battery resumed their march at three a.m. and reached Poolesville 13 hours later. While pitching his tent, Israel received orders to march to the Potomac River with two batteries accompanied by infantry, on a reconnaissance mission. Sheldon and his men staggered back into camp at two in the morning after a brutal 23 hours of marching.

The next day a frustrated Lincoln challenged McClellan when he telegraphed, "Are you not over-cautious when you assume that you can not do what the enemy is constantly doing?" [22]

On Tuesday, the 14th, Lieutenant Israel Sheldon rolled his section down to the river and spent an uneventful night. For Lieutenant Elisha Rhodes, things were at a new low. News of another Jeb Stuart raid in the North reached the demoralized 2nd Rhode Island. "If the army cannot protect the loyal states we had better sell out and go home," he thought. [23] The weather was bad and turning cold. Few men had coats. Elisha was tired of getting marching orders which required striking the tents and cooking and packing rations only to have the order routinely countermanded. The thought of setting up winter quarters in these conditions was depressing. To placate Lincoln, McClellan initiated two offensives against Lee in the Shenandoah on Thursday.

On Saturday about dusk, Elisha received marching orders again and this time they were real. The 2nd passed through Downsville and beautiful Williamsport, reaching Clear Spring where the men camped in a cornfield. By the following Tuesday, the 2nd had reached the Potomac. Elisha wrote, "The weather is cold and the men suffer... this is filling the hospitals very fast." [24]

On the 25th, Lincoln put McClellan on the spot, saying, "I have just read your dispatch about sore tongued and fatigued horses. Will you pardon me for asking what the horses of your army have done since the battle of Antietam that fatigue anything?" [25] Clearly, their relationship was reaching its breaking point. The next day, the Army of the Potomac crossed the river into Virginia. The 2nd Rhode Island was on the leading edge of the general advance, and Elisha described the shallow water as "ice cold." [26] Four days later, McClellan's army was on the east side of the Blue Ridge Mountains. Lincoln, pleased but curious, telegraphed, "What do you know of the enemy?" [27]

On the 29th, Israel received a letter from his sister, Mary, as his battery watched over the Union troops crossing the Potomac. The following evening, Randolph's Battery waded across the waist deep river into Virginia.

The next day, Elisha and the 2nd Rhode Island were back at their Downsville camp and could see the Confederates organizing across the river. Again baffled by McClellan, he wondered what would happen. Safely on the Virginia shore, Israel and Randolph's Battery set up near a bridge to protect the crossing of an ammunition train. He received another letter from his sister, Mary, and to his delight, a box of books. On the evening of the 31st, Randolph's Battery began marching toward Leesburg, making camp about a mile from the town.

By November both armies were spent. Like proud prize fighters, the knees of the Armies of the Potomac and Northern Virginia buckled, but neither would go down. Lee's men rested while McClellan made another timid advance into Virginia, desperately trying to get Lincoln off his back. Elisha had a tooth pulled. "I thought the top of my head was coming off." [28] But later thought of how lucky he was after visiting a Union hospital. Tough marching was once again the order of the day for Israel, and on November 2, Randolph's Battery began an early march to Mt. Gilead. There they remained until three p.m. the next day when the battery began marching toward Millville where they set up camp.

Also on the 3rd, Longstreet's Corps made a stand at Culpeper Court House, creating the opportunity for one last fight before winter stilled the armies. Jackson lingered not far off in the Shenandoah and all indications predicted battle. Captain

John McCall of the 50th Georgia described his regiment's situation near Fredericksburg in a letter to his sister, "We are daily expecting a fight here, as we are in a mile and a half of the Yankees, supposed to be about two hundred thousand. Our pickets stand on one side of the river and the Yankees on the other, not more than a hundred yards apart. We also have a very large force at this place. It is getting very cold in this part of the country now and continues to get colder. I don't know what we will all do here this winter. The boys have nearly all drawn shoes, and are drawing some clothing occasionally but not nearly enough to supply their wants." Echoing the sentiment of most of the men on both sides the captain stated, "I want to come home very bad but I don't know when I will ever get the chance to come." [29]

Elisha's 2nd Rhode Island again crossed the Potomac and encamped near the Manassas battlefield. The hungry regiment was cold and forced to sleep through the first snowfall of the season without tents.

On Wednesday, November 5, Lincoln decided he had had enough. His order would stun the Army of the Potomac. It read, "By direction of the President, it is ordered that Major General McClellan be relieved from the command of the Army of the Potomac; and that Major General Burnside take the command of that army." [30]

The Confederacy also made changes in its army as both Jackson and Longstreet were promoted to lieutenant general. Randolph's Battery camped in Salem, Virginia, and marched to Waterloo the next morning. Israel relaxed in camp on Friday the 7th, serving Rhode Island cavalry officers coffee as the snow fell.

Just before midnight, McClellan received a solemn General Burnside who requested that they have a few minutes in his tent. After some small talk the awkward moment arose to reveal the purpose of the visit. As Lincoln's order was read, a clearly embarrassed Burnside was nearly in tears, but McClellan, ever the gentlemen, weakly smiled at Burnside and maintained his proud demeanor. The order was hurtful, going so far as to direct McClellan not to return to Washington, but to his home in New Jersey. McClellan's controversial military career ended not in glory on the battlefield but in a quiet, humiliating meeting in a snow-covered tent. Shortly after midnight he wrote a letter to his wife, saying, "Alas for my poor country. I know in my inmost heart she never had a truer servant." [31]

The news of McClellan's dismissal devastated the Army of the Potomac. Despite its hardships and lack of success, the army held the general in great affection. On Monday, November 10, McClellan bid farewell to the Army of the Potomac. McClellan reviewed his troops for the last time as the men cheered and threw their hats in the air as he passed. Some men threw down their arms, vowing to fight no more. After an honor guard of 2,000 men escorted him to the train station at Warrenton, McClellan assured them, "Stand by General Burnside as you have stood by me, and all will be well." [32] Elisha lamented, "This change produces much bitter feeling. McClellan's enemies will now rejoice, but the army loves and respects him." [33]

Two days later, Lincoln granted Burnside's request to begin moving overland to Richmond, and on November 15th, the Army of the Potomac began moving out of Warrenton in the direction of Fredericksburg. Both the 2nd Rhode Island Infantry and Randolph's Battery were on the march. Lee watched closely as sporadic fighting broke out along the Rappahannock.

Randolph's Battery marched into the town of Liberty at four p.m. and began setting up camp. Israel and the other men foraged for anything that might make their night as warm and as comfortable as possible—it was bitterly cold. Two men decided that a bed of straw was just what they needed to rest their weary bodies. Frozen and tired, they helped themselves to their night's bedding from a nearby barn, disobeying an order to respect private property.

Caught in the act of stealing, a provost marshall killed both soldiers on the spot. The men of Randolph's Battery were outraged, "[A] New York [regiment] and other troops mauled the provost and would have killed him but he escaped. After which the mob set fire to the barn and stacks and destroyed them," Israel said. [34] Four days later a fight broke out within the ranks of Israel's battery between a private and a quartermaster sergeant; the private was shot and died the next day. The Army of Northern Virginia was trailing the Army of the Potomac, which was battling itself, as both armies converged on Fredericksburg.

Elisha was 15 miles from Fredericksburg on November 19, camping in the rain. Longstreet spent the day securing his position on the heights above Fredericksburg. Burnside and the leading edge of his army arrived and both armies dug in along opposite banks of the Rappahannock River. Lee arrived the next day.

Burnside, aware of Lincoln's impatience with McClellan, wasted no time in demanding the town's surrender. The mayor of Fredericksburg declined, even under the threat of bombardment.

Israel and Randolph's Battery marched all day on the 22nd, arriving at the outskirts of Fredericksburg at dusk. Elisha and the 2nd Rhode Island Infantry were closing in on Fredericksburg—in very bad shape. "I am cold, in fact half frozen," Elisha wrote on November 23. [35] Morale was terrible; the men were homesick and made no attempt to conceal it. But they were happy for Colonel Wheaton, who had been promoted to brigadier general. Although they were disappointed at losing their colonel, Elisha was confident that his successor, Nelson Viall, would prove himself worthy as the new colonel.

During the week, Lincoln conferred with Burnside, who suggested a direct attack on Fredericksburg. Oddly enough, Lincoln proposed a more McClellanesque style operation, but in the end blessed Burnside's plan.

****

On November 26, James Sheldon and the 50th Georgia were assigned to another brigade. Lee decided to form a brigade made up exclusively of Georgians under the command of General Paul Semmes. The 10th, 51st and 53rd Georgia Regiments joined the 50th in what would become commonly known as "Semmes' Brigade." Semmes, 47, was a banker and planter in peacetime and had served as a captain in the Georgia militia. When war broke out he was elected colonel of the 2nd Georgia Volunteers.

General Paul Semmes

Concerned for the well-being of his wife and family, and having been denied a leave of absence, Semmes submitted a letter of resignation to Joe Johnston in February of 1862. Not only was his resignation refused, he was promoted to brigadier general. Tall, strikingly handsome with piercing eyes and impeccable dress, Semmes was an imposing presence. His boots always gleamed and he fancied wearing a red sash and turban, giving him the appearance of a zouave. James and the other men referred to the turban as his "battle cap." [36]

****

On the first day of December, Lincoln issued the annual State of the Union message, focusing on the freeing of the slaves, "We cannot escape history," he warned. "We shall nobly save, or meanly lose, the last best, hope of earth." [37] Skirmishing continued along the Rappahannock.

131

A private in Israel's battery died on December 2nd, and his comrades buried him with honors. Elisha, having been assured that the 2nd would remain near Stafford Court House, spent the day with the rest of the regiment constructing elaborate winter quarters. The men were thrilled with their new homes and looked forward to passing the coming months in relative comfort. Exhausted from their day's work, the men plunked themselves down on their new beds, but before they could close their eyes, an order was given to the regiment to "have three day's rations cooked and be ready to move tomorrow morning." [38]

The next day the skirmishing along the Rappahannock evolved into an engagement. By evening, Elisha and the 2nd were freezing on a hill about twelve miles from Fredericksburg and spent the next day battling the snow, ice and stinging cold.

On December 10, Burnside's army was across the river from Fredericksburg with 100,000 men, animals and artillery, giving Lee the impression that he would attack the town at any moment. Burnside began constructing a number of pontoon bridges under the fire of Confederate sharpshooters and elements of the Army of the Potomac began crossing the next day. Elisha's regiment was the first to cross to cross the river below Federicksburg. Burnside's artillery began firing on the city and by afternoon an entire Union division was in Fredericksburg. Longstreet and Lee braced for a full attack, holding their wildcard, Jackson's army, just outside of town. Israel marched all day until eleven p.m.—Randolph's Battery camped about two miles below Fredericksburg.

On the morning of Thursday, December 11, Private James Sheldon and the 50th Georgia were awakened by the sound of Confederate pickets firing on the enemy crossing the river. One man in James' brigade remembered, "We were ordered to be ready to march about half after four o' clock. Our regiment was formed about daybreak. We then marched a quarter of a mile to the road. We then built us fires and rested for further orders, until one o' clock p.m. We were then ordered in line of battle one mile from camps, three quarters of a mile to the river, and one and one half miles from the city." [39]

The commander of Elisha's brigade, General Charles Devens, stated that about an hour before sunset on the evening of December 11, he received orders, "[to] cross my brigade as the advance guard of the left wing of the army over the pontoon bridges which had been constructed over the Rappahannock… and should rest the right of my brigade line, as soon as I could form it, upon the bank of a ravine, which be designated. The brigade was immediately moved to the bridges, and three companies of the Second Rhode Island Regiment were thrown across in advance…supported at once by the rest of the regiment." [40]

Two columns of Massachusetts and New York men immediately followed the 2nd Rhode Island and the Union men deployed skirmishers. They were greeted by a considerable number of their Confederate counterparts who were posted in gardens amid the cluster of houses just above the bridges. Elisha and his comrades forced the enemy out of their hideouts, allowing other Union regiments to form unmolested.

Having successfully gotten his skirmishers across the river, Devens ordered the 10th Massachusetts to form in line on the riverbank. This was done in good order and the other regiments of the brigade followed rapidly. The remaining brigades of the 2nd Division were also moved across the river and put into line, but this order was almost instantly reversed. Alone, and cut off from the rest of the Army of the Potomac, Elisha's brigade was ordered to hold the bridge and Devens remembered, "during the night (one of the bitterest of the season) the men were awake and under arms, the outpost and pickets being several times engaged with those of the enemy, especially soon after daylight the next morning." [41]

In a heavy early morning mist on December 13, the Battle of Fredericksburg began. Burnside's army faced an enemy entrenched in the strongest natural defensive position imaginable. A sunken road behind a long stone wall at the foot of a hill known as Marye's Heights made one portion of Lee's 75,000 man army effectively unassailable. James Sheldon was on the heights overlooking the stone wall. From mid-morning until mid-afternoon, Burnside ordered wave after wave of suicidal assaults against the wall, proving that he was as aggressive as his predecessor was timid.

Semmes' Brigade poured volley after volley into the Union men below. James was not under fire of any kind except an occasional artillery shell. It was Malvern Hill in reverse. The field below crawled with wounded and resounded with groans and pleadings. Even some Confederates became sickened by the scene; one soldier more than most. Sergeant Richard Kirkland of South Carolina approached his commanding general and blurted out, "I can't stand this."[42] He asked permission to give water to the enemy wounded. He requested permission to carry a white flag, but this violated the rules of war and he was refused. Draped with canteens, Kirkland mounted the wall and calmly walked directly toward a line of Union sharpshooters who set their sights on him. But the way he walked, stoic and alone, caused the riflemen to look at each other with puzzled stares. As he knelt by the first man and opened his canteen, the firing on both sides came to a halt. Repeatedly he returned to a nearby well, filling his canteens as men on both sides watched in amazement. James Sheldon had perhaps the best view of the "Angel of Marye's Heights,"[43] and for an hour and a half, Kirkland worked the field until every man had received a drink. Just as calmly as he came upon the field, he walked back to the wall, and when he picked up his rifle, the fighting resumed.

Elisha Rhodes and the 2nd Rhode Island were ordered forward to protect a battery and were subjected to enemy artillery fire—more annoying than deadly. Israel Sheldon and Randolph's Battery were engaged all day; they lost two men and Israel's horse was wounded. James Sheldon and the 50th Georgia did not enter the fighting but under a heavy artillery barrage four of its men were wounded. Burnside had proved to be a disaster, losing nearly 13,000 men, but had Lee baffled by his recklessness. Lee considered a counterattack but worried that Burnside would renew his attack. On Sunday the 14th, and again the next day, Elisha and the 2nd dug rifle pits expecting the Army of Northern

Virginia to counterattack. On the night of the 15th, Burnside's Army of the Potomac began slipping away.

In the ensuing disaster, Burnside called upon his old friends from Rhode Island to get his army out of Fredericksburg and to the safety of the other side of the Rappahannock. The 10th Massachusetts was the last regiment to cross, followed by a detachment of the 2nd Rhode Island assigned as bridge guard, under Captain Samuel Read. Once safely across, "the bridges were at once taken up. Boats were kept on the other side of the river until after daybreak, to take off any stragglers, but, as reported to me, only a very small number appeared, so carefully and thoroughly had the retreat been conducted...The behavior of the whole command, both officers and men, for spirit and willingness, could not be exceeded... the 2nd Rhode Island, is entitled to the honor of having first crossed the bridge and engaged the skirmishers of the enemy." [44]

The 2nd Rhode Island's distinction of being first and last on the battlefield of Fredericksburg was not lost on the men of the Army of the Potomac. The following day, the 2nd Rhode Island crossed the river. "I am so tired, O so tired, and can hardly keep awake," Elisha wrote. [45]

James Sheldon's side of things was equally unpleasant. The evening of Thursday, December 11th was bitterly cold and James Sheldon had to get up repeatedly throughout to night to warm himself by the campfire. Constant shelling drove the men into their trenches and shouts of "Where is you? Where is you?" [46] were heard between the explosions.

Friday morning, about sunrise, Semmes' Brigade was ordered half a mile upriver to support a battery from Petersburg, Virginia. This battery opened fire about eight a.m. and shelled the enemy off and on throughout the day. Burnside's artillery replied in kind and according to one Georgian soldier, "The [Union] shells fell and busted around us in all directions, but fortunately, hurt none of us, though they fell very close sometimes to us. Saturday, our battery opened fire about one o'clock PM and done good execution. The enemy shelled us most furiously Saturday evening." [47] At about

10 o'clock Sunday evening James' 50th was ordered to relieve another regiment stationed at the lower edge of town. Burnside's men fired at Semmes' pickets about one o' clock in the morning but no one in James' brigade was hit. To avoid giving their position away to the enemy gunners, all fires in the brigade were doused and the men "were obliged to lie almost without fire for six days and nights."[48]

James and his comrades were trapped in this position as danger lurked in every direction. Pickets skirmished all day and sharpshooters did their deadly work up and down the line. "We were visited all day off and on by shells… Our pickets were fired upon again by the enemy about midnight…[and] several balls passed over us," remembered a drummer in the 53rd Georgia. By Tuesday the battle began to subside although the artillery of both sides dueled until about ten o' clock. With Burnside's army back across the river, James and some other men were detailed to help pick up guns and other abandoned equipment. "The enemy was shamefully whipped," observed one of these men. [49] "[We were] on the field in less than fifteen minutes after the enemy stopped shelling our battery. You can't imagine what a horrible spectacle I witnessed. I saw hundreds of men lying dead, shot in all parts some with their heads, hands, legs, arms, etc shot off, and mangled in all manner and shapes. The ground resembled an immense hog pen and them all killed. It put me in mind of hog killing time more than anything else, blankets, haversacks, knapsacks, guns, bayonets, cartridge boxes, belts, caps, hats, and etc. lay scattered in all directions. You may know that our brigade helped themselves to plunder. Some searched the Yanks pockets, and even stripped them to their skin. Nearly every one of our boys helped themselves to Yankee canteens, haversacks, overcoats, shoes, and etc.."[50]

For the next few days every man in Semmes' Brigade was in business, much to the chagrin of the sutler. Because of the below freezing temperatures, blankets were selling for $10, nearly the equivalent of a private's monthly salary. India rubber cloths were also selling for $10, knives for $4, tents for $6 and Union overcoats were fetching up to $20. In spite of this booming trade, the men of Semmes' Brigade were still hard at work. "We have not had but three good nights rest since the 1st day of the battle, on account of having to work on rifle pits," one man complained." [51]

Confusion followed the Battle of Fredericksburg. Was this the aggressive campaign Lincoln had demanded of McClellan? Burnside had considered resuming the attack the next morning but was talked out of it. Lee also had some questions and concerns. The pressure was on to cross the river and counterattack, and the previous day's events made this option very tempting. But after considering Burnside's artillery firepower on the hills and his entrenched 90,000 active troops, Lee thought better of it. As Burnside's army meekly recrossed the Rappahannock, Lee's Army of Northern Virginia watched, haunted by the notion that this giant of an army would yet again return to fight.

****

The Augusta *Constitutionalist* reported on December 14 that the St. John's Hospital was closing, and had "opened its doors [on the] 8th of January 1862." [52] The hospital had been the private home of Hiram Roberts, and had been operated by the Ladies of St. John's, but now the sick and wounded had either died or gone home and the army was in Virginia and the West.

The demoralized Rhode Islanders spent the remainder of 1862 homesick—bickering among themselves. In Washington, Lincoln met with Burnside, trying to understand what had gone wrong at Fredericksburg. Christmas was quiet. Lieutenant Israel Sheldon wrote long letters to his dear Alma. As the year ended, Elisha Rhodes reflected, "One year ago tonight I was an enlisted man and stood up cap in hand asking for a furlough. Tonight I am an officer and men ask the same favor of me." [53]

Israel received a box of socks from Alma, while his brother, James Sheldon of the 50th Georgia, went into winter camp outside of Fredericksburg. The men had plenty of food but no coffee. When tents finally arrived, the men were given Christmas Day off from work and drill. One man in the brigade wrote home describing Christmas in the army, saying, "We can walk across the water on the ice. We are getting enough beef and flour to eat at this time but we have no way to cook it. Our whole company has only one spider (a tripod used for hanging a pot over an open fire) and one frying pan and one oven is all the cooking things the company has got. And that is as much as we can tote." [54]

On Tuesday, December 30, the Union's beloved *Monitor* sank in heavy seas while being towed. The brutality of 1862 ended as both armies went into winter quarters.

6

THEY WERE A SAVAGE LOOKING SET OF BLUE BIRDS

On Thursday January 1, 1863, President Lincoln signed the long-anticipated Emancipation Proclamation—raising the Union's stake in the conflict. On the national scale the war had changed politically, but nothing had changed for the average footsoldier. On this same day, Burnside was trying to get his head out of the noose by writing to Lincoln, hinting that he was eager to be relieved of command.

Both armies went into winter quarters, hoping to regroup, but winter brought with it sickness such as pneumonia and chronic diarrhea. Rations were in short supply. The Northern men struggled through the cold weather while the Southern men felt its sting to the bone. One of the best defenses against the harsh elements was to keep busy. For most of January, James Sheldon was assigned to picket and provost duty in Fredericksburg.

The 50th Georgia's camp was seven miles southwest of Fredericksburg. The men ventured into the woods for firewood—the nearest water supply was a mile away. But by mid-month, James and the men found a better location and began erecting winter quarters that they named "Pine Grove Camp." [1] James and the other Rangers, weary from the ordeal of setting up a new camp, huddled around their fires and talked about what the future might bring. James' brother Israel and friend Elisha passed the time building stables to protect their horses and livestock. Most men believed the armies were back in their old positions and didn't expect another major battle any time soon.

In Tennessee at Stone's River, the first major action of 1863 brought great loss to both sides. The town of Murfreesboro fell to Union troops on the 5th and Lincoln was thrilled by the news.

January passed slowly. James, Israel and Elisha all endured the freezing rains around Fredericksburg. Except for picket duty on the riverbank, they looked forward to a month of much-deserved rest. Fresh food was a rare commodity and the locals seized the opportunity to charge top dollar for their wares. Butter was selling for 60 cents a pound—the equivalent of two day's pay on a private's salary.

For James Sheldon and Semmes' Brigade, the food situation was unpredictable at best. There seemed to be an abundance of beef, flour and bacon but the locals, hit hard by the harsh winter and recent fighting, were unwilling to sell. Bakery treats like ginger cakes that normally sold for five cents were fetching as much as 75 cents apiece. Alcohol was a true luxury item, selling for $20 per quart. A private in the 51st Georgia quipped, "If I had a barrel or two of good whiskey here it would be almost a fortune. But I have not got it nor I can't get it for it is against the law to bring it on the [rail]cars." [3]

On the 17th, Burnside reviewed his army and his visit broke the tedium of winter camp, if only for a few hours. Israel's battery and Elisha's 2nd Rhode Island were ordered to prepare three days rations and be ready to march. Two days later, Burnside made another attempt to cross the Rappahannock River at a point ten miles northwest of Fredericksburg. Within 24 hours heavy winter rains swept the area, turning the roads around Fredericksburg into impassable slop. Wagons and gun carriages sank into the mud. Men and horses had to be pulled out of this quagmire and both man and beast were dropping dead of exposure and exhaustion. Lieutenant Israel Sheldon was shocked at the condition of the men he saw passing his battery in what soldiers were calling "Burnside's Mud March." [2]

Elisha worked his way through mud so deep that sixteen horses couldn't pull a single gun through it. By Friday, January

23, the men were cold, hungry and exhausted. Burnside's second attempt on Fredericksburg ground to an embarrassing failure. Throughout the month, Union and Confederate pickets on the river good-naturedly taunted each other about their governments and military leaders. As Elisha and the Army of the Potomac sat in the rain and mud, a sign went up on his friend James Sheldon's side of the Rappahannock, which read, "BURNSIDE STUCK IN THE MUD" — mules, horses, wagons and men remained mired in the muck.

The Army of the Potomac dragged itself back to its winter quarters and on the morning of the 25th, Burnside conferred with his commander-in-chief, trying to explain his efforts during the failed campaign. Burnside demanded the removal of other generals who he claimed were responsible for the disaster. After listening to his defeated general, Lincoln fired Burnside and replaced him with Joseph Hooker. Burnside, whose star had shone so brightly in the Carolinas, and had accepted Lincoln's appointment with little confidence in his own abilities, had commanded the Army of the Potomac for a mere 90 days.

****

On Monday morning, Lieutenant Israel Sheldon and Randolph's Battery received their first pay in two months. Their first priority was to visit the sutler, the local residents, and the shopkeepers in an attempt to buy some decent food. As Hooker took command of the army his men had full stomachs.

Joseph Hooker of Massachusetts was 49 when Lincoln appointed him commander of the Army of the Potomac. His division had performed admirably during the Peninsula Campaign, South Mountain, and Antietam, where he was wounded in the foot. The newspapers labeled him "Fighting Joe," [4] and although he didn't like the nickname, it stuck. But Hooker also had his critics, not the least of whom was President Lincoln, who warned him, "I think it best for you to know that there are some things in regard to which I am not quite satisfied with you." Lincoln chastised Hooker for his role in Burnside's failure but closed his letter by urging Hooker to "go forward and give us victories." [5] Hooker assumed his new command under this cloud of mixed messages from his commander-in-chief.

Hearing the news of Burnside's firing, the morale of the 2nd Rhode Island sank. It plummeted even further when their new colonel, Nelson Viall, resigned, claiming he'd been insulted by Governor Sprague. The regiment was deeply resentful of Viall's treatment and as he said goodbye to the 2nd, he "cried like a child," [6] according to Elisha. During Viall's farewell address, the men booed Sprague's name three times, and Lieutenant Elisha Rhodes predicted the governor, "will be sorry for his actions." [7] The men of Elisha's company put their woes at bay by constructing an elaborate shelter which they referred to as a "house." [8] The structure was built of large timbers mortared with mud and, it was large enough to hold the entire company. As January 1863 ended, only 40 of the 2nd Rhode Island's remaining 80 men were still fit for service.

On the first day of February, Elisha applied for a leave of absence and expected to obtain it in about a month. One week later, the 2nd Rhode Island was ordered out on three days of picket duty along the river. This assignment turned out to be a pleasant experience as every evening the men sat by their campfires serenaded by the Southern bands across the water.

Still stinging from Viall's resignation, the regiment was further upset when they returned to camp to find their new colonel, Horatio Rogers, waiting for them. Explaining that they felt the appointment should have gone to Lieutenant Colonel Nathan Goff, Jr., Rogers promised to inform Governor Sprague of their disappointment. But for now he was their commander. Rogers was a gentleman and within days, the men were already growing fond of him.

Colonel Horatio Rogers

At mid-month, a two-day snowstorm buried both armies. One man in James' brigade wrote, "The weather is very cold. The snow is on the ground now. It has been knee to half thigh deep for several days." [9] Ten days later, the situation showed signs of improvement, and the soldier wrote, "the weather is a little warmer this morning but I think it will be snowing again before tomorrow morning." [10] In the midst of this stormy weather, one of the 50th Georgia's most popular officers, Major Duncan Curry, resigned due to poor health. Speculating on military operations a man wrote, "We are going to leave here in a few days and the general opinion is that we will go to Charlestown (Virginia, near Harper's Ferry)." [11] One snowy afternoon a snowball throwing incident flared into a full-fledged mock battle. Officers, including General Longstreet, joined in. The fight was the highlight of an otherwise depressing month for the Confederates at Fredericksburg. On February 23, James heard the Yankees firing across the river celebrating Washington's birthday.

On March 3, Lincoln signed an act authorizing that all able men between 20 and 45 years of age were eligible for military service. Most could never have imagined such a "draft" back in the early days of the war. The draft had an unusual clause in that a man could either pay $300 to the government for an exemption, or simply hire another man to serve in his place. A week later, the President offered amnesty to deserters if they returned to their regiments before an April 1 deadline. If they didn't return voluntarily and were later captured, they would be executed.

****

On March 11, Israel Sheldon was granted a short leave of absence and hurried to Pawtuxet to spend a few days with Alma and young son, William. Winter hung on doggedly and the men of both armies had by now invented ingenious ways of combating the weather; the men in Semmes' Brigade built small fireplaces with chimneys to warm their tents.

General Paul Semmes returned to James' brigade after being away for two months. Private James Sheldon and the other Georgians now had plenty of food but were forced to move a mile and a half away from Pine Grove Camp to be closer to an abundant source of firewood. On March 18, Semmes' Brigade marched to United States Ford to guard against sporadic Yankee cavalry attacks.

After a winter of discontent and boredom, Elisha enjoyed the 21st of March when he celebrated not only his birthday, but also the approval of his request for leave. "I am a man today, for it is my birthday and I am 21 years old," [12] he wrote. Elisha hurriedly packed his gear and a few days later was home in Pawtuxet, enjoying a four-day visit with friends and family.

After settling into his mother Eliza's little house near the bridge on Broad Street, Elisha enjoyed a good night's sleep in his own bed. The next day he strolled through the village. The talk of Pawtuxet was predominantly local gossip. Although the recent Battle of Fredericksburg was still a curiosity worthy of discussion with a returning soldier, the residents seemed far more preoccupied with the crowning of a new "High Hook" than General Hooker. They were also preparing for the day tipplers who in a few short weeks would be streaming in from Providence and Worcester, filling the Golden Ball Inn and Charlie Gorton's Saloon with hungry and thirsty customers. But Elisha was home and it was good to stop in and visit Mr. Arnold at his store and to watch Captain Ralph, fur cap and all, working away in his kitchen.

Two visits were requisite. Of course there was Frederick Miller, a father figure to Elisha, who was eager to hear anything and everything about the war. Then, of course, there was Mrs. Sheldon, his next-door neighbor, although conversation regarding the war would be awkward, and if possible, avoided. There would be plenty of war talk with George Sheldon, however, who undoubtedly would inquire as to the whereabouts of his brother Israel. Correspondence with sister, Patience, in Thomasville had all but been cut off, but word was that brother James was in Virginia with a Georgia regiment.

Elisha's four days passed quickly and he was all too soon traveling south to rejoin his regiment.

****

The weather at Fredericksburg was breaking, warming to the point where soldiers explored the surrounding woods and villages. One man in James' brigade got his first look at downtown Fredericksburg, deciding, "This place Fredericksburg is a nice place. It is the second in size in the state… It is badly torn up with shells and balls from the great battle that was fought here some time ago." [13] All indications were that the long winter of inactivity had come to an end.

As April opened, Presidents Davis and Lincoln struggled to hold their nations' war efforts together. There were food riots in Richmond as the effects of the Union blockade took its toll on the citizenry throughout the South. In the North, Lincoln met with Hooker on April 6. The president insisted that the army concern itself with the enemy across the river rather than Richmond.

On the 7th, Elisha Rhodes returned to his regiment. Well rested, he was surprised to find that Horatio Rogers was still colonel. He was even more surprised that during his leave, he had been promoted to 1st lieutenant.

Lieutenants Israel Sheldon and Elisha Rhodes took part in a review of the Army of the Potomac by President Lincoln at Falmouth on April 8. Three days later, Lincoln was back at the White House sharing his thoughts on General Hooker with his cabinet. The following day, a Sunday, Lincoln received a letter from his general which detailed his plan to cross the river to turn the Army of Northern Virginia's left flank. This would be followed by a cavalry attack to roll up the enemy along the river.

As the weather warmed, the attitudes between the enemies along the opposing banks of the Rappahannock softened somewhat. Makeshift wooden sailboats tied to strings were sent back and forth across the river carrying tiny cargoes of newspapers, coffee and tobacco. Fraternization with the enemy was discouraged by officers on both sides, but the fascination the pickets had with their counterparts across the water was often too tempting to ignore. One order which was strictly enforced was that there was to be no gunfire across the river. The mighty "Stonewall" Jackson once presented himself as an easy target to the pickets of the 2nd Rhode Island Infantry, but the men held their fire.

****

By mid-April war operations began again. At Vicksburg, Mississippi, Admiral David Porter's twelve gunboats swept under the city's bluffs. Although facing fierce opposition, he lost only one warship. The river opened, a land campaign by Grant could now begin in earnest. In Virginia, the roads were drying and becoming passable once again. An offensive by Fighting Joe Hooker would soon be in the offing.

The arrival of spring did little to bring down the prices of basic commodities in Fredericksburg. "Times is very hard here. Every thing is very dear. Sweet milk is worth one dollar per quart and butter five dollars per pound and green beef two dollars per pound and chickens three dollars a head and eggs from three to four dollars per dozen and corn meal eight dollars per bushel," [14] wrote a Georgia man earning $13 a month. But at last the weather was improving, "it begins to look a little like spring for the peach trees is beginning to bud and to bloom." [15]

Captain McCall of James' 50th wrote his father a light-hearted, reassuring letter on April 22, saying, "I want [you] to wear [your beard] till I come home and don't think the time is far distant, for I am of the opinion that this unholy war will come to a wind up before long. I think that the Yanks are getting very tired of it…Our Yankees are lying still here. I don't believe that they will fight anymore, there is 300 thousand of them to [be] mustered out in May and I suppose they say they won't fight any more and that they are going home when their time is out." [16] McCall commented on the condition of the 50th Georgia, saying, "There is a right smart of sickness now in camps." [17]

On the morning of April 27, Hooker began moving 54,000 men northwest along the Rappahannock. Israel received his marching orders that evening and was awakened at two a.m. on the 28th. Randolph's battery began its march at six in the morning. By noon, seven miles into the march, the battery went into camp. Another 40,000 men under the command of General John Sedgwick were poised to cross the river near Falmouth, for a direct assault on Fredericksburg. To protect against a counterattack, 40,000 men, or the remainder of Hooker's army, would be held in reserve.

Unaware of the danger, James Sheldon and his brigade spent the 27th fishing and on picket duty. Nothing unusual appeared to be happening on the other side of the river. One of the Georgian pickets wrote, "we stand in speaking distance to each other (enemy pickets) but we do not shoot at each other. I think both is afraid. We are having our fun here seining for fish and catching fish with a hook and lines. We drag them out by the hundreds with seins." [18]

But the next morning, the church bells of Fredericksburg were ringing the alarm as Hooker's men crossed the Rappahannock and marched into a thickly overgrown forest called the Wilderness. "We were in full view of the Yanks," one man said. "I could hear them crossing all night. I went out on scout to see, and walked from 125 to 150 yards of them. They were a savage looking set of blue birds." [19] Marching through the Wilderness, elements of Hooker's force arrived at a clearing which featured the home of the Chancellor family. Hooker's men settled in an area the locals called Chancellorsville.

After dark, the 2nd Rhode Island was ordered about two miles south of Fredericksburg, watching as elements of another division crossed the river over pontoon bridges and boats. The crackle of rifle fire split the crisp night air as Union forces charged into the Confederate works. After a bold stand the Confederates abandoned their rifle pits to the oncoming Union infantry which seized and held the south bank. Hooker now had a foothold both in front of and on Lee's 60,000-man left flank. James' 50th Georgia was camping about a half mile behind of Marye's Heights and were moved and ordered into line of battle at three a.m. on the 30th. James and the other Georgians remained in this position until dusk when the brigade was ordered to march one mile beyond the intersection of the Plank Road and Orange Turnpike. Hooker was reported moving in great force in their direction, driving in Confederate pickets. Private James Sheldon expected a general attack at dawn.

Lee expressed his belief to Jackson that Hooker's main attack would not be at Fredericksburg, but at Chancellorsville, eight miles to the west. Even with Hooker's army divided into thirds, each was large enough to threaten Lee's entire army. Lee's objective was to keep his Army of Northern Virginia between the enemy and Richmond. Hooker's aim was to destroy it where it stood.

Semmes' Brigade began marching toward Chancellorsville at midnight of May 1. The Georgians stopped at the edge of a wooded area overlooking an open field—the enemy could be seen forming lines. Private Sheldon heard the order to open fire on the unsuspecting Union men, who in turn, charged. The Georgians stubbornly held their ground, rolling back the wave of blue. Union cavalry burst upon a Georgian battery banging away in the road, but was immediately driven back. Semmes' Brigade held. After 45 minutes of hot work the Union infantry and cavalry withdrew. But this victory had cost the Georgians dearly. Among the dead was William Slaughter—colonel of the 51st.

Lieutenant Colonel Kearse's 50th Georgia resumed its march as the enemy fell back before them along a road "strewn with knapsacks, blankets, overcoats and other valuable articles."[20] With no enemy in sight, they pursued for another two miles before finding the main force of Hooker's army strongly entrenched near Chancellorsville. Kearse ordered the 50th Georgia to a halt and sent out a strong line of skirmishers to protect his front and flanks. James slept in the open air under a nearly full spring moon.

Jackson was busy—at about midnight, he ordered his troops awake and ready to move. By eight a.m., his men were 5 ½ miles west of Fredericksburg. There they found Confederate General Richard Anderson's three brigades building bold fortifications on the roads to Fredericksburg. By eleven a.m., General "Jeb" Stuart had reported that he was coming in from the west with his cavalry, and wrote to Jackson, "I will close in on the flank and help all I can when the ball opens."[21]

Within minutes, Lee received word that Hooker's army was moving in force toward Jackson. Refusing to be put in a defensive box, Jackson ordered Anderson's men to stop digging entrenchments and prepare to engage the enemy. The fighting in front of Chancellorsville continued throughout the first day of May, and Jackson's aggressive action threw Hooker into a defensive position. December's battle at Fredericksburg was still fresh in the mind of every Union soldier. Hooker waited for

Lee's next move; this time the roles would be reversed and they would let the Confederates come into the slaughter pen. Union general George Meade was furious with Hooker for ending his offensive scheme. Lee, watching all of this, had a fateful decision to make.

As May 1 drew to a close, Lee conferred with Jackson, his most trusted lieutenant general. Staring at a map of the area, Lee voiced his concerns for disrupting Hooker's campaign. "How do we get at those people?" [22] he asked. Jackson listened patiently and intently as Lee thought through his options. Finally, Lee threw caution to the wind and announced a strategy that would make even the stoutest of hearts wince. He would divide his forces at Chancellorsville in two, sending Jackson's Corps 16 miles into the Wilderness directly in the rear of Hooker's army. Lee asked Jackson about the size of force he intended to take with him. "With my whole corps," was Jackson's straightforward reply. Lee pointedly retorted, "What will you leave me?" Lee didn't challenge his lieutenant general, but instead asked for more details, saying, "Go on." [25] Hooker's force now numbered about 73,000 men compared to Lee's 17,000 and Jackson's 26,000.

Jackson smiled when Lee made his proposal and promised that Stuart's cavalry would help protect his march through the hostile terrain of the Wilderness. Jackson told the commander, "My troops will move at 4 o'clock." [23]

****

The night passed quietly. On the morning of the 2nd, about ten a.m., James Sheldon could hear artillery fire, this time down the river on his right. But the firing stopped abruptly. After dark, the sky boomed with heavy cannonading, and the light crackle of musket fire was heard from the same direction as in the morning. With the surrounding woods secured and in friendly hands, James and the other men rested for the night.

By dawn of May 2, Jackson had his battle face on. "Old blue light," [24] drew his face tightly, his lips thinned and his blue eyes blazed. Helping Jackson find his way through the Wilderness to Hooker's rear was a former New York engineer, Jedediah Hotchkiss. Jed had moved to Virginia in 1847 where he taught school in the Shenandoah Valley. He made maps to supplement his income. At a meeting with Lee's braintrust early on the 2nd, Hotchkiss was pleased to report that the locals had told him of a route which would enable a small Confederate contingent to get behind Hooker.

Jackson's march got underway about eight a.m. His men were expected to maintain a standard they had set for themselves: 25 minutes per mile with a ten minute rest for every two miles marched. The roads proved to be good and the maps accurate as his men and a parade of animals and equipment plodded steadily along in the morning sun. Not far into the march, Jackson's column was spotted by Union pickets with Sickles' Corps, and the general sent two regiments to investigate. They tangled with the rear guard of Jackson's column; in particular, the 23rd Georgia which suffered 300 casualties. The brief affair ended with Sickles withdrawing and Jackson continuing his march. Amazingly, nothing further resulted from this brief clash between the two armies.

Throughout the day, James Sheldon and the 50th Georgia took part in occasional heavy skirmishing designed to divert Hooker's attention from Jackson's march. News of the attack on Jackson's column prompted Semmes to intensify his harassment of Hooker.

Late in the afternoon, Jackson's men were poised on Hooker's right flank. Not even a skirmish line preventing them from driving into the exposed flank. Lee's 17,000 men, which included Semmes' Brigade and James Sheldon's 50th Georgia, stood in front and slightly on Hooker's left flank. If Hooker chose not to stand, he would have to either delve deeper into Virginia where his supply line would be cut off, or would have to get his 73,000 men back across the Rappahannock while under attack on two flanks.

By five o' clock most of the pieces critical to Jackson's success were in place, but he still faced two major obstacles. With every passing moment the chance of being spotted increased and the element of surprise lost. Furthermore, darkness would fall in a little over two hours, throwing any coordinated attack into chaos. Scouts watched as Hooker's soldiers went about the business of building campfires to cook their coffee and evening meal. All indications pointed to a pleasant night in Virginia. In the thick woods on the edge of the Wilderness, Jackson spread out his lines, each two miles wide. Witnesses reported that his eyes burned "with a brilliant glow." [26]

Sitting on his mount, "Little Sorrel," [27] Jackson ordered his 26,000 soldiers to fix bayonets. Looking left and right, inspecting the endless lines, he checked his pocket-watch; it was 5:15. Jackson's orders to his brigade commanders were simple: at the sound of the bugles signaling advance, the whole line was to sweep forward. A bugler rode up to the general announcing that everything was ready. Without speaking, Jackson gave only a nod. The bugler sounded the advance. All along the edge of the woods, buglers sounded the same call as frightened deer and rabbits bounded out of the woods in front of Jackson's men.

Realizing what was happening, some of Hooker's men tried to put up a defensive fire. Union artillery let loose several volleys. Jackson's men, whooping the Rebel Yell began pouring into the camps. With bayonets gleaming, the Confederates charged into the flank of the Army of the Potomac. Some Union men were killed as they crawled out of their tents, while others fled or surrendered.

Israel Sheldon and his battery of Rhode Islanders kept a steady fire on Jackson's surging army, fighting "with great vigor." [28] A week before the battle, George Randolph was promoted to major and appointed chief of artillery of Sickles' 3rd Corps. This left Israel's friend, Lieutenant Pardon Jastram in command of the battery. During Jackson's stunning attack, Israel and his men fell victim to a "galling enfilading fire," killing two Rhode Island men and wounding thirteen others. [29] Twenty-four horses were killed, including one which was struck by a cannonball as an officer sat in the saddle. Israel survived unhurt, but it was his most terrifying experience of the war.

Within ten minutes, Hooker's flank was falling back toward Chancellorsville where Lee's 17,000 men waited. By dark, the Army of the Potomac had retreated two miles and regrouped, bringing Jackson's advance to a gradual halt. The lines of both armies were broken, twisted, and at some points, within a stone's throw.

As Fredericksburg glowed under a full moon, Lieutenant Elisha Rhodes and the 2nd Rhode Island were crossing the Rappahannock River just south of Fredericksburg. The rest of Sedgwick's 23,000 men followed. Confederate General Jubal Early and his 10,000 men waited for them.

By nine o' clock, rumors were rife that Hooker was mounting a counterattack. Not knowing the position or condition of his own army, Jackson decided to investigate. The general and a few staff members rode through the woods trying to determine where the two armies' lines stood. While returning to his own lines, Jackson's entourage rode too close to a regiment of tired, scared North Carolinians. A volley of musket fire pierced the quiet woods and Little Sorrel, for the only time in the war, panicked and fled as branches gashed the general's face. Jackson's doctor shouted at the Carolinians, "Cease firing, you are firing into your own men." [30]

Word of Jackson's accidental shooting brought General Lee to the brink of tears. But this news, along with word that Sedgwick was crossing the river at Fredericksburg, and Lee's uncertainty about Stuart, now commanding Jackson's corps, forced his hand. May 3 would be a day of denouement at Chancellorsville.

Private James Sheldon spent the night of May 2 out of harm's way. A man in his brigade remembered that shortly after midnight "another battle came off, on our left, which lasted until one a.m. and ended by the enemy being repulsed, and routed again…All was quiet until Sunday, May the 3rd." [31]

Elisha Rhodes and Sedgwick's Corps spent the night in a nearly deserted Fredericksburg. At first light, the 2nd Rhode Island fell into line on Princess Anne Street, and by eight a.m., the regiment began marching out of the city to support Hooker at Chancellorsville. From the heights above Fredericksburg, Confederate artillery opened upon them and the march was conducted under heavy fire. Pinned down near a small mill pond, Elisha watched as shells burst overhead and splashed in the water. As Union artillery came on line, it was pounded by Confederate gunners on the hills and rendered useless. Scores of men fell—killed or wounded.

John Sedgwick was a fighter. His grandfather had fought in the American Revolution. The 49-year-old general and Connecticut bachelor, who had fought in both the Seminole and Mexican Wars, had already been wounded twice in this one. "Uncle John," as he was referred to by the men of the 6th Corps, was arguably the most beloved of Union generals. Although a strict disciplinarian, he had great affection for his men and refused to see them pinned down and slaughtered in the streets.

When his artillery was unable to elevate enough to return fire, he ordered ten regiments to assault the Confederate guns on the heights. The men of the 2nd watched in awe as wave after wave of blue-clad soldiers charged up the slopes, taking severe casualties.

Commanding Marye's Heights was a 47-year-old Confederate general, Jubal Early. "Jubilee," or "Old Jube,"[32] as his men called him, was a Virginia attorney, and like Sedgwick, was a veteran of both the Seminole and Mexican Wars. He had been wounded at Williamsburg. Early had voted against secession but his first loyalty was to Virginia. On this day at Fredericksburg, the numbers were against him. Sedgwick, below, had over twice the men Early had and even in this nearly impregnable position he wouldn't be able to hold against sustained assaults.

By late morning, the first of Sedgwick's men had reached the crest of the hill and Early's men began falling back. Elisha spotted Union flags flying atop Marye's Heights just as the 2nd

Rhode Island was ordered to join the assault. All eyes were on Colonel Rogers. While he was becoming immensely popular, he had never been under fire with the 2nd. Rogers led them up the slope and within minutes Lieutenant Rhodes and the men were in the thick of the battle. Reaching the crest of the first of a series of hills, the 2nd chased Early's men who were desperately trying to drag their artillery with them as they retreated. The whir and buzz of minie balls filled the air—shells burst everywhere. While charging up the second slope, a shell exploded only a few feet from Rhodes, throwing a "shower of iron" at him. [33] A sharp pain in his foot caused Elisha to jump into the air. Although the pain was severe, he wasn't seriously wounded. He found the culprit, a small iron ball, laying innocently nearby. Putting it in his pocket he vowed to send it to his mother in Pawtuxet. Limping, he rejoined the charge as Sedgwick's Corps took total control of Marye's Heights.

Sedgwick now had access to the Plank Road, which was the main approach to Chancellorsville. Learning that Hooker was in trouble at Chancellorsville, Sedgwick hastened his march. Upon hearing that Sedgwick had broken through, Lee divided his army yet again, to drive the Union men off the Plank Road, his only line of escape in the direction of Fredericksburg. Only "Jeb" Stuart's 25,000 men remained to face Hooker's 73,000 entrenched troops at Chancellorsville—Hooker did nothing.

Semmes' Brigade had also spent a violent Sunday morning and James took part in heavy skirmishing. The Georgian skirmishers pressed the enemy so fiercely that the Union men remained in their rifle pits. A private in James' brigade had a close call during the fighting, "As soon as the Yankee sharpshooters saw us, they fired volleys after volleys at us, and the worst of it was they could see us and fire at us, while we could not fire at them with any effect. We stayed there, four or five minutes, and had twelve men wounded. The bullets sung 'round me as thick almost as hail. They cut bushes all 'round me. The only thing that saved me was a little alder bush about an inch or an inch and one-half thick. It turned a ball that would have killed or wounded me perhaps seriously, as it struck it about waist high. And I was standing about six spaces behind it."[34]

As the morning wore on, the fighting intensified and soon whole Union regiments could be seen retreating. Within minutes, "large and confused masses of fugitives rapidly retreating in the direction of United States Ford, was presented to the view."[35] Seeking to avoid needless slaughter, General Paul Semmes sent forward a flag of truce and demanded the surrender of the enemy still in their trenches. Seeing the hopelessness of his situation, the colonel of the 27th Connecticut and a detachment from another Connecticut regiment, totaling 340 men, surrendered.

By late morning of May 3, Semmes' Brigade was on the Plank Road heading east. The Georgians were fighting with attitude; their losses at Fox's Gap were still a bitter memory.

At noon, Private James Sheldon and the other men of Semmes' Brigade hid in the woods near the Plank Road leading to Fredericksburg. The occasional dropping of an enemy shell kept every man on edge. Men talked and the air was full of rumors. Suddenly, the men fell silent at the sight of General Lee and his staff riding slowly out of the woods toward them. James watched with keen interest as Lee, engrossed in conversation with General Lafayette McLaws, nodded pleasantly and said loud enough for all to hear, "Now, General, there is a chance for your young men to distinguish themselves."[36]

The stirring moment took a touching turn as a group of Union prisoners, being herded at the point of a bayonet, marched past Lee and McLaws. Stopping briefly, one of the prisoners shouted, "That's him! That's Lee! Hats off, boys!"[37] Every single prisoner faced the general and raised his hat to him. An obviously humbled Lee removed his own hat and bowed his head in respectful acknowledgement. The men of the 50th Georgia were so moved by the scene that they cheered the prisoners. Major McGlashan described the moment as "picturesque."[38] As James Sheldon and the 50th Georgia resumed the march to meet Sedgwick, a "defiant cheerfulness"[39] swept over the men.

Three miles west of Fredericksburg on the Plank Road, stood a modest red brick two story building known as Salem Church. Sunday services were ending as elements of Lee's army began arriving. At mid-afternoon James Sheldon and the 50th Georgia arrived preparing to meet the corps of John Sedgwick and Confederate sharpshooters ran through the church, competing for the windows of the second floor. They peered down the Plank Road waiting for Sedgwick's line of blue to come within range— they didn't wait long.

Salem Church (today)
note the bullet holes in the brick

Major McGlashan recalled, "a stirring sight awaited us … The enemy in magnificent force, and three lines deep, at right angles to and crossing the road, with flying colors and glancing bayonets, were driving Wilcox's Alabamians, who were gallantly struggling to delay them, before them. There was not a moment to lose. The enemy was almost in possession of the rising ground in front that would have commanded our position... Our brigade was ordered to the front." [40]

The 50th Georgia was part of the Confederate extreme left, while the 2nd Rhode Island, in reserve, was part of the Union extreme right. James Sheldon and Elisha Rhodes were facing each other. The gunfire was at first slight but quickly became severe. James fell into line of battle under a storm of bullets. General Semmes described the moment, "position was never more gallantly taken or more persistently and heroically." [41]

Lieutenant Rhodes wrote, "After the attack was made by the [Union] front line, we could see troops waver, and soon men began to retreat down the road. The next we knew the Rebels came in sight, and Colonel Rogers was ordered to the front with the 2nd RI." [42] Elisha's regiment crossed a field, reached the crest of a hill, and opened fire on the oncoming Georgians. The two sides fought each other at a distance of a mere 60 yards. McGlashan recalled, "The moment was critical; we could barely reach our line before the enemy. There was no time for brigade movements...The 50th Georgia on reaching their ground found the formation obstructed by a ditch and wattle fence at the edge of the field. Leaping over that, like so many deer, the men formed like lightning on the right by file into line. Receiving a terrible fire from the enemy at 60 yards range, and then, with a wild yell, we charged and drove the enemy over and beyond the line in confusion and ranged up along the 53rd Georgia to receive their next assault. We had lost about 15 or 20 men, but a more gallant deed I never witnessed." [43]

Most of Semmes' men began firing as soon as they formed their line. One soldier described it, saying, "The struggle became furious...With the exception of the battle at Malvern

Hill, I never heard such a noise in all my life. It sounded like a large canebrake on fire and a thunder storm with repeated loud thunder claps, one clap following another. [We] had a beautiful position in a little trench behind an embankment, formed by the fence, so we could load and fire without exposing anything except our heads and arms. In shooting, our company fired averaging from fifteen to twenty rounds apiece at the vandals…You may well guess that we made things count when we let loose at them." [44] During the fight a man standing near James "was shot through the side of the head while tearing a cartridge to load. He died without a groan." [45]

Colonel Rogers impressed Lt. Rhodes and his comrades by carrying the regimental colors into the fight three times. The 2nd Rhode Island was hurt but not broken, and rejoined the charge. As Rogers brought his men out to meet the Georgians again, a soldier from a New Jersey regiment began pleading to him, "For God's sake Colonel, come over and help us out!" [46] The New Jersey men, left behind when Sedgwick's first assault collapsed, were now pinned down in the woods without ammunition. Rogers charged into the woods as the enemy fell back, leaving behind several New Jersey men who had been captured, as well as their company colors. The fight in the woods lasted an hour before Lt. Rhodes and the 2nd Rhode Island, running low on ammunition, were reinforced by the 10th Massachusetts. In the thickest part of the fighting, the 53rd Georgia of Semmes' Brigade crashed into the 2nd Rhode Island, capturing the regiment's United States flag. The Georgians defiantly waved the banner at the Rhode Islanders as the 2nd fell back across a brook and rested, waiting for orders and ammunition.

****

Lee's army continued along the Plank Road and his situation improved by the minute as more regiments were thrown at Sedgwick. But the 50th Georgia was paying a ghastly price for its successes at Salem Church. Major McGlashan remembered, "we were suffering terribly, three color bearers shot down in succession. Gaps were seen along the line strewn with dead and wounded, the men steadily closing up the gaps, and kneeling, were firing with deliberation. The roar of musketry was incessant and terrific. Still the men loaded and fired, not a break or waver in the line, although nearly two-thirds of their men lay dead and wounded around them. Rush after rush was made by the enemy and as often vigorously repulsed. Our rifles were leading up so they were useless, the men throwing them away would pick up the rifle of some dead or wounded comrade and resume the fight." [47]

The 10th Georgia of Semmes' Brigade, burdened by the Connecticut prisoners it had taken earlier in the day, was just arriving at Salem Church. "[But] scarcely had we gotten in position, when the enemy fired upon us at a distance not exceeding 100 yards, which was returned by us in such a manner as to completely break their lines; and seeing the brigade immediately upon my right charging, I communicated the fact to General Semmes, who ordered us to charge, when every man and officer in my regiment leaped the fence and dashed forward at the enemy with a yell, cutting them down as they advanced, and completely routing them... without any support, General Semmes ordered us to fall back, which was done in good order." [48]

Colonel Holt of the 10th Georgia later remarked, "General Semmes was with us in the charge, and, as usual, in the front rank. No officer or man with any pride could skulk behind and see his general display such courage as General Semmes displayed in the charge." [49]

James and the other Georgians had fired nearly 60 rounds of ammunition. Lt. Colonel Frank Kearse sent a courier to Semmes stating that his ammunition was running low. The general ordered him to replenish his ammunition from the ordnance train. If this was not possible, the 50th was expected to continue the fight with whatever ammunition they had left. Surviving men could then, and only then, retire to the rear.

Peter McGlashan also described the desperate situation of James' regiment, saying, "[We] had used up sixty rounds of ammunition, the litter bearers were dispatched for more, the wounded left uncared for. 'I shall have no regiment left,' shouted [Lt. Colonel Francis Kearse] to me, 'if this lasts a half hour longer. Oh, that the sun would set; is there no supports?'" [50]

Sedgwick was whipped. "They are giving way; let us charge them," [51] a soldier of the "Thomas County Rangers" shouted to McGlashan. So the 50th Georgia charged one more time and found Sedgwick's men fleeing to the Rappahannock. "The field was won," Major McGlashan remembered, "But there was great loss within the regiment." [52] Darkness had brought mercy to both armies and it was time to tend to those who had fallen. In a touching moment, Major McGlashan was approached by a litter bearer who, mistaking him for Lt. Colonel Kearse, explained, "Colonel, one of your men, badly wounded, desires to see you before he dies!" McGlashan recalled, "I went back with him and found, stretched on a litter, a private named John Culpepper, of Company H, from Colquit County, Georgia, a plain woods farmer, always present for duty, plain and unobtrusive in his manners. He was terribly wounded; a ball had struck him on the edge of the temple, tearing out both eyes and nose; the very brains seemed coming out. He evidently had not long to live, although quite conscious. 'Is the Colonel here?' he said. 'Yes, I answered, and I am grieved to find you so sorely hurt.' He groped out with his hand. 'Colonel, take my hand.' I took it in both mine and knelt down beside him."

"'Colonel,' he whispered, 'have I done my duty?' I was thrilled to the heart with the dying hero's devotion. 'Yes, and all the time.' 'Oh, that is all right,' he said; 'tell my people, when you return home, that John Culpepper died doing his duty.' He never spoke again dying shortly afterward." [53]

On another part of the battlefield, some men of the 10th Georgia found a Union boy who looked barely fifteen and had the voice of a young child. His uniform was shot to pieces and he appeared to be dying. The Georgians carried him to the rear for treatment. To everyone's amazement, the boy survived.

Sedgwick's 6th Corps and the 2nd Rhode Island fled toward the Rappahannock—they were unable to cross. Sedgwick was caught between the Army of Northern Virginia at Fredericksburg and Chancellorsville. Early Monday, Lt. Elisha Rhodes wrote, "The Rebels have taken possession of Fredericksburg in our rear and we are cut off from the river, but we have confidence in General Sedgwick and shall get out of the scrape somehow. Heavy fighting is going on up the river where Hooker is trying to break through, but we do not know the result." [54]

In the darkness of May 3, the Army of Northern Virginia ended its pursuit of Hooker and fell back to the vicinity of Salem Church. Sedgwick and Hooker struggled to get their men across the river. Paul Semmes' Georgians rested until Monday morning and then built breastworks until late that evening. As no tools were available, James and the men used their bayonets instead of picks and axes, and were forced to dig with their hands instead of shovels and spades. Due to its position, the 50th Georgia once again had the first pick through a sea of guns, bayonets, cartridge boxes, and knapsacks that lay scattered as far as they could see. One man claimed, "Dead Yanks lay very thick. It looked more like a slaughter pen than anything else. The trees were riddled with balls and torn to pieces by shells. Every person that was in hearing distance of the fighting that I have conversed with say that it was the most terrific battle that they had ever heard. It is said that our regiment done the best shooting that [has] ever been done since the war commenced. There was seldom a bullet seen in the trees shot from our side that was above a man's head." [55] The scope of the tragedy was eerily reminiscent of the Battle of Malvern Hill ten months before. "The shrieks and groans of the wounded on the battlefield after the fight was heart-rending beyond all description. You can't imagine what an awful sight it is to visit a battlefield just after a hard fought battle," one Confederate survivor explained in a letter to his family. [56]

On Tuesday, the 5th, Semmes' Brigade took to the road at about 3:30 in the afternoon and marched three or four miles in the hardest rain James had seen fall in Virginia. Soaked to the bone, the brigade halted about sundown. James pitched his half of a little tent, courtesy of Joe Hooker and the Army of the Potomac.

To this day, Lee's movements at Chancellorsville are studied as perhaps the most brilliant military operation in the history of warfare. But at great cost. Most sources agree that Hooker had over 130,000 men at his disposal while Lee had 61,000. The Army of the Potomac suffered 17,000 killed, wounded, or missing, compared to the Army of Northern Virginia's 13,000. In spite of his stellar victory, these were staggering losses for Lee. Elisha's 2nd Rhode Island counted 7 killed, 68 wounded, and 9 missing. James' 50th Georgia fared far worse; of the 316 men who'd answered the morning roll call on May 3, 187 were killed or wounded and four were missing. One of the severely wounded was Private John Brack, Gussie Brack's father. He died nine days later.

Insult added to the sorrow of the regiment. General Semmes had received few reports of the 50th Georgia's action during the day. After the battle, as the regiment was resting, Semmes rode up to Frank Kearse demanding, "What regiment is this?" The lieutenant colonel's adjutant handed the day's tragic report to one of Semmes' staff. Minutes later, Semmes, in an altered tone, ordered, "Colonel bring your regiment to attention." It was done. Raising his cap off his head, Semmes shouted to the men, "50th Georgia, I salute you! This is a most honorable report. I am proud of you!" [57]

McGlashan remembered how angry the men of the 50th were with Semmes, "The men gazed at him steadily, but the idea that the General did not know they had been fighting at all was too much for them; they received the salute in silence." [58]

In spite of their losses, Semmes' Georgians had a lot to feel good about. During the operations of the first three days of May, they took 595 prisoners and 1,500 smallarms and a large number of small tents.

Nine days after the Battle of Chancellorsville, a tired James Sheldon stumbled back into Pine Grove Camp. One man in Semmes' Brigade remembered the march back to Pine Grove, saying, "we marched on our way back to camp, which was some 12 or 15 miles. The roads were very muddy, and it was tiresome marching…We reached camps about dark, wet, tired, worn out and with blistered feet. When we got here, we found it almost a ruin, as no person was there. Our tents were cut to ribbons, by orders of our General. The camp had been plundered by citizens [and] stragglers. We all lost everything we had left in our knapsacks. You may well know how we felt. The tents were all cut for fear they would fall into the hands of the Yanks." [59]

No rations had been issued during the fighting at Chancellorsville and the Georgians had been living off the Yankees. The brigade captured almost 500 Union rifles, and the men fought over the best guns. It was clear to all that the summer of 1863 was going to be a hot one.

7

IT WAS A SAD LIST

May 4 brought continued heavy fighting as Sedgwick and Hooker both sought the safety of the Rappahannock River. Private James Sheldon's 50th Georgia continued to press Lieutenant Elisha Rhodes and the 2nd Rhode Island which was cut off from the river. Knowing their wounded had been left behind and in enemy hands, the spirits of the Rhode Islanders sank even further.

On the evening of Tuesday the 5th, Sedgwick's 6th Corps began crossing the river over a pontoon bridge. The 2nd was again given the deadly assignment of rear guard. Shot and shell fell like rain. Elisha patiently watched regiment after regiment pass over the river. When it was finally their turn, the Rhode Islanders made their way across the Rappahannock where they collapsed from exhaustion. To the west, at United States Ford, Hooker's Army of the Potomac also recrossed the river. Meanwhile, Captain Peter McGlashan of the 50th Georgia observed, "a severe storm of wind and rain [swept the area]…we returned to Chancellorsville and prepared to assault General Hooker in his last entrenched position. But on advancing to his lines we found them deserted. During the storm he had recrossed the river to his original position, and the memorable campaign of Chancellorsville was ended." [1]

Wednesday was raw and windy. Elisha's company was ordered down to the riverbank to retrieve some pontoons, but reaching the water's edge they were greeted by a large force of

Confederates. A Confederate officer on the opposite bank began shouting that if the men of the 2ⁿᵈ agreed to leave the pontoons behind there would be no bloodshed. Elisha acceded to the demand and what followed was the strange sight of two enemies watching each other build fires to keep warm in the pouring rain. He remembered, "we spent the day chaffing each other across the stream."[2] Under the cover of darkness and under occasional rifle fire, the entire 2ⁿᵈ Rhode Island safely escaped their position at Banks Ford by boat. By daylight most of the men were ashore across from Fredericksburg and before noon were back in their old camp at Falmouth. The "Valley Forge"[3] of the new war suddenly looked quite welcoming and Elisha reflected, "Thank God I am alive and well…"[4]

The armies returned to the positions they had held before the battle of Chancellorsville as an uneasy stillness quelled the banks of the Rappahannock. The aftermath of the fight changed strategies and attitudes on both sides. Lincoln left Washington to meet with Hooker, while Lee appointed A. P. Hill to permanently replace the wounded and ailing Jackson as commander of the 2ⁿᵈ Corps. Hooker's army sat vulnerable on the banks of the Rappahannock, but Lee's losses left him unable to take advantage of the situation. With their armies battered in Virginia, Presidents Lincoln and Davis shifted their attention to Mississippi where Grant and William Tecumseh Sherman were pushing hard at Jackson, Vicksburg, and Port Hudson. To oppose them, Confederate general Joseph Johnston was placed in command of the Southern troops in Mississippi.

During the second week of May, word spread that "Stonewall" Jackson was dead—the people of the South were devastated.

****

But there was still a war to be fought. Elisha Rhodes rested in camp near Falmouth, while James Sheldon did the same near Chancellorsville. In the West, it was a different story. On

Tuesday, May 12, Grant won a battle at Raymond, Mississippi, 15 miles from Jackson, the state capital. This engagement drew Grant's attention away from Vicksburg and he attacked Joe Johnston at the capital instead. On May 14, Johnston's force of 12,000 fled north. In a wind-driven afternoon rain Grant's forces occupied Jackson.

Sherman remained at Jackson to collect or destroy Confederate supplies, while Grant focused on Vicksburg. On the 16th, Grant tried to cut the lines of supply and communication between Confederate forces north and south in Mississippi, and a fierce fight took place at Champion's Hill. Forced to withdraw, the Confederates fell back to the Big Black River. Desertions among Confederate troops soared as Grant upped the pressure on Mississippi. On May 18, Grant's army crossed Big Black River and began siege operations at Vicksburg. Union artillery started pummeling the city the next day. Grant also ordered Massachusetts native General Nathaniel Banks to begin siege operations downriver at Port Hudson.

Army life was relatively quiet along the Rappahannock. The men of both sides paused and evaluated their military and personal situations. Lieutenant Israel Sheldon thought long and hard about his future and where he was needed most. He had been a dedicated soldier but he had a little boy back in Pawtuxet. Three weeks before the battle of Chancellorsville, Israel celebrated his 36th birthday. A fellow officer in his battery said of Israel, "Although not a brilliant officer, he performed his part with a conscientious fidelity to his conceptions of duty. The respect for Lieutenant Sheldon among the enlisted men was universal and sincere. His amiable disposition and gentlemanly demeanor will cause them always to hold him in high respect and esteem." Another officer recalled that Israel had his shortcomings as a military man but he was "redeemed by his manly and amiable demeanor." [5]

On May 21, Israel resigned from the army and began preparing for his journey back to Rhode Island, where his Alma, son, William, brothers, sisters and mother waited. The second of Rebecca Sheldon's three soldier sons returned safely home.

The next day Grant attacked Vicksburg only to be repulsed with heavy casualties. Union General Nathaniel Bank's siege operations against Port Hudson were in full swing. But when the embattled Confederate artillerists atop the bluffs of Vicksburg suddenly went on the offensive against a Union gunboat below, Grant's river campaign was temporarily stymied.

****

In the shadow of these events, newspapers North and South took little notice of Lee's reorganization of the Army of Northern Virginia. Streamlined into three corps led by Longstreet commanding the 1st, Ewell the 2nd, and A. P. Hill commanding the newly created 3rd, the army was about to embark on a daring march. Semmes' Brigade moved to a new camp within one mile of Fredericksburg and within sight of the Union camps. In Washington, Lincoln considered firing Joe Hooker.

June began much like May had ended. Grant and Banks continued to pound Port Hudson and Vicksburg. Ambrose Burnside ordered the *Chicago Times* to close its doors after running anti-Lincoln editorials. Lincoln sought the advice of General John Reynolds regarding Hooker's future as commander of the Army of the Potomac. Reynolds, a 43-year-old Pennsylvanian, was one of the army's most distinguished officers. A Mexican War veteran and "Indian fighter," Reynolds was commandant of cadets at West Point when Ft. Sumter was attacked. He was put in charge of defending Washington in the early days of the war and was taken prisoner during the Seven Days' Battles. After being exchanged, he rose in rank to divisional and corps command. Lincoln had few generals as solid as John Reynolds.

James Sheldon turned 23 years old on Tuesday, June 3. Lee's Army of Northern Virginia began moving out of Fredericksburg. With Lee's objective to the north and the safety of Richmond to the south, he boldly headed his army west. At Falmouth, Hooker was worried. When word of Lee's movements reached Lincoln, the President ordered Hooker to attack Lee's

168

army on the move, rather than attempt to retake Fredericksburg from the small Confederate force that had been left to defend it.

Lieutenant Elisha Rhodes anxiously watched as the events of June 5 unfolded. Two rumors swept through the ranks; there would be an advance on Richmond, and, several of their own corps' deserters were to be executed later that day. Morale was pitifully low and Elisha wrote that "it is worse for a soldier to wait for a battle to begin than it is to do the fighting."[6] About mid-morning the following day, the 2nd Rhode Island left its camp at Falmouth and marched down to the Rappahannock at Franklin's Crossing where it halted. Elisha watched curiously as much of Hooker's Army crossed the river over pontoon bridges, finally taking the abandoned Fredericksburg. Both armies sporadically lobbed artillery shells at each other as Lee's main army crept to the west and north.

The next day, Sunday June 7, Confederate forces attacked Grant at Milliken's Bend, Mississippi, and Grant suffered over 500 casualties until the Union Navy shelled the enemy into submission. On Monday, Lee and Ewell's Corps entered Culpeper Court House and established a base as the Army of Northern Virginia began its bold campaign into the North. This stop at Culpepper featured a grand spectacle as General "Jeb" Stuart paraded his cavalry before Lee and his staff. Stuart's cavalry would be indispensable to Lee during the coming campaign.

****

Semmes' Brigade was worn out from the road. Private James Sheldon and the 50th Georgia broke camp on the night of June 3 and marched within a mile of Chancellorsville. On the march they had passed the Chancellorsville battlefield where many dead enemy and horses remained unburied. The next day Semmes' men marched fifteen miles and camped before sundown on Mountain Run Creek, two miles from Rockwood Forest on the Rapidan River. One man in the brigade wrote "these lines leaves me tolerable well but very tired from the long march we have had. We have just got here. We have left Fredericksburg and are going on in the direction of Manassas where I think will soon be a big fight but I hope we will not be in it. It is about sixty five miles further." [7]

On Tuesday, June 9, Hooker, seeing Lee moving north, sent his cavalry to investigate. "Jeb" Stuart's cavalry was sent to meet him and what resulted was the largest cavalry engagement ever to take place on American soil. Stuart held his ground at Brandy's Station but, for the first time, Union cavalry proved to be his equal. Union losses were about 900 killed, wounded or missing, while Stuart lost slightly over 500 men.

Under constant shelling, Lt. Elisha Rhodes and the 2nd Rhode Island continued to quietly watch the Army of Northern Virginia slither out of Fredericksburg, making its way northwest toward Pennsylvania. Richmond was now lightly defended and easy prey for Hooker, but Lincoln was more concerned with Lee's advancing army than the Confederate capital.

For two days beginning on the 14th, the armies clashed at Winchester, Virginia. The Confederates seized over 20 guns and 300 loaded wagons. Badly mauled, the Union force fell back towards Harper's Ferry as the Army of Northern Virginia began crossing the Potomac near Williamsport, Maryland. Hooker's army left its position of seven months and began moving north in pursuit. As the Army of Northern Virginia approached Pennsylvania the citizens of the state began to panic. The government at Harrisburg prepared to evacuate the city as Lincoln called for 100,000 volunteers to ward off the growing threat.

By the 17th, the Army of the Potomac was outside Fairfax Court House, 25 miles from Washington. Lt. Elisha Rhodes described the journey from Fredericksburg as "one of hardest marches we have ever known... [I am] almost dead from the heat. I never suffered more in my life than I did on this march." [8]

Two days later, Ewell, A. P. Hill and Longstreet continued north while skirmishing with scattered Union forces. On Wednesday, the 24th, A. P. Hill and Longstreet's Corps began crossing the Potomac. That same day, the 2nd Rhode Island and the 6th Corps marched to Centreville, discarding any unnecessary equipment to quicken their march. Rumors circulated that Lee was in Pennsylvania.

For the next week, the Army of the Potomac marched north and west in pursuit of the Army of Northern Virginia. Confederate cavalry continuously harassed the rear of Hooker's army and the 2nd Rhode Island served as rear guard, fighting as it marched. "Jeb" Stuart's cavalry left the main body of Lee's army, positioning itself between Hooker's army and Washington. On Friday the 26th, General Jubal Early and his troops entered the small crossroads town of Gettysburg. The next day, with Washington in danger and the North invaded, Lincoln fired Joe Hooker.

The new commander of the Army of the Potomac was Major General George Gordon Meade. At 49, Meade had risen from brigadier general to corps commander. He was short-tempered, often unapproachable, and generally disliked by his peers. Yet Lincoln chose him over John Reynolds to lead the Army of the Potomac through the coming storm. Unlike General George McClellan, who was seriously considering challenging Lincoln for the presidency in 1864, Meade could hold no such aspirations, having been born in Spain.

The march to Pennsylvania was taking its toll on Semmes' Brigade, which had numbered 1334 during late June. James Sheldon's 50th Georgia, having suffered badly at Fox's Gap and Salem Church, had only 302 men fit for duty. The oppressive heat caused many men to fall out of the march from exhaustion or sunstroke. On the 20th, the brigade crossed the flooding Shenandoah River at Berry's Ford, only to recross the next day to repel a rumored threat from Hooker. With Hooker nowhere in sight, the Georgians again pushed north across the river on the 22nd. The following day James was issued one of the new rifles that had arrived from Winchester, Virginia.

On June 26, Semmes' men were excited as they crossed the Potomac River at Martinsburg and camped at Williamsport,

Maryland. This was Union soil but didn't feel like it. It wasn't until the following day, the same Saturday on which Lincoln fired Hooker, that the first elements of Lee's Army of Northern Virginia officially invaded the North. Semmes' Brigade marched through Hagerstown, Maryland, where it captured large quantities of supplies and food. James' 50th marched another 14 miles, and later that same day the Georgians entered Pennsylvania at Greencastle. Semmes' men finally made camp five miles from Chambersburg, about 25 miles due east of Gettysburg. James, Gussie Brack, John Chastain and others went on a raiding party. Their objectives were the locals' vegetable gardens.

Paul Semmes expected his men to be the same gentlemen in Pennsylvania as they would be in Georgia and gave strict orders against looting. However, he allowed his men to forage for necessities. A private in the 53rd Georgia described the brigade's predicament, saying, "It hurts them (the locals) very badly to see rebels occupying their country. We do not destroy anything but what we need to eat and wear, such things as vegetables and chickens. An old Dutch woman got after me today while I was getting onions from her garden. She gave me fits, but I made this reply, 'Yes,'em, Yes, 'em, our generals don't allow us to take anything the people will sell.' The people look very sour and crest-fallen and as if they hope we get whipped." [9]

Elisha Rhodes and the 2nd Rhode Island, 409 strong, crossed the Potomac on a pontoon bridge at Edwards Ferry, and then resumed a march averaging twenty miles a day.

Sunday morning, George Meade awoke to news of his appointment as commander of the Army of the Potomac. His first order of business was to gather as much information about the condition and positions of his army as well as the Army of Northern Virginia. His army of 90,000 men had also crossed the Potomac and was scattered in the area of Frederick, Maryland, one day's march behind Lee's 70,000. Early summer rains slowed the progress of both armies.

By evening Lee received word that the Army of the Potomac had crossed the river. Some leading elements of his own army were camped a mere five miles from the Pennsylvania capital, but rather than continue on to Harrisburg, he ordered his army toward Cashtown and Gettysburg. Jubal Early had marched through Gettysburg and was now in York, and the solid defensive ground he had left behind at Gettysburg now was held by a small Union cavalry force under General John Buford. Lee wondered and worried—where was "Jeb" Stuart and his cavalry? Stuart had wandered far to the east, skirmishing occasionally with Union cavalry, but rendering himself useless to Lee when plans changed.

On the last day of June, Meade ordered the 1st Corps of John Reynolds to rush to Buford's aid at Gettysburg as both Lee and Meade sought to be the first to occupy the town and its surrounding hills. Lee ordered all of his forces to converge on Cashtown, nine miles west of Gettysburg, and June 29 proved to be a footrace in the mud between 160,000 soldiers.

****

Lieutenant Elisha Rhodes and the 2nd Rhode Island were camped at Manchester, Maryland, about 20 miles southeast of Gettysburg on the Baltimore Pike. In spite of the hard marching, Elisha managed to enjoy himself. As the 2nd approached the Pennsylvania border he wrote, "The country is beautiful, and the people are very kind to us and appear glad to see us. Young ladies stand at the gates and furnish the men with cold water and loaves of bread as we pass. It has rained for a week and the roads are muddy. After marching for twenty miles it is not pleasant to lie down at night in the wet without any cover. I am tired—in fact I never was so tired in my life. But Hurrah! It is all for the Union." [10] Elisha also appreciated being in friendly territory, noting, "It is entirely different from our treatment in Virginia." [11]

Private James Sheldon and the 50th Georgia had also put in several days of tough marching reaching Fayetteville, about 20 miles west and slightly to the north of Gettysburg.

Union General John Buford's cavalry waited three miles west of Gettysburg on the Chambersburg Pike and spent the last hours of June staring through the darkness of a steady summer drizzle. He put pickets on the east side of a stone bridge which spanned Marsh Creek. As Lee gathered his army at Cashtown, a few of his footsore brigades heard of a trainload of shoes at Gettysburg.

At 5:30 a.m., Lieutenant Marcellus Jones of the 8th Illinois Cavalry thought he saw something across the stone bridge. Straining his eyes through the mist, the image became clearer—a man on a horse. Other men could be seen walking beside the horseman. Seeing a Confederate officer shouting orders to marching infantry, Jones didn't hesitate to act and asked a sergeant to hand him a rifle. At 700 yards, Jones took aim on the officer. He fired and missed as the Confederates spread themselves into a skirmish line a mile and a half wide—the Battle of Gettysburg had begun.

Buford understood his situation all too well and he didn't like it. Seventy-five-hundred Confederate infantrymen were advancing on his force of less than 3,000 dismounted cavalry, a quarter of them would be needed to look after the horses. Gettysburg was neither army's first choice as a field of battle, but it did feature two opposing ridges running north and south about a mile apart. To the south were two hills overlooking the entire area, and all that lay between them and the Army of Northern Virginia was Buford's tiny force. The Union general would make his stand along McPherson's Ridge on the Chambersburg Pike and wait for Reynolds' 1st Corps, due to arrive at any hour. Buford had one advantage, the Spencer repeating carbines his men had recently been issued.

At eight a.m., two Confederate brigades were ordered forward to attack Buford. A sustained burst of rifle fire from McPherson's Ridge stunned and staggered the Confederates, but still they came on as Buford's men reloaded their repeating rifles, firing at multiple targets. Buford took heavy casualties but held his position. Two hours later, as Buford's line was faltering, the

1st Corps arrived. Reynolds was soon killed and General Abner Doubleday assumed command of the 1st Corps.

An hour later, the heavy fighting subsided—both armies poured onto the battlefield. The Army of Northern Virginia held a numerical advantage of three to two. By noon, things began to heat up again with the arrival Major General Oliver Howard and his 11th Corps.

Howard sent two of his divisions to extend the line of the 1st Corps along Seminary Ridge. He held the remainder of his corps in reserve on Cemetery Hill. Before his troops were deployed, Howard received a message from Buford that Ewell's Corps was advancing directly on the Union, right where Howard was sending his divisions. Howard sent urgent messages to other Union corps that were marching to Gettysburg, pleading for their swift arrival.

By two o' clock, Ewell smashed through Howard's divisions on Seminary Ridge, pushing them through Gettysburg and overwhelming the entire 11th Corps. Terrified Union soldiers fled across the open fields. South of the town along Cemetery Hill, they were relieved to find that Howard had left a division and a few pieces of artillery in reserve under the command of Brigadier General Adolph von Steinwehr. Steinwehr had spent the late morning and early afternoon hours overseeing the construction of earthworks and organizing lines of shelter behind groups of trees and stone walls. These positions were hastily adopted by the shaken men of the 11th Corps.

The 2,500 residents of Gettysburg suddenly found themselves hosting nearly 75,000 guests, with at least that many more on the way. One of these residents was Tillie Pierce, 15, who lived with her family above her father's butcher shop in the center of town.

One week before the battle, low murmurs were running through both the Young Ladies Seminary and the town that Lee's army was somewhere in Pennsylvania. Anxiety gripped Gettysburg and Tillie's teacher kept one eye on her class and the other on the window. The atmosphere in the classroom was one of stifled worry as the afternoons ticked away. Suddenly, the teacher stunned Tillie and the other children by abruptly declaring, "Children, run home as quickly as you can." [12]

The order "did not require repeating," Tillie recalled, adding, "I am satisfied some of the girls did not reach home before the Rebels were in the streets." Upon reaching the safety of her home, Ms. Pierce slammed the door shut and ran to the sitting room. Her curiosity won out over fear, however, and she went to a window and peeked out between the shutters. "What a horrible sight!," she thought to herself. "There they were, human beings! Clad in almost rags, covered with dust, riding wildly, pell-mell down the hill toward our home! Shouting, yelling most unearthly, cursing, brandishing their revolvers, and firing right and left." [13] These Confederates left Gettysburg the next day in the direction of York, Pennsylvania.

By three o'clock, General Robert E. Lee sat on his horse, Traveller, on a hill along the Chambersburg Pike. Only hours earlier at Cashtown, Lee had become unsettled by the sound of artillery fire in the direction of Gettysburg, but with Longstreet's Corps still on the march and "Jeb" Stuarts's cavalry out of contact and blind as to what was happening ahead of him, Lee asserted there would be no "general engagement today." [14] But as he anxiously peered through his field glasses, he liked what he saw. It was here that he would destroy the Army of the Potomac once and for all. Longstreet disagreed, offering a plan of defense. Lee gazed toward Cemetery Hill and stated, "No—I am going to attack him there!" He predicted, "I am going to whip them or they are going to whip me." [15]

An hour later, command of Union forces at Gettysburg changed hands again, as General Winfield Scott Hancock was sent by Meade to take charge until the commanding general himself arrived later in the day. The 39-year-old Hancock exuded a confidence that flirted with cockiness—with his army crumbling, Meade needed such a personality on the field. One officer noted of Hancock that soldiers "felt safe when near him." [16] The Union collapse stopped at Cemetery Hill and Hancock rode back and forth along its crest, rallying his men to dig in and fight. During the hostility of the first day, the Union's 1st and 11th Corps lost nearly 10,000 men killed, wounded or missing.

Throughout the late afternoon of July 1, the Union men on Cemetery Hill employed the saw and axe as much as the musket. From Culp's Hill to the north and the smaller of two hills to the south known as the "Round Tops," [17] Hancock's battered army stubbornly clung to the high ground. The Army of Northern Virginia spread out in a line from downtown Gettysburg along Seminary Ridge, ranging from one half to one mile to the west. The opposing lines were formed in the same shape.

Knowing just how narrowly the Army of the Potomac had escaped destruction, Lee believed the end of the war lay just beyond Cemetery Ridge and wanted one more final push through Hancock's bloodied lines. Early in the afternoon, Lee urged General Richard Ewell to seize the high ground on Cemetery Hill. Ewell, whose corps had already suffered badly throughout the day, insisted that his men were spent and his one fresh division had not yet arrived. The Confederate advance of July 1 sputtered and stopped as the blazing sun sank in the western sky. Ewell's decision not to attack Hancock on Cemetery Hill became an immediate controversy, and adding injury to insult, Ewell was shot in his wooden leg, which he dryly described as painless.

As the day ended, Lee and Longstreet debated the strengths and weaknesses of their position—blind without Stuart's cavalry. Meade, en route to Gettysburg, ordered all available Union forces to join him there. Before dawn, the Army of the Potomac swelled to 85,000 men; they would face nearly 70,000 of Lee's Army of Northern Virginia.

****

Earlier that same afternoon, with Colonel Manning back in command, James Sheldon and the 50th Georgia reached Marsh Creek, three miles from Gettysburg. Semmes' Brigade numbered less than 600 men. These soldiers had pushed themselves to the edge of exhaustion and wilted in the oppressive heat—many nearly collapsed under the weight of their knapsacks. Black clouds hung in the eastern sky and man-made thunder rumbled in the distance as an excited cavalryman rode through the weary ranks of the 50th. After pleading with the horseman for details about the Yankees, he would only share, "They were running like hell the last time I saw them!" [18] From his haste, it was obvious that the horseman had seen enough Yankees for his liking. The brigade bivouacked under the Pennsylvania stars—James wondered what morning would bring.

The 2nd Rhode Island was camped near Manchester, Maryland, when the fighting at Gettysburg began. Elisha wrote, "Rumors of the fighting in Pennsylvania have been heard all the [recent] days, but the distance was so great that we knew little about it. The men were hungry and tired and lay down to rest early in the evening (July 1). At nine o'clock orders came for us to move and we, in great haste, packed up and started on the road towards Pennsylvania." [19]

The men of the 2nd Rhode Island plodded throughout the warm summer night. Some soldiers had been without sleep for more than 24 hours and "were falling over their own shadows… Little is said by anyone, for we are too weary to talk, only now and then an officer sharply orders the men to close up. Daylight brought no halt and what little hard bread we had was taken from the haversacks and eaten as we marched on." [20]

Meade arrived at Gettysburg after a twelve-mile moonlit ride and took command from Hancock. In a hastily called council-of-war, Meade pressed his generals for assurances that his army was entrenched on sound defensive ground. Strong in the center along Cemetery Ridge, and holding even higher ground on the extreme left and right ends of his line, Meade was satisfied.

Lee's plan of attack for July 2 was for Longstreet to assail the Union flank near a wheatfield along the Emmitsburg Pike with two divisions under John Bell Hood and Lafayette McLaws. At the same time, Ewell was to keep Meade busy by attacking his right near Culp's Hill. But things went awry from the start, as Ewell and Longstreet were slow to get moving and Ewell was dealing with an unmanageable number of wounded. A Confederate division commanded by General George Pickett had not yet arrived and Longstreet was reluctant to go into battle with, as he described it, "one boot off." [21] Lee's stomach discomfort had worsened and some feared he was experiencing a recurrence of a mild heart attack that had disabled him the previous March. After riding with his staff to survey the terrain, Lee returned to his headquarters late in the morning only to learn that Longstreet had yet to move out, while Meade had strengthened his own defenses—the general was beside himself.

Hours passed and the day dragged. Then, poisoning Lee's mood further, Stuart suddenly returned proudly presenting the general with 125 wagons he had captured. Witnesses described the meeting as "painful" to watch—the wandering cavalier caught the full wrath of the red-faced commander. Stuart offered to resign and if Lee was tempted to accept this resignation circumstances would not allow it. Lee would have to settle for a strong rebuke of Stuart's latest "ride." [22]

****

At about three p.m., without orders, Union General Sickles sent four companies of sharpshooters out in front of his 3rd Corps to probe Longstreet's strength. Although Longstreet was not there, Sickles' men encountered stiff resistance from some Alabamians. Thinking this was the beginning of a major engagement, Sickles moved his entire corps a half mile forward of Meade's army, fully exposing it to Longstreet who was finally getting into position. Longstreet couldn't believe his luck, as Meade, looking on in horror, personally rode out to reprimand Sickles, who by then had recognized his folly and offered to return to his original position. As the two men argued, Longstreet's artillery erupted in a fury. A shell burst near Meade, sending his panicked horse running. Sickles' Corps was alone and in big trouble as Longstreet hit him at the peach orchard, the wheat field, and a clump of boulders known as Devil's Den.

Semmes' Georgians had been roused at four in the morning, but delays prevented the brigade from breaking camp until sunrise. General Joseph Kershaw's brigade was serving with Semmes as part of McLaw's Division. Kershaw, in his mid-thirties, was an attorney before the war and came from an old money South Carolina family. He had served as a legislator and fought in the Mexican War. Of that July morning in Gettysburg he said, "we reached the hill overlooking Gettysburg, with only a slight detention from the [wagon] trains in the way, and moved to the right of the 3rd Corps, and were halted until about noon. We were then directed to move under the cover of the hills toward the right, with a view to flanking the enemy in that direction, if cover could be found to conceal the movement. Arriving at the hill beyond the hotel, at the stone field on the Fairfield road, the column was halted while Generals Longstreet and McLaws reconnoitered (surveyed) the route. After some little delay, the major-general returned, and directed a countermarch, and the command was marched to the left, beyond the point at which we had before halted, and thence, under cover of the woods, to the right of our line of battle."[23]

Private James Sheldon and the 50th Georgia arrived at a schoolhouse on the road leading across the Emmitsburg Road. Nearby was a peach orchard, which the enemy held, and Semmes and Kershaw's brigades were ordered to attack the enemy at that position in an attempt to turn his flank. At the same time, a Confederate battery was moved along the road, parallel with the brigades' line of march. About three p.m., the head of the column came into the open field in front of a stone wall and in full view of the enemy. Semmes and Kershaw's men quickly formed a line of battle in front of the wall under cover of their skirmishers, who were exchanging fire with those of the enemy drawn out along the Emmitsburg Road.

A soldier in James' regiment described the moment, saying, "I knew a battle was imminent. Lt. Colonel Kearse addressed each company, telling the men to fight and win."[24]

James went into battle at the Peach Orchard as Elisha Rhodes and the 2nd Rhode Island were just arriving at Gettysburg.

The Peach Orchard

The Rhode Islanders could hear gunfire in the distance and the pace of their march quickened. Elisha suddenly felt light-headed and queasy and he collapsed in the road. The regimental surgeon treated him and gave Elisha a pass for admittance to an ambulance. "I lay upon the road side until several regiments had passed when I began to revive. I immediately hurried on and soon came up with my Company 'B.' The boys received me well and I went on without further trouble." [25] Elisha's illness could be attributed to the dinner of raw pork and wormy biscuits the regiment was issued the previous night.

Numb with fatigue, the Rhode Island men reached Littlestown, where the firing in their front grew louder and more distinct. Within minutes, Elisha witnessed scores of wounded being carried by all types of vehicles to field hospitals in the rear. The immensity of the battle ahead of them was becoming frighteningly evident—Elisha reached Gettysburg at about two p.m. They had marched a grueling 34 miles without a halt and the rubber-legged soldiers threw themselves on the ground exhausted. But almost immediately, they were ordered to their feet and sent forward. "We followed the road blocked with troops and trains until four p.m., when the field of battle with the long lines of struggling weary soldiers burst upon us," said Elisha. [26]

The 2nd went into position as a reserve unit near the Round Tops behind Sedgwick. "We were at once put into position on the extreme left, and lay on our arms all night on the field of battle," remembered Colonel Rogers. [27] Reverend Augustus Woodbury of the 2nd described the greeting the regiment received, saying, "when the battlefield came fairly into view, hunger, fatigue and exhaustion were forgotten; the column actually broke into double-quick, and with shouts and cheers took position in aid of the imperiled left wing. Never was an arrival more opportune, or reinforcements more welcome." [28]

Longstreet had spotted Sickles' blunder and ordered two divisions forward into the Peach Orchard, the Wheatfield, and Devil's Den in an attempt to seize the lightly defended high ground of the Round Tops. Paul Semmes was in full battle regalia as he led his Georgians through the woods near the farm of the Rose family. At Lt. Colonel Francis Kearse's command, James and the 50th Georgia followed. The air filled with the murderous whirr of the minie ball and shrapnel flew in all directions. The noise became a din, as explosions muffled the screams and groans of wounded men. Dirt and smoke flew into the Georgian's faces as they pushed on toward a small stream called Plum Run. A member of the 50th recalled the desperation of the afternoon, saying, "We were ordered to advance. We moved forward over a hill into an open field where we were under fire. We came to a road with high fences on both sides; the firing was getting hotter. I wondered if I would ever get across the fences. We were going toward a peach orchard, but were ordered to right oblique. The firing was very hot and dangerous." [29]

Since March 4, 1862, on the courthouse steps in Thomasville, Frank Kearse led his "Rangers" with an air of invincibility. But on this hot July afternoon in Pennsylvania, his life was cut short when he was struck by a shell fragment or minie ball—no one could tell for sure. What was certain was that a portion of his skull had been shot away, killing him instantly.

The death of their beloved lieutenant colonel stunned James and the men. One soldier remembered, "The men in front retreated, and finally our men gave way about two hundred yards. We passed a stream (Plum Run) which was bloody from wounded men drinking, but I drank some too." Some of the men began to rally, determined to avenge the fallen Kearse, and a soldier urged his comrades, "Let's show we can fight in Pennsylvania as well as in Virginia." [30]

Major Peter McGlashan wasted no time taking command of the regiment. He gallantly followed the brigade's bold General Semmes who was dashing "through the line like a maddened tiger, shouting 'Look, to the front, men! Look to the front! Forward, Forward!'" [31] Although suffering heavy losses, the 50th Georgia prevented a flanking movement by the enemy, saving the 3rd South Carolina from certain disaster. An officer of that regiment reported, "about 40 men of the Fiftieth Georgia Regiment, under command of its major, came in on our left, and engaged the enemy. We remained in this position, under a heavy fire of musketry at short range in front, and an enfilading fire of grape and shrapnel from the batteries that the left had failed in entirely silencing, until about dusk, when we were ordered by General Kershaw back to another line a short distance in our rear." [32]

With the Round Tops in jeopardy, Meade swung a portion of his line to the left in their defense. The peach orchard changed hands six times. By late afternoon, the Union line had fallen back to the base of the hills where they repulsed repeated assaults by Hood's Texans.

Suddenly things looked bright for Semmes' men as they broke through a regiment of Pennsylvanians. But in an instant, a single bullet changed everything when Paul Semmes was brought down with a wound to his upper left thigh. Conscious, but bleeding profusely, Semmes writhed in pain. He was tended to with great care and placed upon a stretcher made from a captured Pennsylvania flag. General Paul Semmes was carried from the field, put aboard one of the first available ambulances, and transported across the Potomac River to the safety of Martinsburg, Virginia. The assault on the Round Tops failed and the second day of fighting was coming to a close. [33]

General Joe Kershaw, in temporary command of Semmes' Brigade, looked around, "It was now near nightfall, and the operations of the day were over. Gathering all my regiments, with Semmes' brigade, behind the wall, and placing pickets well to the front, I commenced the melancholy task of looking up my numerous dead and wounded. It was a sad list." [34]

Private James Sheldon had once again been one of the lucky ones, leaving the field without a scratch. Others had been less fortunate. Three hundred and one of James' fellow 50th Georgians had reported for duty on the morning of July 2, by day's end, 10 were dead and another 68 had either been carried from the field or left wounded—an appalling casualty rate of 25%. Captain John McCall, still recovering from being shot in the face at Sharpsburg, was wounded again. As a whole, Semmes' brigade had suffered terribly, counting 55 killed, 284 wounded and 91 missing.

Darkness brought further misery. Kershaw reported, "About dark, I was ordered to move my brigade to the left, to the peach orchard, where I remained until noon of the next day, when I was ordered to return to the stone wall." [35] A soldier in James' regiment remembered, "It was a moonlight night. When I went back to my own regiment the dead and wounded were lying all around, many crying for water. Sergeant Bailey gave some to a Union soldier who assaulted him with his fists. About ten o'clock I heard a voice asking what regiment we were. It was [Lt.] Colonel Fleming who had not been in the battle. He had orders to bring the regiment back to the brigade near the spring. We started back. I walked with Fleming and asked him about Colonel Kearse." He continued, "I said, 'Colonel, will this war never end?' I was very sad about my dead friends. We got back to a (The Rose) farm house, where we lay all night in line of battle." [36]

Whatever gains Lee had made on the first day were now gone. Not only had he been repulsed at the Round Tops, he was similarly stymied on the extreme right at Culp's Hill by 60-year-old General George Sears Greene's New Yorkers. Although he made some small inroads, his campaign was on the brink of failure. Lee then blundered further. He believed that Meade's army had been bolstered to such a degree on the flanks that the center, on Cemetery Ridge, had been left vulnerable. He argued to Longstreet that a fresh division could break through Meade's line after pounding the hill with a fantastic artillery barrage. Furthermore, a renewed attack on Culp's Hill might fool Meade into thinking the attacks of the second day's fighting were being resumed. But after the fierce fighting of two days, where was a fresh division to be found?

One division of Longstreet's Corps was late to arrive on July 2. Six thousand men were fresh and ready for action under the command of 38-year-old General George Pickett. Pickett's own military experience had been limited, graduating from West Point in 1846, finishing 59th in a class of 59. Pickett hardly inspired confidence but Lee believed he was the obvious choice to save the day.

Lee insisted that 15,000 men could do the job. Longstreet disagreed, telling Lee, "General, I have been a soldier all my life. It is my opinion that no 15,000 men ever arrayed for battle can take that position." Years later Longstreet would write, "Never was I so depressed as upon that day." [37]

Across the field, Meade worried. His army, although holding on, had been badly wounded. If Lee was able to deliver another blow like those of the previous two days, there was no guarantee that the Army of the Potomac could withstand it. Summoning twelve of his generals to his headquarters at the Leister house, he sought their advice. By the light of a single candle, the fate of a nation was debated until after midnight. The consensus was simple: stay and fight. As the council-of-war broke up, Meade turned to 2nd Corps General Gibbon and stunned him by predicting he would be attacked the next day. Gibbon asked Meade how he knew. "Because he has made attacks on both our flanks and failed, and if he concludes to try it again, it will be on our center," Meade reasoned. [38]

Elisha Rhodes and the 2nd Rhode Island were armed and ready to fight before the sun was up on Friday, July 3. Reverend Woodbury was impressed, saying, "Despite the picket firing, the groans of the wounded, the movements of the troops around, and the riding to and fro of staff officers intent upon dispositions for the morrow, the men slept comparatively well, and in the morning were in good trim for their perilous and harassing duty." [39]

Rumors flew throughout both armies; the enemy was retreating, was being reinforced, and so on. There were wounded to care for and dead to bury. At the peach orchard, James Sheldon and his fellow "Thomas County Rangers" tended to their own. Perhaps the saddest of their woeful work was parting with their young lieutenant colonel. "The next day we gathered up our dead and buried them," a member of the 50th wrote. [40] "I found a blanket on the field and we buried Colonel Kearse in it. I covered his face with an old shirt. During the burial I heard the battery start firing." Frank Kearse was 26 years old. [41]

Lee's plan of attack went wrong from the beginning. The renewed assault on Culp's Hill began much too early and proved ineffective as a ruse for his true aims on Meade's center. Nevertheless, at 1:40 p.m., his plan was put forth and his artillery on Seminary Ridge belched fire and smoke, hammering the Union men on Cemetery Ridge without mercy. The attack came so suddenly and forcefully that some men died still clutching their noon rations. Within minutes, Meade's artillery responded in kind—the hills of Pennsylvania shuddered. Never before had there been such a sound in the western hemisphere and the cannonade was said to have been heard as far away as New York City. A man in James' 50th Georgia recalled, "This battle was the greatest artillery battle the world had known." [42]

During this artillery battle, James' division was ordered to the right, about 300 or 400 yards where it formed behind a stone wall. James and the 50th remained there until ordered back to its position of the previous afternoon, west of Emmitsburg Road.

Although the 2nd Rhode Island was not on the front line, it was under constant bombardment as shells burst lively around the men. The 2nd was moved from point to point. Nearing Meade's headquarters, a shell exploded directly over Elisha's head, showering him with hot iron. In a test of nerve, most of the incoming struck the road on which the men were moving. "Solid shot would strike the large rocks and split them as if exploded by gunpowder. The flying iron and pieces of stone struck men down in every direction," Elisha said. [43]

For over an hour, the artillerists dueled and Israel Sheldon's old battery suffered badly with several men wounded. At 2:45, Meade suddenly ordered his own guns to cease firing to conserve rounds for the infantry attack he believed was imminent. Across the open space between the armies, heavy black smoke hung in the thick 90-degree air, obscuring all view of each other— 15,000 men of the Army of Northern Virginia gathered in the woods of Seminary Ridge, praying, writing last letters home or just waiting. A rumor that Meade was retreating spread through the ranks and men prayed that Cemetery Hill would be theirs without a fight. Just maybe, a peaceful one-mile walk across an open field would finally bring this war to an end.

On Cemetery Hill thousands of eyes strained to see anything along Seminary Ridge through the acrid smoke. As if on cue, the afternoon breezes arrived, sweeping the air clean and Union men beheld a sight so magnificent in its evil splendor that those present would never forget it. Before them were 15,000 men, clad in butternut, standing with arms, their regimental flags flapping and fluttering in the July breezes, with bayonets sparkling and gleaming in the sunlight. The muffled voices of officers barking final orders were drowned out by the wafted sounds of regimental bands playing their hearts out. The men of the Army of the Potomac swallowed hard.

Pickett sought Longstreet for final orders at about three p.m. "General, shall I advance?" he begged. Longstreet could only manage a fateful nod. "I shall lead my division forward, sir," Pickett confidently declared. [44]

It was over quickly. Pickett broke Meade's center, but only briefly. With just 5,000 men, it was Hancock's moment to shine as he rode up and down his line, seemingly impervious to the danger. Union reserves swarmed onto Cemetery Ridge, devouring the Confederate attack. Elisha witnessed, "Our lines of infantry in front of us rose and poured in a terrific fire."[45] Pickett's charge was a disaster and Lee knew it immediately. Greeting the returning remnants of his attack, and nearly in tears, he pleaded, "It's all my fault." [46]

Colonel Horatio Rogers of Elisha's regiment said, "July 3, was the hottest of the battle, and this was the severest engagement of the war. The brigade to which we are attached was constantly in posts of danger, but being used as a reserve, it was always sent to the points most pressed, and, though much exposed, was not directly engaged, but lay, seeing the fight progress, until our services were more actively needed, but we were not called on to fire a shot. Never have I seen or heard of severer fighting. The field was bloody in the extreme." [47]

In the confusion of the retreat, Lee found Pickett and tried to console him by reminding the general that he must reorganize his division. A shattered Pickett could only blurt out, "General, I have no division." Fifteen regiments of Pickett's Division took part in the charge—all had lost their commanding officers. Two brigadier generals and six colonels were dead and about half the men who crossed the field were dead, wounded or missing. Of Pickett's own 6,000 men 3,000 did not return. [48]

Union casualties were comparatively low. Generals Hancock and Gibbon were wounded but would recover. The 2nd Rhode Island had five wounded and one man killed; Charlie Powers, a 20-year-old laborer from Providence. Rogers assured his superiors that his regiment was still in fighting trim. "Though the regiment has marched hundreds of miles in the last month, and performed much arduous duty, it is, I am happy to state, in excellent health and spirits." [49]

The battle of Gettysburg was over—the casualty figures were beyond comprehension. Of the 85,000 men of the Army of the Potomac, 3,155 were killed, 14,529 were wounded and 5,365 were missing, for a total of 23,049. The Army of Northern Virginia, previously 65,000 strong, suffered 2,592 killed, 12,709 wounded, and 5,190 unaccounted for, bringing the total casualties to 20,451. Incredibly, only one civilian was killed during the fighting.

In the early morning hours of the nation's 87th birthday, James Sheldon and Elisha Rhodes watched as clouds gathered over Gettysburg. The two soldiers sat a little over a mile apart—drops of rain began to splash upon their faces. Staring through the dark, cloudy night, Rhodes wrote, "Oh the dead and dying on this bloody field." [50]

The 2nd Rhode Island Monument at Gettysburg

8

KISS THIS CORNER

John Imboden couldn't believe his eyes. All around him on Seminary Ridge was the famous Army of Northern Virginia—immortalized in song and prose throughout the South—now sitting bloodied and broken in Gettysburg, Pennsylvania. In the hearts of the Confederacy, warm memories of Chancellorsville and "Stonewall" Jackson suddenly seemed distant. All eyes were once again cast upon Robert E. Lee, looking for a reason to hope.

The forty-year-old Imboden, a Virginia attorney in better times, had been a brigadier general for a mere six months. His brigade of cavalry had gained some notoriety, first with Jackson in the Shenandoah Valley and later from its raids in western Virginia during March and April. Racing to Gettysburg, Imboden's 2,100 men arrived too late on the afternoon of July 3 to engage in any fighting, but by fate made their place in history anyway. Imboden was ordered to Lee's headquarters and told to wait for the general to return from the field. Lee had spent the last hours of the afternoon consoling the demoralized and wounded men of Longstreet's attack. Imboden and his staff waited until after midnight on the 4th of July. Unceremoniously, the weary general finally galloped onto the grounds. Imboden was stunned by Lee's sudden presence, realizing, "When he arrived there was not even a sentinel on duty at his tent, and no one of his staff was awake. The moon was high in the clear sky and the silent scene was unusually vivid…The moon shone full upon his massive features and revealed an expression of sadness that I had never before seen upon his face."[1]

As distraught as he was, Lee did not panic but instead calmly regrouped and prepared for Meade's expected counterattack. He was emotionally and physically exhausted, but, as if reflecting the condition of his army which still had enough artillery for one day's fight, he was not defeated. The survivors of the afternoon's charge returned to their camps where they cooked rations, cleaned their guns and rested. Lee contracted his lines, ordering Ewell's men away from Cemetery Hill and Longstreet out of the tangled woods at the base of the Round Tops. When dawn broke all eyes on Seminary Ridge were cast on Cemetery Ridge. The battered Army of Northern Virginia hoped Meade would launch a charge as they had the day before—the order never came. A light sprinkle dotted the air and by afternoon it was pouring. James Sheldon hovered near the stone wall. Elisha Rhodes sought shelter in a sunken portion of the Emmitsburg Road. Bodies were strewn everywhere.

Imboden's orders: Lead and protect the Army of Northern Virginia's somber wagon train out of Pennsylvania and across the Potomac to the safety of Virginia. By late afternoon his line of wagons was ready to roll. Those too injured to walk were loaded aboard the ambulances and wagons moving out in single file. General Edward Porter Alexander, who had commanded much of the artillery the day before, described the scene, saying, "Every vehicle appeared to be loaded to its capacity. It was about 4 PM on the 4th before the head of the train was put in motion from Cashtown. Meanwhile, what would have seemed a visitation of the wrath of God had come upon us, had we not preferred the theory which has been previously to, that storms may be generating by heavy firings. Now there came suddenly, out of the clear sky of the day before, one of the heaviest rainfalls I have ever seen. Probably four inches of water fell in twelve hours, and it was sure to make the Potomac unfordable."[2] Some of the mortally wounded were removed from the wagons at Williamsport, and many less seriously wounded died from the effects of the journey.

Imboden added, "After dark I set out from Cashtown to gain the head of the column during the night. My orders had been peremptory that there should be no halt for any cause whatsoever. If an accident should happen to any vehicle, it was immediately to be put out of the road and abandoned... Many of the wounded in the wagons had been without food for 36 hours...From nearly every wagon as the teams trotted on, urged by whip and shout, came such cries and shrieks as these: - 'Oh God! Why can't I die!' 'My God! Will no one have mercy and kill me!...Stop! Oh! For God's sake stop just for one minute; take me out and leave me to die by the roadside.' No help could be rendered to any of the sufferers. We must move on. The storm continued, and the darkness was appalling." [3] Imboden's parade was 17 miles long.

****

In Richmond, President Davis spent the 4th of July scrambling for any information he could find regarding Lee's invasion of Pennsylvania, but he could only establish that a great battle had been fought. In Washington, Lincoln began wondering why Meade wasn't going on the offensive in Pennsylvania.

If Meade hadn't delivered the political results that Lincoln so badly needed, Ulysses Grant once again came through for the president. Twenty-thousand stubborn Confederates gave up the fight and marched out of the city of Vicksburg.

Newspapers North and South brimmed with headlines of the events in Gettysburg and Vicksburg. On July 6, Washington's *Evening Star* boasted, "GREAT and GLORIOUS NEWS! – The Union Armies Victorious In The Greatest Battle of the Century!" [4] The Philadelphia *Inquirer* featured an image of the United States flag above the headline, "Waterloo Eclipsed!!" [5] Not to be outdone, South Carolina's *Charleston Courier* proclaimed, "Thrilling And Glorious News, Confederates Victorious!" [6] *The Courier* detailed how Lee captured 40,000 Union soldiers who would be transported to Martinsburg, Virginia, as prisoners of war. If all this good news made the reader feel tempted to celebrate, he or she only needed to scan the front page further to find "the most complete assortment of imported wines and liquors," and the "Old London Cordial Gin" the *Evening Star* advertised. [7]

As the top man in each executive mansion read his papers, civilians back at Gettysburg finally believed it was safe to emerge from their cellars. Tillie Pierce and a friend climbed one of the surrounding hills to view the landscape. She recalled, "as we stood upon those mighty boulders, and looked down into chasms between, we beheld the dead lying there just as they had fallen during the struggle. From the summit of Little Round Top, surrounded by the wrecks of battle, we gazed upon the valley of death beneath. The view spread out before us was terrible to contemplate! It was an awful spectacle! Dead soldiers, bloated horses, shattered cannon and caissons, thousands of small arms. In fact everything belonging to army equipments, was there in one confused and indescribable mass." [8]

Elisha spent the 4th as a skirmisher on the sunken Emmitsburg Road, taking occasional potshots whenever a straggling Confederate came into view. "It is impossible to march across the field without stepping upon dead or wounded men, while horses and broken Artillery lay on every side," he described. [9] The holiday was marked by the firing of a national salute that put a lump in the throats of the weary Army of the Potomac, but for the sore-footed men of the 2nd Rhode Island, the high point of the evening was the opportunity to enjoy a well-earned night's sleep.

****

On July 5, Lee's tired army continued its retreat toward Hagerstown, Maryland. Almost everyone had lost a friend and James Sheldon's 50th Georgia, which had been hit particularly hard, was no exception. The men of the 10th, 51st, 53rd and 50th had formed a tight bond after they'd been brigaded together.

Having gone through so many fights their numbers were severely diminished now. Their appearance was ragtag; some of the men were barefoot. Like other brigades, its cohesion and strength came from its leadership, and although each man struggled with his personal grief, all shared the common loss of their beloved General Semmes. As James Sheldon and the other men marched in the rain toward the Potomac, much of the chatter was about the well-being and whereabouts of their leader, who many saw fall near the Rose Farm.

Semmes had been carried by ambulance to the home of Mary Ogden across the Potomac in Martinsburg, Virginia. His wound was severe and in the days following his arrival at the Ogden home his prognosis changed daily. On Sunday, July 10, Semmes felt well enough to pen a letter to his wife, Emily. But later that afternoon, he abruptly asked for his sword and Bible. Placing the sword at his side and clutching the book in his hands, he softly spoke to the others in the room, saying, "I consider it a privilege to die for my country." [10] Shortly after speaking these words he drew his last breath.

In the brief time Mary Ogden had shared with the wounded general, she grew increasingly fond of him and upon his death felt compelled to write an account of his last days to his wife. Ogden explained that Semmes didn't eat much but he seemed to enjoy the raspberries and cream her sister had brought him. He talked about Georgia. Ogden offered the widow a vision of Semmes' remains in her sitting room, saying, "I wish you could see the quantities of beautiful flowers brought here this morning." [11] Before sealing her letter, Mary Ogden enclosed a few evergreens and locks of the general's hair.

As they continued their sad march to the Potomac, James and the other men shared reminiscences of General Semmes and his distinct, booming voice, but word quickly spread through the ranks that their friend was no more.

As the march meandered south, men presumed dead or captured began returning to their regiments. These men were pressed for information regarding the battle, and more importantly, fallen and missing comrades. In the aftermath of Longstreet's futile charge, all military cohesion was broken and entire companies of men simply disappeared. Hundreds of other Confederate men, hopelessly separated from their units, deserted and started walking home. Whether these men saw an opportunity forever lost at Gettysburg, or had simply grown too weary of soldiering, desertion now seemed a viable option.

By July 5, a Sunday, James Sheldon's weary feet were approaching Hagerstown, Maryland, where the 50th Georgia camped for one week. Lee's wagon train of wounded straggled twenty miles behind at Chambersburg, Pennsylvania, vulnerable to attacks by detachments of Meade's cavalry. The local citizenry also got into the fray with sporadic assaults on the wagon train, at one point cutting the spokes off twelve wagons. But to Lincoln's frustration the bulk of the Army of the Potomac didn't budge from Gettysburg. By late Sunday afternoon and into the morning of the 6th, the Army of Northern Virginia began arriving at Williamsport and the banks of the Potomac. As John Imboden had feared, the heavy rains of recent days had swollen the river to flood stage, making it "impassable except by two small ferry-boats." [12] To make matters worse, five brigades of Union cavalry carrying eighteen pieces of artillery were believed to be approaching.

Imboden didn't panic, but instead used his predicament to his advantage. Due to the raging waters, the enemy could only approach from the north. Imboden quickly collected his teamsters, some dismounted cavalry, two infantry regiments, and any wounded man capable of carrying a rifle, to create the "impression of a large force." [13] His men wrestled with their artillery, bringing it into line and putting on a grand display of firepower. It worked, and although a "sharp fight ensued, the teamsters acquitted themselves handsomely. The enemy was driven back and held off until the approach of Stuart's cavalry in the afternoon caused the Federal cavalry to withdraw." [14]

James Sheldon and his exhausted comrades caught a breather as the firing died away in the distance. A soldier in the 50th remembered, "This was the fifth day since the beginning of the battle and I had not washed my face the whole time and was not able to until the next morning. In the afternoon we came to a town and one of the men who was ahead got some fresh biscuits at the house of a woman who was a Southern sympathizer. He told us where to get some. We marched on until sundown, on the mountains again. We camped near a hotel at a watering place, South Mountain, a delightful place to camp. The next morning I was able to wash my face, and we started down the mountain toward Hagerstown." [15]

The 2nd Rhode Island was once again on the road as Sedgwick's 6th Corps pursued Lee. On the morning of the 5th, Elisha got a glimpse of the bigger picture of the battle as his corps began moving out. "We have had rain and the roads are bad, so we move slow. Every house we see is a hospital, and the road is covered with the arms and equipments thrown away by the Rebels." [16]

****

Lincoln had his share of problems, both political and military, but most embarrassing was a family matter that spilled over into both of these areas. His wife's half-brothers fought for the South.

The Todds were prosperous Kentuckians and one of the state's founding families. Confederate surgeon Dr. George Rodgers Clark Todd was, like the country he had disavowed, born on the 4th of July. His mother died of childbirth complications the following day. Like many families in the border states, the Dred Scot decision and John Brown's Harper's Ferry raid divided and ultimately tore the Todds apart. After Ft. Sumter fell George and his three brothers offered their services to the Confederacy, although their half-sister, Mary, was the First Lady of the United States.

George's anti-Union passions were extreme and he showed no restraint from exhibiting them. Sick and wounded Union prisoners from the battle of 1ˢᵗ Manassas were the first to feel his wrath. George and his brother, David, were accused by several Confederate officers of neglectful, even cruel, treatment of some of the Northern men under their care. On at least one occasion, he was known to have kicked the corpse of a Union prisoner while cursing, "damned abolitionists."[17] In another incident, he was accused of ordering a Union officer out of his hospital bed and having him bound and gagged. The man died the following day. Enraged, some Confederate officers took their complaints directly to President Davis, but the president could hardly afford to lose a surgeon of Todd's ability so he transferred him to the field. In the summer of 1862, Dr. George Todd became Surgeon Todd of Semmes' Brigade and remained in that role until September 30, 1863.

Todd's appointment to Semmes' Brigade had an immediate impact. By curing a private's swollen jaw with medication rather than surgery, men were less hesitant to seek medical care. Near Fredericksburg in 1862, Todd became the victim of the brigade's Great Brandy Heist in which a keg of his "medicinal" brandy was stolen from his tent. After the Battle of Salem Church, Todd found himself working alongside a captured Union surgeon, who caustically described the experience as a "pleasure." The doctor remembered Todd as "short, rather inferior looking with an impediment in his speech." While operating with Todd, he explained that he had recently met Mrs. Lincoln, to which Todd quipped, "Well I don't know as I feel the better or worse for that. She is a poor weak-minded woman anyhow." [18] All three of Dr. Todd's brothers lost their lives as a result of the war.

The 2ⁿᵈ Rhode Island passed through Fairfield and Liberty, Pennsylvania, reaching Emmitsburg, Maryland, where Elisha and the men camped on July 6. Skirmishing broke out ahead of them at Boonsboro, Hagerstown and Williamsport. The next morning they were again in hot pursuit of the enemy, marching through Franklin's Mills, Mechanicsville, and passing the

Catoctin Iron Works, where iron plates had been manufactured for the *Monitor*. Beginning their ascent of Catoctin Mountain, Elisha felt the tension between the Rhode Islanders and the locals, writing, "Now the people stare at us as we march past." [19] No biscuits or water were offered along the route.

Catoctin Mountain itself proved to be just as unwelcoming. A six-hour hike in the darkness pushed the regiment to its physical limits as the men crawled up its steep walls, struggling with their gear. A few hours past midnight, the 2nd halted, feeling they were "used up and could go no further." [20] But before dawn, Colonel Rogers was again rousing his men and sending them down Catoctin's west face. Marching downhill, the trek was less arduous, but the footing proved difficult at times. Arriving at the village of Middletown, the men of the 2nd plopped down their packs and rifles. Some napped away the afternoon while others played cards, cooked rations, or wrote letters. Lieutenant Elisha Rhodes reflected on the state of the war, "I wonder what the South thinks of us Yankees now." [21]

As events in the East slowed to a game of tactical cat and mouse, things continued to heat up in the West. Following Grant's success at Vicksburg, another star began to twinkle on the national stage. Newspapers around the country were reporting that Union General William Tecumseh Sherman, an avowed admirer of Grant, had taken a large force of Grant's army and was relentlessly hunting Joe Johnston and his army near Jackson, Mississippi. An optimistic Lincoln predicted, "Now, if General Meade can complete his work, so gloriously prosecuted thus far, by the literal or substantial destruction of Lee's army, the rebellion will be over." [22]

****

Lee was trapped. The pontoon bridge to be used for his escape had been destroyed by Union cavalry and he could only watch the flooded Potomac roll by, as Meade's Army of the Potomac slowly but steadily flowed into Maryland. Skirmishing was breaking out at Boonsboro, Funkstown, Falling Waters and Williamsport. Lt. Elisha Rhodes evaluated the situation. "I do not see how they (Lee's army) can escape us this time."[23] As if victory was now inevitable, Rhodes could afford compassion for his foe, writing, "Everybody except the Rebels are in good spirits, and they must feel lonesome after their defeat." Elisha envisioned the end of the war as he feasted on a luxury of bread and butter. But just as Meade was making final preparations to bring the hammer down on Lee, the waters of the Potomac began to recede slightly, and with the return of the sun the water levels suddenly dropped dramatically. On July 10, Lee nervously eyed the river and Meade hurriedly brought up his army.

Private James Sheldon and the 50th Georgia waited for the river to recede while they camped in an apple orchard on Antietam Creek, not far from the battlefield of the previous year. One soldier recalled, "Across the creek was Funkstown, Maryland. In the course of the morning we were marched across the creek and through the town, and saw a Confederate battery on a hill. We formed in line of battle and advanced. At the same time both batteries opened up." The 50th was met sharply by Union skirmishers and things heated up quickly. "[Our] line was in a farmyard, under fire of skirmishers, behind stones and a fence. I saw a hen and some chickens, which made me homesick." [24] The sentimental moment ended abruptly as the air filled with the zip and whir of minie balls. But as thick as the firing was, the enemy was nowhere to be seen. Sheldon and the men of the 50th kept up a steady fire, but quickly decided their position was too exposed to hold and a retreat to the farmyard was ordered. An officer remembered the moment, saying, "[We were] angry at being recalled. Then some men started firing but we couldn't see the enemy… A little later when I happened to look down the line I saw a man from Thomas County killed dead. He was the only man killed in that place. We stayed there until sundown, and then were withdrawn to the same camp, across the creek from the orchard, where we stayed two days in line of battle, behind a stone wall." [25]

For the first time since the war began, and unbeknownst to both, Pawtuxet natives James Sheldon and Elisha Rhodes were shooting at each other. A man in the 2nd Rhode Island recalled, "[We] found the enemy at Funkstown, drawn up in a line of battle, with his front slightly entrenched. Lee had reached Williamsport and was showing a bold face in order to cover his crossing. Our cavalry had inflicted considerable damage upon his wagon trains, he had but few pontoons on the Potomac, had lost several pieces of artillery and many prisoners. The river was swollen by the rain and altogether his position was not encouraging." [26]

The fight at Funkstown was sharp and quick. When it was over, Elisha wrote, "Last night we had a skirmish, and the 2nd RI lost three men, one of them from my Company B." Elisha had seen more than his share of death, and privately questioned Meade's intentions, writing, "I do not understand our movements but suppose them to be all right. Time will tell however." [27]

As the men of the 50th huddled along the shelter of the stone wall, trading rations, playing cards and smoking, one soldier, William Stilwell, spent the afternoon writing a letter to his wife:

> "I have suffered very much hard marching in mud and rain, my clothes has not been dry until now in five days and nights, war is like the infidels faith, it will do well until you come to test it and then it makes the heart sick... We will stay over on this side [of the Potomac] and have another fight or two. I think General Lee is going to fight the Yankees all this summer on their own land and make the people feel the effects of war. We made them feel it wherever we went. I have lived high on pork, fowls, butter and so etc. I said I was going to live high if I ever come over here."

> "Mollie, a few more battles and our Regiment will all be gone, it isn't much larger now than our company was when it come out.

Oh, the sorrow of war, who can tell, if this war lasts much longer there won't be many left. We don't know how the war is going on at Vicksburg nor nowhere else. We don't know anything but what we see as we don't get any papers. I hope they are all getting along well for I do want this war closed this year. I want to be with my family next year by that time if not long before."

"I have endured enough, I have suffered enough for any one man yet there is another that has suffered more. I ought to be and I trust I am very thankful that I have fared so well but Oh, my Mollie and my Tommy and my mother, if it was not for thee I could give up my life more freely on the battlefield. I lay down night before last very wet and tired. I dreamt that I was at home and how glad I was but when I woke I found that I was still lying in mud and water [and] I was greatly disappointed."

"Oh my Mollie and my babes, what I would give to kiss thee. This wicked war, this wicked war! God grant that we meet again. I am always your absent lonely and ever faithful husband. Until death goodbye my dear Mollie."

At the bottom left of the page was a small inscription which read, "kiss this corner." [28]

Not far from where William Stilwell sat writing this letter to his wife, Lt. Elisha Rhodes echoed similar sentiments, writing, "My poor little company will soon be gone if we do not get recruits." [29]

An anxious week passed and James remained on constant alert, convinced that the Army of the Potomac was coming. Semmes' Brigade was given the responsibility of blocking the advance of Meade's army between Martinsburg and Winchester. Finally, word arrived that Vicksburg had fallen. The news had a demoralizing effect and one soldier in the 50th wrote, "I was very much discouraged and thought that if Meade attacked we would be defeated." [30]

Private James Sheldon and the 50th Georgia remained camped in the orchard near Funkstown for two days following their skirmish with the 2nd Rhode Island. Rejoining Lee's retreat toward the Shenandoah Valley, they broke camp and marched along the creek through Sharpsburg before stopping for the night. Fearing another attack, the 50th was again on the move the next morning, seeking a better position to make a stand if Meade's army appeared. James and the other men went to work felling trees and moving dirt and by late afternoon they were nestled in relative comfort behind formidable earthworks.

General Meade was in a quandary. Should he attack Lee while the Army of the Potomac was not yet at full strength and risk disaster, or wait a few more days and risk letting the trapped Army of Northern Virginia get away? As Reverend Woodbury saw it, "Meade was new to command...and ignorant of the ground," [31] and therefore reluctant to make a bold strike. So, as he had at Gettysburg, Meade summoned his generals for a council-of-war. Generals Wadsworth and Howard argued for attacking but were voted down by the others. Meade suggested the army make a grand demonstration of force and attack Lee if the opportunity presented itself. But in the end, Meade decided to wait. Then, after a few hours of agonizing self-doubt, he reversed himself and ordered a full scale engagement for Tuesday, July 14. He had given Lee and the flooded Potomac a stay of one more day.

Longstreet's reserve artillery commander, Edward Porter Alexander remembered, "Another rain-storm had set in before dusk, and it kept up nearly all night. It was the dark period of the moon and the blackness of the night was phenomenal. The route to the bridge was over small farm roads, rough, narrow, and hilly. Already from the incessant rains they were in bad condition, and now, under the long procession of heavy wheels, churning in the mud, they became canals of slush in which many vehicles were hopelessly stalled." [32] In a surreal scene, massive bonfires were built along the roads and riverbanks, guiding the way to the bridge as if passing through some demonic ritual.

A soldier in James Sheldon's 50th Georgia described the escape, saying,

> "This march was the most memorable march I had during all the war. It had been raining a good deal. It was very muddy, misty and rainy. We marched in mud, knee deep. One of my shoes came off, but I found it again. We went very slowly. I once fell into some entrenchments and struck my canteen against my side and hurt myself. Another time the road was so slippery that I slipped and fell flat. About midnight we came to a hard road. The officers got together, sang songs, told jokes and were jolly – and I with them. When daylight came we had not reached the Potomac River. All were covered with red mud, and we had no breakfast that morning. I ate slippery elm bark that one of the men gave me. Soon we reached the Potomac but couldn't wade across as it was so swollen, but some pontoon bridges had already been made and we crossed to a place called Falling Waters. Just as we crossed we saw Lee and his staff watching us, and we saluted as we passed. We then marched several miles, camped and had something to eat." [33]

On Tuesday morning the Army of the Potomac attacked. But when they reached Williamsport, there was no enemy to be found. All that remained of Lee's army were 1500 men who had failed to get across the river. In disgust, Elisha could see that the enemy had safely made it to the banks upon the Virginia shore.

Lee's great northern campaign had ended. Meade's epic victory of ten days earlier ended with the faint odor of lost opportunity. President Lincoln angrily scribbled a message to his top general, saying, "Your golden opportunity is gone, and I am distressed immeasurably because of it."[34] However satisfying it felt for Lincoln to write these angry words, he never sent it.

If the emotional rollercoaster of the presidency had dropped him precipitously in the ten days following the 4th of July victory, Lincoln sank even deeper when news from New York City reached the White House. The military draft had gone into effect on Saturday the 11th and rioters had left much of the city in flames. By Thursday, nearly one thousand New Yorkers lay dead or wandered the streets severely injured in what is still the worst civilian violence in the United States on record.

Faced with his own set of grave concerns, Confederate President Jefferson Davis pleading the case for unity wrote to one of his senators, "In proportion as our difficulties increase, so must we all cling together, judge charitably of each other, and strive to bear and forbear, however great may be the sacrifice and bitter the trial."[35] General Lee also had important issues on his mind and wrote to Davis, assuring him that the Army of Northern Virginia was in good condition, "but want shoes and clothing badly."[36]

****

On July 18, Major William Fleming of the 50th Georgia finally had a chance to write home while the regiment camped at Funkstown, Maryland, saying, "Our lines are again along the famous Antietam creek. It is not supposed that General Lee intends to recross the river. He is getting ready it is thought for another advance. The army has suffered severely but what is left is in good spirits."[37]

Filling the void left by Semmes' death was 51-year-old Goode Bryan. A fellow Georgian born in Hancock County, Bryan had graduated 25th in his class at West Point in 1834 and for a time had Edgar Allen Poe as a classmate. This was a relatively quiet period for the United States military and Bryan quickly tired of soldiery. He resigned his commission and returned to civilian life to begin a career as a civil engineer with the Augusta & Athens

Railroad. In 1839, he moved to Alabama, intent on a peaceful life of a planter, while dabbling in both military and political affairs. His talents as a soldier were quickly recognized and by the mid-1840s he was a colonel of militia. He later served in the Alabama House of Representatives. When the war with Mexico beckoned in 1846, Bryan served as a major with the 1st Alabama Volunteers and later as assistant quartermaster on a general's staff.

General Goode Bryan

After the war, Bryan returned to his plantings in Alabama until 1849 when he moved to Jefferson County, Georgia, and soon after, Richmond County. When Ft. Sumter was attacked, he entered the Confederate Army as a captain in the 16th Georgia Infantry. The following February he became the regiment's colonel and as part of Magruder's Division led his Georgians through the Seven Days' Battles, Fredericksburg, Chancellorsville and Gettysburg. Colonel Bryan assumed command of Paul Semmes' old brigade after Gettysburg, but the paperwork promoting him to brigadier general was not finalized until August 29.

On Sunday, July 19, after days of marching, waiting, and wading, the Army of the Potomac crossed the namesake river.

Elisha Rhodes and the 2ⁿᵈ Rhode Island marched over a pontoon bridge during the afternoon and then pushed on to Wheatland where the regiment spent the night. Colonel Horatio Rogers' men hit the road again the next morning. For the next four days the marching continued as Meade hoped to intercept Lee's rear guard. "The scenery was fine, and in spite of the heat I enjoyed the march," wrote Elisha. The abundance of blackberries on the bushes lining the roads was an unexpected treat, and having no other rations, "everybody ate their fill. They were good too, for we were nearly starved." [38] Near the town of Warrenton, Virginia, the 2ⁿᵈ Rhode Island made camp on a hillside. It was impossible not to notice the effect that the recent campaigning had taken on the regiment. Since the end of the Peninsula Campaign the year before, the regiment suffered from 36 desertions and 107 discharges due to disability.

With a head start of several days, the exhausted Confederates welcomed the warm embrace of the Shenandoah Valley. Friendly faces and pretty girls greeted the Army of Northern Virginia with offerings of home-baked breads, sweets, blankets, and clothing. The war in Pennsylvania and Maryland was behind them; it was time to rest and regroup if the South was to fight on.

James Sheldon, for the first time in a very long time, was enjoying himself. For two weeks, the men of the 50ᵗʰ Georgia had "a wonderful rest," as one man described it. [39] Their uniforms could no longer be described as such, often being one-legged trousers worn with tattered shirts and jackets—many men were barefoot and severely footsore. During this stay in the Valley, a precious shipment of shoes arrived in camp. Manufactured in England, the shoes had been run through the blockade in North Carolina and shipped to Richmond. Having never seen pointed shoes before, Sheldon and his friends looked skeptically at each other as they sought out a pair their size.

During this brief respite both armies continued to feel each other out. Meade sought to control the trails leading to the Valley, probing Lee's strength and position, while Lee worried about Meade getting between the Army of Northern Virginia and Richmond. Lee wrote to President Davis that he had hoped to get his army east of the Blue Ridge Mountains, but the cresting rivers had made the movement impossible. He went on to explain how badly his army needed rest and replenishment.

As July closed, the 2nd Rhode Island enjoyed its time in camp where the men could "sleep nights without being expected to be called out at daylight." [40] The camp was enveloped by two steep hills bursting with blackberries and Elisha described it as "the most romantic place I ever saw."[41] But even here some of the men suffered from sunstroke as the afternoon sun beat down brutally upon them.

The 50th Georgia marched over the Blue Ridge Mountains into Culpeper County where it stopped at a place called Waller's Tavern which lay between Gordonsville and Richmond. The regiment was low on rations and the hot sun took its toll on many of the Georgians. Newly promoted Colonel Peter McGlashan ordered those suffering from "sun pain" [42] to ride in ambulances.

Near Waller's Tavern and Warrenton respectively, Lieutenant Elisha Rhodes and Private Sheldon spent the end of July and early August basking in the delights of the Virginia summer. James and his friends passed their days going into town and mingling with the locals. The general store was frequented daily by the Georgians who sampled its wares, the favorite being watermelon. As James counted his coins, he was struck by the curious sight of something few men had ever seen before, a female clerk.

On August 13, as Bryan's Brigade camped near the Rapidan River, a soldier in the 53rd Georgia wrote to his father, "This summer's marching to Pennsylvania and Maryland has jerked the flesh off of me... We have been drawing plenty to eat, for the last 4 days. I hope we may continue, as it is a late thing. As a general thing, the flour and meal that we draw for three days rations, lasts us one and one half days and sometimes two days. We draw beef for three meals and generally eat up at one meal. I have nearly got used to eating bread and water by its self. I have done without many a meal of victuals, mostly on the account of our Quartermaster getting whisky. Whisky played the wild with our flour, meal, bacon, beef, peas, soap. The commissioned officers draw sugar sometimes, but sugar is too good for privates and non-commissioned officers." [43]

Morale in Bryan's Brigade was not good though, and a man expressed his temptation to mutiny and his burning desire to return home. "It is reported and said to be true, that [some soldiers] held a mass meeting at Orange Court House, and they declared they would go [back] into the Union again if the privates and non-commissioned officers were not better treated and respected... Pa I want you to see if you can get a man to come and take my place for a month or so, until I can come home. I will pay any money, $50 or 75 dollars, and rather than miss it, 100 dollars, if he will come and take my place, for one or two months, at the above rate a month. I want you to be sure, and see if you can get one please," he wrote in a letter to his father. [44]

In their hillside camp, Elisha Rhodes and the 2nd Rhode Island unexpectedly became hosts. The 37th Massachusetts Infantry had been severely beaten up during the summer and its numbers were greatly reduced and the surviving Massachusetts men were reassigned to Elisha's brigade. So battle scarred were these men that they had taken to wearing ramshackle metal plates on their chests and the regiment became nicknamed "the Ironclad Regiment." [45] But almost immediately, the Virginia heat caused the Massachusetts men to reassess the value of such heavy armor and they threw the metal plates away. Ever resourceful, the Rhode Islanders turned them into frying pans.

This was a time for the men of both sides to grieve for lost friends and daydream of home. Most importantly, to laugh, as they did one day at mail call when Elisha Rhodes opened a letter to learn he had been drafted.

9

WE ALL STAND AS
HEARTY AS BUCKS

⧖ ◦◦◦ ⧖

The oppressive August heat was straight from Hades. The air was thick and leaves hung lazily from the trees on Thursday, August 6. The men of the 2nd Rhode Island answered morning roll call and those not designated for picket duty lounged about their sticky camp hoping for a breeze. In the afternoon, soldiers napped or went about the business of organized boredom, as many described army life. The sky grew dark in the distance.

Far-off lightning crackled and the sound of thunder rumbled between the mountains as the first drops of rain began to gently pelt the tents. To veterans like Elisha Rhodes, serving his third summer in the Virginia sun, it was apparent with the first gush of cold air that something was wrong. A funnel cloud appeared over the crest of the steeped hillside and swooped through the camp like a clumsy giant on his way to the dinner table. There was no time to seek shelter and little to be found anyway. Tents and makeshift shacks were twisted and torn from the ground as horses and mules whinnied and kicked at their hitchings. Men covered their eyes as sand and dirt stung their faces, while letters, laundry, and knapsacks took flight in a swirling mass. Within a minute it was over. One of the first to begin surveying what was left of the camp was Reverend Woodbury. He saw overturned tents, uprooted trees and debris, but apart from some shaken nappers and a few bruises, he noted that all was well "in the neighborhood."[1] Rethinking the wisdom of camping in their picturesque location, the 2nd Rhode Island marched a short distance to build a new camp on the plain below.

It was fitting that the tumultuous events of July and early August were culminated by a tornado. A relative peace settled over northern Virginia, as the two armies sat like worn-out prize fighters, eyeing each other from their stools but unable to answer the bell. It was, as Reverend Woodbury put it, "quiet, as though it was a time of truce between the opposing armies."[2] Private James Sheldon and Lt. Elisha Rhodes spent the month of August in leisure. Peter McGlashan, now the 50th Georgia's colonel, immediately appointed his brother Andrew as his adjutant. Major William Fleming was now lieutenant colonel. For Georgians and Rhode Islanders, drilling and parading once again became the daily routine while nearby ponds and streams allowed them an opportunity to swim and fish. Shipments of new clothing went a long way to brighten the attitude and appearance of the disheveled soldiers who spent most of their free time fixing up their surroundings. The men took great care constructing their camps, often replacing tents with log and stone structures which soon became the envy of local civilians living in shacks. They built their quarters in rows, divided by streets that were often named after the roads back home.

For the first time, some of the men of Bryan's Brigade expressed their doubts about the war. As the Georgians rested near Culpeper Court House, a soldier in the 51st Georgia wrote, "I think the war can not last much longer. We have not been whipped yet but the yanks is a whipping our army every where else an I think we will soon have to give it up. They have got so many more soldiers than we have got it is thought among us that we will soon have to give up and if we ever have to give up I want us to do it now before any more of us gets killed."[3] The next day, on August 9, Bryan's Brigade marched to within 20 miles of Fredericksburg. The men were starving, and one man from James' brigade wrote, "we have not had more than half enough to eat since we turned back. But we all stand as hearty as bucks. We spend all we can for something to eat to keep from perishing."[4]

In Union camps such as the 2nd Rhode Island's, life was improving. A social scene of sorts emerged as men invited neighbors over for dinners and evenings of drinks and card games. During the day, baseball was the game of choice as companies squared off against each other. Some games were played between different regiments, and old hometown rivalries, combined with a heavy dose of regimental pride, attracted big crowds.

Another popular gathering was the prayer meeting. The 2nd Rhode Island was particularly lacking in spiritual matters. The men had grown bitter toward Chaplain Jameson and were relieved when he resigned. Elisha complained that Jameson "never did any good in the regiment."[5] A spiritual mutiny erupted, spearheaded by Elisha and Colonel Rogers who were concerned that they were facing death without religious guidance. Elisha's enthusiasm for a new church became contagious and men took to the nearby forests, felling trees and splitting logs. The timbers were dragged or carried into camp where they were sawed and sanded smooth into benches, lecterns and an altar. A shaded grove evolved into "The Temple of the Lord,"[6] and the services held there became so popular that it was common to see ladies from Warrenton seated next to Confederate prisoners at Sunday School Bible readings. "Soldiers are not the worst men in the world,"[7] prayed Lt. Rhodes.

The lazy days of the Virginia summer yielded a wide variety of treats for those who only weeks before were nearly starving. The men of the 50th Georgia discovered watermelons at Waller's Tavern and the countryside offered fat peas, cool cucumbers, and squash. Ripe melons of all types were common and mouthwatering peaches, pears and plums were in abundance. Apples were often made into cider and men on both sides filled their canteens. Some, desiring a more potent refreshment, jugged their cider for fermentation. The war seemed a thousand miles away.

The 50th Georgia remained in its camp 20 miles from Fredericksburg. One man in the brigade wrote, "the weather is very hot here and it has been the rainingest time I ever saw and we have no tents at all. We have some Yankee oilcloths that shelter some of us." But the weather wasn't the only thing weighing on the soldier's mind as he stated, "I dread the next battle for when the yanks try us again I think they will try us with a very heavy force." [8]

Elisha's midsummer hiatus was briefly interrupted when he received word from Pawtuxet that his younger brother, James, was gravely ill. Elisha was given a ten-day furlough, and on the morning of August 19, he boarded a train at Warrenton to begin his journey home. Most of his leave was spent in a bedside vigil, but within a week his brother's illness subsided and Elisha rejoined his regiment at month's end.

As the Armies of the Potomac and Northern Virginia rested in the positions they had held prior to the Gettysburg Campaign, the military hierarchies sought to reorganize themselves. Lee, in poor physical health and battling a severe bout of melancholy, offered his resignation to President Davis. But with few options available to him, Davis wouldn't hear of it. Lincoln began pressing for the activation of black regiments and Grant began to break his gigantic army into smaller ones capable of operations throughout the South and West.

The United States Navy's blockade choked off raw materials desperately needed in Southern cities, while England and France watched. Ft. Sumter continued to be systematically reduced to rubble in Charleston harbor and Grant tightened his grip on the Mississippi. But the world's eyes were on Tennessee, anxiously waiting for the next moves of Confederate General Braxton Bragg and his Union counterpart, William Rosecrans.

Just as Grant had brought siege to Vicksburg, President Davis hoped that General Bragg's army could bring some relief to the embattled Pemberton there. To prevent this, Rosecrans had been ordered to keep Bragg busy in Tennessee. In a series of battles known as the Tullahoma Campaign, Rosecrans forced Bragg to withdraw south of the Tennessee River in late June. When Vicksburg fell, Rosecrans became free to move his Army of the Cumberland to Chattanooga, Tennessee, an invaluable crossroads of rail and communications for the Confederacy. From the start of the operation, Rosecrans baffled Bragg by moving his army west of the city instead of east, where a junction with Burnside was possible. Confused and nervous, Bragg asked President Davis for more troops for his Army of Tennessee. With few troops available in the West for such a maneuver and an uneasy quiet in Virginia, Lee considered the possibility of detaching a portion of the Army of Northern Virginia. Quietly, the Chickamauga Campaign had begun.

It had been five weeks since the Battle of Gettysburg and morale in the Army of Northern Virginia was severely tested. "This is indeed a dark day for the Confederacy. Hundreds of our men are deserting and those who remain are discouraged and disheartened. To give up is but subjugation. To fight on is dissolution," wrote a man in James Sheldon's brigade on the 13th of August. [9]

Although events in the East had ground to a relative halt, there was still news. Reports from South Carolina described the daily bombardment of Ft. Sumter; President Lincoln went out to Treasury Park and test-fired a new Spencer Rifle; and the *Hunley*, the first submarine ever to sink an enemy vessel, sank in Charleston harbor. But it was news from Kansas that shook both nations. A force of nearly 450 men made up of Confederate cavalry and Missouri terrorists rode into the town of Lawrence on Friday, August 21. Using the old border dispute with Missouri as a reason, they killed 150 civilians and destroyed nearly one million dollars in property.

****

James Sheldon and the 50th Georgia ended the month of August in "a pretty campground... fourteen miles from Frederick Hall Station sixty miles from Richmond near the railroad leading from Richmond to Gordonsville." The health of the regiment was generally very good. "But we do not get more than half enough to eat," said one man. "We get one pint of corn meal and about a half a pound of bacon in the place of the beef a day and that is short rations for a hearty man. We generally eat it up at one mess and do without the rest of the day." [10]

September opened with Rosecrans' Army of the Cumberland's crossing of the Tennessee River near Chattanooga. The nearly week-long crossing itself was uneventful but Union General Burnside seized Knoxville, Tennessee, cutting the railroad line between Chattanooga and Virginia. On September 9, Bragg, viewing his situation in Chattanooga as untenable, moved his army out of the city and into the state of Georgia. As dire as Bragg's military disposition appeared at first glance, Rosecrans' success had created its own set of problems for the Union general. While the Army of the Cumberland entered parts of the city, it did not control it, and much of the river and railroad was still in Confederate hands. More troubling for Rosecrans was the discovery that Bragg had not retreated deep into Georgia, but instead was posted behind Chickamauga Creek several miles southeast. Worse, Rosecrans' army was now spread out over forty miles of mountainous terrain.

Men frequently paid unofficial visits to other regiments, spreading local news and gossip. These "newswalkers" talked of going to join Bragg but the average footsoldier could only speculate and worry. In a letter to his wife, one Georgia man wrote, "All eyes are turned to Bragg's Army in Tennessee. From what I can hear a great battle will be fought near Chattanooga. Should his Army be defeated woe be to Georgia." [11]

****

That morning, in Richmond, President Davis conferred with his generals and after listening to opposing arguments, decided that part of Longstreet's 1st Corps would go to Tennessee. Private James Sheldon's peaceful summer came to an abrupt end.

The weeks following Gettysburg were filled with dances and festivals. Day and night, the parties continued, as if men tried to blot out their losses. Horseback rides with the ladies in the countryside always featured a picnic. Leave of absences were plentiful and Richmond offered its theaters and restaurants to those who could afford to get away and take in the night life. Many a Georgian soldier's heart was taken by one of the countless Virginia girls, "Ah! those were lovely days," recalled one officer on Longstreet's staff. [12]

But the war beckoned and General Goode Bryan summoned Colonel Peter McGlashan to his headquarters to tell him the news from Longstreet. McGlashan gave his 50th Georgia orders to prepare to break camp. Two hours later the men were in what was called campaign trim. Private James Sheldon was issued a new blanket, one change of underwear, a tin cup and plate, a knife and fork, and a small haversack. Within the haversack was a pouch containing a small towel, soap, a comb and a toothbrush. Many soldiers carried a popular item provided to them not by the government, but by someone from home; an invaluable little packet known simply as a "housewife," [13] which contained a needle and thread along with instructions for sewing buttons and darning socks. The haversack itself was lined with several pockets and compartments to be filled as they best suited the individual soldier. But often these pockets held their most precious possessions — images of loved ones, letters from home, or a journal the soldier was keeping. A friend was always shown where this compartment was in the event the soldier was killed. Other pockets held tobacco or candy that could be easily reached on a whim. Along with the haversack, some journeying warriors wore a forage cap, an unsoldierly accordion-like hat that could be filled with berries or any other small treats gathered along a march to be consumed at a later time. No space was wasted, and all of this equipment, blanket included, weighed no more than seven or eight pounds.

James and the men of the 50th had established tender bonds with the people of Waller's Tavern and the surrounding farms and villages. Friendships with innkeepers and schoolchildren alike were difficult to walk away from. As the 50th Georgia prepared for its journey to reinforce Bragg in Georgia, hearts were broken, tears were cried, and promises not to be kept were made anyway. For soldiers like James Sheldon, the sadness of parting was lessened somewhat by the prospect of going home.

Longstreet understood the situation and he also understood Robert E. Lee. Longstreet had lost his argument for defense at Gettysburg and was taking no chances this time around. He believed Meade would be cautious. If ever there was a time to safely divide the Army of Northern Virginia this was it. Convinced that Lee would not take such a bold risk, Longstreet made his case directly to Secretary of War James Seddon. Insisting that losing Chattanooga and the interior lines it supplied would be the death of the Confederacy, Longstreet got his plan approved. If done covertly, Richmond would remain adequately defended. Plus, Longstreet contended, Rosecrans' army was disorganized and spread out, ready to be picked apart. Although Lee and Longstreet had sharp disagreements, their respect for each other never wavered. Before embarking on his secret journey, Longstreet went to Lee's tent to say goodbye. The meeting was private. Their respective staffs were told to wait outside, leaving no record of their conversation, but as Longstreet left the tent Lee accompanied him to his horse, Hero. The two men appeared to be in good, yet somewhat subdued, moods. As Longstreet put his foot in a stirrup, Lee offered him fatherly encouragement. "Now, General, you must beat those people out in the West." [14] With those words, Longstreet was off to Georgia.

The men of the 50th Georgia weren't sure where they were going, but rumors persisted that Bragg was in trouble in either Georgia or Chattanooga. The regiment took to the road for Hanover Junction where it boarded a freight train already packed with soldiers crammed into the hot boxcars. As the locomotive built up a head of steam, Private James Sheldon and his friends scrambled to the roofs of the cars, braving tree branches, low tunnels and the broiling sun. The train rumbled to Richmond at 20 miles per hour, arriving after dark.

The next morning, amid great fanfare, the 50th Georgia marched through Richmond and after crossing the James River made camp. The journey ahead of them resembled more of a grand expedition than a military maneuver. The main body of

Longstreet's Corps, 12,000 men, was the largest redeployment ever attempted by rail in the history of warfare. The distance from Waller's Tavern to Chattanooga by direct rail was nearly 550 miles. Needing to shroud the mission, the route went through Wilmington and Augusta, Georgia, nearly twice that distance. The assemblage of so many men was a reunion of sorts. Not since the fighting at Gettysburg had Longstreet's brigades been so concentrated and they made an impressive sight. Rested and replenished with reinforcements, along with new artillery pieces gleaming in the Richmond sun, one Confederate officer boasted, "No better troops could be found anywhere."[15] Another officer bemoaned the fact that the operation hadn't been better planned, thinking that if it had come on the heels of Gettysburg, Rosecrans wouldn't have known what hit him. In spite of the second guessing, morale was once again running high. The men reboarded the trains on September 11, hoping to give Rosecrans the surprise of his life.

It seemed as if all of Richmond turned out to send its boys off to Chattanooga. Railcars of every type and size were loaded beyond capacity. Freight cars, baggage and mail cars, and even a few empty coal cars were hitched up and as they pulled away, smiling, laughing, grimy soldiers could be seen clinging to the sides of the cars. A man in the 50th Georgia recalled the journey with fondness, writing, "[We] went on to Petersburg on the train. We took another train there and traveled three or four days and nights to Atlanta, Georgia, through Augusta. On the trip people cheered us and the men yelled. At Greensboro, North Carolina, two or three-hundred girls dressed in blue, from a seminary, charged down the street—a beautiful sight. Now and then we came to a town where there were tables set out for us. We arrived at Augusta at noon and stayed two or three hours, and then went on a freight train to Atlanta."[16] If they needed to be reminded of what they were fighting for, James Sheldon and his regiment couldn't escape it on their journey through Georgia.

The expedition was going much better than they could have expected. As Longstreet's command rolled south, the outburst of affection produced an overwhelming sense of homesickness in some of the men. Many of these soldiers had not seen their homes in more than two years. As the trains neared their hometowns the temptation to hop off the train for a quick family visit was simply too much for many of the men.

The train stopped for a few hours at Greensboro where another hero's welcome and long tables of meats, fruit and fresh baked breads waited for the men. Hours later, the trains were rolling through farm lands and small towns before grinding to a halt in Atlanta, where the 50th camped in a downtown public square. James Sheldon and the 50th Georgia were bursting with state pride, accepting gifts and warm greetings from pretty girls and politicians who wanted to hear stories of far off places like Chancellorsville and Gettysburg. The push was on, however, as Bragg and Rosecrans were having at each other and the sound of cannonading could be heard in the direction of Chattanooga.

The 50th did not spend the night in Atlanta. As soon as coal was loaded and the tracks ahead were clear, the engines were fired up and the cars began creaking toward Chattanooga. The mood of the soldiers changed as the grim reality of war pushed the images of girls in blue dresses and patriotic songs out of their thoughts. Conversations grew quieter as men prepared themselves for what they knew would be another bloodbath. To have survived so many battles on distant soil the thought of dying in Georgia had never occurred to these men. But suddenly the prospect of returning home, only to be killed, was very real. Men slept, wrote last minute letters and prayed in silence as the steel wheels grinded and rolled over the rails. As the sounds of war grew louder, a captain in Bryan's Brigade got into a long argument with a Union prisoner about the war. The men in the car listened politely and intently. Americans all, one soldier remembered, "It was very interesting and a lot of the men of both sides listened." [17]

A man in James' brigade took a moment to scribble a quick letter home, writing, "I am afraid we will have to go to Tennessee and if we go there I think we will have some hard fighting to do." [18]

As the men of the 50th rode the rails, skirmishing increased south of Chattanooga and a major battle grew imminent. Ambrose Burnside, once Lincoln's commander of the Army of the Potomac, but now relegated to somewhat of a handyman or all-purpose general, offered to resign again. Lincoln wouldn't hear of it. Meade moved the Army of the Potomac from the Rappahannock River to the Rapidan near Culpeper Court House on Sunday, September 13, causing Lee great anxiety. For Lt. Elisha Rhodes the move to Culpeper Court House was merely a change in venue rather than an end to the peaceful summer. The following day skirmishing increased on the land between the rivers.

Twelve miles south of Chattanooga, near a creek in Georgia called Chickamauga, Rosecrans was anxiously pulling together his stretched-out army while Bragg pleaded for reinforcements to anyone who would listen.

By dusk on Thursday the 17th, Rosecrans had successfully concentrated three corps totaling 45,855 men close enough to support each other on the Chickamauga. Disaster loomed for Bragg as he and several of his commanders began blaming each other for this situation. The first of Longstreet's trains began arriving and Bragg, attempting to rein in his temper, began making plans to attack Rosecrans. In the morning, keeping three divisions in reserve, he moved his 34,000 man Army of Tennessee along with some of Longstreet's newly arrived troops, to the area across from Rosecrans on West Chickamauga Creek. Fierce skirmishing broke out all along the creek—the Battle of Chickamauga began.

In the pre-dawn hours of September 19, uncertain of the other's strength, both sides shuffled brigades along six miles of West Chickamauga Creek. At about first light, Union General George Henry Thomas sent one of his divisions forward. His men encountered dismounted Confederate cavalry under Tennessean Nathan Bedford Forrest's command. Surprised by Thomas' sudden appearance, Forrest was forced to fall back, signaling for help. During the course of the day, three full Union corps were brought up and Bragg committed everything he had except two divisions. Along a three mile line through thick, steamy woods, the two armies pounded away at each other. Men fell at a shocking clip, reminiscent of the bloody fighting at Sharpsburg. Bragg hoped to pierce Rosecrans' lines and seize the roads to Chattanooga but was sharply repulsed. The cost in lives was staggering. As darkness fell, little strategic gain could be claimed by either side. That evening, Rosecrans was determined to strengthen his line and ordered his men to build earthworks. Across the field, Bragg organized his army into two wings with General Leonidas Polk in command of the right and, unknown to Rosecrans, General James Longstreet and a portion of his command on the left. Bragg ordered both generals to attack at daylight.

On the left, Bragg renewed his assault on the Union line. Rosecrans, believing he had a gap in his line, moved units to fill it, but this created a hole in his line and a portion of Longstreet's men smashed through. Union forces, under the command of George H. Thomas, desperately clung to two strategic hills. Bragg ordered repeated attacks on these positions but Thomas and his men held until after dark. Under the cover of night, Thomas evacuated his men and retired to Chattanooga, leaving Bragg in control of the surrounding heights.

Morning revealed staggering losses. Although the Battle of Chickamauga was a Confederate victory, it was pyrrhic in the truest sense. Of 58,222 Union soldiers, there were 1,644 dead, 9,262 wounded, 4,945 reported missing, and nearly 500 cavalry lost, bringing the total losses to a mind-boggling 16,351. In addition, 36 cannon, 8,000 rifles and about 150,000 rounds of ammunition were lost, captured or destroyed. Of Bragg and Longstreet's 66,326 men, 2,389 were dead, 13,412 were wounded and slightly over 2,000 were missing or taken prisoner for a total of 17,801 casualties.

For James Sheldon, the four days of riding the rails turned time into a blur. The darkness and occasional flecks of light through the cracks in the boxcar blended with the shards of moonlight breaking through the treetops. Conversations dwindled and died away; after 72 hours, there was little the soldier next to you didn't know about you, your girlfriend or your plans for after the war. There were snores which drew some laughs and periodic groaning as men moved about stretching their cramped legs. Above all else, there was the constant rhythmic thwack of the steel wheels on the track. After the third or fourth day, the rhythm slowed, and the scraping sound of metal on metal announced that the long journey from Virginia to Georgia was nearing its end.

The train halted, then jerked forward only to stop again. Amid the sounds of heavy doors sliding open and slamming shut, muffled shouts could be heard beneath the shuffling of anxious feet on the car's roof. Artillery boomed ominously in the distance as the passengers resigned themselves to an eternity spent in and on the boxcars. James Sheldon and the men of the 50th Georgia were freed from their captivity as the train's doors opened. Officers barked orders to get out of the cars. The scene greeting James was surreal. This was no train station, and there were no pretty girls or finely laid tables waiting for them. Quietly, he and the other men murmured to each other as to their whereabouts. What was this place? There was no platform, nothing more than a series of sorry-looking warehouses and shacks. There were horsemen, teamsters, and wagons of every sort, working against each other in a hot-tempered struggle to get somewhere in a hurry. Every man in sight was covered with soot or soaked with blood. Doctor's tents overflowed with mangled men insane with pain. Bodies were stacked and discarded limbs lay in heaps. And yet, there was an air of joy about the scene. Men, drunk with whiskey and the aphrodisiac of war, hooted and let out the Rebel Yell and all within earshot knew that Pickett's Charge was avenged. Before his pointed shoes hit the ground at Catoosa Woodshed, James Sheldon learned they had arrived too late. The Battle of Chickamauga was over.

Roll call was taken and James' duty as part of Bragg's Army of the Tennessee began. Rosecrans provided the homecoming festivities and a man in the 50th Georgia remembered, "We marched on toward Chattanooga, hearing cannon sometimes and expecting a battle. We marched a little distance, stopped among some trees and formed a line of battle. We lay down all day under very severe shelling, and although most of them went over, it was the most unpleasant experience I had ever had." [19]

The 50th spent the night at Catoosa Woodshed, caring for the wounded who were still streaming in. "They told us about the fighting," a man in the regiment explained. "The next morning we were marched through the battlefield, but we were in the woods and didn't see where the hardest fighting had been. We marched all day following Rosecrans, and when we were close to Chattanooga camped all night. We started on the next morning." [20]

****

President Lincoln was frantic as telegrams and reports of disaster poured into the White House. He wired Burnside in east Tennessee, urging him to "Go to Rosecrans with your force, without a moments delay."[21] The *Richmond Daily Dispatch* reported, "The enemy was completely routed and in full retreat. We have captured over 40 stand of colors, we have taken over 6,000 prisoners." [22] In a haunting description, the reporter continued, "The battlefield that night by moonlight—the glittering beams shining on the ghostly faces of the dead, distorted in expression from the wounds of their torn and mangled bodies, with heaps of the wounded and dying, with scattered arms strewn everywhere, broken artillery carriages and caissons, dead limbers, and all that makes up the debris of a bloody contested field—was terrible and appalling." [23]

The *New York Times* took a different view of events, saying, "The Union army achieved a substantial success instead of being beaten – the enemy being more damaged in killed, wounded, etc. The army is in excellent spirits, and the highest anticipations are entertained." [24] Soldiers on both sides who happened upon a newspaper scratched their heads.

On September 20, Lt. Colonel Fleming of James' 50th Georgia wrote to his wife, detailing the regiment's activities and revealing his loneliness. "[We] arrived at this point about an hour ago. The men are now cleaning up their guns and cooking rations preparatory to marching to the front. Our army is about 12 or 15 miles distant. Yesterday there was quite a heavy engagement. A number of our wounded took the cars from this point to Atlanta today. Rosecrans is falling back before us but I am afraid not so much because driven as to secure a formidable position. This has been his tactics heretofore. This brigade will reach the front I suppose to-morrow and will take part in the fighting... I must not neglect to inform you that I am writing this seated before a nice warm fire—made in a regular chimney. I have at last got a tent and our mess gave two men four dollars to put us up a clay chimney. You have no idea how comfortable it makes our tent. It is a much larger fire place than that in our room. Last night we had a pleasant time sitting around the fire, smoking our pipes and talking." [25] The homesick lieutenant colonel then closed his letter, "Why don't you write me?"

A scared soldier in James Sheldon's brigade also wrote to his wife from Chattanooga, saying, "we should all pray for this wicked war to stop." [26]

On the evening of Wednesday, September 23, President Lincoln convened his cabinet to discuss the Army of the Cumberland's predicament. After a lively discussion, it was agreed that the 11th and 12th Corps be sent to Rosecrans' aid. Adding further urgency to Rosecrans' situation were unsubstantiated reports of Confederate prisoners taken at Chickamauga claiming to be Longstreet's men. Lincoln informed Rosecrans that he was covertly sending him 60,000 more men. He also wrote to General Burnside, expressing his profound disappointment that he had failed to reinforce Rosecrans, saying, "[I have been] struggling... to get you to go assist General Rosecrans in an extremity, and you have repeatedly declared you would do it, and yet you steadily move the other way." [27] After venting his anger, Lincoln characteristically decided not to send the message.

Lincoln was further distressed by the front page of the *New York Post* of September 26, which told in detail of the 11th and 12th Corps' secret mission to join Rosecrans. Feeling defeated on all fronts, military, personal and domestic, Lincoln decided to set out on another tack and wrote Burnside again. This time the tone was softer, almost apologetic, saying, "My order to you meant simply that you should save Rosecrans from being crushed out, believing if he lost his position, you could not hold east Tennessee in any event." [28] Burnside replied that he didn't know what the problem was and denied any lapse in responsibility.

As James Sheldon rode hundreds of miles on the rails, and two worried presidents paced the halls of their mansions, Lt. Elisha Hunt Rhodes and the 2nd Rhode Island Infantry lazed away the breezy Virginia afternoons and sultry nights. As thousands of men fell dead or wounded along Chickamauga Creek, the Army of the Potomac enjoyed the most romantic, even idyllic, period of its existence. Not since the days of McClellan back in 1861 and "oysters on the Potomac," [29] had the army enjoyed such pleasant duty. On a warm late September afternoon, Elisha wrote, "This is a beautiful day with weather just right... On our march to this place we passed through the village or town of Sulphur Springs which before the war was a famous summer resort. Traces of its glory and beauty can still be seen in the ruined and blackened walls of its hotels. We did not stop long enough to visit the famous springs. This camp is named in honor of Major-General Sedgwick, the commander of the 6th Army Corps. He is very popular with the men, and whenever he appears loud cheers are given for 'Uncle John' as he is familiarly called by the soldiers." [30]

As September drew to a close, memories of Gettysburg were eclipsed by the recent events of Chickamauga and the jostling of thousands of men on both sides by railroad. For Private Sheldon and Lt. Rhodes, their often paralleled careers that had taken them on marches along the same dusty roads and crossings of the same rivers now put them on very different paths.

For James Sheldon and Peter McGlashan, returning to their home state and neighboring Tennessee was an eerie experience. The peaceful farms with dales and country lanes they remembered were now replaced by bombed out barns and broken fence rails trodden by thousands of angry men in blue uniforms. Chickens and cattle had been stolen, farms plundered, and freshly cut roads plowed through what had once been cornfields and pastures. Two years of privations caused by the Union blockade had given much of the citizenry a ghostly appearance. For the 150 men of the 50th these sights hardened their resolve to fight on.

One night James Sheldon's 50th Georgia sheltered itself against an incessant enemy fire, but during a lull in the bombardment, McGlashan moved his men forward seeking to escape the sheets of iron that Rosecrans' artillery would soon resume raining down on them. One officer in the 50th recalled, "That night we were moved out into an open field, and had to dig trenches… The ground was very hard and we had only bayonets to dig with, but we had not done much before we were ordered to another place."[31]

James had grown accustomed to seeing and hearing beauty amid the carnage of his daily surroundings and he took pleasure wherever he found it. "While we were in the field we heard drums and a brass band of Rosecrans' army," a Georgia man said. "I had never heard such a sound in my life."[32] This was the Union Army tattoo, a signal sounded on a drum and bugle summoning soldiers to their quarters at night.

Bryan's Brigade was ordered to build a camp and wait for orders while Rosecrans and Bragg continued their dance. By the next morning, McGlashan's men, showing a respectful disregard for constant shelling, took position in a rich forest and cut down trees to form breastworks. For the month of October, these beautiful woods with their towering pines would be home to James and the 50th, whose only rations were bacon and sour cornmeal. On October 2, a man on Colonel Bryan's staff observed the state of affairs at Chattanooga in a letter to his family, writing, "I think we will shell the city in a day or two. I long to see the

Confederate flag wave over Chattanooga. The Yanks still hold the city but it is reported that we have their supplies cut off. We whipped them very badly last Saturday. I have had some narrow escapes from shells."[33]

On Saturday, October 3, President Lincoln issued a proclamation establishing a new national holiday, Thanksgiving. Jefferson Davis spent the weekend preparing for a trip that would take him to Charleston, South Carolina, and to the outskirts of Chattanooga, Tennessee, in an attempt to raise the morale of Confederate troops.

Now that Longstreet's secret mission to Georgia was revealed, Lee expected Meade to go on the offensive. Having read the *New York Post* report of two Union corps being sent to Rosecrans, and believing the best defense was a good offense, Lee decided to attack. Boldly defiant, the Army of Northern Virginia crossed the Rapidan on October 9 and headed northwest, hoping to smash the right arm of the Army of the Potomac and roll it back toward Washington. Meade, having a numerical advantage of two to one, expected just such a move and sounded the alarm throughout his command. As the air of the Virginia Indian summer began to fill with the nearly forgotten sounds of rifle fire, the men of Meade's army were reminded that there was still a war going on.

Skirmishing broke out along the Rapidan making Meade nervous, convinced his right flank was in danger. Unsure of Lee's intentions, Meade went on the defensive and pulled his army back to the banks of the Rappahannock River. The area between the two rivers was now hotly contested as both armies pushed and probed each other. Lee, instead of attacking the Union's right flank, swung around, putting Manassas and Washington in his sights. For a moment it appeared the Army of Northern Virginia would get between Meade and Washington, but Meade quickly closed the gap. On Wednesday, the 14th, the inevitable clash began.

Five miles southwest of the old Bull Run battlefield, the Battle of Bristoe Station was hot and quick. It was a Union victory but the two armies once again fell into a state of quiet after the battle of Bristoe Station. Alarmed, Lincoln called for 300,000 more volunteers.

Reverend Augustus Woodbury summed up the events in northern Virginia in October, 1863, saying, "Lee's intention was not to fight, but to embarrass [Meade]." The Union general hesitated to attack, preferring to withdraw from his advanced position and to occupy a position nearer Washington and its defenses. Woodbury explained, "Lee was supposed to be inferior in strength, but, by skillful maneuvering his army, prevented battle, yet forced a retreat." Although by no means a decisive strategic victory, Lee had seriously damaged and disrupted Meade's supply depots and communications, thereby "effectively postponing any important hostile operation on our part during the favorable autumnal weather." [34]

Although the 2nd Rhode Island camped near Bristoe Station, it was not engaged, and Elisha and the men knew little of the battle fought there except from what he'd heard from the newswalkers. The 2nd Rhode Island existed as if in the eye of a hurricane as their peaceful stay in Virginia rolled on. On the last day of September the regiment marched in the rain from Culpeper Court House, taking up a position along the Orange & Alexandria Railroad and given the mundane duty of guarding tracks.

The 2nd was building a new camp and Elisha enjoyed his status as an officer which provided him with a crew of privates. His men constructed an eighteen-by-ten-foot-wide house for him, or a "shebang" as he called it. The peak was twelve feet high and featured a window and door with curtains. Elisha wrote, "One of my men found me a desk, so I am living in style…All of the officers have built quarters, and it looks now as if we were to stay here during the winter and guard the railroad. I hope so, for this is the first easy duty we have ever had, and we need rest." [35]

The 2nd had finally been assigned a new chaplain, John D. Beugless, replacing the unpopular Jameson. Elisha introduced him to the men at a prayer meeting where he shook hands while receiving an enthusiastic welcome. Beugless quickly fit in, becoming a popular member of the regiment. Elisha enjoyed the chaplain's company so much that he took him foraging through the ghost town of Brentville, and they returned with a wagonload of windows and doors for the shebang.

Chaplain John Beugless

A growing concern for the men of the 2nd was the survival of the regiment itself. For many of them, including Elisha, their three-year term of service was nearing its end and they would be going home. This situation existed throughout the army and the government was seeking ways to get men to re-enlist. A leave of 30 days, along with a bonus of $400, the equivalent to three years salary for a private, was offered to any man who chose to stay on. Meetings were held and arguments made for going home as a group, re-enlisting as a group or disbanding the regiment altogether. Elisha's opinion was strong and pointed, telling the others, "I hope we shall decide to remain, for I could not be contented at home if mustered out and should rather be in the 2nd Rhode Island Volunteers than seek service in any other regiment. I want to remain and see the end of the war." [36] The future was uncertain, but for the time being the men seemed interested in keeping the 2nd Rhode Island alive as a fighting regiment.

By mid-October, the men of the 2nd heard reports of renewed fighting. Elisha wrote, "We are too far in the rear to know much about it," adding, "The enemy does not molest us. Only pretty girls with pies for sale invade our camp." [37]

****

Although trench life was a relatively new experience for Private James Sheldon and the 50th Georgia, they found it tolerable; the only complaint being lousy rations. But soon boredom revisited the men, and the narrow confines of their earthworks made its effects insufferable. Each day passed much like the day before and the tedium began taking its toll on the morale of the regiment. An occasional gunshot in the distance or the arrival of a courier would stir things up for a few minutes before the morass resumed. Rainy days were the worst. The trenches would fill with standing puddles which brought about a day long chorus of mutterings from James and the other men, wondering aloud how long they would have to stay in this hole.

In the past the men avoided picket duty if they could, but now it was an opportunity to escape the drudgery. It also gave a man a chance to forage, stretch his legs, and get some exercise. One afternoon in late October, James and his fellow Rangers were ordered out on picket. Warily stretched out in a line, they began a slow, deliberate walk in the direction of the Army of the Cumberland.

The enemy is always the great unknown in war. The dead kept their secrets and the wounded are often too injured or terrified to offer up much information. The prisoner of war, always a great curiosity, is usually tight-lipped and proud. The chance to talk to a living, breathing enemy soldier in arms is remote, at best.

But on this autumn day near Chickamauga Creek, Private Sheldon and his picket line found themselves face-to-face with about a dozen men in blue uniforms. They must have been a curious sight to the Union men, as the Georgia men were wearing their own new uniforms of blue jackets, light blue trousers and pointed shoes.

Muskets were instinctively raised amid the clatter of gear being jostled, and the men nervously prepared for a firefight. But a hush fell upon Sheldon's line and the weird sensation of something that had never happened before gripped the men. One of them recalled, "[We stood] about two hundred yards from the Yankee picket lines, but didn't fire." [38] There they were, staring each other down, speechless. The Georgians whispered to each other, wondering if they were caught in a trap, looking to their left and right waiting to be flanked. Fingers itched on triggers while hearts pounded. Tense moments passed until a Union man slowly raised a newspaper over his head and then held it out in front of him as an offering. No one flinched until one of James' officers asked if any of the men had a newspaper. A Georgian sacrificed his paper and gave it to him. The officer held the paper above his own head and waved it. This was acknowledged with a nod from his counterpart across the way and the two men began a slow, tentative walk toward each other. Steel-eyed stares were exchanged, sizing each other up, until the men accepted each other's hand and the newspapers were exchanged.

The pickets on both sides broke ranks and the men slung their rifles over their shoulders. They walked the hundred yards to engage the enemy—in conversation. There were the obvious questions about home and war news, and quickly the conversation turned toward the more pressing issues of coffee, sugar and tobacco shortages. Knapsacks were opened and the trading began. Cautious smiles and nervous laughs helped break the tension and it wasn't long before ambrotypes and tintypes of family appeared. As pleasant as the truce between the two picket lines had been, there was fear on both sides of being caught. Fraternizing with the enemy was one of the most severe infractions and someone certainly would be made an example of if charged with committing the act. The Georgian's and their Union counterparts discreetly shared information as to where and when the other would be on picket duty.

For days afterward, the same men would venture into a predetermined section of forest and with a designated whistle or other signal, a white flag would slowly emerge. This arrangement worked for both sides and it was made clear that other pickets were not aware of the agreement. Precautions needed to be taken to avoid getting shot. But word got out, and there was an abrupt end to the socializing on the picket line. It was also discovered that other regiments had their own secret friends across the way and the informal agreements between the pickets were often fairly elaborate. When a swimming hole was discovered, it became an item of contention. The two sides decided which days were for Union use and which days would be strictly for Confederates. Years after the war, men of both sides talked of the day Johnny Reb met Billy Yank and shared a smoke or a "chaw."

On October 12, Bryan's Brigade camped about three miles from Chattanooga, one and one half miles from Lookout Mountain in a place called Dry Valley. The brigade was situated at the center of its division. A private in James' brigade wrote to his father, "We have more sickness in camps than [we] have had for some time. Citizens that have lived here, say that this is a sickly place." [39] Describing life on the frontlines, he continued, "Both sides are in line of battle. There has been some little cannonading on our left, this evening. There was considerable cannonading this morning, which sounded as though it was in the yanks rear. It seemed to be a good ways off. We have cannonading on one side or the other every day. We are well fortified here... We have a splendid position, and plenty of men and artillery. All we ask them to do, is to attack us. If they don't attack us shortly, I think we will bluff them and attack them in the rear. As I hear it reported, that we are building pontoons for bridges, as fast as we can." [40]

"The Army of the Potomac has again skedaddled to the rear," wrote a dismayed Lt. Elisha Rhodes on October 16, 1863.[41] Meade posted his massive army on the heights of Centreville, Virginia, and waited to see where Lee's Army of Northern Virginia might be. Two days later, John Sedgwick's 6th Corps, including the 2nd Rhode Island, was dug in at Chantilly. Lee fell back to the Rappahannock River and Meade saw an opportunity to catch him on his heels. The whole army moved forward on the 19th, and Elisha Rhodes and the 2nd Rhode Island crossed Cub Run Creek, Bull Run and for the third time, marched across the old battlefield at Manassas. The nights were bitterly cold and the men suffered severely. Most of the roads were jammed with traffic—the march was repeatedly halted. With nowhere to go, Colonel Rogers ordered his men to make camp and rest. This little-remembered march was one of the most miserable experiences of the war for Elisha who, in addition to suffering from the freezing temperatures, was without rations. A nearby cornfield was plundered and Elisha roasted several ears in his campfire feeling "more dead than alive." [42] Throughout the week, skirmishing was almost continuous. By the evening of the 20th nothing had been resolved in terms of territorial gains or losses, but the fighting in northern Virginia slowly died away, leaving 1,400 Confederate and 2,300 Union men killed, wounded, or missing.

On Wednesday October 21, the exhausted men of the 2nd reached their old camp near Warrenton, delighted to be back "in our old camp with the stone house." [43] The good feeling was short-lived, however, when they discovered their camp had been borrowed during their absence by a couple of Mississippi regiments who used much of it for firewood, including the new church benches. Cold rains began to fall and the nights felt winter-like. The Mississippians had burned most of the nearby trees and the gathering of firewood meant a daily journey into the forest. Elisha was happily surprised to be issued a new heavy winter overcoat. There was no place like home, in spite of the vandalism. Elisha had caught a bad cold on the march and needed a good rest.

On Sunday, October 18, Ulysses Grant ascended in power to command the Military Division of the Mississippi, taking charge of all Federal military operations from the Mississippi to the mountains in the east. The war would never be the same. Understanding the expectations of his new boss, George Thomas announced from Chattanooga that he would "hold the town till we starve." [44] Grant immediately wired his commanding generals to leave no doubt as to who was in charge.

After days of dodging enemy raiders and traveling torn up roads, Grant and his entourage arrived in Chattanooga on the 23rd. Five hundred miles to the northeast, in Washington, Lincoln urged General Meade to begin planning an attack on Lee. To the southeast, on the 26th, Charleston, South Carolina, shuddered as a major bombardment of Ft. Sumter began. The battle fronts of the war now stood in triangular configuration.

As October closed, James Sheldon and Elisha Rhodes might as well have been living in different worlds. Pickets of the 50th Georgia befriended some of their Northern counterparts, while the camp of the 2nd Rhode Island was invaded by herds of marauding pigs who had escaped their farms. The hungry Rhode Islanders envisioned pork chops and bacon on their tin plates but found themselves on the wrong side of the law for shooting at them. One thing James Sheldon didn't have to worry about was the northern Virginia cold that Elisha was enduring. "I have a huge fire of oak wood burning in my hut, but every time some one opens the blanket that serves as a door I imagine myself at the North Pole," Elisha joked. [45]

On Wednesday, November 4, Longstreet was ordered to take his command to east Tennessee in an attempt to push Burnside out of his stronghold at Knoxville. The 50th Georgia waited to move out. Orders were given and countermanded as hours turned into days. Grant, at Chattanooga, waited nervously for Sherman to arrive and put pressure on Bragg, perhaps forcing him to recall Longstreet.

In Virginia, Meade ordered Elisha's 6th Corps to move toward Lee's lines near Rappahannock Station, where it arrived about three p.m. A Confederate welcoming committee was there to meet them and the result was a "brilliant affair" according to Reverend Woodbury. [46] The 6th Corps' prize was 1600 prisoners, four cannon, eight regimental flags and piles of small arms. Elisha, elated to get back into action, described the fight as "hot for an hour, and shot and shell flew lively." [47] In the afternoon, the 1st Corps came on line to support the attack, and made "a daring and successful assault upon the enemy's entrenchments upon the north bank of the Rappahannock." [48] At the same time, the 2nd and 3rd Corps entered the fray, forcing the Southerners to retreat and leave 400 more prisoners behind. Woodbury explained, "General Meade had planned a battle with the enemy along the Rappahannock, and expected from it decisive results. The reports from the enemy's generals show it to have been extremely mortifying to them, as it took them by surprise, and inflicted upon them considerable damage." [49]

Once again it appeared that the elusive Lee had been cornered. On the following morning, November 8, Sedgwick's 6th Corps set out to finish off the retreating Army of Northern Virginia, but a severe fog blanketed the area making it impossible to see more than a few feet in any direction. The 2nd Rhode Island was ordered to a spot along the river known as Kelly's Ford, where it guarded a New York battery. The next morning Elisha and the men crossed the river on a pontoon bridge and went out on picket duty. Colonel Rogers told Elisha that he could either be promoted to captain, in command of his own company, or he could become the regimental adjutant. As adjutant, he would be given a horse and Elisha decided it was time to give his sore feet a rest. "Old Abe…a fine bay horse with a white mark on his face," was purchased by Lt. Rhodes who liked to boast he could "run like a deer." [50] Life as a private seemed a lifetime ago. Elisha enjoyed the spoils of upper-echelon military life which included not only a horse and wooden hut, but the daily opportunity to dine with Chaplain Beugless and Colonel Rogers discussing the progress of the war and the affairs of the regiment.

On Thursday, November 12, the 2nd Rhode Island was once again moving. The regiment marched back to Rappahannock Station and pushed on with the rest of the army to Brandy Station. Over the next two weeks, the railroad and bridges were rebuilt and a supply depot reestablished. The men named their new camp "Sedgwick" in honor of their corps commander. The days and nights passed quietly with the only real excitement being the visit of high ranking Russian Army and Navy officers. The Russians had come to observe and a parade and review was held at headquarters in their honor. News also reached Camp Sedgwick that one of their favorites, former Rhode Island governor and now United States senator, William Sprague, had married the beautiful daughter of Treasury Secretary Chase in Washington and that President Lincoln attended the wedding.

Elisha entertained himself by attending prayer meetings and going sightseeing on his new horse. One afternoon he visited John Botts, a former congressman from Virginia, who regaled him with a story of how he once put a Confederate general in his place after his 2,200-acre estate was destroyed by artillery fire. Later, Elisha found a farm selling fresh milk at 35 cents a quart, which he declined, but he returned to Camp Sedgwick with another horse named Charley, which he could use for pulling a wagon.

The Army of Northern Virginia was "retired beyond the Rapidan," according to Reverend Woodbury, and General Meade wanted one more fight before winter to push Lee back toward Richmond. [51] He proposed seizing the heights of Fredericksburg where he could be readily supplied but Lincoln overruled the operation.

The Virginia nights grew increasingly cold. As snow fell the men of Colonel Horatio Rogers' 2nd Rhode Island huddled around huge bonfires in an effort to keep warm. In Tennessee, Colonel Peter McGlashan's 50th Georgia remained camped on scenic Lookout Mountain waiting for orders to follow Longstreet to Knoxville. In the three months since the Battle of Gettysburg, Elisha and James had been spared from much of the fighting, spending their days in the warm paradise of the Virginia mountains or lazing away in the Georgia and Tennessee forests. In Gettysburg itself, President Lincoln delivered some very brief remarks at the dedication of a new national cemetery. On a stage in Providence, Rhode Island, a hit play about the war opened to sell-out audiences—*Paradise Lost.*

10

THEY WERE BRAVE MEN

J ames and Elisha both heard stories about Grant. Newswalkers
on both sides described the new commander as a hard-nosed,
cigar-chomping general who held chivalry in low regard.
Some even joked that his initials stood for "Unconditional
Surrender."[1] His battle-worn appearance was a sharp contrast to
the likes of his predecessors—George McClellan in particular.
He was once described as, "a man forced to watch something
that did not interest him at all." Most telling, two privates who
got close enough to get a good look at their new boss told their
friends, "He looks as if he meant it."[2]

When Longstreet began moving his corps east to
Knoxville, President Davis and his military advisors were certain
Grant would detach some of his forces at Chattanooga to
intercept him and reinforce Burnside. But Grant wouldn't hear
of it, and Burnside would have to make the fight at Knoxville his
own. The Confederate brain-trust hadn't seen anything like this
before. Until now, *they*, and not the Union command, had decided
how and where the war would be fought. Even his fellow Union
generals felt the change. Once, after being warned that there
weren't enough pontoon bridges available for the retreat of his
army across the Rapidan River should a campaign fail, he calmly
informed his generals, "If I beat General Lee I sha'n't want any
pontoons; and if General Lee beats me I can take all the men I
intend to take back across the river on a log."[3] Grant understood
the numbers and they were not good for the Confederacy. One
of his first acts upon taking command was to request that the

government no longer engage in the practice of releasing and exchanging prisoners of war.

****

The men of the 50th Georgia left Chattanooga the same way they had arrived and Private James Sheldon found himself once again crammed into a boxcar. Sounds of battle could be heard in the distance, as the 50th Georgia slowly rolled away from Chattanooga on Wednesday, November 4. One soldier remembered, "As we looked back we saw shells bursting over Lookout Mountain where we had been." [4] The same soldier gave a detailed account of the 50th's journey to Knoxville, where along the way the train was halted because Grant's men had torn up the tracks, "We had to march some of the time. At night we stopped near a railroad, it was raining. We got on some boxcars, but there wasn't room for all to sit down, so I half-kneeled all night. The train didn't move. Toward morning the rain stopped and I climbed on top. At dawn the train moved into mountainous country. At about eleven in the morning we overtook another train full of soldiers. I saw some men pointing to the sky, I looked up and saw Venus shining. We were in a deep ravine between two mountains." [5]

As the train carried James away from Lookout Mountain he could see Alabama and North Carolina in the distance. Painfully, the vistas of Georgia and thoughts of home faded from view as the boxcars rolled into the mountain passes of Tennessee. Despite the breathtaking scenery, the journey itself was an awful experience. The men of the 50th disembarked at Sweetwater, Tennessee, and camped for a week. A shipment of flour arrived and the famished men tore into the bags. They went to work making biscuits, dumplings, and a camp favorite, "sloosh," a mixture of cornmeal, flour and bacon grease slowly cooked over a fire on the end of a bayonet. But within an hour after eating this evening's meal, many of the men were doubled over in pain, vomiting or running to the latrine with diarrhea. The processed wheat had been tainted with a nasty bacteria, shutting down the 50th Georgia more effectively than the Union Army ever had. For the remainder of the regiment's stay at Sweetwater, the men had to subsist on water.

Happy to leave Sweetwater, the 50th Georgia began a twenty-mile march to the town of Loudon where it expected a clash with Burnside's men. About a day's march and twelve miles from Loudon, the regiment spent the night in a huge pumpkin patch bursting with the most enormous gourds James had ever seen. Pumpkin stew was the order of the day featuring lots of salt, the only spice available.

By late the next morning, Lt. Colonel William Fleming, in command while Colonel McGlashan was on leave, led his men to the outskirts of Loudon. Feeling uneasy, the men looked at their strange surroundings. The town was quiet and Burnside's men had fallen back to a stronger defensive position across the Holston River. Reaching the water's edge no one was surprised that all the bridges had been burned. Longstreet ordered pontoons to be assembled and late in the afternoon James and the 50th Georgia crossed the river. "But the enemy had withdrawn, so there was still no fighting," remembered one veteran. [6]

Longstreet's men were hungry and a major battle loomed. His supply trains lagged behind his corps and foraging was hindered by the fact that his men were on Southern soil. If this had been Pennsylvania, his men would plunder local farms as had become the custom for both armies when on enemy ground. The Tennesseans did their best to provide sustenance but they too were in desperate need of raw materials. Luck played a hand in filling the empty bellies of James Sheldon and the 50th Georgia when, as they marched toward Knoxville, a flock of sheep suddenly surrounded the regiment. Lieutenant Colonel Fleming learned that the flock was the property of a farmer with strong Union connections and with fixed bayonets each company was ordered to attack the unsuspecting sheep. Only animals they could eat or carry on the march were slaughtered. Pumpkin stew paled in comparison to the roasts and lamb legs and their aroma wafted in the air that evening. The next day some half-starved Texans asked Sheldon and his friends if they had any meat. When the Georgians boasted of their feast the night before, the Texans thought they were being put on and marched away.

Longstreet had hoped to overtake Burnside as he fell back toward Knoxville and the giant earthen fortifications the Union general had constructed to enclose the city. On the morning of November 16, the 50th Georgia caught up with the rear guard of Burnside's retreating army which made a stand, effectively punching the pursuing Georgians in the nose. The first burst of artillery spoke with a terrifying roar and was soon joined by other field pieces spitting fire and hot iron over and near the Georgians. James hit the ground and instinctively began digging. For almost 12 hours the men stayed in this position as the ground shook and a mixture of dirt, rocks, and shrapnel flew around them. By midnight the firing withered and stopped. An angry Private James Sheldon wanted a fight.

In the morning the Union artillery fire resumed, but this time it was answered by some of Longstreet's batteries. A man in the 50th Georgia described the action, saying, "We were formed into line of battle in some woods, so we thought there would be a battle. The firing kept up for some time. We were ordered to advance; we were in a field with a Yankee battery on a hill a quarter of a mile away. We advanced as if we were on dress parade, until the firing was too hot, then we lay down flat in the field, and nobody was killed. It was now about sundown. We lay on the ground until dark, when the enemy withdrew." [7] This small engagement was known as Campbell's Station.

The 50th camped that night in some nearby woods, resuming its march in the morning. Knoxville was still about thirty miles away. Burnside's men again appeared and a brief skirmish broke out before they skedaddled once again in the direction of Knoxville. James Sheldon and the 50th crossed the meandering Holston River by flatboat, finally arriving at the foot of Ft. Loudon with the rest of Bryan's Brigade on the 17th. James and the other men gazed at this monster of a fort and no one liked what they saw.

The fort's high walls were nearly vertical and the fields in front protected by an entanglement of telegraph wire, tied from one tree stump to the next. If these outer defenses could be breeched, the attackers must then descend into a ditch partially filled with water. This created, in effect, a moat twelve feet wide and four-to-ten feet deep. Once the wall was scaled, the attacker would be on the fort's parapet and greeted by bayonets, small arms fire and desperate hand-to-hand combat. All of these obstacles would have to be overcome while under close range artillery fire from the fort's big guns.

The 50th Georgia camped on a hill near the Holston River about two miles from the fort, looming ominously in the distance. James dug earthworks with his comrades and passed the next few days nervously waiting for orders. There was a battery in their camp, and one afternoon James and a few men shouted into each other's ears about how, after all this time as soldiers they were still amazed at just how loud these cannons were. "The noise was very hard on the ears," said one soldier. [8]

Suddenly, one man nudged an elbow into the ribs of the man next to him who looked up in awe. He did the same to the man standing next to him and so on throughout the small group. No one could quite believe it, but General Longstreet had quietly joined them to watch the battery do its work.

Later that day some of Burnside's men were seen in the distance, heading for cover in the direction of the fort. The 50th was ordered in hot pursuit but Private Sheldon and the 50th halted after coming under heavy artillery fire. At one point a cannonball slowly rolled past them.

Before assaulting Ft. Sanders, Longstreet intended to bring siege to it and the city of Knoxville which it was shielding. He began constructing a series of cannon pits along the Holston River and the men of the 50th were busy digging and carrying dirt and rocks along its banks. James and the men crossed the Holston so many times, that they eventually decided to stretch ropes across the river so they could pull a large flatboat, laden with men and supplies, back and forth. In spite of the hard work, not a single man took his eyes off Ft. Sanders. The Confederates dug each night, and morning revealed that their lines were inching closer and closer to the base of the fort. Within the ranks of the 50th Georgia, "Rumors were spreading among the men that we would attack first, and the men kept expecting it."[9]

****

During the third week of November, word of a Union victory near Chattanooga was carried by the newswalkers through the camps of both armies. Reports of the "Battle Above The Clouds"[10] prompted cheers of "Remember Chickamauga! Remember Chickamauga!"[11] on the Union side, while the Confederates were relieved to hear that Bragg had managed to save most of his army. All eyes now turned toward Knoxville, which, as a railway hub, was suddenly a vital center of interstate commerce.

On Friday, November 27, the rain cast a pall over the already somber men of the 50th Georgia. Many in James' regiment, battle-tested and hardened by war, were convinced that here, at Ft. Sanders, was where they would meet their deaths. One man vividly recalled the mood and the eerie events of the 48 hours that followed, "The day before the battle it rained very hard. I was at a little spring with Captain Waldron, one of my best friends in the war. We were talking about the reports of an attack, and Waldron had a feeling that he would be killed. I told him to throw off the feeling, but we were both depressed. It continued to rain hard all day. My blanket got very wet. At sundown the ground was so wet that there was no place to sleep, so I took two fence rails, put a tent cloth over them and slept on the rails. The men built big fires. A man from Bass [County, Georgia] came over to my fire, he was very depressed and said to me, 'Lieutenant, if we attack that fort I will be killed or severely wounded.' At three o'clock in the morning we were awakened by an orderly, and told to be ready to start at a moment's notice."[12]

The 50th's assault of Ft. Sanders was part of a 4,000-man operation that Longstreet hoped could overwhelm the small force defending it. The fort held a mere 335 of Burnside's infantrymen and 105 artillerymen manning 12 cannons. Most of them were from Massachusetts and Michigan, under the command of 24-year-old 1st Lieutenant Samuel Benjamin. Living on less than a quarter of their normally allotted rations, these men were starving. But they understood their situation and used the fort to every advantage they could think of. Expecting an attack the next morning, the men filled the ditch with water which partially froze during the night. Benjamin roused his men hours before first light in strict silence, posting them at their gun positions.

Grim faced, James and the other men counted the contents of their cartridge boxes and cap pouches while making sure they were dry. Guns were checked and rechecked. Within minutes the 50th was marching out of the woods, "toward the road and turned toward the fort, so we knew the battle was on. Everything was very still. We were only two miles from the fort," recalled one of the men in James' regiment. [13] The march continued—the road twisted and turned—large houses and buildings blotted out the fort in the distance. Townspeople stood and watched as the men passed glumly. Occasionally a word of encouragement was offered, but it was more compassion than patriotic fervor. One man in James' regiment recalled, "We turned to the right and just as day broke we saw the fort not a hundred yards away. Everything was still, when right in front of me a man fired from the picket line, he didn't know we were so near. This was very depressing to the soldiers just before a battle." [14]

"Order-Forward, guide center!" was heard up and down the line and finally, the order to charge. [15] For some unknown reason, the artillerymen inside the fort held their fire but rifle fire began raining down from the parapet. James and the other men moved slowly through the tangled maze for 150 yards. When they reached an open area, they rushed the fort with bayonets fixed announcing their arrival with a shrill, bone-chilling Rebel Yell. According to one officer in the 50th Georgia, "[George] Waldron and I were running along together and he was wounded. I thought he was killed. Just after this we struck telegraph wires that had been laid, but some of our men got up to the fort. Many men were in a ditch around the fort, I saw a Union shell drop into the ditch and explode. The men and I lay down flat behind the ditch, and we were under the deadliest fire that I saw in the whole war. Just before we lay down I heard a bullet strike a man at my side, it was the man from Bass [County], and he was killed." [15]

The Georgians were halted by the ditch and the frozen ground was slippery. Inside the fort the Union men were busy. All along the wall artillery and musketry fire showered the struggling mass below. Hand grenades, blocks of wood, axes and metal objects, were hurled over the parapet, killing and mangling many of Longstreet's men. On the south side of the fort Confederate pickets silenced the Union artillery and sharpshooters but a deadly fire continued from the west wall. "Those that succeeded in climbing up the parapet to the crest were shot down, and rolling back dragged all below them back into the ditch," remembered one Confederate general. [16]

A newspaper called *The Southern Drummer* reported, "The forward column of Confederates mostly tripped over the wire entanglements and fell into the ditch, or jumped in an attempt to scale the wall of the fort. Thus the ditch, which was twelve feet wide and ten feet deep, was literally packed full of struggling men. The wall of the fort was fully sixteen feet high and it was impossible for men to scale it. From the parapets and embrasures men shot the struggling men below. Double-shotted charges of canister from cannons in the angles of the fort raked the trenches filled with men. Twenty-pound shells, fuses out and lighted for twenty seconds, were thrown over the doomed combatants. Still they struggled to scale the fort. Men climbed upon each other's shoulders, and a few reached the parapet, only to be shot or knocked down again." [17]

A corporal in a battery inside the fort described the fight from the Union's perspective, saying, "I was standing up against the breastwork and saw the shell coming just as plain as day. We could hear them coming before they got anywhere near us and what a noise they make. While this shelling was going on the rebels were forming for a charge on the fort and the first our folks knew of them they were within 20 yards of the picket line and less than 300 from the point of the fort. And on they came with a yell 3 columns deep and one in reserve... the rebels came over the logs, wire and stumps and planted their colors right on the outer slope of the fort...But all of this did not last more than half an hour for those that were alive in the ditches began to call for quarter and the order was given to cease firing... There was arrangements made right off to cease hostilities till 7 o'clock in the evening. As soon as the firing stopped I went up on the parapet to look at them. And such a sight I never saw before nor do I care about seeing again. The ditch in places was almost full of them piled one on top of the other...They were brave men. Most of them Georgians. I would give one of the wounded a drink as quick as anybody if I had it. That is the only thing they ask for when first wounded." [18]

One man who was near James Sheldon remembered, "we were ordered to retreat. We had been there only twenty minutes. We jumped up and dashed down the hill, then cannon opened up on us. I was caught in the telegraph wire and fell forward down the hill."

The soldier continued, "We retreated down to a low field, protected from fire, and the firing ceased. We were ordered to build fires and we got breakfast. My blanket was frozen. In an hour or so we were taken back to the position on the hill that we had come from. In the morning Longstreet sent a flag of truce for permission to get the dead and wounded. This was granted and among others we got Captain Waldron." [19]

The battle was over in twenty minutes. Confederate losses were 813 including over 200 men who were trapped and taken prisoner in the ditch. Eight Confederate officers were dead. Burnside lost only thirteen men, eight of them killed, six of whom were found in the ditch. He reported that, "The ground between the fort and the crest was strewn with the dead and wounded, who were crying for help, and after the repulse was fully established I tendered to the enemy a flag of truce for the purpose of burying the dead and caring for the wounded." [20] The ninety-two Confederate dead were buried in haste, and not very deeply. As the bodies were being interred, a wounded dog dragged itself around in agony. An embittered Union soldier angrily kicked the injured animal into an open grave, muttering, "Let the sleeping dogs lie together." [21] A few days after the battle, body parts began emerging from the thawing and refreezing grounds around the fort and wild hogs began gnawing the human remains. A Knoxville undertaker was hired at the rate of $4 per body to build pine coffins and bury the Confederate dead.

Although the attack on Ft. Sanders was over, Longstreet's siege of Knoxville wasn't. Knowing that Burnside's men were physically and mentally exhausted, for the next three days he ordered mock assaults on the fort hoping to break the morale of the starving men inside. The Union men had been without sleep for days and were forced to survive on bags of corn intended for the horses. On frayed nerves and empty bellies, somehow the Union soldiers kept going and their defense of the fort grew more creative by the hour. At night turpentine-drenched cotton was set ablaze and fired from the fort's cannons over its ramparts, lighting up Longstreet's position. A locomotive was sacrificed for the cause. Its wheels and axles were cut off and were dangled from the edge of the fort's wall by ropes. Axe wielding men stood ready to cut the ropes sending the wheels careening down into the ranks of an advancing intruder. On December 3, a Thursday, General Longstreet learned that Sherman was indeed on his way to Knoxville—Longstreet ended his operations.

Ambrose Burnside was the big winner at Knoxville. His once-promising career had plummeted since the early days of the war but his stand at Knoxville redeemed him. Within the fort the men rejoiced and their spirits soared. Now that they could finally relax they debated what they wanted first—it was about 50-50 between sleep or a hot bath. Sherman, who was only 15 miles away, praised Burnside, saying, "I am here and can bring 25,000 men into Knoxville, tomorrow, but Longstreet having retreated, I feel disposed to stop... Accept my congratulations at your successful defense and your patient endurance." [22] The United States Congress interrupted its session to state that, "The thanks of Congress be, and they hereby are, presented to Major General Ambrose E. Burnside, and through him to the officers, and men who have fought under his command, for their gallantry, good conduct, and soldier-like endurance." [23] President Lincoln urged his countrymen to "assemble at their high places of worship, and render special homage and gratitude to Almighty God for this great advancement of the National Course." [24]

The war devastated Knoxville. Both sides plundered and stripped its food supply and raw materials. Almost all of the city's livestock were either slaughtered or taken away by soldiers of both sides, and bands of guerrillas terrorized the citizenry long after the actual fighting had stopped.

The 50th Georgia remained encamped on the hill for the next several days, bracing for a counterattack that never came. The newswalkers said that Sherman was moving on Longstreet's rear flank to break his siege of Knoxville. Many believed the thunder in the distance was actually Sherman's artillery twenty miles away and closing. Longstreet knew it was time for his army to withdraw and regroup. On December 3, James and the 50th Georgia broke camp to act as rear guard, protecting their army as it crossed the Tennessee River for the last time. The men of the 50th held a position under the watchful eye of Burnside's men, who were within shouting distance, and both sides engaged in an afternoon of name-calling that was more good-natured than one would have expected under the circumstances. The 50th remained on rear guard for "a day and a night," [25] leaving at daylight and reaching their hillside camp in the evening darkness. Marching back to camp, one man thought he'd tripped on a log, but when he picked it up to inspect it he was horrified to discover it was a human foot.

Lieutenant Rhodes' days of tranquility in the Virginia forests were about to be interrupted. President Lincoln, uncomfortable with the prospect of Lee's Army of Northern Virginia's 48,500 men spending the winter on his doorstep, had been hounding General Meade to push Lee back toward Richmond. But even without Longstreet's Corps of 22,000, Lee was still a tiger Meade was not eager to engage. Risking even a minor defeat on the eve of a winter of inactivity would have huge political repercussions and probably cost Meade his job. Lee, facing Meade's 85,000 men, couldn't afford a defeat either. But if Meade didn't want a fight, perhaps he could outmaneuver Lee back to Richmond. Thoughts of Chancellorsville haunted Meade's plans—being outnumbered never seemed to worry Lee.

Whatever fears Meade had were quietly put aside and on Tuesday, November 24, he ordered his army to start moving out, but two days of heavy rains muddied the roads and he was forced to wait. It wasn't until dawn on Thursday that the Army of the Potomac began crossing the Rapidan River, hoping to get around the right flank of the Army of Northern Virginia. The 2nd Rhode Island was "all packed and ready," [26] according to Elisha. The men were anxious to get out of their camp as the recent heavy rains had turned it into a sea of mud. "We live in mud, sleep in mud, and almost eat in mud," [27] Elisha wrote. The 2nd crossed Mountain Run and later that evening the Rapidan, via a pontoon bridge at a place called Jacob's Ford. That night Elisha and the men made camp on the south bank. The following day, their 6th Corps was joined by the 2nd Corps.

When Lee received word of Meade's flanking movement, he immediately began sending elements of his army east along the south side of the Rapidan to stop him. Skirmishing began breaking out at little-known places such as Robertson's Tavern and Payne's Farm. More significant fighting took place near a church in the Wilderness. It was along a small stream called Mine Run, near Locust Grove, that Lee chose to make his stand and Meade decided to attack him before his position became unassailable. Spearheading Meade's attack was General William Henry French's 3rd Corps. Confusion directed the events of the day—French led his corps down the wrong road on his way to Mine Run. He ran straight into a Confederate division led by

General Jubal Early. Meade's fall campaign bogged down and would now have to be fought on Lee's terms.

On Friday, the 3rd Corps engaged the enemy. Sedgwick's 6th Corps, including Elisha's 2nd Rhode Island, followed and supported it with artillery fire. Aside from artillery support, Elisha's corps remained in reserve. The Confederates retired and Meade ordered the pursuit resumed the next morning.

At one in the afternoon on Saturday, the 28th, Elisha and the 2nd were back on the road near the Wilderness. Along the march, the men of the 3rd and 6th Corps were joined by the 1st Corps. The three corps headed for Mine Run looking for Lee—he was waiting for them.

At dusk, Meade found Lee strongly posted on the west bank of Mine Run. Convinced that a frontal attack would be costly, Meade decided on another tack. He ordered Warren's 2nd Corps to make an eight-mile march around Lee's right wing to make a "demonstration," [28] hoping they would find a weak point in his lines. Arriving on the Confederate right, about noon, Warren came in contact with Lee's skirmish line which immediately fell back. "By noon the entire force was in line of battle in front of Lee's right wing, and some lively skirmishing and cannonading ensued,"[29] observed Reverend Woodbury. Once again, there was "Music in the Air," [30] and the men of the 2nd laughed as some English observers headed for the safety of the rear amid taunting and catcalls. According to Reverend Woodbury, Lee's superior knowledge of his surroundings and his strongly defended position created "an extremely difficult one for attack." [31] "Jeb" Stuart's cavalry harassed Meade's left flank and rear, thwarting any hope he had of a coordinated offensive. The day ended without any decisive results. Soldiers stretched out in the mud and made themselves as comfortable as possible.

On Sunday morning, the 2nd Rhode Island was marching again. The regiment passed through Robertson's Tavern taking to a plank road for ten miles until reaching Mine Run. The regiment formed a line of battle and waited all day for orders under enemy artillery fire. As formidable as Lee's lines were, General Warren still sought a fight. With two divisions and three corps at his disposal, Warren ordered an attack for eight o' clock the next morning. Sedgwick's 6th Corps would follow Warren's lead with great "vigor," [32] according to Reverend Woodbury.

At dawn, Warren took out his fieldglasses and looked across the field at Lee's position and was stunned by what he saw. During the night Lee had been busy. There "seemed to be more men, thicker abatis, heavier cannon and higher breastworks," [33] than the evening before. Eight o'clock came and went as an artillery duel intensified throughout the morning and early afternoon.

As the 2nd Rhode Island waited for orders, the men withstood the din of bursting shells and the deadly hiss of minie balls. Elisha could see Lee's entrenchments and was not eager to try and take them. Seeking shelter, he recalled, "Our mess servant found a house, and what was better, a *turkey*. This they roasted, and with sweet potatoes and new bread and butter they appeared to us about 2 PM. Colonel Rogers invited Colonel Johns of the 10th Massachusetts to dine with us. The good things were spread upon a rubber blanket and we gathered around. The chaplain began to say grace when bang went a gun, and a shell from the enemy howled over our heads. The chaplain did not falter but went on with his prayer, when two more shells struck near our horses. We lay close to the ground until he had finished, when I called for my orderly to 'Move my horse.'" The absurd dinner was resumed as the participants were forced to dodge the shells and pull the rubber blanket by its corners behind the crest of a knoll. "Our Batteries soon got to work and our dinner was eaten while the Artillery duel went on." [34]

For two days, the armies nervously watched each other as Meade prepared to withdraw. On November 30, the 2nd made up the second line of battle on the left flank, getting into a skirmish during the afternoon. Artillery mixed it up but the affair never blossomed into the battle it had promised to be. The next day Meade's army began recrossing the Rapidan. Reverend Woodbury recalled, "At dark on December 1st the whole army abandoned its position, hurriedly retired, crossed the Rapidan at daylight, and, having placed the river between itself and its opponent, halted for rest until nearly noon, when it resumed its march to its former position." [35]

The temperature was dropping dramatically and the cold air stung the faces of the men as they marched—struggling to stay awake after days with little or no sleep. At one point during the march, Lieutenant Rhodes realized that Colonel Rogers was missing. Elisha remembered the colonel telling him that he needed to water his horse and that he would catch up to his regiment a little later. Elisha found the colonel and his horse in the middle of a brook, both fast asleep. After waking them and resuming the march, Elisha also fought off fatigue by walking his horse rather than riding. The roads, badly cut up by wagon wheels, froze solid causing men to trip or twist their ankles. The men cursed the march and after plodding along for 30 miles reached their old camp near Brandy Station about ten a.m. on the 3rd of December. The men were "used up," [36] wrote Lt. Rhodes.

Meade, facing public ridicule and the President's ire, was quick to blame General French's 3rd Corps for the failure of his Mine Run operation, citing its failure to get into position and get the jump on Lee. The campaign had only managed to dampen the spirits of the Army of the Potomac. Elisha Rhodes wondered, "I do not understand the late movements, but I presume General Meade does, and that is sufficient for me." [37] By contrast, the Army of Northern Virginia experienced a great morale boost having turned back Meade in spite of not having Longstreet's Corps on the field with them.

The Rhode Island men were thrilled to be back at Camp Sedgwick, sleeping and resting their sore feet and aching backs. As the first week of the new month drew to a close they built "very comfortable huts for their winter quarters, and prepared to make the best of what threatened to be an unusually severe season," according to Reverend Woodbury. [38] Elisha had a warm hut built for his adjutant's office where he spent his days and in the evening he shared his shebang with Surgeon Carr of Pawtuxet. Before Christmas, over one hundred draftees and new recruits arrived and the grizzled veterans of the regiment joked at how green and homesick the new men looked. Snow fell and cold winds whipped through their creaky shelters—Colonel Rogers tried to bring order and daily routine to Camp Sedgwick. "We drill when the weather will permit and sleep and smoke when it storms," Elisha wrote, resigning himself to another Virginia winter. [39]

As 1863 drew to a close, the officers of the 2nd Rhode Island held a meeting and many agreed to remain in the army and to not disband the regiment when its term of service expired the following June. At Elisha's urging they voted to keep the 2nd Rhode Island intact for the duration of the war after he argued, "[The war] has dragged along, and no one can tell when the end will come. But when it does come I want to see it, and so I am going to stay." [40]

Elisha celebrated Christmas by taking a ride on his new pride and joy, Kate, a beautiful, lightning-fast horse he'd gotten in exchange for Old Abe, one of his other horses. "I have one of the finest horses in the army," he proudly announced. [41] On Christmas Day, he hosted a dinner party with several officers of the regiment as guests.

****

As the 50th Georgia and Bryan's Brigade began their march back to Virginia they took stock of their losses. For the month of November, General Bryan reported 121 of his men wounded, 64 missing and 27 killed. These losses, mostly at Ft. Sanders, coupled with the frigid temperatures, made for a depressing march. As in northern Virginia, the roads were rut-filled and frozen, making walking treacherous. Rumors flew through the dispirited column that Burnside's men were hot on their trail and any stragglers would end up in a Northern prison. Private Sheldon and the 50th pushed on toward the Virginia state line hoping to reach the town of Bristol. After three days of hard marching, believing that Burnside's men had given up the chase, the brigade rested. Near Bean Station, Tennessee, the Georgians built fires and huddled together in bunches, trying to keep warm. They wrote letters, slept, and redressed wounds and blistered feet. Those who could muster up a little energy went foraging and Irish potatoes were the big find. Some were traded for tobacco or coffee, but the soldiers found them to be a delicacy and baked, mashed and fried them. "I hadn't tasted any for three years," said one of James' comrades. [42] A brief skirmish with the enemy enabled the regiment to capture some badly needed supplies.

While camped near Bean Station, the 50th Georgia and Longstreet's Corps received orders which sent them marching back toward Knoxville. On or about December 9, Major John Spence took command of the regiment as Lt. Colonel Fleming resigned his commission and Colonel McGlashan was still on furlough back home in Georgia. In the cold morning light the regiment retraced its steps of a few days earlier. Shortly after noon cannonading could be heard far off in the distance, presumably at Knoxville. To James' surprise he was much closer to the action than the sounds of cannon fire had led him to believe. Suddenly, the Georgians were in a fight. One soldier recalled, "We got nearer and nearer the cannon, and when we were very near we also heard the rattle of musketry…we marched to the right, up the mountainside—a flank movement. Some of our men were engaged in the front. After we got around on the side of the enemy the firing stopped. It was nearly sundown. We waited until dark, and then marched down to an open field where the battle had been, but the enemy had retreated. We ate our supper, but had nothing with which to build fires, so we went to sleep." [43] Two days later the 50th Georgia once again crossed the Holston River near Knoxville.

In a thick-wooded area the 50th made its winter quarters among chestnut trees near the town of Russelville, Tennessee. It was two days before Christmas. The Georgians took great pride in constructing their own small village, much like the 2nd Rhode Island at Brandy Station, Virginia. But rations were almost non-existent and homesickness spread like influenza throughout the camp. Christmas Day was filled with sadness but some of James' buddies were determined to cook a Christmas dinner, however sparse. The two half-starved men turned their nearly empty flour bags inside out and shook what little remaining powder they contained into a pot of boiling water. A third man tossed a bacon rind he had been saving for such an occasion into the pot. After boiling this concoction for half an hour or so, the three men glumly spooned their lowly Christmas feast. Grinning a toothy smile from ear to ear, a corporal tried to cheer his messmates by toasting, "Well boys, this is right smart better than no eatin!" The group laughed and wished one another a Merry Christmas— 1863 came to a close. [44]

11

A WONDERFULLY
TENACIOUS LIFE

As 1864 opened, life in Richmond went on as normally as possible. The *Richmond Whig* announced that *The Bride of Lammermoor* was opening at the New Richmond Theatre and would soon present *Lady of Lyons*, *The Corsican Brothers*, and *Nothing to Nurse*. The newspaper also reported the grim reality of wartime: "The prices of provisions continue to advance…beef is retailing at $2 per lb…Oysters, $16 to $20 per gallon…Turkeys range from $18 to $35 apiece…Butter is now selling at $6 per lb., and eggs at $3 per dozen." [1]

There were changes on the battlefield. Gone were major players like Pope and Hooker. Blunders at Chattanooga cost Rosecrans his command and Bragg was reassigned. Even Longstreet performed poorly in the West—he arrived too late to make a difference at Chattanooga and was bludgeoned at Knoxville. The only real constant was Lee, who continued to befuddle the Army of the Potomac. In the North names like Grant, Sherman, and now Thomas, were spoken in the same breath with reports of Union successes.

Private James Sheldon and Lieutenant Elisha Rhodes opened the New Year 380 miles apart in their respective winter quarters at Russelville, Tennessee, and Brandy Station, Virginia. For both men monotony soon led to boredom. Only the constant drilling broke up days otherwise spent in a relentless battle against the elements. Wind, sleet and snow made the chores of cooking and foraging miserable. Both armies were in woeful condition and sickness was rampant in the camps. Going into the new year their diets were poor—James had the worst of it. A new market in Brandy Station was to open soon and expected to fulfill many of the 2ⁿᵈ Rhode Island's needs. James and the 50ᵗʰ Georgia, on the other hand, were forced to survive on limited rations most of the time as foraging in Confederate Tennessee was strictly forbidden.

Out of hunger and boredom men became quite creative in finding new ways of preparing the most basic food. One such item was the potato, thinly pared and fried to a crisp, then heavily salted or, if available, dipped in vinegar—potato chips. Another such concoction was a beverage which, according to some, resembled coffee. Acorns, available by the bushel, were washed in their shells, dried and peeled, and then roasted with a small amount of bacon fat.

A man in Kershaw's Brigade described the fare on which the men survived, explaining, "While in the Tennessee our diet was somewhat changed. In the East, flour, with beef or bacon, was issued to the troops; but here we got nothing but cornmeal, with a little beef and half ration of bacon. The troops were required to keep four days' rations cooked on hand all the time. Of the meal we made cart wheels (a mixture of sugar, molasses and cornmeal baked over a campfire), dog heads, ash cakes, and last, but not least, we had cush...it has been said 'if you want soldiers to fight well, you must feed them well'; but this is still a mooted question, and I have known some of the soldiers of the South to give pretty strong battle when rather underfed than overfed."[2]

Of this mysterious dish known only as "cush," the soldier decided to surrender his recipe, instructing, "Chip up bacon in fine particles, place in an oven (pan) and fry to a crisp. Fill the oven one-third or one-half full of branch water, then take the stale corn bread, the more moldy the better, rub into fine crumbs, mix and bring the whole to a boil, gently stirring with a forked stick. When cold, eat with fingers and to prevent waste or to avoid carrying it on the march, eat the four days' rations in one sitting."[3] Tongue planted firmly in cheek, the man critiqued this concoction as being "fit for a king."[4]

The author of the "cush" recipe wasn't shy about explaining how the strictly enforced anti-foraging orders were circumvented. "[Being caught foraging] was one of those cases where orders are more regarded 'in the breach than in the observance.' Officers winked at it, if not actually countenancing the practice, of 'foraging for something to eat.' Then again the old argument presented itself, 'If we don't take it the Yankees will,' so there you were." [5]

A man in the 51st Georgia put it another way, saying, "Our rations of meat is nothing. I can put one day's allowance of meat in my mouth at one time." [6]

It was in these extremely trying days that Peter McGlashan turned to his most trusted friend in the regiment. Private James Sheldon was promoted to commissary sergeant in mid-February and suddenly faced the challenge of keeping the men of the 50th Georgia fed. The job was unrewarding, and at times seemed impossible, but a pay raise and a chance to be part of the colonel's staff made the job tolerable.

Sergeant Sheldon knew he would spend a miserable winter in Tennessee. The "itch" of body lice was going around and men were suffering badly from it. Worse, there were no medicines for three weeks. Boredom set in with a vengeance. There wasn't much to do in winter quarters and, when available, the men lost themselves in books and newspapers, often costing fifty cents for just two sheets. Desertion was becoming a temptation for many men and Longstreet quickly made examples of those who dared try it. Two men of the 50th Georgia were arrested for desertion and brought back to camp, condemned to death by firing squad. Both pleaded for their lives. One of the soldiers, whose family was politically connected, persuaded officers to write to Longstreet requesting that he be pardoned and his sentence was commuted. The other man, having no such influence, was executed. General McLaws ordered his entire division to witness the event.

On the third day of the new year, a private in James' brigade wrote to his father describing the brigade's living quarters, saying, "winter quarters are built on the side of a sloping hill...between 12 and 14 feet long, 5 feet wide, and 6 and one

half high. It is plenty roomy for two and no more…[the] house
and chimney are both built together… Our house is gabled up,
like a common country house, with large saplings and is covered
with a good Yankee fly… Our mansion is daubed with mud, and
is nearly airtight. The chimney forms the west end of our house,
draws fine, and throws out more heat than any one I have seen.
It is as warm and snug as any house…We have a small cistern to
hold water at the north end of our menagerie, it is dug out of a
large poplar with an axe. It is arranged so that we catch water in a
gutter when it rains, and pours all the water into our cistern…The
cistern saves us the trouble of going one half mile for water." [7]

The winter weather played upon the armies equally and
tents and clothing remained constantly wet or frozen. The men
spent much of their time crouching or standing around campfires.
The soldiers were forced to withstand the ever-present smoke
and ash—styes and infections left many men with runny, sore
and reddened eyes.

The lack of medicines forced men to create their own camp
remedies. A mixture of pulverized charcoal, milk and turpentine
was said to cure a sore throat. Treacle and vinegar relieved a
troublesome cough, and charcoal and soda made a headache
go away. The soldier's nemesis, diarrhea, was often met with a
concoction of salt and vinegar, shaken in boiling water. Both
armies were worn out. Terms of enlistment were about to expire
for the three-year volunteers and even the most fervent in their
patriotism desperately longed for home and their families. The
Confederate Army tried to cure the epidemic of homesickness
by issuing thirty-day furloughs. Two men per company were
allowed to leave for one month, but there were problems with
the numbers. The 50th Georgia, for instance, had about 25 men
per company at the beginning of 1864, which meant it could be
one year before everyone received their furlough. But the system
was better than nothing, and although there was some grumbling
and complaining, it worked. One of the first to go on furlough
was Colonel Peter McGlashan and he returned just before
Christmas. James patiently waited his turn, wondering where

he would go. He quickly dismissed any thoughts of visiting his mother in Pawtuxet, Rhode Island. Perhaps he would never see her again.

****

Lincoln had called for 300,000 more volunteers in October, 1863, but everyone knew that civilian volunteers could hardly replace battle-seasoned veterans. To entice officers to reenlist, the army assigned recruiting officers to each regiment. Lt. Edmund Prentiss of the 1st Rhode Island Heavy Artillery resigned his commission and became a lieutenant in the 2nd Rhode Island, assuming the daily duty of recruiting officer. In doing so he struck up a friendship with Elisha, whose heart was set on the continuance of his beloved regiment. Colonel Rogers offered Prentiss and Rhodes a chance. If enough officers could be persuaded to stay, the regiment would continue. If not, the returning officers would be transferred to other regiments and the 2nd Rhode Island would cease to exist. Rogers asked Prentiss and Rhodes to provide him with a list of all the officers and daily progress reports.

The two men made the rounds making their pitch to the men. The army had given them a bargaining chip of a 30-day furlough to present to the officers. As they sat by the glow of their campfires, most of the men grumbled that they'd *done* their part. But there was more. Prentiss and Rhodes explained that the deal also included a signing bonus, in fact, *three.* The United States government offered a bonus of $402 to any man who would re-enlist. The State of Rhode Island would add another $300 and the soldier's hometown would contribute another $100. To put the $802 bonus in perspective, one must consider that a private's pay was $13 a month. Thoughts of cash stirred up old patriotic feelings in many of the men and four days after Christmas, Rhodes and Prentiss had talked 56 men into staying. By January 5, 1864, the re-enlistment deadline, their list had swollen to 80, 52 of whom were founding members of the regiment. The 2nd Rhode Island Infantry would see the end of the war.

As winter settled in around Brandy Station, Reverend Woodbury predicted, "All signs showed that the year 1864 was to witness the most earnest endeavors, which the government at Washington could put forth to crush out the rebellion." [8] He contended that Lincoln's Emancipation Proclamation now gave the conflict a "moral" interest, [9] not just a political one. Commenting on how drastically the war had changed, he stated that, "The rebellion had a wonderfully tenacious life." [10]

Colonel Rogers hadn't been feeling well since the Mine Run Campaign, and rumors were circulating that he was suffering from malaria that he'd contracted while serving with the 11th Rhode Island in South Carolina. Whatever it was, the colonel tried to keep his illness to himself. But he finally faced the fact that he was too sick to remain in command and on January 15, he resigned. Speaking to his regiment before departing for Rhode Island he said, "Comrades, the colonel commanding, having resigned, is about to leave you. During the year he has had the honor to command the 2nd he has been proud of the Regiment." [11]

Rogers congratulated his men on their brave conduct at such places as Salem Church and Gettysburg as he wished them farewell, saying, "Comrades, if it be possible, may your fame grow brighter still and may the same Divine Providence protect you in the future that it has so mercifully preserved you in the past." [12] Rhode Islanders at home read about Rogers' resignation in the *Providence Journal* the following day. Referring to his unenviable task of replacing the popular Viall a year earlier, the *Journal* noted that Rogers "took command under circumstances peculiarly trying and discouraging." The newspaper concluded that his reasons for resigning "are at home and with himself entirely." [13] In peacetime Horatio Rogers was a respected lawyer in Providence. Less than four months after resigning as colonel of the 2nd Rhode Island Infantry, he was elected attorney general of Rhode Island. He was not yet 30 years old.

Second in command of Elisha's regiment was Lt. Colonel Samuel Read. But since July 31, 1863, Read had been appointed inspector general of the 3rd Division of Sedgwick's 6th Corps and would not be returning to his regiment until March. This left command of the 2nd Rhode Island to Major Henry Jenckes of Providence, who had already experienced quite a military career. As quartermaster sergeant, he was taken prisoner at Manassas and brought to Libby Prison in Richmond. He somehow managed to escape, and returning to his regiment was rewarded with a promotion to 2nd Lieutenant. Before the end of 1861, he had risen to 1st Lieutenant and by May of 1863, he had attained the rank of major. Chaplain Beugless assured the men of the 2nd that Major Jenckes was "fully capable" to lead them, and told others that Jenckes had the "utmost trust and esteem of the regiment."[14]

Major Henry Jenckes

Aside from the departure of Colonel Rogers, life in the winter camp of the 2nd Rhode Island went on uneventfully. In mid-January, the army, prompted by the Christian Commission, issued each brigade a large canvas for the purpose of constructing a chapel. Elisha and his friends went to work immediately. Each canvas was large enough to shelter 300 men and was to be supported by log walls and timbers cemented together to keep out the cold. Benches were sanded smooth and every effort was made to make worshippers comfortable. Pine boughs made for a plush carpet and their scent filled "Hope Chapel," named in honor of the Rhode Island state motto. A fireplace was erected near the altar which was covered in red flannel. Tin canisters "were somehow transformed into chandeliers and candelabra," [15] and also used as reflectors for the lighting, creating a mystical effect. Captain John Beveridge donated some seats that his men had removed from a deserted church while in a skirmish with the enemy; at least that was his story. While this contribution to Hope Chapel was somewhat questionable, it was quickly accepted. Upon its completion, Hope Chapel began offering services on Sundays and weekday evenings. Sunday School was held on Sunday afternoons and Elisha was named superintendent.

The structure hardly ever sat empty and began serving as sort of a community center—during the day, it was a school for grammar and algebra. Reverend Beugless offered a course in bookkeeping. The "Rhode Island Lyceum" [16] met on Monday nights and offered lectures on varying subjects which were debated with "considerable ingenuity and skill."

But even the unveiling of Hope Chapel did not keep the men from their favorite pastimes such as checkers, cards and baseball. Practical jokes were also a good way of relieving the boredom and snowballs seemed to be constantly in the air. Blocking up a friend's chimney (causing his shebang to fill with smoke) was always good for a laugh, while a newly invented gun that squirted water claimed many an unsuspecting victim.

In late January, several of the officers' wives came to camp for a short visit, and Reverend Woodbury claimed they "enlivened the camp and freshened the routine of its duty with their presence." [17] Elisha's opinion of the women's contribution to this settlement in the wilds of Virginia was more direct, saying, "This gives an air of civilization to our headquarters." [18]

It remained cold, however, and almost every morning the men awoke to single-digit temperatures. It snowed frequently. But the days passed happily and the new market at Brandy Station helped to make life at Camp Sedgwick tolerable by providing tobacco, sweets, stationary and books to those who could afford such luxuries. Chaplain Beugless noticed the improvement not only of his regiment, but of the entire 6th Corps, and noted, "never has the army been so well cared for as this winter, either morally, mentally and physically." [19] A doctor in a neighboring regiment, the 27th New York, concurred, saying, "never were the men so well contented, or in so good spirits." [20]

On February 10, Lieutenants Edmund Prentiss, T.J. Smith, Elisha Rhodes and Captain John Shaw, left Brandy Station to begin their thirty-five-day furloughs in Rhode Island.

Captain John Shaw

Elisha found Pawtuxet as he left it, with the war existing only in the pages of the *Providence Journal*. Rebecca Sheldon and her family were still next door, and the village was bustling with activity. Henry Johnson banged on his anvil. Dr. Carr strolled down Broad Street, tipping his hat to friends and patients as he went about his daily rounds. Elisha watched the water roll over the falls near his mother's house by the bridge, just as it always had. It was good to be home.

The return of these men was acknowledged by Rhode Island dignitaries; a parade through Providence and a reception at Howard Hall was held in their honor. The men received plaudits from Governor Smith, Bishop Clark and other notables, including officers from the 3rd and 4th Rhode Island Regiments. But the men of the 2nd were the talk of the event and "a bountiful collation was spread for their entertainment," [21] according to Augustus Woodbury. Senator William Sprague was so delighted to see these Rhode Island heroes that he had their furloughs extended by three weeks. Elisha, who just three years earlier rode the omnibus to Providence to enlist, could never have imagined himself being the center of attention at such an event.

Back in Camp Sedgwick near Brandy Station, the 2nd Rhode Island spent a quiet February, interrupted only by the occasional false alarm. But on the 26th, orders came to prepare to move, and the entire 6th Corps was on the road by nine o'clock the next morning. The day was "as bright and beautiful as winter ever saw," according to one man. [22] The purpose of the 6th Corps' march was to make a demonstration which hopefully would draw attention away from the real offensive. Led by Union General Judson Kilpatrick, nicknamed "Kill Cavalry" [23] for the severity of his rides, 3,500 cavalrymen planned to attack Richmond and free the Union prisoners held at Libby and Castle Thunder Prisons. Bad intelligence convinced Lincoln and his advisors that only a token force protected the prison area, but the Confederate government got wind of the operation and Kilpatrick's Raid fizzled.

Major Jenckes and the 2nd Rhode Island crossed Mountain Creek, passed through Culpeper Court House and made camp at the base of Cedar Mountain. On Sunday, the 28th, the regiment marched through James City and arrived at a place called Robertson's Creek about two in the afternoon. The men were sent out on picket duty and rumors were flying that Union cavalry, commanded by a dashing young general, was in the area. After a brief clash with 25-year-old George Armstrong Custer, the Confederate cavalry retreated. But with Kilpatrick's Raid aborted, the 2nd Rhode Island and the rest of Sedgwick's 6th Corps began marching back to Brandy Station on Tuesday, the first of March. Two days later they arrived back in their old camp about six in the evening.

On March 12, Ulysses Grant was appointed chief of the armies of the United States. His first order of business was to inspect his troops. Although deeming it to be in excellent condition, he did want to reorganize its structure, "[My] Headquarters will be in the field, and, until further orders, will be with the Army of the Potomac." [24] Grant did, however, leave General George Meade in command of that army.

Meanwhile, these were not great times for a Southern general. "Detached from General Lee, what a horrible failure, what a slow old humbug is Longstreet," [25] were the sentiments of Mary Chesnut, the wife of one of President Davis' top advisors during the dwindling days of 1863. Longstreet was in trouble. His campaign to join Bragg at Chickamauga had failed and his disastrous operations around Knoxville baffled most of the men in his army. Many of these men began to doubt his leadership. When Longstreet, mired in east Tennessee, learned that Grant had been put in command of all the Union armies, he knew the Confederacy was in for a struggle. "That man will fight us every day and every hour till the end of the war," he said. [26]

****

Though wanting for winter clothing and shoes, Longstreet's command was in good spirits. Expecting the Russelville area, which rests on the south side of the Holston River, to be barren and inhospitable, the men were pleasantly surprised to learn they were wrong. The local farmers held adequate stocks of hogs and chickens. Wild turkeys were in abundance and moonshine flowed freely. An endless supply of hickory and oak was cut and split, keeping the rows of shebangs and shanties warm. Yet there were doubts; winter was only beginning and the war seemed to be going nowhere. Just about everyone wanted to go home.

In the camps around Russelville, including that of Sergeant James Sheldon and the 50th Georgia, record cold temperatures, a harsh wind and occasional snowfall introduced the worst winter in over a decade. When ordered out on picket duty, James and the men once had to hold their frying pans in front of their faces as they marched to shield themselves from the stinging sleet. On that same detail, the regiment was forced to bivouac and awoke to find themselves covered in snow. Returning to camp, the men of the 50th discovered a pleasant diversion from their suffering. "Some of the men had never seen snow before, and that morning the whole regiment started snow ball fights; soon the brigade was having a snow battle with another brigade, led by a brigadier general," wrote one soldier. [27]

Confederate uniforms had become almost nonexistent and men pretty much wore whatever could be scrounged together. They made shoes out of cowhide or simply tied rags around their feet. Food continued to be scarce with cush being the most common staple. Local farmers, believing the money would soon be worthless, refused to sell their vegetables for Confederate dollars. For short stretches, the men were forced to survive on a single ear of corn per day. Occasionally, sheep were available for purchase but the animals had been so poorly fed that the men complained the mutton had a bad taste to it. Tobacco was also in very short supply, and the weather continued to brutalize James and the other Georgians. On the 22nd of February, one man in James' brigade wrote, "My Dear it is the coldest weather I have seen this winter. I met the snow when I got to the line of North Carolina which was last Wednesday. The snow is very deep and the creeks and river is frozen over although the weather is now moderating." [28] James' good friend, John Chastain, fell victim to the unforgiving weather and was hospitalized at Farmville, Virginia. Although he recovered fairly quickly, he was ordered to spend the next few months at the hospital as a nurse.

During the third week of March, winter was showing signs of ebbing. Although Richmond was belted by a heavy snowfall on the 22nd, the days grew longer and the first hints of spring appeared. At Culpeper Court House, Virginia, General Grant announced that he would make his permanent headquarters there, and both armies slowly began gearing up for springtime operations. Elisha celebrated his 22nd birthday.

On the last day of March, a man in James' brigade described the condition of the army in a letter to his family back in Georgia. "The army lacks a great deal of being whipped. They will whip whenever they get a chance, instead of being whipped, and down in the mouth. I think our prospects for peace this year is better than it ever has been." [29]

At Russelville, Tennessee, Sergeant James Sheldon and the 50th Georgia Infantry were preparing to break camp. No one was going to miss Tennessee. "We began to march toward Bristol before the winter was over," recalled one lieutenant. [30]

On April 3, James Sheldon and the 50th Georgia arrived at the town of Bristol, which spills over into both Tennessee and Virginia. The men set up camp, and for the first time in a long time felt optimistic. After all, they had tents, good food, and new recruits were said to be coming in. Most of all, they would soon be reunited with the Army of Northern Virginia.

A drummer in James' brigade wrote about their new camp at Bristol, saying, "A portion of our baggage has been shipped to Lynchburg. We have had very disagreeable weather ever since I have got back. It has rained every day, with the exception of yesterday. It looks cloudy and very much like raining today. The country is rough and rolling, somewhat similar to that at Russelville. The inhabitants are generally either wealthy or good livers. We have drawn plenty of food since we got back; such as it is, from beef and graham bread. The boys say they get bread and beef dried alive on its feet. There is a great deal of difference, between living in camps in a little tent, than living at home with all the luxuries of social happiness, where peace and plenty reigns." [31]

On Wednesday, April 6, a train slowly pulled out of Providence, Rhode Island, bound for New York City. Among the passengers was a carload of officers of the 2nd Rhode Island heading for Virginia. The car was full of laughter and singing as the men celebrated the last night of their furloughs. The men were in a boisterous mood and most carried their own supply of liquor. Lieutenants Elisha Rhodes and T. J. Smith stood by the doors to ensure that no one would get sentimental and decide to stay home. On the morning of April 8, the contingent was safely back in Camp Sedgwick—ready for the business of war.

****

The 50th didn't remain at Bristol long, according to one soldier in the regiment, "It snowed on the way, with unusually large flakes. We got on the train at Bristol. I climbed on top, although it was rather cold." [32] The regiment disembarked at Lynchburg, happy to be on Virginia soil, and after camping for one night, began marching to Charlottesville. The march brought out scores of pretty girls, bringing back memories of the great sendoff off the previous fall. From Charlottesville, the 50th made its way to Gordonsville, settling on the site of its camp of two years before. Tired and footsore, James welcomed a good, long rest. Only days after being back in their Gordonsville camp, every man in the regiment suddenly jumped to his feet, cleaned his weapon and made the most of his shabby appearance. Robert E. Lee was coming to personally inspect Simms' Brigade, undoubtedly Sergeant Sheldon's biggest thrill since putting on a Confederate uniform.

A man in the 51st described the new camp, saying, "we left Greenville last Monday and got here last night. It is sixty miles and it has bin snowing all the time and the weather very cold and the roads was in the worst fix you ever saw. It has been mud and water and snow to our knees nearly all the way." Describing the dwindling food supply the man said, "We are getting almost nothing to eat now. We draw what they call three days rations out at a time [and] then eat one time [and] we then have to do without the remainder of those three days unless we steal it from a citizen which we do to keep from starving. Bread is the worst of it. We kill a hog whenever we can find one but we have to be very sly with it for if it is found out on us we are punished very much for it." [33]

A colonel in Bryan's Brigade, James Simms of the 53rd Georgia, faced with the unenviable task of holding his regiment together, summoned his brother Arthur Benjamin Simms from Covington, Georgia, to serve as his adjutant. Ben was the youngest of the three Simms brothers who had enlisted in the Confederate Army. In 1862, Richard, the middle son, was killed during the fighting at Fox's Gap in Maryland. In this same battle, Sergeant Ben Simms of the 53rd Georgia was taken prisoner. He was held at Johnson's Island prison camp on Lake Erie until he became seriously ill and was exchanged. After his release, Ben was hospitalized in Richmond until he was sent home. In 1863, he made an attempt to return to duty as a fighting man but was too weak to remain in the ranks. Having spent most of 1863 and part of 1864 sick at home, Ben Simms jumped at the chance to get back into the war as his brother's adjutant.

Colonel McGlashan was also in need of a adjutant and called upon *his* own brother, Andrew. Andrew McGlashan had been a member of the 24th Georgia Cavalry Battalion, and while living in Britain had served with the Royal Artillery. He stood five-feet, ten-inches tall with a dark complexion, hazel eyes and light brown hair. Andrew loved battle and aside from some eccentric behaviors he was a soldier's soldier.

In mid-April, brother Peter had fallen ill with a severe case of diarrhea, which could so weaken the immune system it often proved fatal. On April 15, he was granted a 30-day furlough to recover.

The 50th Georgia was living large. There was plenty to eat, and cornmeal, rice, bacon, and even coffee and sugar seemed to be in abundance. But by the third week of April, James was doing all that he could to procure rations for his men. The situation grew increasingly desperate after Simms' Brigade was moved to Gordonsville, Virginia. Said one man in the brigade, "our rations is very short hear now we draw a little bacon an a little corn meal an some sugar an some coffee but not enough to do much good." [34] Even with this setback, the men stayed busy preparing for the coming campaign.

In Camp Sedgwick, near Brandy Station, Lt. Colonel Read had returned and was busy drilling and disciplining his regiment. The days were getting longer and warmer, and privates and presidents alike knew that General Grant would very soon move his great armies. As Reverend Woodbury put it, "The great struggle was fast approaching, and the army was put in the best possible state to engage in it." [35]

12

A LICK AND A PROMISE

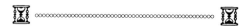

The bitter winds and record-breaking temperatures of the winter of 1864 had finally passed. Freshets of icy water rode streams and rivers, racing for the ocean. Birds nested and the thawing landscape began sprouting flower blossoms as the forests leafed out. Conditions were ideal for military operations.

Believing that he'd finally found a general who could carry the war to the enemy, Lincoln committed himself to pressing the Confederacy as never before. The war would now be fought on many fronts, effectively putting Richmond in a strategic box, stretching the depleted Southern armies to the breaking point. In Louisiana operations began against Shreveport, a major supply depot and gateway to Texas.

At Hampton Roads, General Benjamin Butler was preparing an overland campaign reminiscent of McClellan's Peninsula Campaign two years earlier. Off the coast of North Carolina, the United States Navy prepared to deal with a heavily armed ironclad, the C.S.S. *Ablemarle*, which was flexing her muscles and threatening to break up the blockade.

Near Chattanooga, 100,000 men assembled under the watchful eye of General William Tecumseh Sherman. Sherman was preparing for a march that would force his men to subsist solely on the bounty of its unwelcoming hosts. [1]

In Virginia, Grant ordered General Meade to prepare to move the Army of the Potomac across the Rapidan River and around the right of the Army of Northern Virginia. The war was to be fought everywhere and it was time to get ready. Spring promised to be busy and nowhere was this more evident than in the soldiers' camps at Gordonsville and Brandy Station, Virginia.

With word that the Army of the Potomac was moving, Robert E. Lee wasted no time sending his army marching to meet them. Sergeant James Sheldon checked the wagons, packed his gear, and hit the dusty roads with the rest of his regiment. One soldier in the 50th Georgia remembered, "we were marching to Fredericksburg, but guessed that there would be a battle." [2] General Lafayette McLaws, embroiled in a court-martial after mishandling his command at Knoxville, was replaced as division commander by South Carolinian, Joseph Brevard Kershaw. The men of the 50th Georgia knew Kershaw well; he had commanded them briefly when Semmes had fallen. They looked up to Kershaw for his intelligence, bravery, good looks and strong voice—he cut an inspiring figure on the battlefield. Sergeant Sheldon's brigade remained intact with the 50th serving alongside the 10th, 51st and 53rd Georgia Infantry under the command of Brigadier General Goode Bryan.

Before dusk on May 2, James could see heavy clouds of smoke in the clear northern sky. By dark, Confederate observers could see lines of light from men carrying torches along the roads north of the Rapidan. Dust clouds could be seen in the distance at dawn—Grant was coming. In the Confederate camps around Gordonsville, orders were quickly passed to cook three days' rations which some men chose to eat immediately rather than carry. The men were also to leave their winter blankets and heavy shirts behind. Only days before, on April 29, General Lee had come to Gordonsville to personally inspect Longstreet's returning army. One man remembered, "Everything possible that could add to our looks and appearances was done to make an acceptable display before our commander in chief. Guns were burnished and rubbed up, cartridge boxes and belts polished, and the brass buttons and buckles made to look as bright as new. Our clothes were patched and brushed up, so far was in our power, boots and shoes greased, the tattered and torn old hats were given here and there 'a lick and a promise,' and on the whole I must say we presented not a bad looking body of soldiers…The artillery stationed on the flank fired thirteen guns, a salute to our commander in chief, and as the old warrior rode out into the opening, shouts went up that fairly shook the earth. Hats and caps flew high in the air, flags dipped and waved to and fro, while the drums and fifes struck up 'Hail To The Chief.' General Lee lifted his hat modestly from his head recognizing the honor done him, and we know the old commander's heart swelled with emotion at this outburst of enthusiasm by his old troops on his appearance." [3] Longstreet's men were happy to be back in Virginia.

On May 4, a half hour after midnight, Lieutenant Elisha Rhodes awoke to the sounds of reveille, and by four a.m., his camp was empty. The 2nd Rhode Island left Brandy Station and marched twenty hot, dusty miles to the Rapidan where the regiment crossed at Germanna Ford. The 2nd Rhode Island was now part of General George Getty's 2nd Division, and brigaded with the 7th, 10th and 37th Massachusetts. This new brigade was commanded by Brigadier General Henry Eustis.

In Bryan's Brigade there was talk of a great battle to come, and the men of the 50th Georgia leaned heavily on their faith. They held a prayer meeting in the woods, and as they marched, a voice from the ranks repeatedly warned, "Prepare to meet thy God," sending a chill down everyone's spine. [4] The Rhode Islanders held a similar meeting and Elisha vowed to leave his fate in the hands of God.

As Grant's 122,000 men crossed the Rapidan and marched around Lee's right, 66,000 Confederates left Orange Court House and Gordonsville to meet them. Between the two armies lay hundreds of acres of tangled forest and swamp, overgrown with thick vegetation. Within this wet woodland stood oak, maple, ash, cedar and fir trees, strung together in a maze of vines. Only a few crude roads penetrated this barrier, and often ended in thicket. Grant's army spent the night camped in the Wilderness.

Although this was new territory to the general, the Army of the Potomac knew it all too well. They had been soundly defeated here at the battle of Chancellorsville and broken caissons and shattered wagons were everywhere. As the Union men settled in for the evening, a ghostly presence made itself known. Human remains protruded up through the spring thaws, their uniforms still discernible. Whippoorwills sang their sad melodies as melancholy fell upon the men sitting quietly, staring at their campfires, and some shared premonitions of the upcoming battle with those close to them. The general feeling was that this tangled jungle filled with dead was the last place on earth they should be fighting. One soldier described the mood of the men, saying, "[there was] a sense of ominous dread which many of us found almost impossible to shake off." [5]

Adjutant Ben Simms sat in his brother's headquarters' tent and jotted off a short letter to his sister, "Yankees and Southerners are all agreed that this will be the last year of the war. I hope to pray it may be for we have certainly had war enough. The Yanks expect to crush us or else give it up. We can and certainly will remain firm and hold our own, if we do I think all will be well with us." [6] Sleep, for both sides, was difficult to come by.

Before dawn on May 5, the 2nd Rhode Island and Sedgwick's 6th Corps marched to the intersection of the Stevenson Plank Road and the Orange Turnpike and ran into enemy pickets. As often happened, the pickets of both armies had spent the night a mere three miles from each other without detecting the other's presence. Resuming its march, Sedgwick's 6th Corps entered into a "thick and almost impenetrable underbrush," according to Lt. Rhodes. [7] On their left, the 5th Corps encountered what was thought to be Lee's rear guard and a sharp fight quickly erupted. Not knowing that this was, in fact, Ewell's Corps, Warren's 5th Corps attacked the Confederates with vigor until thrown back by stiff resistance. With a full battle developing on their left, the 2nd Rhode Island and the 6th Corps advanced further into the Wilderness. Reverend Woodbury remembered, "The tangled paths were only too well known to Lee, and he hoped to stop Grant on his way, and even force him to retire, as he had done to the other commanders, in previous battles." [8] About two o'clock in the afternoon, Elisha's 2nd Rhode Island and the 10th Massachusetts went into line of battle—the 7th and 37th Massachusetts stood directly behind them.

Trying to get artillery into the Wilderness quickly proved to be both difficult and ineffective and the Union men quickly abandoned the idea. The enemy was hidden by the forest and heavy smoke hung low in the sticky air. At about three p.m., the 2nd Rhode Island was ordered to charge through the brush and attack an unseen enemy, while the 6th Corps was "gallantly brought into action," relieving Warren on the right of the 5th Corps. [9] With a sharp snap, a minie ball clipped Elisha Rhodes on his forefinger, stripping off the skin. Briefly stunned, he shook off the pain, saying it "only hurt me a little." [10]

Amid the screaming and confusion, regiments became entangled in swamps while brushfires impeded the advance. Elisha and the 2nd Rhode Island were on the extreme right of Grant's line. Lee intended to hammer it. It was three o' clock in the afternoon and unseasonally hot. Directly in front of the 2nd was General Richard Ewell's Corps, pouring volley after volley into the Rhode Islander's ranks—men started to fall. Ewell's flankers got around the Rhode Islanders' right, and a bullet struck a company captain, killing him instantly. When Chaplain Beugless knelt over him to administer last rites, he was shot through the wrist. For three hours soldiers on both sides cut through the brush and fired on each other. By late afternoon, the Rhode Island men held on to their flank which was posted on the skirmish line. "Up and down the forest paths, among the underbrush, the contest was waged, but with no decisive results on either side." [11]

About eight o' clock, darkness draped the woods and the fighting slackened, but the blind firing through the woods continued. Wounded were strewn everywhere—their pleas and bone-chilling screams could be heard in the darkness as the dry underbrush caught fire, spreading and growing. As the flames gasped for oxygen, air was drawn into the Wilderness creating a stiff wind. Amid the smoke, blackness, and biting briars, survivors could only sit and listen to the helpless wounded burning in the Wilderness. A man in the 2nd Massachusetts Artillery remembered, "Flames sprang up in the woods in our front, where the fight of the morning had taken place. With crackling roar, like an army of fire, it came down upon the Union line. The wind drove the blinding smoke and suffocating heat into our faces. This, added to the oppressive heat of the weather, was almost unendurable. It soon became terrible. The line of fire, with resistless march, swept the thickets before its advance, then reaching out its tongue of flame, ignited the breastworks composed of resinous logs, which soon roared and crackled along their entire length…The fire was the most terrible enemy our men had met that day, and few survivors will forget this attack of flames." [12]

Some of the wounded shot themselves to escape death by fire, and the sickening stench of burning human flesh hung in the steamy, dirty air. Once again, soldiers witnessed horrors previously unimagined. The day ended—neither side could claim victory.

****

Meanwhile, in the pre-dawn hours of the same morning, Longstreet's Corps began moving out of its camps at and around Gordonsville. Those returning from a night of foraging reported heavy firing in the direction of the Rapidan. This, it turned out, was a cavalry engagement checking Grant at the river fords. These reports, coupled with the 50th Georgia's marching orders, led James to believe that the campaign had opened. Throughout the day the men marched along overgrown roads, across fields and through tangled woods—by five p.m., the regiment had marched 28 miles. Sergeant Sheldon and the others were so tired from the march that they couldn't bother pitching tents. As James, Peter McGlashan and the other sore-footed men closed their eyes, they received an order to be ready to move at midnight.

"Promptly at midnight we began to move again, and such a march, and under such conditions, was never before experienced by the troops. Along blind roads, overgrown by underbrush, through fields that had lain fallow for years, now studded with bushes and briars, and the night being exceedingly dark, the men floundered and fell as they marched. But the needs were too urgent to be slack in the march now, so the men struggled with nature in their endeavor to keep in ranks. Sometimes the head of the column would lose its way, and during the time it was hunting its way back to the lost bridle path, was about the only rest we got," one man remembered. [13]

No one had seen a place like this before. James was already exhausted from the forced march the day before, and now had to exert all of his strength just to keep up. At first light the 50th took to the plank road leading from Orange Court House to Fredericksburg. Free from the briars and overgrowth, the men marched with a swinging step. Bryan's Brigade was at the rear of Kershaw's Division's march.

From intelligence reports and interviews with prisoners, Grant was convinced that Longstreet's Corps had not arrived. Seizing what he saw as an opportunity, he ordered an all out attack to begin at five a.m. on May 6. The start of the attack was unusually punctual; crisp and sharp in clear contrast to the clumsy and oft-delayed attacks of previous commanders. Taking the brunt of the initial onslaught was General Cadmus Wilcox's division of mostly North Carolinians. Wilcox's men broke and ran, desperately trying to reorganize their lines. Seeing the collapse of their right wing, the men of Heth's Division, also mostly North Carolinians, ran for the rear. At his headquarters, General Lee was told that the situation was desperate; his right was crumbling and his left was being pummeled by Sedgwick and Warren's Corps.

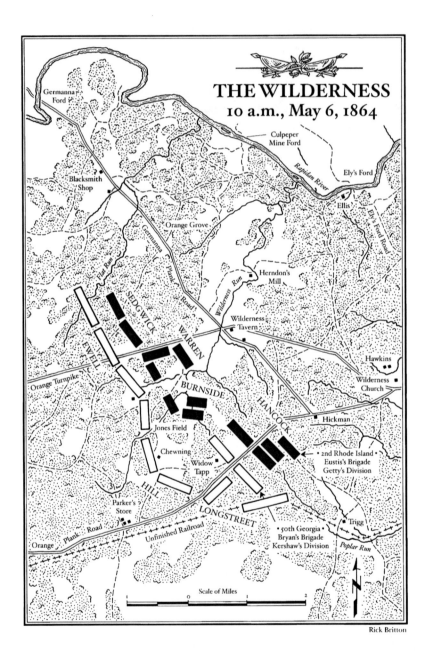

THE WILDERNESS
10 a.m., May 6, 1864

Germanna Ford

Culpeper Mine Ford

Ely's Ford

Rapidan River

Ely's Ford Road

Blacksmith Shop

Ellis

Orange Grove

Germanna Plank Road

Flat Run

Herndon's Mill

Wilderness Run

SEDGWICK

Wilderness Tavern

WARREN

Hawkins

EWELL

Wilderness Church

Orange Turnpike

BURNSIDE

HANCOCK

Jones Field

Hickman

Chewning

Widow Tapp

• 2nd Rhode Island •
Eustis's Brigade
Getty's Division

HILL

Parker's Store

LONGSTREET

Trigg

Orange

Plank Road

Unfinished Railroad

• 50th Georgia •
Bryan's Brigade
Kershaw's Division

Poplar Run

Scale of Miles

Rick Britton

Mounted on Traveller, Lee watched from a ridge brimming with artillery. He scanned the fields before him with his field glasses and looked to his rear hoping to see Longstreet. Grant's men were breaking through everywhere in the 70-square miles of the Wilderness. Along the broken Confederate lines, brigadier generals and colonels feverishly plugged holes and vainly moved their tangled lines around. All military cohesion was broken in the woods as many men had lost contact with their friends, and above the din was the constant shouting of men asking what regiment they were fighting with.

A sudden rumbling of activity came from the rear, and some Confederates feared the worst. Amid the chaos of the moment one man with a keen eye spotted a parallel column of dirty men with gleaming bayonets rapidly approaching. Their flags, flapping in the morning air, proudly announced that they were Texans. "Here they come!" shouted the man. [14] Lee's men whooped and cheered as the leading elements of Longstreet's Corps trickled in, steadily taking position, 10,000 rifles strong.

Sergeant Sheldon and the rest of the corps arrived in dramatic fashion, and Lee became uncharacteristically animated. A Texas brigade was just ahead of Bryan's Brigade of Georgians. "General, what Brigade is this?" Lee inquired of General John Gregg. "The Texas Brigade," Gregg replied. "I am glad to see it!" answered an anxious Lee. "When you go in there, I wish you to give those men cold steel," he ordered. Gregg turned in his saddle to face his men, shouting, "Attention, Texas Brigade! The eyes... of General Lee... are... upon you!! Forward... march!" With renewed confidence, Lee told an aide, "Texans always move them!" The Texans refused to move out, however, until Lee agreed to move to the safety of the rear amid a thunderous cheer. In tears, one soldier remarked, "I would charge hell itself for that old man." [15]

Forming a line of battle, the Georgians waited for General Bryan to order them forward. One man observed, "After several months of comparative rest in our quarters in east Tennessee, nothing but one week of strict camp discipline was required to put us in the best fighting order." [16] The cartridge boxes of the men were filled with forty rounds; another twenty were kept in their pockets, "all ready for the fray." [17] James stood for nearly ten minutes, and one of the hushed soldiers remembered, "I looked up and down the line and noticed that the men's faces were pale." [18] Suddenly, Bryan ordered, "Charge!" and with the whoop of the Rebel Yell, the brigade attacked with a fury. Wild-eyed courage dispelled the fear which had blanketed them just moments before. "We were ordered to charge and went a little way into the woods," remembered one company captain. [19] The zeal of the 50th Georgia was temporarily quelled as the enemy greeted them with a wall of minie balls swarming like hornets. The captain remembered, "The men hesitated when the shots began. I was trying to get to the front to lead them, all officers were usually behind the men. Just as I was getting through, seeing a man strange to me, I took off my hat and yelled 'Come on, boys!' They all followed and I got ahead. We were under heavy fire in a minutes, and were 'in for it' for two or three hours." [20]

Charging down a slight slope toward an unseen enemy, "Men fell here and there," according to one Confederate, who added, "officers urging on their commands and ordering them to 'hold their fire.' When near the lower end of the declivity, the shock came. Just in front of us, not forty yards away, lay the enemy. The long line of blue could be seen under the ascending smoke of thousands of rifles; the red flashes of their guns seemed to blaze in our very faces. Now the battle was on in earnest." [21]

By late morning, things were going in the 50th Georgia's favor. "At eleven o'clock the enemy retreated and we advanced a mile. We came to a pond where there was heavy firing," reported an officer. "Here we were relieved by another division, as we were very much exhausted. The whole army was engaged around here. My orderly sergeant came up to me and said, 'My gun's busted.' I said 'Throw it down and pick up another.' Then [another man] came and said 'Our ammunition's out.'" [22] Many of the men seemed to be experiencing both madness and euphoria. Colonel McGlashan's brother, Andrew, was seen lopping imaginary heads off shrubbery shouting, "Spurr!" [23] After the battle, another man in the 50th Georgia was asked why he had been smiling during the fighting and claimed he had no recollection of smiling. When told that during the most intense fighting, he was spotted playfully looking under the smoke to try and see the Yankees' feet; he couldn't remember that either.

The Wilderness became a whirlwind of death, with no sense of time or command. There seemed to be no way out. Men killed each other with the minie ball, the bayonet or the butt of a musket. One of Longstreet's men described the struggle, saying, "The roar of small arms, mingled with the thunder of the cannon that Longstreet had brought forward, echoed and re-echoed up and down the little valley, but never to die away, for new troops were being put in rapidly to the right and left of us. Men rolled and writhed in their last death struggle; wounded men groped their way to the rear, being blinded by the stifling smoke. All commands were drowned in this terrible din of battle —the earth and elements shook and trembled with the deadly shock of combat...Still the battle rolled on...Both armies stood at extreme tension, and the cord must soon snap one way or another, or it seemed as all would be annihilated." [24]

James and the 50th Georgia worked their way back beyond the range of the firing. Collapsing from exhaustion, the men struggled to take in the horrors they had just witnessed. After a rest of three or four hours and a few bites of their rations, the men were ordered back into the fight. After refilling their cartridge boxes they were soon back on the same ground where they had fought earlier. But the battle had ended, fading away in the distance. Even in quiet, the shattered forest remained a frightening place. "The trees were speckled like smallpox from bullets," said one man. [25] Some men rifled through the pockets of the Union dead or took their shoes. Sergeant Sheldon and his regiment, following Colonel McGlashan's lead, "marched on further and advanced another hundred yards in line of battle, but didn't strike the enemy, so returned and went into camp for the night." [26] Miraculously, James was spared yet again on the field of battle. Others in his regiment were not so lucky; three men were killed and nine wounded. One of the dead and two of the wounded were members of the "Thomas County Rangers." Lieutenant Colonel Pliney Sheffield was severely wounded and his right arm had to be amputated. As a whole, Bryan's Brigade lost 96 men, with 25 killed, 60 wounded and 11 missing.

Two miles to the north, Ewell's Corps hammered away at Sedgwick's 6th Corps. As it had the day before, the 2nd Rhode Island, as part of Henry Eustis' division, held the far end of the Union right. Grant, hoping to gain the advantage before Longstreet's Corps arrived, intended to renew his attack on Lee's left flank at five a.m. From the beginning, Generals Warren and Sedgwick had difficultly consolidating their attack. During the night General Burnside arrived with three divisions of the 9th Corps but had difficulty positioning his men between Warren and Hancock. Lee's mastery of defense and the difficult terrain stymied the Union attack. The Union line stood with Sedgwick on the right, and Hancock, Warren and Burnside on the left. General A. P. Hill faced Hancock and Richard "Old Bald Head"[27] Ewell resumed his face-off of the previous day against Sedgwick. The fighting grew hot in a hurry. Reverend Woodbury noted that the fighting the day before had merely been a warm-up for this day's main event, adding that Lee intended to "deliver an overwhelming blow on the left of the Union army,"[28] pushing it back to the banks of the Rapidan. On this morning Lee had gotten the jump on Grant, attacking Sedgwick's 6th Corps at 4:45 a.m., hoping to distract the Army of the Potomac until Longstreet got into position.

Lieutenant Rhodes and the 2nd Rhode Island were in the thick of things. After spending a sleepless night among dead and wounded, the 2nd was forced to advance into Ewell's attacking corps. With his head down, Elisha watched as his 6th Corps charged Ewell's lines as a wall of solid shot, canister and small arms fire filled the air. Initially, the 6th Corps gained ground. Elisha wrote, "Our men fell in all directions, but we kept on. Our lines were driven back and fresh troops sent in, but these shared the same fate. Soon we were ordered forward but had to return. A third time we tried it with the same result, losing many more men every time. When we retreated the Rebels shelled us and added to the confusion. Officers with drawn swords and pistols were urging the men forward, but poor fellows it was no use, for it was certain death." [29] A Union general rode into the 2nd Rhode Island's lines on a majestic white horse, trying to organize a charge. Minutes later, the horse was running around spooked and riderless while the general lay dead on the field.

Desperate, the Rhode Islanders reformed their lines a fourth time and charged, only to see the left of their line crumble. Ewell's men lurched forward and the 2nd Rhode Island's line fell back on itself, surrounded on three sides by a "U" formation of the enemy. Elisha and other officers stood by their color-bearer, drawing their pistols and swords, refusing to yield. Another great push of the 6th Corps came up from behind them and Ewell's men were again hurled back. Six times, the 2nd Rhode Island charged Ewell's lines, only to be driven back with great loss. Their ammunition spent, the Rhode Islanders began running for the rear. "The way we did leave! Everybody traveled as fast as possible. Many were captured, but I came out all right," said Elisha. [30]

Lee's line managed to entrench, although the 6th Corps made "unavailing attacks upon the strongly posted lines in front," remembered Reverend Woodbury. "Our men fought bravely and persistently. But, after the first advantage of the morning, there was no further gain." [31] A quiet fell over the Wilderness as both armies tried to sort out their tangled and broken lines. Brushfires and friendly fire paralyzed field commanders.

Eerily reminiscent of events of one year before, a prominent Confederate general went prowling through the jungles of the Wilderness, trying to reorganize his scattered army and determine the strengths and location of the Union lines. At some points the lines overlapped each other, and captives and captors exchanged roles from minute to minute. No one was where they should be and no one identified themselves until certain of who their hosts were. A group of horsemen galloped into a detachment of the 12th Virginia who were seeking safety from a brushfire, not far from the spot where Stonewall Jackson was wounded the previous May. The sound of riders approaching through the thicket was often answered by a volley of musketry. In a single defining moment, the already sagging hopes of the Confederacy were dimmed even further as a minie ball ripped through Longstreet's throat and shoulder. His arm went limp and his mouth filled with blood. General Joseph Kershaw, who was nearby, screamed at the riflemen to stop firing, "They are *fri-e-en-nds!*" [32]

****

At about four in the afternoon, Lee personally took command of Longstreet's Corps and renewed his attack. Like a wounded animal, the Army of Northern Virginia stung Grant's lines with "considerable impetuosity," according to Woodbury. [33] Ewell was determined to get around Sedgwick's right flank and just before dark inflicted serious damage to the Army of the Potomac. Near the position of the 2nd Rhode Island, Elisha witnessed two Union brigades being "surprised, overpowered and broke to pieces." [34]

Grant was frantic. Pacing and grumbling nervously, General Meade tried to calm him. Being the taller of the two, Meade leaned over Grant and offered him reassuring advice. While doing this, Meade noticed one of Grant's coat buttons had come undone; as a parent might do, Meade bent forward and buttoned it. When an officer burst in and excitedly told Meade that the army was crumbling and that all was lost, Grant fumed in silence until he could stand it no longer. As the officer began his forecast of what the great Robert E. Lee was about to do to the Union Army, Grant let him and all who were listening have it, bellowing, "Some of you always seem to think he is suddenly going to turn a double somersault and land in our rear and on both our flanks at the same time." [35] Turning his wrath on the officer, Grant ordered him to, "Go back to your command and try to think what we are going to do ourselves, instead of what Lee is going to do!" [36]

With his corps breaking up around him, Sedgwick tried to rally his men by appearing at the front. Disregarding his own safety, Sedgwick ordered retreating men back to the fight and demanded that officers take charge of their commands. He challenged his 1st Division to remember the honor of their 6th Corps. "Don't be in a hurry, boys—let them come well up before you let them have it." [37] In an instant, this division slammed into the "exhultant foe" [38] and forced them back out of the earthworks. This bitter repulse and the coming darkness ended the second day's fighting at the Wilderness. Longstreet's men fell back to their entrenched lines. When the firing finally died away, Sedgwick's men cheered him wildly. Slightly embarrassed by the fuss, the general waved his hat and, as a member of his staff put it, "blushed like a girl." [39]

As the firing died away, men of both armies staggered around the blackness of the Wilderness in search of wounded buddies or the safety of their regiments. Chaplains offered comfort to the wounded and administered last rites to the dying. Later, in the stillness of the woods, Reverend Augustus Woodbury reflected upon the events of the past 48 hours. "It was a strange battle…The nature of the ground virtually forbade any fighting with artillery or cavalry. It was almost wholly a conflict of infantry. Carried on among the trees and swamps, it was also, in a measure, an independent kind of contest. Officers could scarcely see their own men. The smoke hung low in the branches of the trees and in the thick growth of bushes and underbrush. Very little direction could be given by the officers, and it was only by the utmost care that any formation could be preserved. In several places fire would kindle among the thickets, and the horrors of burning were added to the pains of wounds." [40]

For a second night fires burned out of control in the Wilderness. Union wounded lay helpless in the woods as fires surrounded them. Confederate men, sickened by the sight, tried to reach them, only to be driven back by the guns of Grant's men. The men could only watch as blue flame engulfed blue uniforms. One man remembered, "Dead trees in the woods were aflame like torches. Often, as soldiers watched, fire would run along limb after limb till the whole tree was outlined in blaze. The reflection of the fire gave the clouds a sickening yellow cast. As the flames advanced there was a low swell of sound, a crash of limbs as if the artillery still were in action. The nearer men ventured to the fire, the louder were the frantic cries of the wounded who could not creep away as fast as the flames approached. Some of the wounded could not drag a broken back, or crawl with shattered limbs. These men could only pray and plead for succor or frantically seek to clear an open space around them as the fire drew nearer every minute. It was in vain. Two hundred of them soon were suffocated or were burned to charred trunks of flesh." [41]

****

The 2nd Rhode Island numbered less than 500 officers and men before the Battle of the Wilderness. When the fighting ended, it counted 13 killed and 55 wounded; several of those killed had re-enlisted only days before. Collectively, Eustis' Brigade suffered 80 killed and 287 wounded. The evening following the end of the fighting, James Sheldon, Elisha Rhodes and their regiments rested. But for most, sleep didn't come easily, if at all.

The two days of fighting at the Wilderness did little except drain the dwindling manpower of the Confederacy. The Army of the Potomac could hardly claim victory and some would even argue that the Wilderness was a Union defeat. But something was different. Just one day after being bloodied by the Army of Northern Virginia, Grant ordered his army to continue its march south, on the right of Lee's army, toward Richmond. "If we were under any other General except Grant I should expect a retreat, but Grant is not that kind of a soldier, and we feel that we can trust him," wrote Elisha. [42] Grant's new war was just getting under way.

Dawn of May 7 broke quietly over the Wilderness. "Both parties rested upon the ground," Reverend Woodbury recalled. "The contest had been very sanguinary, although it had been noticed, that generally in the army more men had been wounded in proportion to the killed than in other battles." [43] The day was passed quietly and anxiously by both armies. Grant would not retreat and Lee refused to acknowledge defeat but, both sides knew that Grant would not risk leaving his army in the Wilderness. Through their field glasses Lee's staff could see a parade of Union artillery being hitched up, undoubtedly bound for the sleepy little village of Spotsylvania Court House. There, several roads linked up with the Richmond & Petersburg Railroad, carrying badly needed Confederate supplies and reinforcements. Some reports indicated that Grant moved before all of his dead were buried. At dusk on the 7th, the Army of the Potomac was on the road bound for Chancellorsville.

Lee had command problems. In Longstreet's immediate absence he had personally taken command of the 1st Corps, but Lee's duty was to command an army, not a corps, and he moved quickly to replace Longstreet. He turned to Major General Richard "Dick" Anderson. [44] At 43, Anderson had already seen more than his share of warfare. Graduating from West Point in 1842, he had served in the Mexican War and the little-remembered Mormon uprising in Utah in 1857. Now, on May 7, the 1st Corps was his.

Unsure of Grant's exact intentions, Lee was determined to keep his army between the Army of the Potomac and Richmond. He ordered Anderson to have his corps ready to march early on the morning of May 8, choosing the 1st Corps because of its position on the extreme right of Lee's army. Lee ordered Anderson to begin his movement at three a.m. but Anderson wanted an earlier start. About an hour before midnight, the 1st Corps began making its way along a freshly cut road through the Wilderness. Anderson's plan was to forego resting his men until they had made significant progress toward Spotsylvania, but the new road caused a problem. "I found the woods in every direction on fire and burning furiously, and there was no suitable rest for us," he reported. [45] The road was narrower than anticipated and most of the stumps protruded above grade; tree trunks obstructed travel. Undaunted, Dick Anderson pushed on through the night until finding a place to bivouac near his destination. About three miles from Spotsylvania Court House, the 1st Corps came upon an expanse of open fields. "We marched all night and came to Spotsylvania Court House. I saw "Jeb" Stuart's cavalry there, going back to the rear, which meant a battle," recalled a member of the 50th Georgia Infantry. [46] The sound of gunfire echoed in the distance but Anderson, knowing his men needed rest and breakfast, ordered his column to halt.

Back on the road an hour later, with Sergeant James Sheldon's 50th Georgia near the head of the column, Anderson received a message from an excited, out-of-breath, barefooted courier. A small contingent of Confederate cavalry was just ahead down the road, while a large force of Grant's infantry was forming to charge. Anderson didn't hesitate and Bryan's Georgians broke into a run. Minutes later, James Sheldon and the 50th met the nervous cavalrymen, one of whom rode up to the Georgians pleading, "Run for our rail piles, the Federal infantry will reach them first, if you don't run!" [47] as he pointed to stacks of abandoned fench rails. Crowding up against the stacks, the men fixed bayonets. James could see brigade after brigade of blue-clad soldiers taking up similar positions across the field. At some points the lines were a mere 60 yards apart, but for the moment Lee's men had gained the better ground because of Anderson's decisiveness. Although it was only mid-morning, it was already brutally hot and Colonel McGlashan became ill from the heat and nearly passed out. As the men of the 50th braced for an attack, they talked about how they had demoralized the enemy at the Wilderness. One man claimed, "we heard that Grant was giving his men whiskey to make them drunk so they would fight." [48]

The Army of the Potomac arrived on a ridge at Spotsylvania only to find the enemy entrenched and waiting. Reverend Woodbury of the 2nd Rhode Island looked at the Confederate stronghold and summed up the situation. "Warfare," he declared, "although accepted as a science, is still oftentimes dependent for its issues upon what seems like the caprice of fortune." [49] Elisha and the 2nd Rhode Island were also racing to Spotsylvania on May 7. Knowing a gap had developed between the 6th and 9th (Burnside's) Corps, the 2nd Rhode Island was ordered on picket duty to probe this gap. The woods were crawling with "Jeb" Stuart's roaming cavalry, and the prospects of a Rhode Islander having his head lopped off by a swordsman in the night chilled every man to the bone. Lieutenant Colonel Read ordered his men to put their canteens and tin cups into their haversacks to keep them from rattling.

About midnight, the 2nd was ordered to return to their corps and fell into line on the Germanna Plank Road, preparing to march for Spotsylvania. Elisha was given a frightening assignment, and recalled, "I was ordered to ride in advance down the road and to endeavor to find Col. Joseph B. Hamblin, the corps officer of the day. As the Rebel Cavalry were known to have passed the road in our rear I did not like the job given me, but knowing I must obey I drew my revolver, pulled the hammer back and rode on. About half a mile to the rear, as I was riding in the shadow of the trees, some one put a pistol in my face and demanded 'Halt.' I quickly leveled my pistol and said: 'Who are you?' A man replied 'Give me your name or I will fire.' Knowing that my name could do no harm I replied 'Rhodes.' The man stepped out from behind his tree, and I saw that it was Col. Hamblin. He said: 'Adjutant, I came near shooting you.'" [50]

His heart racing, Elisha got down from his horse and led the colonel into the woods to wait for the 2nd to come along. Once reunited with his regiment, Lt. Rhodes and the regiment marched all night until catching up with the rest of the 6th Corps near Spotsylvania where the men were rewarded with freshly brewed coffee. Elisha was amazed by the number of Confederate prisoners being shuffled about. At eight a.m., General Warren believed he saw a detachment of Confederate cavalry isolated from Lee's main body. He sent a division forward to engage it, but to his horror watched many of his tired men slaughtered as thousands of Anderson's entrenched men rose up and fired volley after volley into the Union ranks.

Although held in reserve about a mile to the rear of the fighting, James and his comrades got a taste of artillery fire. "It started to rain," a Georgia man said. "Grant fired right down our line, and a cannon ball knocked an oil-cloth cape off the back of a colonel of a Mississippi regiment. He laughed and picked it up again. Another ball knocked off the top of a tree near me and hit a man. We moved nearer the enemy toward the right, into a trench full of mud." [51] For James and his fellow Georgians, "It was the most miserable night of the war—mud, bullets, and rain, no supper, no breakfast." [52] Later on the morning of May 8, the 50th Georgia was moved into Spotsylvania Court House and ordered to hold the main crossroads at the center of town.

During the morning of Monday, May 9, thousands of troops on both sides continued to converge on Spotsylvania. The lines formed and reformed. Lee's lines took on the shape of a horseshoe. Grant, constantly replenished his own lines with a seemingly endless stream of reinforcements and planned for an attack the following morning. Although there was no general attack by either side, skirmishing was flaring all along the lines, making it too dangerous for anyone to venture from the safety of their rifle pits. The men of the 2nd were comforted by the presence of Israel Sheldon's old battery, arriving just in time to repulse an assault on the 2nd's position. The Confederates were sent reeling by a thunderous roar of six hundred rounds of iron. Beaten back at great loss, they decided to leave the Rhode Islanders alone. The 50th Georgia was also under fire. "About nine o'clock we moved back further and formed in line of battle. We had to lie down to escape sharpshooting," a lieutenant in James' regiment said. [53]

Later that morning, 6th Corps commander Sedgwick sought to soothe the nerves of his men by braving the hail of sharpshooters' minie balls while riding back and forth along his line. An aide suggested that he was putting himself in danger. "Why they couldn't hit an elephant at this distance," Sedgwick assured his staff. [54] Seven hundred yards away, a Confederate sharpshooter peered through his sight at the defiant figure across the field. The marksman gently squeezed the trigger, sending a bullet through Sedgwick's skull. His men were stunned. Even the usually stoic Grant was shaken by the news, asking, "Is he *really* dead?" [55] Elisha later wrote in a letter, "He was one of our best Generals, and his death was a great loss to the Army...We are all sad for Uncle John, as he was called, [he] was beloved by all the Army." [56] Reverend Woodbury attested that Sedgwick was "fairly idolized by the men" and they admired his "modesty, manliness and unpretentious courage."[57] Although he was a strict disciplinarian, Sedgwick was known for his generosity, easy going personality, his love of playing cards and bachelorhood. Those close to him claimed he was the most popular general in the entire army. He was 47 years old.

Union General John Sedgwick

Attempting to fill the void in command of the 6th Corps was General Horatio Wright. At 44, he had graduated second in his class at West Point in 1841. He led troops at Gettysburg and Mine Run before serving on a board overseeing the seacoast defenses. Now, at Spotsylvania, he was promoted to major general.

Both armies spent the remainder of Monday building fortifications and strengthening their lines. Lee's lines were particularly impressive and unique in their formation. Bent in a "U" shape, some men on both sides quickly began referring to it as the "Mule Shoe." [58] It contained one spot along its length which jutted out on an elevated plain, dubbed "the salient." [59] Holding this ground was the battle-tested corps of Richard Ewell, who recognized the terrain's features as an ideal place to post artillery and he ordered twenty-two cannons positioned there. The "Mule Shoe" was almost a mile in depth and nearly a half-mile wide; a perfect space for batteries to operate with their teams of horses and caissons. Grant thought the salient could be taken.

Twelve regiments, specifically chosen for the operation, were put under the command of 45-year-old Colonel Emory Upton of New York. Upton's plan was for four lines, each consisting of three regiments, to hit the salient and then spread out their attack to the left and right. Once Upton's charge had broken through the center, General Gershom Mott's division would follow, crushing what was left of the "Mule Shoe" and preventing Lee from reinforcing it. On May 10, at 4:30 in the afternoon, Upton began organizing his troops. An hour later these men were stealthily marching toward Ewell's artillery. About six that evening they burst into the Confederate works like wildmen.

A member of the Virginia Howitzers remembered Upton's attack, saying, "Toward the close of the day everything seemed to have quieted down, in a sort of implied truce. There was absolutely no fire, either of musketry or cannon. Our weary, hungry infantry stacked arms and were cooking their mean and meager little rations. Someone rose up, and looking over the works—it was shading down a little toward the dark—cried out: 'Hello! What's this? Why, here come our men on a run, from—no, by Heavens! It's the Yankees!'" [60] The Union attack had been so sudden that the Confederates did not have time to run for their stacked muskets. Southern men were shot and bayoneted in their sleep, and those surprised at their campfires were forced to use cooking utensils for weapons.

"There was an old Captain Hunter," recalled the artillerist, "it seems difficult to determine whether of the Texas or the Georgia regiment—who had the handle of his frying pan in his hand, holding the pan over the hot coals, with his little slice of meat sizzling in it, when the enemy broke over. He had his back to them, and the first thing he knew his men were scampering past him like frightened sheep. He had not been accustomed to that style of movement among them, and he sprang up and tore after them, showering them with hot grease and hotter profanity, but never letting go his frying pan. On the contrary, he slapped right and left with the sooty, burning bottom, distributing his favors impartially on Federal and Confederate alike—several of his own men bearing the black and ugly brand on their cheeks for a long time after and occasionally having to bear also the captain's curses for having made him lose his meat that evening. He actually led the counter-charge, leaping upon the works, wielding and waving his frying pan, at once as sword and banner." [61]

Upton's attack went off precisely as planned, in spite of being wounded himself. Unfortunately, General Mott was not up to the task and efforts to support Upton failed miserably. As a result, Upton couldn't hold the trenches or the artillery he had so brilliantly captured and with a few prisoners in tow, he retreated back to the Union lines. In spite of the failure of the operation, Grant promoted him to the rank of general on the spot. Impressed by Upton's tactics, Grant decided to employ the same mode of attack after a day of regrouping.

In spite of the sporadic gunfire, May 11 turned out to be a day of rest. Reverend Augustus Woodbury recalled, "The day passed with some lively skirmishing in different parts of the field, which had, to a degree, withdrawn Lee's attention from the designated objective. A shower of rain had cooled the air and laid the dust, lasting into the evening...In other parts of the line the bivouac fires were lighted, the bands of music filled the air with patriotic strains, and the soldiers succeeded in obtaining a little rest—greatly needed after the toils of the week." [62] The newswalkers claimed that "Jeb" Stuart was dead; killed in a cavalry skirmish at Yellow Tavern. His death was yet another blow to the crumbling Confederate military hierarchy, and to the men of the 2nd Rhode Island, word of Stuart's death was greeted as another indication that the end of the war was almost in sight.

Shortly after four a.m. on May 12, the corps of Hancock and Burnside, shrouded in a blinding mist and light drizzle, began making their way along the two-day-old footprints of Upton's men. Because Ewell's position had proved impregnable, Lee was convinced that Grant would not hit it again and would instead attack his *right* flank. Taking no chances, he had withdrawn Ewell's twenty-two guns to the rear so they could be shuffled around at a moment's notice. Hancock and Burnside took Ewell totally by surprise.

Woodbury recalled, "Without firing a shot, and in silence, broken only by a mistimed cheer, the men rushed on, over and into the enemy's works, capturing, almost at a single stroke, 3,000 men, two general officers, Johnson and Stewart, twenty guns and thirty flags. The officers were disturbed at their breakfast." [63] For a time it seemed like a Union success. Hancock reported to Grant that he had the situation well in hand and was ready to go after Jubal Early's division. "The point taken proved to be a salient of the enemy's works, and one of his most important positions," Woodbury wrote. [64] Lieutenant Rhodes and the 2nd Rhode Island waited in reserve to support Hancock's attacking column on the right flank.

Grant's plan was for Hancock's men to hit the salient and fan out, opening a hole for Burnside to come pouring through. But after Hancock's initial success, his men failed to spread out and Burnside, like a football running back, found no opening in the line to hit. Early was able to gain a flank on Hancock's men and poured a deadly fire into them. A reserve division of Confederate General John B. Gordon was thrown into the fray, forcing the Union men to fall back. It was still only six a.m. when Grant ordered Warren's 5th Corps, along with the 6th Corps, to Hancock's aid—Elisha and his men were on the move. A Confederate officer described the fighting, saying, "there was one continuous roll of musketry from dawn until midnight." [65] The most intense hand-to-hand struggle of the war raged for a full 18 hours. By mid-morning, Lee saw the very real possibility of his army being cut in two and without a unified front his flanks would be battered into submission. Lee took to the field himself and began directing a series of five deadly counterattacks, all at a cost the Army of Northern Virginia could not afford to pay.

Several hundred yards west of the salient was a sharp bend in the "Mule Shoe"—etched in history as the "Bloody Angle." [66] Ewell's best and battle-hardened men were charging out of their works to take the fight to the enemy. Lieutenant Elisha Rhodes' 2nd Rhode Island smashed headlong into these men—fighting bayonet to bayonet.

It rained hard as Ewell's men were pushed back, only to come on again and again in the torrential downpour. By noon, the standing water in the trenches was turning red, and on more than one occasion opposing flags touched each other over the works. The Confederates hit and fell back, only to come charging once again. The Rebel Yell howled above the din. Woodbury wrote, "The retreating wave marks were deep with blood. The rain came down again. Thousands of feet trampled down the gory mud. The enemy, finding our men too tenacious of their gains, turned his attention to our left flank, and fiercely attacks Burnside." [67] Although Burnside's own attack fell short, he managed to withstand the counterattacks and hold his position.

Lieutenant Colonel Read's 2nd Rhode Island saw the worst of the fighting. At six a.m. Elisha's brigade "took possession of the Rebel works." The Southern men desperately wanted it back. [68] All afternoon the Confederates hit them on the left and left-center. Elisha wrote, "How the old 2nd Rhode Island did fire. I fired over a hundred rounds myself. [Lt.] Colonel Read was firing when he was hit. At the same instant a bullet struck me in my right breast, tore my coat, glanced on my pocket book and bruised my right arm. It whirled me round, and I thought I was dead but soon found that I was all right. The ammunition was exhausted and the officers passed it up to the men in boxes." [69]

A New York brigade to the right of the 2nd was driven from the field and the men were forced to withstand a terrible enfilading fire, "but our boys never moved," Elisha said. "For three hours the Rebels were within twenty feet of our regiment. It seemed to me that the day would never pass away." [70] About four p.m., reinforcements came to the aid of the Rhode Islanders and they were sent to the relative safety of the rear. Elisha and most of the other men fell into a deep sleep, in spite of the rain. Elisha dreamed he was home in Pawtuxet.

A reporter for *The Army and Navy Journal* telegraphed, "Every inch of muddy and gory soil was fought over with desperation, and yielded only when impossible to hold it. Neither the rain nor the wretched mire of the roads delayed the rapidity or intensity of the fight. The rival bayonets often interlocked, and a bloody grapple over the entrenchments lasted for hours, the rebel battle flags now surging up side by side with our own, and anon, torn and riddled, disappearing in the woods…Our men would reach over this partition, and discharge their muskets in the face of the enemy, and in return would receive the fire of the rebels at the same close range. Finally the men began to use their muskets as clubs, and then rails were used." [71]

In his report of the fighting of May 12, a Union general said, "Nothing but the piled up logs of breastworks separated the combatants. Our men would reach over the logs and fire into the faces of the enemy, would stab over with their bayonets; many were shot and stabbed through the crevices and holes between logs; men mounted the works and with muskets rapidly handed them kept up a continuous fire until they were shot down, when others would take their places." [72] At one point a mighty oak, 22" wide at its base, came crashing down after being ravaged by small arms fire.

Although not engaged in the most severe fighting, Sergeant James Sheldon saw action at Spotsylvania. After the action of Tuesday, May 10, the 50th was "moved nearer the enemy to the left in some woods. We stayed an hour and then came back," remembered an officer, adding, "on the way back, when we came to a stream, [we] saw the enemy up the creek. I thought we would be fired at and we were, and my lieutenant was wounded (Lt. Hillary Cason was struck in the right groin by a minie ball) as he jumped across."[73] This was the last of the 50th Georgia's direct participation in the fighting at Spotsylvania Court House. "After this we were taken a mile to the rear and went into camp, that is 'placed in reserve.'"[74] James was finally able to enjoy a decent meal and rest. One officer wrote, "what a luxury it was to rest and feel safe from being killed! We stayed there twenty-four hours, and got one good night's sleep."[75] But at Spotsylvania, no one was ever really safe. A private in the 53rd Georgia wrote, "I have made many narrow escapes and passed through many dangers. I had one of my friends killed by my side the other night while asleep. He and I was sleeping together. The ball struck him in the breast. He awoke me struggling but before I could get [a light] he was dead. Poor fellow never knew what hit him."[76]

During the thickest part of the firing, Lt. Rhodes was ordered to deliver a message to a Union battery. While doing so, he became the target of sharpshooters and took cover hanging off the side of his horse as he rode. But, in his haste, he lost his new hat. Having spent the small fortune of $7.50 on it, he chose to test the skill of the riflemen and managed to retrieve the hat with the tip of his sword. Returning to his regiment he found the officers receiving a flag of truce from a line of approaching Confederates. In an instant, the flag was lowered and guns raised as the Confederates whooped the Rebel Yell and charged at the Rhode Islanders. Elisha's friend, Captain John Shaw, leapt upon a stump waving his sword in an attempt to rally the men. Seconds later he was dead, blood squirting from his chest. Elisha took the captain's pistol, vowing to give it to Shaw's father.

At midnight the firing died away. The 2nd Rhode Island held tight to the rifle pits they had seized earlier in the day. It wasn't until after the struggle ended that the regiment realized the cost of its stubbornness. A quick roll call told the story: Lt. Colonel Read was severely wounded, only days before he would be commissioned a full colonel. Elisha's good friend, Captain

John Shaw, the 27-year-old jeweler from Providence, was dead. Along the length of the rifle pit were the tangled bodies of countless Confederates and 12 dead Rhode Island men. Another 13 were badly wounded. In the four days of fighting, the 2nd Rhode Island lost a total of 20 killed and 14 wounded; their worst losses since 1st Manassas almost three years earlier. James Sheldon's 50th Georgia suffered the loss of one man wounded and three missing.

The next day was Friday the 13th. The rain continued to beat down upon the bloody grounds of Spotsylvania. There were so many wounded men that some pitifully crawled away into the woods to die alone. Both armies rested in the deep mud, seeking out friends and trying to comprehend the scope of the tragic events. Elisha Rhodes saw a trench full of Confederate dead— 3,000 he was told. "May God save me from another such scene," he thought. [77] Lee and Grant reorganized their lines but neither were willing to give battle. Adjutant Ben Simms described the new Union commander in a letter to his mother, "Grant fights with a great deal of stubbornness and perseverance, he seems to regard the loss of life as quite a small thing compared to the accomplishing of his designs. He seems to regard the extravagant loss of life with a great deal of indifference. I think he has been beaten well but have no idea how long he will continue to fight us. He seems willing to sacrifice all his men for Richmond." [78]

On May 14 there were some small attacks but nothing of any strategic consequence. On Sunday the men of both armies worshipped, wrote letters, smoked and napped. Monday, the 17th, saw more of the same.

On the morning of the 18th, Grant tried one more time to break Lee's lines. The assault failed as Confederate artillery "mowed the men down in rows," Elisha said. [79] Unable to scale an array of abatis, most of the Union men ended up pinned down under a killing fire. Lieutenant Edmund Prentiss, another of Elisha's friends, was hit twice, once by a piece of shell in the groin and again by a round of grapeshot that struck him in the temple. As he was carried off the field with these horrific wounds, he was still alive.

The attack crumbled and the 2nd Rhode Island withdrew from the field. The regiment counted two more men killed, four wounded, and one man missing. Tragically, many of these men were only days from going home. In another life, these men were weavers, farmers and sailors from quiet villages such as Apponaug and Greenville. "Many a poor fellow who had looked forward to his return home, and had counted the days, found a resting place for his shattered body beneath the ensanguined turf, while his spirit went up above the strife 'Unto God who gave it.'" [80] Embittered, the motto of the 2nd Rhode Island became "Death or Richmond." [81]

While the eyes of both countries were focused on Spotsylvania Court House, other important events had changed the face of the war. In Georgia, Joe Johnston prepared to face off against Sherman. Union General Nathaniel Banks' infantry and the Union Navy's gunboats were in retreat on the Red River. Union artillery pummeled Ft. Sumter with more than a thousand rounds over four days. The teenage cadets from the Virginia Military Institute fought to victory at New Market, Virginia. The Shenandoah Valley looked warlike, while in Richmond, "Jeb" Stuart was buried in Hollywood Cemetery overlooking the James River.

The Sunday after the last battle, James Sheldon was free to walk around Spotsylvania. What he saw was ghoulish. One Union soldier was found lying dead behind a tree wearing two homemade steel plates on his chest—a hole ran through his skull. At the Bloody Angle, the ground was strewn with Union dead. A man in the 50th Georgia described the scene, saying, "They were swollen from the rain and had been there three days, and couldn't be buried. They were thick—I tell you it was awful! There were pools of water in the trenches which were bloody, and right at the angle were old field pines that were speckled from top to bottom with bullets." [82]

James Sheldon's 50th Georgia made camp near the line of battle at Hanover Junction on May 23.

The fighting at Spotsylvania had cost Grant dearly and the nation howled at the news. After ten days, 2,700 men were dead, 13,500 wounded and another 2,250 were missing. On the Confederate side, the numbers indicated success, with total losses of 8,000 men killed, wounded and missing. But this was 18 percent of the Army of Northern Virginia, which would not be able to replenish its ranks. On the 19th, Grant began preparing to once again march around Lee's right flank—inching ever closer to Richmond.

13

THE ANGRY FEATURES
OF THE FOE!

As Grant's army began moving away from Spotsylvania, Sergeant James Sheldon and the 50th Georgia came under attack again. But this time the enemies were "Graybacks," as some itchy men would call them. Pediculus humanus, commonly known as body lice, preyed upon the men of both armies and everyone from generals to privates endured their humiliation at one time or another. After Spotsylvania the 50th fell victim to a severe infestation, and the company cook's kettle did double duty as naked men stood around a pot full of boiling salt water. The less modest of the men held their clothes hanging from a stick above a campfire listening for a sound much like popping corn as the little menaces burst and fell off. Others simply threw their clothes away and begged, borrowed or stole a new uniform, although the term "uniform" hardly applied to the rags most soldiers were wearing by mid-1864. Most men withstood the "Graybacks" in good humor, having mock lice fights and "Grayback" races which took place on a tin plate. One man was said to have cheated by heating his plate to make his louse run faster.

Having withstood the parasite invasion, the men of the 50th refocused on the other enemy. "The next morning we started back toward Richmond. We marched hard all day. We passed Lee's headquarters, and he was standing in front of his tent. The men cheered him," remembered one man in James' regiment. [1]

The Army of the Potomac was also on the move. By nightfall of May 19 the ground which had been the left was now held by the troops who had been on the right only hours earlier. In a pouring rain Hancock's 2nd Corps marched toward the little hamlet of Bowling Green. Lee harassed Grant's movement by attacking the right and rear of the Army of the Potomac with a portion of Ewell's. A division of the Union 2nd Corps made a strong stand against Ewell's men, forcing them to back off. At about midnight of Saturday the 21st, Grant's army began moving south toward the banks of the North Anna River, arriving at Bowling Green late in the afternoon, fending off skirmishers as it marched. Once entrenched, the army's lines faced west.

Lee was also in a hurry to get to the North Anna. One soldier in the 50th remembered, "We camped that night (the 21st) and marched all the next day until afternoon when we arrived at the North Anna River. After crossing it we formed in line of battle with our backs to Richmond…We were in a large primeval forest, thirty miles from Richmond, and we built breastworks of trees." [2]

Grant's weary men pushed on, arriving at the North Anna on the 23rd. Along its banks, the 5th Corps and Lt. Elisha Rhodes' 6th Corps were on the right flank at a place called Jericho Mills. Burnside's 9th Corps was near Ox Ford and the 2nd Corps encamped near the railroad and the Chesterfield bridges. The march had taken Elisha through a part of Virginia that had somehow been untouched by the war. The men of the 2nd were moved by the sight of rolling green fields and pastures, abundant with crops that held a promise of plentiful harvests to come later in the summer.

On Monday afternoon, Grant began a pontoon crossing over the river and after forming a line of battle a "sharp engagement"[3] immediately erupted, resulting in the capture of a significant number of Confederates. A man in the 50th described Grant's arrival on the North Anna, writing, "That afternoon about five, we heard shots across the river, our skirmishers were retreating." [4] Hancock's 2nd Corps had done most of the fighting, losing about 300 men as a result.

As Grant continued his crossing, Lee's men vainly tried to stop him. According to one of James' comrades, "We were ordered to load guns, but we couldn't see across the river on account of bushes. A terrible fire was opened on us, bullets whistled over our heads, but we were perfectly safe, and no one was hurt. It seemed almost like fun, compared to some experiences we had had." [5]

The battle for the bridges had begun and James Sheldon was in the thick of it. "We were here by the river a day or two. Firing lasted until sundown, but no one was hurt. We had only one shovel to a company. There was a railroad bridge near, and each side was trying to get it. The enemy wanted to use it and we wanted to burn it. After a day or two, Lee gave up the bridge and formed [his lines] in a half moon shape, and Grant crossed and got inside the half moon," said one soldier. [6] By nightfall, the Chesterfield bridges were in Union hands.

On May 24, Burnside's 9th Corps crossed the North Anna near Ox Ford while Elisha's 6th Corps remained on the north bank behind Warren's 5th Corps. Geography favored the Army of Northern Virginia. On the points of the North Anna where Grant had planted his army, the river bends sharply into a crescent shape. This allowed Lee to refuse his flanks, or draw them in toward his center. By throwing his center forward at Ox Ford he could protect the railroad at Hanover Junction and divide Grant's right and left wings. The bend was so tight that the ends of Lee's lines approached each other, forcing Grant to actually cross the river twice to get at Lee's center. A Union cavalry reconnaissance confirmed that Lee's position was simply too strong to attack.

Conceding the uselessness of his position, Grant once again reverted to a flanking movement, planning to swing to the east around Lee and cross the Pamunkey River less than ten miles from Richmond. "On to the Pamunkey," [7] became the new cry of Grant's army. The men of the 50th Georgia waited to see what was going to happen next. "We saw very little of them (Grant's men) as we were in thick woods. Although we were there for several days, not many were hurt, as we dug breastworks and the bullets were spent," said a Georgian officer. [8] Sharpshooters were everywhere and men of both sides traveled from tree to tree seeking shelter around their camps.

On the evening of May 26, the Army of the Potomac was once again set in motion. About ten o'clock the following morning, under orders of strict silence, the 2nd Rhode Island and the 6th Corps marched into Hanovertown led by the cavalry of General Philip "Little Phil"[9] Henry Sheridan, who had just returned from an 11-day expedition. General Grant liked the style of this diminutive warrior, and one of his first appointments after becoming general-in-chief of the United States Armies was to appoint the five-foot-five Sheridan to chief of cavalry of the Army of the Potomac. When Sheridan was taken to the White House to be introduced to Lincoln, the president quipped an old army joke, saying, "Who ever saw a dead cavalryman?"[10] Little Phil fumed in respectful silence, but later, over a few drinks with friends, predicted, "I'm going to take the cavalry away from the bobtailed brigadier generals. They must do without their escorts. I intend to make the cavalry an arm of the service."[11] It was said that Sheridan's cavalry often "moved at a walk, conscious of its power, as if it had all the time in the world."[12] With summer rapidly approaching, Sheridan's star was about to really shine.

****

On May 28, Grant's army crossed the Pamunkey River. One of the first orders of business was to move its supply base from Port Royal to White House Landing, which looked familiar to the veterans of the Peninsula Campaign of two years before. The next day the Army of the Potomac began a steady, slow, forward advance. Observing this movement, Lee did not "see fit to attack,"[13] and instead, chose to wait for Grant six miles south at Totopotamoy Creek, with the Chickahominy River and Richmond at his back.

By Monday, Grant was as close to Richmond as McClellan had been in 1862. Wright's 6th Corps held the right of the line toward Hanover Court House while Hancock's 2nd, Warren's 5th and Burnside's 9th were on the left. Cavalry was posted on both flanks. About noon the cavalry on the left flank got into a fight, each side losing between 80 and 90 men. Later in the afternoon Warren's Corps was attacked but able to hold, due in large part to a counterattack made by Hancock's 2nd Corps.

James Sheldon had been marching a day and a half in the direction of Richmond when the 50th got near the town of Mechanicsville and came under fire. The men quickly occupied some rail fences for protection. The regiment did little except wait out the harassing skirmishers; listening to the occasional thwack of minie balls striking the wooden rails. After dark, the 50th resumed its march and after several miles set up camp. At first light, the men began building earthen defenses. They were not fired upon, and for a few hours it was as if James and the regiment had a day off as they were free to walk about and mingle with men from other regiments. In the morning, the men of the 50th continued their march toward the southeast without incident, and at dusk made camp a few miles north of the Chickahominy River.

On the Union side, Hancock found himself under attack at midnight, repulsing the Confederates and taking several hundred prisoners in the process. Burnside was also engaged with some minor success. As a result, much of the Army of the Potomac awoke on the 31st to find itself within a mere eight miles of Richmond. Grant planned to destroy the Army of Northern Virginia, making the capture of Richmond little more than a formality. But as they gazed at the Richmond skyline from a hillside, the men of the 2nd Rhode Island knew that "true distance is measured by the character of the obstructions which fill the way," as Reverend Woodbury said.[14] Grant dryly joked that Richmond could be taken in two or three days, but only if Lee agreed to it.

On the morning of the last day of May, the Army of the Potomac lurched forward one-quarter to three-quarters of a mile, seizing rifle pits and advancing closer to Lee's lines. Under the cover of darkness, Elisha Rhodes' 6th Corps moved from the right to the left of the line, joining troops of Ben Butler's 18th Corps. This move was to secure a passage across the Chickahominy River, near a vital crossroads about three miles north of the river; an area once known as "Cool Arbor," and by 1864, "Cold Harbor." [15] Lee intended to stop it.

Bryan's Brigade tramped through the early morning darkness toward Cold Harbor. General Bryan had been battling his latest attack of gout and temporarily handed the reins of his brigade over to Colonel James P. Simms of the 53rd Georgia.

The morning was already warm and the day promised to be hot and humid. As the Georgians approached the small crossroads, still several miles to the southeast, James could hear gunfire in the distance, growing louder and clearer with each step. Occasionally, wounded men, alone or in small groups, would pass them, heading for the rear. But as the sun rose higher in the morning sky, the 50th plodded along. At different points along the march the regiment was ordered to hit the ground as reports were received of a strong enemy presence ahead of them. Each report proved unfounded, however, and the march resumed. As the 50th neared Cold Harbor the sounds of battle grew more intense. In spite of this thunderous racket, a brass band could be heard, adding a touch of surrealism to the scene.

At mid-morning James and the 50th Georgia arrived at Cold Harbor. "We were on an old road, with woods in front of us and a field behind us. We worked hard at the breastworks which were made of logs and dirt," recalled a man in the 50th. [16]

On May 31, Sheridan's cavalry, still basking in the glory of having vanquished "Jeb" Stuart, galloped into Cold Harbor with infantry following behind. Lt. Elisha Rhodes and the 2nd Rhode Island marched throughout the night, creating a light brown dust cloud which coated their uniforms and dry throats. The dust was so heavy that it "hung upon the leaves of the trees like snow," according to a surgeon in the 6th Corps. [17] Fifteen miles later the men reached Cold Harbor where many dropped from exhaustion, directly across from the rifle pits of James Sheldon's

50th Georgia. It was mid-afternoon of June 1. Slowly and behind schedule, other elements of Grant's army began arriving and immediately went to work digging rifle pits.

"Thus closed the month of May—altogether the most arduous month's campaigning the Army of the Potomac had ever experienced. Scarcely a day had passed without fighting, more or less severe. The enemy was 'obstinate,' General Grant said. Every foot of ground had been disputed, and Lee's serried ranks stood unbroken before our slowly advancing columns," observed Reverend Woodbury. [18]

Grant's first assault on Lee's lines got underway late in the afternoon. Elisha Rhodes' 6th Corps and the 18th Corps prepared to charge out of their entrenchments up a slight slope through newly felled trees and other defenses that Lee had placed in their path. But just moments before the signal was given, the 2nd Rhode Island and its entire brigade was ordered to another position to protect threatened artillery. Arriving there, Elisha and the men of the 2nd "charged front and advanced on the enemy and drove them from our flank." [19] An officer in the 50th Georgia described Grant's attack, saying, "In the afternoon we were attacked and our skirmishers were driven back to the breastworks. We were all ready to receive the attack, but it didn't reach my regiment. There was, however, a heavy engagement at the right. Suddenly we saw our men over there retreating, all except the regiment next to us. When McGlashan noticed it he acted independently. He gave me the command, 'Take companies B, C, and E (Thomas County Rangers) up the line and hold the enemy in check.' We rushed up a hundred yards and found ourselves in the midst of the enemy in the woods. We jumped into the breastworks and fired, the enemy stopped firing and moved toward us. I saw that we would be taken prisoner, so I ordered a retreat." [20]

Colonel Peter McGlashan put the 50th Georgia into line, forming a right angle and a formidable line of defense, persuading the attackers to take their business elsewhere. As James watched Grant's men fall back to their breastworks in the woods, a South Carolina regiment came up behind the

Georgians as reinforcements. The men of the 50th waved their hats and cheered the Carolinians. Seizing upon the emotion of the moment, the Carolina men cheered the 50th, urging them to join their charge. "Fiftieth Georgia, forward!," Colonel McGlashan shouted, and the Carolinians and Georgians charged across the fields whooping a shrill Rebel Yell. [21] "The whole line thundered with the incessant volleys of musketry, and the shot and shell of artillery shrieked and howled like spirits of evil," wrote the 6th Corps surgeon. [22] The Union line broke and fell back in disorder, leaving their works to the Southern men. Sergeant Sheldon and the 50th Georgia left the captured works to the Carolina men and moved back to the breastworks they had built earlier in the day.

Elsewhere along the line, the fight was on. At one point, as the Union men approached the Confederate works 30 yards distant, "a sheet of flame, sudden as lightning, red as blood, and so near it seemed to singe the men's faces," was unleashed on them. [23] Back and forth the lines surged and bent, as men killed and died until darkness ended the fight. The attack was only a partial Union success, capturing some of Lee's rifle pits and a few hundred prisoners, but a success nonetheless. By late in the day, there was fighting along the entire line and by dusk the Army of the Potomac could lay claim to a modest advantage. "As darkness came on, the conflict still raged, and sheets of flame rolled from one end of the line to the other as the discomfited rebels strove to regain their lost ground." [24] The 6th and 18th Corps lost 2,200 men, but Lee's losses, although unknown, were fearful as well, even more so when coupled with the fact that these men could not be replaced. During the fighting of June 1 at Cold Harbor, the 50th Georgia suffered the loss of one man killed, six wounded and had nine taken prisoner. One man in the 2nd Rhode Island was wounded.

Grant saw an opportunity, and expecting the arrival of the remainder of the army during the night, he ordered an all out attack on Lee's crippled army for daybreak the following morning.

But it was not to be. Neither trained or designed for speed, the Union Army slowly lumbered into the vicinity of Cold Harbor. As a result, the attack was postponed until four in the afternoon. Shortly before that time, reports came into Meade and Grant's headquarters that many of their brigades were simply too beat up or exhausted to fight. "The men of the 6th and 18th Corps, tired and worn out from marching, fighting, and the hard night's work in throwing up entrenchments, had spent the early part of the day in quietly watching the enemy, or lounging behind the breastworks, glad of an opportunity for rest." [25] The armies sized each other up throughout the day of Thursday, June 2, as skirmishing flared up and down the lines. It was brutally hot, and dark clouds in the west promised to bring relief by way of a late spring thunderstorm.

The men of the 50th Georgia had spent most of the day in reserve but under heavy artillery bombardment. During the afternoon the regiment was sent back to a deep gorge where the men felt relatively safe. After two days of marching and fighting under a broiling sun, the worn out men of the 50th stacked arms and rested. The hungry soldiers built cooking fires while Commissary Sergeant Sheldon spent his 24th birthday distributing what few rations were available. The 50th Georgia lost two men killed by sharpshooters while retrieving water. The same day, June 2, a man in the 2nd Rhode Island suffered a similar fate.

In the growing darkness, Hancock planned to launch another attack such as he had in the Wilderness, but nature intervened with thunder, blinding lightning, and a driving rain, keeping the armies in their muddy trenches. Later, as the rain cooled the evening air, Grant was finally ready to go. The designated time was 4:30 a.m., but the earlier delays would prove costly.

The first streaks of light in the Virginia sky revealed Lee's 59,000 troops staring nervously through woods and across open fields at the Union entrenchments facing them. In these trenches, clutching their muskets, crouched an equally anxious 108,000 Union men. Elisha Rhodes' 6th Corps was on the left of the Union line with Hancock's men, and the two corps stayed tightly connected to their cavalry. Much of Lee's own lines were partially sheltered by woods and a portion obscured by a slight crest. But instead of the disorganized line of defense that Lee had hurriedly thrown together two days earlier, this was a strong fortification. Lee's lines were engineering marvels, as "every ravine, knoll and hillock, every bog and water course, every clump of trees and patch of brambles, [were designed] so that unending cross fires could be laid on all possible avenues of approach." [26] One newspaper reporter described "intricate lines within lines…works within works." [27] Worse for Grant, in his haste to put together one final crushing blow, he did not have reconnaissance reports of any real merit. As flecks of morning sunlight sliced through tree branches, tens of thousands of Union men labored up the modest slope into Lee's deathtrap.

At about 6:30 a.m., Union soldiers came in contact with their Confederate counterparts and the sharp crack of rifle fire announced the opening of battle. The 2nd, 18th and 6th Corps charged out of their entrenchments into the jaws of the Army of Northern Virginia. The sound of musketry quickly became deafening, followed by the thunder of artillery, and wild cries from thousands of throats. Hancock's veterans knew that when their general ordered a charge they were to hit the enemy ferociously, driving them without mercy, and in this first assault on Lee's lines they did just that. According to Reverend Woodbury, these 2nd Corps men made "a splendid charge" up the hill, sweeping A. P. Hill's men from the summit and taking a series of earthworks, a flag, and 300 shocked prisoners. [28] Hancock's men stubbornly held this ground until Lee's flanking troops concentrated a murderous fire on them, driving them back.

Hancock's men fell back 150 feet and immediately began digging in, fully aware of what was coming. Elisha's 6th Corps tried to break Lee's line directly in its center, hitting James Sheldon's 50th Georgia and Anderson's Corps. At the same time, the 18th Corps attacked Early's 2nd Corps. On the left, Warren and Burnside's men were also hitting Lee's line with limited success. But the day was turning into a disaster for the Army of the Potomac. Maps were useless and there were swamps and streams where no one expected them. Lee's angry gunners seemed to be everywhere.

But there was also confusion on the Confederate side. "We were behind a hill and safe, but received orders to advance up the hill. At the top there was an open field, then a downward slope. We could see everything from there, but were in the line of bullets," a man next to James Sheldon remembered. "We ran fast down the hill and when we arrived found a small ditch already full of men, so I lay flat behind the men in the ditch, it was perfectly safe if lying down." [29] The orders for the 50th Georgia had been a mistake and nearly a disaster. During a slackening of the firing the regiment was ordered to move about one-half mile to the right where it went into line with the 8th Georgia. But the fight was just as hot along this section of the line and as James arrived there was another attack. The 50th waited until the Union men got within a few hundred yards of their breastworks. Colonel McGlashan shouted the order to fire, and Grant's men were stopped cold. Many of them hit the ground and others retreated. The wounded and dead lay in rows, as they had stood in battle. "One [man] waved a handkerchief as a sign of surrender and to stop firing, which ceased," claimed one man in the 50th Georgia. "Then instead of surrendering some jumped up and ran back, so we started firing again, but the colonel told us to stop wasting shot." [30]

Covering the retreat, some of Grant's men began firing from the woods. The men of the 50th witnessed a wounded Confederate, staggering toward the position of the Georgians from their rear. The man repeatedly fell to one knee, only to struggle back to his feet, waving a small piece of white cloth, but before the 50th's litter bearers could go to his aid, the wounded man was shot dead.

Wave after wave of dusty blue uniforms charged Lee's works as low smoke, known as rank fog, clogged the air. The roar of artillery and the rattle of small arms was deafening. Even

313

three-year veterans had never heard anything like this, as rifle fire rolled like one continual crash of thunder. After the first 15 minutes of Grant's charge, nearly 7,000 Union soldiers were down.

At about noon, Grant ordered the offensive to be halted. Years later, Grant would confess, "I have always regretted that the last assault at Cold Harbor was ever made." [31] But the day was not yet over. Knowing that Grant's army had crippled itself by suicidal charges, Lee decided to go on the offensive. An officer in the 6th Corps recalled, "Suddenly, at eight o'clock, the rebels in front of our Sixth corps and of the Second corps, leaped over their works and rushed with a yell toward our lines. At the same time their artillery opened upon us… our men were glad to show them the difference between being the assailants and the assailed…many grey-coated soldiers who advanced to the charge, were left by their retreating comrades, dead between the two lines, while others were ordered in as prisoners. The rebels returned to their place, and again all was still." [32]

The 50th Georgia played no part in this fighting and an officer wrote that they were "kept in reserve as we had borne the brunt of the first two days' fighting." [33] James and the other men of the 50th found a safe place in the woods and while hurriedly cooking rations, they had a lot to talk about. The three-day Battle of Cold Harbor was over, resulting in Grant's first defeat. His total loss of 7,000, compared to the relatively acceptable Confederate loss of 1,500, angered many in the North and for the first time the expression "that butcher Grant," echoed North and South. [34] In Richmond, news of the victory at Cold Harbor held a hollow ring as the combined losses of the Wilderness, Spotsylvania and Cold Harbor continued to drain Lee's army. The Confederate draft yielded pitiful results and Grant's refusal to exchange prisoners was taking its toll. The outlook for both Jefferson Davis' government and the Army of Northern Virginia was grim, in spite of Grant's staggering losses at Cold Harbor.

The most intense fighting had drawn to a close but would continue sporadically throughout the coming week. James

Sheldon's colonel reported, "our line was in such close proximity to the enemy's works that a constant fire was kept up during the day between us and the enemy, resulting in loss to us, and to be supposed in greater loss to them, as we finally almost silenced their sharpshooters entirely." [35]

On June 7, Grant requested a truce to bury the dead. Confederate and Union burial details eyed each other warily as they went about their gruesome work. In some instances the soldiers approached each other with words of kindness or regret. "It seemed almost like murder to fire upon you," confessed one Confederate to a Union soldier. [36] In three days of fighting, the 2nd Rhode Island's losses were four killed, three wounded and three taken prisoner. The 50th Georgia lost two killed and two wounded. "Our troops are in excellent spirits and perfectly confident," wrote Adjutant Simms. [37] But the war had changed. From now on, at the first hint of battle, men on both sides instinctively began to dig or build earthworks, and the men understood that assaulting a dug-in adversary bordered on suicide.

****

Although the numbers themselves were not fearfully high, the 2nd Rhode Island had reason to feel their losses more deeply than other regiments. Elisha reflected on the events of June 3, writing, "We have had a terrible battle today, and the killed and wounded number in thousands. For some reason, perhaps because so many men go home tomorrow, the 2nd R.I. has been kept in the reserve." [38] Two days later, 265 men of the 2nd Rhode Island left for home. Of the 326 men remaining on the roll, only about 150 were present for duty. The senior officer, Captain Henry Young, was temporarily detached to the 4th Brigade of the 2nd Division as inspector general. In his absence, command of the 2nd Rhode Island Regiment devolved upon 22-year-old 1st Lieutenant Elisha Hunt Rhodes. As excited as he was by this opportunity, Elisha worried that the army might "think me too young" for such responsibility, but nevertheless believed that "if everything works out well I shall climb higher." [39]

The evening of June 4 was the last night that the original 2nd Rhode Island would camp together. There was much laughter and song, along with a lot of grim faces, some streaked with tears. Many men who were staying had written letters for their departing friends to give to family and loved ones back home. The evening was filled with awkward moments as the reenlisting men knew that they might not survive the war. Reverend Woodbury wrote, "And so they parted—some turning their faces joyfully to friends and kindred, the others to the stern realities of duty yet to be performed and the angry features of the foe!" [40] As a gift from the regiment, the tattered battle flags of the 2nd, each with its own story of glory and loss, were furled and given to the departing soldiers. No honor could have been higher than to escort these banners back to Rhode Island. The next morning, only one tenth of the original 2nd remained in the field.

A week later, Providence shone with its "brightest holiday aspect." [41] Flags were everywhere and crowds lined the streets hoping to catch a glimpse of the returning heroes. At a reception in the men's honor, Governor Smith introduced former Colonel Horatio Rogers to thunderous applause. "The dear old tattered flag, never once disgraced, and wreathed all round with glory, will be sacredly preserved and handed down to posterity, who will gaze upon it and tell the story of your deeds, as they will that of your revolutionary fathers," proclaimed a beaming Rogers. [42]

In spite of all the pomp and reverie, there was still a war being fought, and on June 10, the *Providence Journal* speculated that the 2nd might continue as a detached battalion, perhaps on provost, or prison duty. "Captain Young, we are informed, is the senior captain, and will have command of the battalion, if he leaves the staff service in which he is engaged. If he does not, Adjutant Rhodes will be the senior officer." [43] This was already old news to the army but for the first time the citizenry of Rhode Island was hearing of this up-and-coming young officer, Elisha Rhodes of Pawtuxet Village. For the time being the 2nd would remain intact and in the field as "a distinct and separate, if only a battalion organization." [44] Due to this reorganization, many of the remaining men were rewarded by a raise in rank and pay. Among these promotions was that of "Captain" Elisha Rhodes, to be made official on June 26.

****

The week following the fighting at Cold Harbor passed uncomfortably as sharpshooters on both sides preyed upon unsuspecting targets. As mortars pounded their lines, the two armies spent their days and nights caring for wounded and burying their dead. James Sheldon and the 50th Georgia camped across a field from a Union fort nestled on the edge of the woods. "A battery of our mortar guns was opposite the fort. The third evening (June 6) this battery opened up, it was a most beautiful sight to see mortars going through the night," remembered one officer in the 50th. Colonel Simms' adjutant, brother Ben, was hoping that the Union general would renew the fight. [45] "I do want Grant to make his best efforts on Richmond and then if he fails I want him to retire and let our army have some rest. I think he is certainly one of the most inhuman wretches now living. He is willing to make any sacrifice in blood that will gain him laurels." [46] Revealing how little he really knew about the Union general, Simms said, "I think that he will make a grander failure than McClellan." [47]

On Monday, June 11, elements of the Army of the Potomac began moving to the rear, and word quickly spread through the ranks that there would be no further attempts to break Lee's lines at Cold Harbor. But the Union men, understanding Grant, did not see this movement as a retreat. Once again, Grant's army would be crossing the Chickahominy and James Rivers in pursuit of Lee. The army moved "almost in complete secrecy," [48] but Confederate scouts eventually caught wind of it, convincing Lee that Grant was about to launch an attack on Richmond from the east.

Twenty miles south of Richmond is the city of Petersburg, Virginia. The city of 18,000, half which were slaves, served as the crossroads of five rail lines. About 10 miles to the northeast of Petersburg was City Point, on the banks of the James River. Grant began his Petersburg operations on June 11. Making this plan all the more appealing was the Union presence at City Point, where Grant could off-load ships full of men and supplies onto railcars, sending them directly into his lines. Taking the lightly defended Petersburg would not carry with it the glory of a victory at Richmond, but Petersburg's fall would be the demise of the Confederate capital all the same. If all went according to plan, the James would be the last major river the Army of the Potomac would cross in anger.

On the morning of June 12, the men of James Sheldon's 50th Georgia got a surprise. Said one soldier, "we woke up one day, at the end of a week, and found the enemy gone, they had withdrawn, and were moving toward Petersburg." [49] Just as they had raced to the Wilderness, Spotsylvania and Cold Harbor, the two armies were once again moving south and east where Grant would determine the final destination. Due to Bryan's illness, James Sheldon's brigade joined the pursuit under the command of Colonel James Simms. Some of the other Georgia men explored part of the vacated Union position. One man recalled, "some of our men, went over the [Union] fort, there was not much damage done to it...In a wheatfield there were green spots where men had been buried two years before. I saw two skulls," said one man. [50] On the 16th, the 50th Georgia left Frayser's Farm and began marching in the direction of Petersburg, reaching there on the 18th. Arriving at Petersburg "the enemy made an attack, which was very easily repulsed. The brigade occupied this line until the 23rd," remembered Colonel James Simms. [51]

Simms, 27 years old of Covington, Georgia, had been an excellent soldier. He had enlisted in the 53rd Georgia Infantry as a captain on May 12, 1862, and on October 8, became its colonel. Simms made his presence felt immediately, bravely leading his regiment at Fredericksburg two months later and capturing a United States flag at Salem Church the following May. He led his regiment at Gettysburg and Chattanooga before being wounded during the bloody assault at Ft. Sanders. As the Army of Northern Virginia began a grueling march southward, young Simms was at the helm of his brigade of Georgians.

Colonel James Simms

During the late afternoon of Monday, June 13, Captain Elisha Rhodes' regiment and the 6th Corps began crossing the Chickahominy over pontoon bridges, arriving on the north bank of the James the next day. On Wednesday, the 2nd Rhode Island crossed the James River above Ft. Powhatan.

The following morning, the Army of the Potomac approached the James River as if it was the gateway to the promised land. "As we began to descend from the high lands toward the plain, on which stands the little cluster of houses called, in Southern fashion, Charles City, we beheld, in the distance, the James river, lying in all its loveliness, spreading widely between its banks. A magnificent prospect opened before us," wrote a man in the 6th Corps. [52] From the Rapidan to the

James, the two armies had clashed for over a month, leaving a trail of death in their wake. But the Union Army's tactics were as much of a mystery to Captain Rhodes as they had been after the battle at Sharpsburg, Maryland, almost two years earlier. "When will wonders cease. Thirty-six hours ago the Army of the Potomac was within nine miles of Richmond, and now we are forty miles distant," he wrote. [53]

Having quick-marched there with "all dispatch," the 18th Corps was the first of Grant's army to arrive at Petersburg on June 15, and was joined in the evening by two divisions of Hancock's 2nd Corps. But Grant's armies failed him once again when Hancock was unable to get his corps into action. The small Confederate force at Petersburg wasted no time, and General Pierre Beauregard, commanding that department, continued constructing fortifications to protect the city from what was certain to be another bloodbath. Although Grant was angered by his army's lack of tenacity, he was heartened by a telegram from Lincoln, saying, "I begin to see it. You will succeed. God bless you all." [54]

Captain Rhodes' 2nd Rhode Island spent the pleasant evening of June 16 on the north bank of the James River near Charles City. Waiting their turn to cross over a newly laid pontoon bridge, the men slept, relaxed and, most enjoyably, bathed and washed clothes in the cool waters of the James River. The following evening, the regiment took its place in line and marched across the river. After halting briefly for breakfast, Elisha and his regiment put in a full day's march in the stifling heat and choking dust. The 2nd was only three miles from the outskirts of Petersburg when they ran into the first of Lee's defenses. The footsore 6th Corps rested for the night, knowing that morning might bring battle. Throughout Friday the 17th, Grant continued his assaults on the thin Confederate's lines. Occasionally, Beauregard's line would break and an end to the Confederacy appeared to be at hand, but confusion among Grant's generals prevented the Army of the Potomac from charging through. Time was running out on Grant's hope for a quick, crippling blow upon the city.

Sergeant James Sheldon's 50th Georgia was already closing in on Petersburg, having made a hard march from Cold Harbor. Not fully knowing Grant's intentions, Lee could not simply outrace him to Petersburg; he needed to cling tightly to Grant's advancing army should it suddenly start for Richmond. One man in James' division remembered, "The march started out as a forced one, but before daylight it had gotten almost to a run…When we got four miles from Petersburg we saw soldiers in front of us jump on the [rail]cars to Petersburg, but then heard that Grant was approaching the town. [We] were in the front division of the army. We expected the train to come back but it didn't, and we heard no firing at Petersburg."[55]

As Simms' Brigade camped about six miles from Richmond, Adjutant Ben Simms wrote, "Our army is still in good spirits and in very good health. We are getting good rest and plenty to eat. I mean by rest undisturbed sleep. Man can stand almost anything if he gets plenty to eat and sleep enough."[56]

Reaching the city limits of Petersburg around sunrise on June 18, the Army of Northern Virginia found the city to be anything but evacuated. Filthy and soaking with sweat, James Sheldon, Peter McGlashan, Gussie Brack and the other veterans basked in the last hero's welcome they would ever receive. An officer of the 50th Georgia said, "On the streets were ladies of every walk in life, some waving banners and handkerchiefs, some clapping their hands and giving words of cheer as the soldiers came by with their swinging step, their clothes looking as if they had just swum the river…If Richmond had become famous through the courage and loyalty of her daughters, Petersburg was equally entitled to share the glories of her older sister, Richmond." [57]

Pierre Beauregard sighed in relief. Not since 1st Manassas and Shiloh had so much responsibility been put upon him, and his force of 3,000 men could hardly be expected to fend off Grant's coming onslaught. But by the morning of Saturday, June 18, as reinforcements poured in, Beauregard's defense of Petersburg had grown to about 50,000—the Union army numbered nearly 90,000.

Grant had waited long enough, if every detail had yet to be finalized, so be it; today was the day. Lee arrived with the bulk of the Army of Northern Virginia, convinced that Richmond was not Grant's objective. With every passing hour, Lee's lines were stiffened. James and Elisha spent the morning in an anxious state of relaxation as only veterans could. James was awed by the sight of Beauregard as he inspected the breastworks with his staff. He and the other men heard that Beauregard's men had never been in a fight before and wondered how they'd stand under fire.

Elisha and the men of the 2nd checked their weapons, filled their cartridge boxes and canteens, and waited for some long overdue mail. The newswalkers said their corps would be held in reserve and the men were glad for it.

Lt. Thorndike "TJ" Smith

Elisha remembered, "About noon I was standing with Lieutenant Thorndike J. Smith on a little knoll in rear of our works when we saw his father who is a private in the regiment and acting as Postmaster coming across the plain in our rear… Our cook carrying some pork, hard bread and coffee was with him, and as the bullets whistled past his head would duck and dodge. I was laughing at his strange antics when Lieutenant Smith asked me to tell his father not to come to the front again until dark. Before I could reply I heard a *thud* and saw Lieutenant Smith falling. I caught him in my arms and called for a stretcher. He was shot through the back, the bullet penetrating his lung. I sent him to the hospital, and we fear he will die. He is a fine fellow and a brave man and is to me like my own brother." [58]

Grant's assaults on the morning of the 18th were disastrous as brigades moved out piecemeal or not at all. Attacks went off hours behind schedule while generals idly waited for orders. During the afternoon, James and the 50th took their positions in the trenches with Beauregard's men. "We had been in the breastworks only a few minutes when Grant's men came surging across the field; they lay down and did not retreat. This was near sundown; no one in the breastworks was hurt. The new troops (Beauregard's) expressed delight at having old soldiers with them. Night came on but the Union men had not retreated." [59]

Under the cover of darkness, Colonel Simms was ordered to move his Georgians further up the right of Lee's line. Simms oversaw the construction of his brigade's defenses, stating, "The enemy had thrown up works within sixty yards of ours, and when we were placed there the works were incomplete and we were compelled to complete them under incessant fire of musketry and artillery, and on some parts of the line the works were begun without any protection whatever." [60] An officer in James' regiment remembered just how frightening the work was, saying, "Just as we got there a terrific fire opened on us from the whole line of battle not seventy-five yards away, but we were lying flat behind a small slope. And so we were safe." [61] Words of encouragement were hard to muster, but Colonel McGlashan talked calmly and reassuringly to the men of the 50th, reminding them how bravely they had always performed under fire. Eventually the firing died away and with his Scottish brogue, the colonel ordered his regiment to its feet. Throughout the night, the men dug, piling up earth to protect them during the next morning's fight.

About four in the afternoon, Captain Rhodes' division was ordered to attack a line of works in front of them. Through waves of minie balls and artillery shells, the men pushed forward, only to be driven back with heavy loss. The 2nd somehow managed to hold on and form a line about half its original distance from the Confederate works, and immediately began digging. After dark, the regiment's left flank was attacked but presented a rigorous defense. The Confederates were repulsed. For the first time, Elisha witnessed black troops in combat and was impressed by what he saw. Amid constant shelling, half of the men of the 2nd tried to sleep while the others stood watch, bracing for another attack. Elisha thought how elusive Petersburg was, just as Richmond had been twice before. "Petersburg is only about two miles away, but yet it is afar off." [62]

At first light, Sergeant James Sheldon cautiously peered over the works, gazing in disbelief. Throughout the night, less than 100 yards away, Grant's men had dug their own trenches. All along Lee's entrenchments, men gripped their rifles, waiting for Grant's thousands to come charging out of their trenches with their new bayonets gleaming. An hour passed, and then another, as curious looks expressing disbelief went up and down the Confederate line. Could it be that Grant wasn't coming? By mid-morning they had their answer. There would be no more Cold Harbors—the siege of Petersburg had begun. During the three days of fighting at Petersburg, Grant's losses were 1,700 killed, 8,500 wounded and 1,200 missing or captured. The losses of the Army of Northern Virginia are unknown, but believed to be significantly less. Five men in the 2nd Rhode Island were wounded, while the 50th Georgia lost one man killed and three wounded. In one month of fighting, Grant's army had lost nearly 60,000 men. The North was aghast. But Lee was kept continuously on the defensive and a bold strike, a la Chancellorsville, had never become an option.

The two armies faced each other on the northeast and east sides of the city in a line that stretched five miles. Anywhere along the line where there was a slight crest or hill, artillerists posted batteries and built elaborate forts. "Our division is nearer the city than any other part of the line," wrote Ben Simms. [63] Raw materials for these earthen works was scarce and nothing was wasted in their construction. The bodies of some Confederate dead were used in one part of the Union line as they were smothered with dirt above ground and then had logs piled on them. Union soldiers explained that the practice was merely an innovative method of burying the dead. The trenches and forts which paralleled each other were often less than 400 feet apart. Simms recalled, "there has been nothing but artillery and sharp shooting going on between the lines. Every day some are killed or wounded." [64] The weather was getting quite warm, and Simms observed, the "roads are dusty and will be very disagreeable without rain pretty soon." [65]

Inside the trenches one could fully appreciate their engineering. On the wall facing the enemy, logs were stacked up, creating a solid barrier, and dirt was piled against it to secure the logs. These trenches were several feet wide, following zigzag patterns which confounded enemy artillerists. At various points the trenches had rooms constructed as bomb shelters or "bombproofs." [66] A few yards in front of the trenches were even more impressive defenses. A six-foot-deep by ten-foot-wide ditch was dug, and its dirt was piled in front of it. Mixing logs into this dirt pile created a mound eight-feet-high and twelve-feet thick. Topping off this mound were sandbags packed end to end, except for the occasional rifle slit. A hundred or so yards closer to the enemy, clusters of felled trees with their sharpened branches presented a nasty barrier. Heavy logs lashed with pointed sticks aimed menacingly at the enemy's line. Because of their close proximity to each other, both sides recognized the strengths of the other's works. At one point along Lee's line, slightly to the southeast of Petersburg, was Cemetery Hill, which boasted one of his most formidable forts, Elliot's Salient.

If there was safety in the trenches, there was little else this subterranean existence could offer. The forts were like ovens and temperature often reached 110 degrees. Dust was *everywhere*. It was powdery with a texture of "soiled flour," [67] and one Union soldier found that so much dust got into his mouth that "you do not want your teeth to touch each other." [68] There was also the constant, sickening, stench of unburied dead baking in the sun.

In the trenches of both armies, boredom and sickness set in almost immediately. Hours of letter writing, card games and smoking were never enough to fill the day. And there was the relentless firing of sharpshooters. "Seven of our men were killed by sharpshooters [during the first four days of the siege], two were officers. We couldn't dig the breastworks out in the open, but had to dig from the cannon pits out. All day, the first day, the sharpshooters kept up heavy fire. A man who was not a sharpshooter (a spotter) would look for a head showing, and then the sharpshooter would shoot," recalled an officer in James' 50th Georgia. [69] One afternoon a lieutenant colonel of a South Carolina regiment, drank himself into a stupor and decided to go for a walk. Before anyone could stop him, he began walking across an open field. James and his friends "strained their eyes watching him, and bullets peppered all around him, but he was not hit at all. He went up a gradual ascent and disappeared over the top," a man in the 50th laughingly remembered. [70]

Elisha was also witness to the *weirdness* of Petersburg. One afternoon, a man in a Massachusetts regiment showed him a wooden headboard he had carved into a headstone for himself as a joke. The following day the man was killed.

About two weeks into the siege, the Georgians decided to hold a revival in the rear of the lines. The event was a rousing success and afterwards James and some of the other men went into the woods for a small prayer meeting. The night seemed magical in the Virginia forest and the moon provided enough light for the men to read their Bibles. It also provided just enough light for a sharpshooter to kill one of them.

Once again, picket duty became an envied assignment and went a long way toward breaking the monotony. The pickets themselves promptly made the usual arrangements with their counterparts to avoid trouble with one another. Men would routinely let the enemy know when officers were around, as everyone understood that some officers still held the strange notion that pickets should be shooting at each other.

The trenches became feeding grounds for germs as discarded food scraps, human excrement and unburied dead invited disease. Yet somehow, the men of both armies remained relatively healthy. Lemons and fresh vegetables were occasionally available and the dry summer kept illness at bay—boredom was a more difficult problem. Some Union soldiers discovered that firing their ramrods produced a whirring, fluttering sound in flight and the practice became a favorite pastime. Abandoned ramrods were in seemingly endless supply, and a few men developed a real talent for the sport. The most accomplished ramrod shooters would occasionally hold impromptu clinics, during which some unsuspecting Confederate would become an unwitting participant.

Another group of Union men, the coal-mining 48th Pennsylvania, envisioned digging a tunnel under Elliot Salient, filling it with black powder, and blowing it up. Others had simpler aspirations, hoping only that their letters might reach home. The process of mailing a letter was simple. A soldier, after finishing his letter writing, would make an envelope and tie it to a small stick, passing it from man to man along the line of trenches until it found a postmaster. Incredibly, most letters reached their destinations.

Nighttime in the trenches was more lively. The heat relented and after a day of being peppered by sharpshooters, a soldier could blow off steam by squeezing off a few rounds into the darkness. Some regiments had standing orders to fire a designated quota of shots per day, resulting in sporadic heavy firing along the Petersburg lines throughout the night.

As June came to a close the newswalkers talked of the war on other fronts. Union General David Hunter's force of 8,500 won an important victory in the Shenandoah Valley. At Lynchburg, Hunter ran into Confederate General Early's 2nd Corps which had been sent west to stop him. Unable to storm the city, Hunter decided to retreat.

In Georgia, Sherman continued to position himself for his showdown with Confederate General Joe Johnston. On June 10, in Mississippi, the Union Army had been sent reeling by a force half its size, led by the cavalry of General Nathan Bedford Forrest. At Ft. Sumter in Charleston Harbor, where it all began, the Confederates replaced their ragged flag for the umpteenth time, refusing to buckle under the relentless Union artillery bombardment. On the high seas, the pride of the Confederate navy, the C.S.S. *Alabama*, captained by the late Paul Semmes' brother Raphael, was sunk off the coast of France by the U.S.S. *Kearsarge*. Another symbol of the Confederacy was gone.

Excited by Grant's progress, Lincoln couldn't resist getting a firsthand glimpse of Lee's Army of Northern Virginia, trapped in front of Petersburg. On June 20, he sailed down to City Point to meet with Grant and Meade, and later toured the lines around Petersburg on horseback.

Then suddenly, the war seemed to go quiet. The fighting of May and June, with its merciless and relentless marches under a murderous sun and choking dust, had been beyond the scope of anything anyone could have imagined in 1861. Yet somehow, in spite of tens of thousands of deaths and untold human suffering, the war was still not over. In fact, without much fanfare, Jubal Early's Confederates opened the month of July by flirting with the town of Harper's Ferry and gazing upon the Potomac River. Beyond it, only sixty miles downriver, was the lightly defended capital of the United States.

The men in the trenches celebrated the nation's 88th birthday in very different moods. The morale of the Army of Northern Virginia was surprisingly good. As bleak as things looked at first glance, many of Lee's men were convinced that once Johnston had destroyed the arrogant Sherman in Georgia, his army would unite with theirs, turning the tables on Grant. In the 6th Corps of the Army of the Potomac the atmosphere was optimistic, even festive. Captain Elisha Rhodes enjoyed the National Salutes and then dined with his fellow officers in a feast of oysters, ham, potatoes, chicken, canned turkey, bread, tapioca pudding and apple pie. The enjoyment of the quiet afternoon meal was made complete with cold lemonade and cigars. By contrast, James Sheldon and the 50th Georgia ate whatever meat and cornbread was available. The day before, Ben Simms wrote to his sister saying that tomorrow (Independence Day) "the Yankees will amuse themselves by shelling the city…they will rain them down in torrents."[71] Everyone hoped this would be the last 4th of July of the war.

14

EARLY WAS LATE

Captain Elisha Rhodes looked at his new cap. The cross insignia of the 6th Corps had been changed from white to red, indicating his new assignment. The 2nd Rhode Island found a new home with the 3rd Brigade of the 1st Division, which included their old friends the 37th Massachusetts, along with the 5th Wisconsin and the 82nd and 119th Pennsylvania. Commanding this brigade was Oliver Edwards, the 29-year-old colonel of the 37th Massachusetts. Edwards had led the 37th at Fredericksburg and Gettysburg and made a name for himself at Spotsylvania. He had also commanded a brigade during the New York City draft riots. The first order of business for this new brigade was to squash any ideas Jubal Early had about attacking Washington. The Confederate general had crossed the Potomac River near Sharpsburg, Maryland, on July 6.

Elisha and the 2nd Rhode Island marched to City Point where they boarded a steamer on July 10, bound for Washington. The voyage was as an unexpected pleasure. The views from the ship's rails were so breathtaking that the tired soldiers thought them "too pleasant to sleep." [1] As they passed Fortress Monroe sailors in their dress whites could be seen on parade. "I never saw a more beautiful sight," Elisha decided. Many of the Rhode Island men got seasick, but Elisha, being an "old salt," roamed the ship to his heart's content. [2] He enjoyed the company of the ship's captain who, to his amazement, had known his father. Storytelling and smoking filled the hours, and Rhodes wished he could "…prolong [the voyage] for a month." [3] But at midnight of the 12th their transport gently glided into the 6th Street Wharf at Washington. Gunfire could clearly be heard in the distance.

Captain Elisha Rhodes and his 2nd Rhode Island Regiment stepped onto the docks at 6th Street. How things had changed since a wide-eyed Elisha Rhodes first visited Washington in 1861. He never could have imagined returning as a commanding officer. Even more telling was his refusal of an escort to Ft. Stevens where Early was expected to attack. The cosmopolitan Rhodes politely explained that he knew the city well and that a guide wasn't necessary.

Jubal Early had every reason to feel good. He was not easy to get along with and lacked the human touch of a Lee or a Sedgwick. He was described as a "snarling and stooped" man. [4] Blunt and sarcastic, he was disliked by many of his peers and drove his soldiers hard. In spite of his shortcomings, no one doubted his devotion to his army and to the Confederate cause. On June 27, Early began a sideshow in the Shenandoah Valley, hoping to divert some of Grant's attention and manpower away from Petersburg. While he hoped for success, he never really expected to achieve any important strategic gains. On June 18, Union General Hunter's force of 10,000 had attacked Confederate General John Breckinridge's 2,000 men at Lynchburg, intending to take or destroy the railroad junction there. What Hunter didn't know was that part of Early's 10,000 man force had already arrived there as reinforcements. Hunter quickly realized that he was in for much more than he had bargained for and ended his operations at Lynchburg, withdrawing into the safety of West Virginia. Suddenly the road to Washington, defended to a large degree by clerks, misfits and invalids, was wide open, blocked only by a series of forts that ringed the city.

On July 11, Early peered through his field glasses from a hill north of Washington. What he saw was a sight few Confederate soldiers had yet seen in three years of fighting—the dome of the United States Capitol. The citizens of Washington were in a panic and the city teetered on the brink of chaos. Drawing close to the city's defenses, Early ordered his sharpshooters to find perches from which they could fire into the Union forts. He sent out skirmishers as his artillerists rolled their pieces onto whatever high ground could be found. "Old Jube" decided to launch his attack at first light of the next morning.

Throughout the afternoon of the 11th, the Union 6th Corps disembarked at the wharves and began marching through the streets of Washington in Early's direction. As "long lines of tanned men in ragged, dusty, sun-bleached uniforms were coming ashore," the civilians of the city barricaded their windows and sought the safety of their cellars. [5] At one point, a venturesome man became curious enough to pop his head out of a window after hearing the pounding of feet and wagons squeaking past his home. This was not Early's dreaded raiders. "It is the old Sixth Corps!... Those are the men who took Marye's Heights!" became the buzz throughout the city. [6]

People emerged from their homes in droves, pushing tobacco into the hands of the Rhode Islanders as they passed. The women ladled out cool drinks of water for the thirsty men. As the men approached Ft. Stevens, the firing grew louder and the hearts of the 2nd fluttered as they caught a glimpse of the fort they had built three years earlier and named in honor of their beloved first colonel, John Slocum. As they got closer to the fort, they saw a man who looked like President Lincoln on the parapet. In fact, the resemblance was downright uncanny. To the rear of the fort sat a carriage containing a party which included someone who looked an awful lot like the First Lady. Quizzical eyes dashed back and forth for a few seconds before the goose bumps set in as the awestruck men realized that this *was* the president and his wife. The 6th Corps' commander, General Horatio Wright, was at the fort when the President's party arrived and he politely invited Lincoln to join him on the parapet to get a better few of the action. Assuming the President would decide the risk was not worth taking, Wright was stunned when Lincoln jumped at the opportunity. It was the first time that Lincoln had seen men being killed and he was deeply moved by what was happening before him.

The towering Lincoln was visible to Early's sharpshooters, who probably couldn't believe that this giant on the parapet was Abraham Lincoln. A man standing only a few feet from Lincoln was shot and minie balls buzzed all around. In spite of Wright's repeated requests to the President to seek shelter, Lincoln wouldn't budge. Finally, Wright threatened to have armed soldiers escort him off the parapet if he refused to leave on his own. Lincoln finally relented, much to Wright's relief.

****

"July 12th came bright and glorious," wrote an officer in the 6th Corps, but General Early's day was beginning to sour. [7] He'd received a message during the night that part of the Union 6th Corps was headed his way. This worried him, but not enough to call off his attack. It wasn't until his sharpshooters spotted the Greek Cross on the caps of their adversaries that he realized these men were not clerks and invalids, but 6th Corps men. Early faced both a military and public opinion nightmare should his little army be crushed or captured at Washington. The fight in front of Ft. Stevens was short but intense. Elisha wrote, "Our column passed through the gate of Ft. Stevens, and on the parapet I saw President Lincoln standing looking at the troops... We marched in line of battle into a peach orchard in front of Ft. Stevens, and here the fight began. For a short time it was warm work, but as the President and many ladies were looking at us every man tried to do his best. Just at dark I was ordered to take my regiment to the right of the line which I did at a double quick. I never saw the 2nd R.I. behave better." [8]

Confederate prisoners later said, that when the Union line in front of the fort refused to break, they knew they were in for a fight. "The Greek Cross of our corps told the story," Elisha proudly boasted. [9] The 6th Corps reportedly lost 200 men killed and wounded, while the 2nd Rhode Island Regiment lost two men wounded. In the darkness, Early's men began heading for Rockville, Maryland, and the fords of the Potomac River, along the way retrieving over seventy wounded Confederate prisoners from a field hospital. As Early crossed the river in retreat, Washington's citizens breathed easier. Their city had been spared from Confederate capture by mere minutes. Elisha quipped, "Early was Late."[10]

In spite of Early's setback at Ft. Stevens, the affair was quite an embarrassment to the Union braintrust. "General Lee is demonstrating to the Yankee nation that their modern Ulysses is not quite up to all the tricks of war," observed Adjutant Ben Simms.[11]

On July 19, it rained for the first time in over two months. It had been oppressively hot and the crops were suffering, and "The dust was excessively annoying," according to Ben Simms. But now the roads were a bit less of a miserable trek.[12] Colonel James Simms recalled, "On the morning of the 23rd [I] received orders to move, and set out for the north side of the James."[13] For the last five weeks, the young lawyer from Covington, Georgia, had watched over his brigade as its men manned the trenches and took turns guarding the Weldon Railroad that connected Petersburg to Weldon, North Carolina, 81 miles to the south. But it wasn't bad duty, as it allowed James and the other men of the 50th Georgia to escape the trenches, if only for a few hours. One officer in the 50th recalled, "Stray shells came there occasionally, but we had a good rest."[14] Colonel Simms held a harsher view of his brigade's tenure at Petersburg, saying, "The number of casualties occurring in the brigade at this place will give some idea of the difficulties which had to be contended against. There were 15 killed and 31 wounded, most of which proved fatal."[15] Another soldier described life in the trenches, recalling, "Another annoyance was the enemy's sharpshooters, armed with globe-sighted rifles. These guns had a telescope on top of the barrel, and objects at a distance could be distinctly seen. Brush screened their rifle pits, and while they could see plainly any object above our works, we could not see them. A head uncautiously raised above the line, would be sure to get a bullet in or near it."[16]

"During the time we were making and strengthening the works a pathetic incident occurred that shall never be effaced from my memory," Colonel Peter McGlashan recalled from his time at Petersburg. A boy, only 16 years old, would struggle to keep up during the severe forced marches. The colonel kept an eye on the young soldier and whenever it seemed as if the boy could go no further "I would dismount and make him ride until rested and strong again…Always in his place in the fighting line, I would look for him at the close of an engagement and feel relieved to find him unhurt."

One afternoon, while at work in the trenches the boy was sent to the rear for some purpose. Obviously daydreaming, he sprang out of the earthworks, becoming a target for dozens of sharpshooters who immediately fired at him. James Sheldon and Peter McGlashan watched as bullets tore up the ground all around him, until he fell forward, shot through the back. The men rushed out of trenches and brought him back into their lines. "Calling for a litter we laid him gently on it; he was fatally wounded and dying. Turning his eyes toward me he made a motion as if he would speak. Bending down over him I said: 'Willie, what can I do for you?' Making a last effort he threw his arms round my neck, saying: 'Colonel, I love you.' It was his last words, as he died on the way to the hospital," said McGlashan. [17] To fatherless young men and boys in the 50th such as Gussie Brack and James Sheldon, Colonel Peter McGlashan filled that role. In turn, James looked after young Gussie who had just turned 18 years old.

In spite of the misery of the Petersburg trenches, where the men were issued a quarter of a pound of meat per day, the mood of James Sheldon and the other men was surprisingly upbeat. A man in James' division said it best: "As gloomy as our situation looked, there was no want of confidence in the officers and the troops. The rank and file of the South had never considered a condition of failure. They felt their cause to be sacred…the South could not fail." [18]

But something in Petersburg wasn't quite right. The newswalkers talked of a mine being dug by the enemy and there were rumors that Sheridan's cavalry was heading north to pursue Early, or to strike at Richmond. In fact, the coal miners of the 48th Pennsylvania had finally gotten their wish and spent weeks tunneling toward the Confederate lines, one shovel of earth at a time.

To draw attention away from the tunneling, Hancock's 2nd Corps, along with two divisions of Sheridan's cavalry, crossed over to the north side of the James River under the cover of darkness on July 26 and 27. The 50th Georgia and Simms' Brigade, having crossed the river on the 23rd at Chaffin's Bluff with the rest of Kershaw's Division, were waiting for them. "The enemy advanced, but the major-general (Anderson) disposed of the troops in such manner as to extend the line to such an extent as to make them believe that we had so great a force as to deter him from an attack; and thus he delayed the enemy until reinforcements came to our aid," recalled Colonel James Simms. [19]

Sergeant James Sheldon was forced to endure a bombardment like he'd never before experienced. Along a little known bend in the James River, 15 miles southeast of Richmond called Deep Bottom, the 50th came under attack by the United States Navy's gunboats. As massive shot and shells exploded around them a soldier in the 50th described the ordeal, saying, "We dug breastworks about a half mile from the river, and the shelling was from the gunboats. Gunboat shelling is more severe than any other, it tore up the ground a good deal but did not damage the men." An officer walked among the men, insisting that, "No two shells ever strike the same place." [20] Throughout the night of the 26th, the men of the 50th withstood the brutal pounding.

In the morning, the shelling ceased but Simms' men awoke to another crisis as enemy skirmishers advanced in the direction of his brigade's camp. "I was ordered to send out two regiments to drive them back. Colonel McGlashan was sent out with the 10th and 50th Georgia Regiments, with which he attacked their line, and succeeded in capturing the greater part of the enemy's skirmish line, which had so advanced, and for the skillful manner in which he managed to accomplish this he deserves credit," Simms proudly insisted. [21] An officer in the 50th recalled the coolness with which Colonel McGlashan led his regiment, saying, "[He] saw the enemy skirmishers advancing on our right and ordered me to take three companies and go to meet them. We ran, fired into their flank, and they retreated. The colonel soon followed, charged into their flank and took twenty prisoners, who were all Germans and couldn't speak English. It is very demoralizing to receive fire on your flank. After they retreated we formed a skirmish line, advanced to the woods and made breastworks of fence rails. The enemy skirmishers were across a field in another wood. They kept up fire all day, if any of us stood up we were exposed." [22] The 50th did not suffer a single casualty in this engagement and on Friday the 29th the regiment recrossed the James River and camped on the Telegraph Road near Chester Station, as it began making its way back to Petersburg.

****

On the morning of July 30, the earth shook. A Confederate officer reported, "The explosion took place at 4:45 AM …The 'Crater' made by eight thousand pounds of gun powder was one hundred and thirty-five feet long, ninety-seven feet broad and thirty feet deep. Two hundred and seventy-eight men were buried in the debris." [23] Grant intended to blow a hole in the Confederate line by tunneling beneath the Confederate fort. But the attack sputtered and failed, and Grant stated later that it was "the saddest affair I have witnessed in the war." [24] When compared to the killings in the Wilderness or at Cold Harbor, the casualties were not excessive and newspaper reports had numbed America to a great extent. But when examined in their own right, the casualties that resulted from the disaster of the Crater were staggering. There were 3,800 Union men killed, wounded or missing. Confederate casualties were estimated at about 1,500. Grant returned to his siege operation.

August opened with James and Elisha separated by 140 miles. James and the 100 or so men of the 50th Georgia rested in camp near Chester, Virginia, while Elisha and the 2nd Rhode Island, slightly over 300 strong, were enduring the most intense heat of the war at Frederick, Maryland. For the first few days of the new month, Elisha relaxed in camp or went sightseeing in Frederick despite occasional thermometer readings of 130 degrees in the sun. James spent his days near Chester, alternately resting and guarding the Richmond & Petersburg Railroad. The newswalkers reported of Bryan's resignation and replacement, while another rumor spread through the Confederate trenches that Grant had been killed.

****

Lincoln was infuriated. The disaster at Petersburg, coupled with Jubal Early's Washington raid, were intolerable embarrassments to the war effort. Although the situation at Petersburg remained a stalemate, Lincoln and Grant agreed that something had to be done about Early. First, David Hunter had to go. The man for the job, Grant insisted, was Phil Sheridan and his world-class cavalry. Early must be hunted "to the death,"[25] demanded the president. Furthermore, if Early's army thrived on the Shenandoah's bounty of farms and crops, then they also must be destroyed. Sheridan would take the war directly to the civilian population of the Shenandoah and its "sacred soil," [26] as some Virginians were known to boast. On Sunday, August 7, General Philip Sheridan was given command of over 48,000 men, designated as the Army of the Shenandoah. Sheridan assembled his army near Harper's Ferry and Halltown, West Virginia, and by Wednesday the Army of the Shenandoah began moving 25 miles southwest toward Winchester, Virginia, in the northern Shenandoah Valley, searching for "Old Jube."

On Thursday, August 4, 1864, the 2nd Rhode Island was reborn. While camped along the Monocacy River, Captain Elisha Rhodes received word from 6th Corps Headquarters that the 2nd would remain an independent entity and not be merged with another regiment. Elisha told Rhode Island authorities that the 2nd would be "the same as other regiments although not so large." [27] At nine o' clock the following evening the 6th Corps began moving toward Harpers Ferry to join Sheridan. The Rhode Islanders, accustomed to being first or last, took its position in the column as the rear guard.

The men of the 2nd awoke on Saturday, shivering and soaked to the bone after being forced to bivouac in a steady rain. After fording the Monocacy, the regiment marched on an eight-foot-wide towpath along a canal running parallel to the Potomac River. The path was hot and the pounding of thousands of feet stirred the dust. The next day, the 2nd Rhode Island marched into Harpers Ferry and the newswalkers quickly told them the story of the new commander—word was that Sheridan was a short but tough-looking fellow.

That same day, one man in Sheldon's brigade wrote home saying, "We are camped on the Richmond and Petersburg Railroad, five miles from Petersburg, about one mile from the line of battle." [28]

In Richmond, President Davis was alerted to the large Union force assembling in West Virginia, and immediately recognized that Early was in trouble. But bringing his army back to the Richmond/Petersburg area would send a defeatist message throughout the Confederacy and allow Grant to have his way with the entire eastern theater. Lee ordered the cavalry division of Fitzhugh Lee and James Sheldon's division, commanded by Joe Kershaw, to begin operations east of the Blue Ridge Mountains. In overall command of this force would be 1st Corps commander, General Richard Anderson. Grant watched this movement carefully, not knowing if Anderson's entire corps was going north which, if true, would create a new set of problems.

On August 6, the 50th Georgia broke camp, and under the watchful eye of Colonel McGlashan, the regiment boarded a train at Chester Station. "When the orders came to march the men did not know where we were going, except that it was in the direction of Richmond," wrote an officer in James' division. [29] Upon arriving in Richmond, the men changed trains; their destination remaining a mystery. Rumors flew throughout the train and along its rooftops; the consensus was that they were headed for Fredericksburg. At the train station at Richmond they were greeted by a large crowd, mostly children. A lieutenant in the regiment commented to no one in particular that he wished they could *all* be children again.

The 50th Georgia disembarked at Gordonsville where they'd gone hungry two years earlier. James and the other men of Kershaw's Division learned they were being sent to the Valley to reinforce Early. As they marched through Culpeper Court House, they were saddened at the sight of a once-beautiful forest, now stripped bare by Grant's men who had camped there. The march continued for 75 miles through Chester Gap until around the 12th, when they reached Front Royal and the Shenandoah Valley.

One man in the division described their new surroundings, saying, "we were moved about one mile distant to a large spring, near the banks of the beautiful and now classic Shenandoah. After long and fatiguing marches, the soldiers here enjoyed a luxury long since denied them on account of their never ceasing activity. The delight of a bath, and in the pure, clear waters of the Shenandoah, was a luxury indeed." [30]

The struggle between Sheridan and Early was in full swing. On August 10, Sheridan had ventured from Harpers Ferry to Berryville, capturing or burning anything of military value. Four days later, upon learning of Anderson's move north, he began withdrawing back toward Harpers Ferry. Meanwhile, Early waited near Strasburg for Anderson. Captain Rhodes and the 2nd spent most of the four days in Milltown, near historic Winchester. The local citizenry were decidedly pro-Union which came as a pleasant surprise to the men who were given home cooked meals and in some cases, a room. Elisha, being an officer, was invited to dinner at the home of a Mr. Hollinsworth and his wife, where Mrs. Hollinsworth entertained the men at the piano. But even as Elisha and his friends were lost in wistful thought, skirmishing was already breaking out nearby.

On Saturday, August 13, the 2nd Rhode Island resumed its march, escorting a wagon train to a place by a stream near Middletown. "The valley is very beautiful," wrote Elisha. "A perfect garden." [31] Rumors spread that Early's army was assembling on the other side of a stream called Cedar Creek. The following Wednesday night the 2nd Rhode Island and the 6th Corps began a 24-hour march back to Harpers Ferry, as Sheridan waited to see what Early was up to. Elisha said he felt "so sleepy that I could not sit in my saddle."[32] He decided he needed to get away; anywhere where there wasn't a war going on would do. Philadelphia came to mind as he closed his eyes, and the next morning Captain Rhodes requested a five-day furlough.

****

The 50th Georgia's rest at Front Royal ended on Wednesday the 17th as Kershaw's Division was ordered north to Winchester to observe Sheridan's movements. "We have had rather a rough country to pass through, being very mountainous and rugged —we have not marched more than fifteen miles on any day," [33] Ben Simms told his sister. The regiment arrived the next day and enjoyed "two days near the old city which had become so dear to the hearts of all the old soldiers through the hospitality and kindness of her truly loyal people," recalled an officer. [34] Another man remembered, "We heard cannons in the distance toward Winchester...Cavalry had been sent to intercept us several times, but had been repulsed every time." [35] In spite of the impending clash with Sheridan, the veterans of the 50th took their lot in stride. They enjoyed whatever pleasures they could find, taking advantage of the cool waters of the Shenandoah River. "[We] camped on the banks for about a week. We had a fine time and went in swimming every day." [36]

While at Winchester, the men of James' brigade awoke one morning to a surprise. The brigadier general was gone again—this time for good. His brief return to the helm of the brigade was to put his affairs in order and use his influence to choose his successor. Bryan's battle with gout rendered him ineffective as a commander, and he finally requested an examination by his division's chief surgeon in mid-August to obtain a certificate of disability so that he could submit his resignation. To his relief the doctor concluded that Goode Bryan was "incapable of performing his duties."[37]

Two days after his examination, Bryan wrote a letter from his headquarters near Winchester to Secretary of War James Seddon, recommending Colonel Peter McGlashan as his successor. "Colonel McGlashan is a very gallant Officer, a good disciplinarian, a man of education and his appointment would in my opinion be highly satisfactory to the entire brigade."[38] But Colonel James Simms' brother and adjutant, Ben, saw things differently, saying, "I have heard that General Bryan has recommended another man, but it is none of old Bryan's business as to who shall succeed him in command... It was nothing but a mad fit that caused him to recommend another."[39] A petition circulated through the brigade's camps, urging Secretary Seddon to appoint Simms as Bryan's replacement. Ben claimed that with the exception of the 50th Georgia, the 10th, 51st and 53rd signed the document unanimously.

Bryan departed on the morning of August 21 and, at least temporarily, the command of the brigade was left in the hands of Colonel Simms. That same day, Kershaw's division left its camp near Winchester and began marching in the direction of Charlestown with Simms' Brigade in the lead. About seven miles into this march, James Sheldon's 50th Georgia encountered a brigade of Union cavalry. In a sharp contest the Georgians drove the enemy about six miles, where they encountered a division of Union cavalry strongly posted with artillery. Simms wisely halted his brigade and waited for Kershaw to bring up the remainder of the division. When it arrived an advance was ordered, prompting a hasty retreat of the enemy in the direction of Charlestown.

James' 50th Georgia and Simms' Brigade camped for the remainder of August near Charlestown, resting and taking their turn on the skirmish line. On the last day of August they returned to Winchester.

****

Elisha got his five-day furlough on August 21 and was offered a cavalry escort to the train depot at Harpers Ferry, but he would have to wait until the following day. Eager to begin his journey, he made his way to the train accompanied only by an armed orderly. A brush with enemy pickets nearly resulted in his capture but by Monday the 22nd Elisha was a free man in Philadelphia. From there he traveled to Camden, New Jersey, where he enjoyed the life of a civilian for a few days. On August 27, he returned to the 2nd at Harpers Ferry.

****

As September dawned, Phil Sheridan's Army of the Shenandoah seemed content to remain at Charlestown, where its presence was sufficient to keep Early at bay. Confederate General Richard Anderson received orders to begin moving some of his corps south to rejoin Lee at Petersburg, and it was crucial that his departure be concealed from the watchful eyes of Sheridan's scouts. But to the surprise of both generals, elements of the two armies collided near Berryville, Virginia. Simms' brigade of Georgians was quickly caught up in the action. Sergeant James Sheldon and the 50th left Winchester on September 3 and moved toward Berryville, arriving about dusk. In the twilight, Union troops suddenly appeared a few hundred yards in front of Simms' men. Colonel McGlashan hurried his regiment into line of battle, and in conjunction with the rest of the division, attacked furiously. Kershaw's attack was impossible to resist and "the enemy only held their position long enough to fire one round, then fled precipitately." As darkness closed the fight, James and his comrades slept upon the field that they had just won. The next morning the enemy was found dug in along a nearby road. "We remained in line confronting them [the] next day and night, and were then ordered to withdraw, and returned to Winchester," recalled Colonel Simms. [40]

As James marched along the hot, dusty roads toward Winchester, he witnessed Sheridan's new war firsthand. One officer in James' regiment wrote, "As we went along we found all the barns and mills burning, which made the men very angry and excited." [41] The fighting at Berryville continued the next day and the brigade suffered four killed and twenty-six wounded. The 50th lost one man, 24-year-old Sam Griffis of Company B, who was hit in the finger and required amputation.

On the second day of September, Adjutant Ben Simms wrote to his sister complaining about the worthlessness of the Confederate dollar. "If we only had Greenbacks we could get anything we wish to eat at what seems to be a Confederate trifling price. These people have no confidence in our permanently occupying the Valley, and they [are] certainly right, therefore a reasonable person cannot expect them to receive Confederate money, because they cannot use it," he said. [42]

Three days after Simms wrote to his sister, Captain Rhodes and the 2nd Rhode Island Regiment narrowly escaped being captured. Colonel Edwards ordered Elisha to take his regiment about one mile from camp to set up an outpost for the purpose of observing enemy cavalry. This operation also included the 5th Wisconsin, also commanded by a captain. Charles Kempf was a robust, proud German who immediately informed Captain Rhodes that he had received his captain's commission at an earlier date than Elisha, making him the senior officer. Upon arriving at the designated position, Elisha suggested deploying the two regiments on a hill concealed by shrubbery which could be protected by sending skirmishers into surrounding woods. Determined to assert his superior rank, the captain of the 5th Wisconsin took charge and posted the two regiments in thick woods, basically leaving the men blind.

About noon there was a flurry of activity and a soldier came running into the 2nd's position shouting, "The Rebels are coming!" [43] Confederate infantry and cavalry were pressing into the woods, surrounding the two Union regiments. Captain Kempf sought out Captain Rhodes, asking his advice and relinquishing command on the spot. Elisha led the men back to the position on the hill he had originally argued for and ordered them to dig breastworks. Back in camp the sound of gunfire could be heard, and it was assumed that the two regiments were in trouble. But cut off from the main body of the army, little could be done to help them, and the Rhode Island and Wisconsin men were forced to hold the little hill until after nightfall. In the darkness, small groups of the men slipped away from the hill making their way back to the lines of the army. Scattered to the wind, the regiments were believed to have been destroyed or captured by the enemy. Colonel Edwards was notified that Elisha and his expedition were now in enemy hands. Safely back in camp, a tired Elisha described the affair as, "A right smart time."[44] Captain Charles Kempf of the 5th Wisconsin, a native of Milwaukee, eventually attained the rank of lieutenant colonel. But September 5, 1864, was not his best day.

****

On the 9th, a private in James Sheldon's brigade wrote to his father from a camp near Winchester, describing the condition of the men. "This country suits me smartly. I get plenty various things to eat. We draw plenty of flour, beef, salt, tobacco. There are more apples up here than I ever saw, read or heard tell of before. The country is full of them. I get plenty of butter and eggs, tomatoes, apples, etc.... So you may know we are faring sumptuously, every day to what we did at Petersburg. The boys of our camp are all well, and in fine spirits." [45]

James was involved in a fight on the 19th, near Culpeper Court House after his brigade had been ordered to intercept a body of the enemy that was marching toward Stevensburg. "The brigade was put in motion immediately and moved at double-quick for nearly two miles," Simms said, "but upon arriving within about 500 yards the enemy were opposite to us in the road, having proceeded so far as to render it impossible to cut them off. Finding that this was the only opportunity we would have of inflicting damage upon them, I gave orders to fire. We killed and wounded several of them. Our loss was nothing." [46] In this fight, Simms' Brigade had intercepted 300 Union cavalry on the Stevensburg Road, capturing 100 horses and mules as well as three ambulances and thirty Union men.

On Wednesday, September 21, while Sergeant Sheldon and the 50th marched south toward Petersburg, they got into a scrape with a dashing, ego-driven young brigadier general of cavalry. With his dapper dress and golden ringlets of hair, George Armstrong Custer was a sight to see. Once described as looking like "a circus rider gone mad," [47] he was nonetheless fearless in battle, having had 11 horses shot from under him before the war was over.

One captain in the 50th told of the event from a foot-soldier's perspective, remembering, "My regiment was in advance and we struck Custer's cavalry. Cavalry seldom fight infantry and this was the first time for me…They had thirteen shots to our one, and were a most celebrated cavalry." The man recalled how close the 50th Georgia came to meeting its demise at the blond cavalry general's hands, saying, "One time we got scattered in a field and Custer started to charge, but stopped or we would have been destroyed. However, he retreated and we followed for three or four miles." [48] The 50th Georgia turned and resumed marching south, not knowing that Early's army was in trouble again.

Early had been betrayed by the unlikeliest of sources. A young Quaker school teacher in Winchester had gotten word of Kershaw's departure from Early, leaving "Old Jube" and his army vulnerable. Rebecca Wright passed this information on to Sheridan's staff and an excited "Little Phil" pleaded his case to Grant to attack Early while he was weak. Never one to favor long discussions, Grant bluntly acknowledged Sheridan's request with a simple "Go in." [49]

By mid-September, Early was in a bind. As Union soldiers terrorized and burned the Shenandoah, a small Confederate army was all that stood in their way. For Early to abandon the citizens of the Valley would be to abandon the very heart of the Confederacy. He had no choice but to somehow stave off Sheridan's men, who were carrying breach-loading carbines capable of firing multiple shots without reloading. Early was already outnumbered three-to-one and these weapons increased Sheridan's advantage almost to the point of absurdity. Early's own army consisted of 12,000 worn out, poorly equipped soldiers resting at Winchester. Another concern was news that Grant had just visited Sheridan, presumably discussing a Union offensive. On September 18, Sheridan's scouts reported that Early had distanced himself from two important elements of his army; the divisions of Gordon and Rodes, which had marched 13 miles north of Winchester.

But Early knew what Sheridan planned to do. The Confederate division of Stephen Ramseur stood in front of Early. Sheridan would hit Ramseur with one corps, drawing Early out, and then strike the Confederate left with another. Early hoped to bring Gordon and Rodes' divisions into the Union flanker's rear and "outflank the flankers and rout them." [50] Both armies deployed during the night of Sunday the 18th, knowing that the morning would bring a battle. Captain Rhodes of the 2nd Rhode Island received orders to have his regiment ready to move at a moment's notice. These veterans knew what was coming and discarded anything deemed unnecessary for the march; guns were checked and cartridge boxes and canteens filled.

The 2nd was moving before dawn and shortly after eight a.m. crossed Opequon Creek, where Ramseur's skirmishers and artillerists were waiting. Things appeared to be going badly as terrified men from the front came falling back through the Rhode Islanders' position. During the excitement, a shell fragment knocked a Union captain off his horse. His frightened horse ran off, taking with it everything the man owned. The furious captain unleashed a barrage of obscenity that approached poetry, as Elisha and the other men broke into fits of laughter. As shells burst all around them, the veterans of the 2nd shrugged off the artillery fire as if it were rain.

About noon, Elisha's division was ordered into the fight. Charging into Early's men with gleaming bayonets, they drove the enemy back in the direction of Winchester. "The 2nd R.I. reached a little knoll near a house, and finding a heavy stone wall in my front I formed behind it and opened fire," said Elisha. "While in this position the 37th Mass, one of the best regiments I ever saw, and armed with Spencer Seven Shooting Rifles, had advanced well to the front and could be seen about a mile to my right, laying upon the ground exposed to the rife of the Rebel guns in a redoubt." Elisha watched these Massachusetts men in awe as they fought their way toward the city. Suddenly a booming voice jolted Captain Rhodes out of his trance, "For God's sake, Rhodes, take the 2nd R.I. and go help [Lt. Colonel] Montague [of the 37th Massachusetts]." [51]

Amid the whistling of artillery and minie balls, Elisha ordered his regiment to its feet. With his heart pounding, Captain Rhodes led his men through some woods at the rear, until they were near the 37th Massachusetts' ordnance wagons. They could see the Massachusetts men pinned down. Helping themselves to the 37th's ordnance wagon, the Rhode Islanders filled their cartridge boxes and Captain Rhodes ordered the men into a skirmish line on the double-quick to the right of the 37th.

The men of the 2nd crawled on their stomachs under heavy fire until reaching the Massachusetts men. Lieutenant Colonel Montague, in a defiant stance, was the only man on his feet when Captain Rhodes announced that he was at his service. Montague waved him away in disgust, complaining nothing could be done as his men were without ammunition. Elisha promptly ordered his men to distribute ammunition to the Massachusetts men and within minutes the New Englanders put a steady fire on the Confederate battery. Soon, the *Southerners* were out of ammunition and a white flag appeared over their redoubt. At the Battle of 3rd Winchester, or Opequon, the 2nd Rhode Island suffered the loss of seven men wounded. Among them was a novelty of sorts, a colorful 42-year-old corporal from England named Tom Parker. Another was 22-year-old Private Tom Lewis, the son of Foster and Phoebe Lewis of Smithfield, Rhode Island. Lewis died in a field hospital later that day. A third man, Private Joe Barton, was a 21-year-old fisherman from the quiet seacoast village of Bristol. Barton died a week after the battle in an overcrowded hospital in Philadelphia.

Sheridan's plan of attack at Winchester was going as planned, but by eleven o' clock it became apparent that the 6th Corps had made a glaring mistake. General Horatio Wright, in direct violation of Sheridan's orders, had brought his entire corps' wagon train into Winchester, clogging the roads and blocking the advance of the 19th Corps. Seeing this gap in Sheridan's lines, Confederate Generals Gordon and Rodes charged into it, disrupting and nearly crippling the Union attack. As a result, General George Crook's Army of West Virginia, which was poised to deliver the knockout blow on Early's unsuspecting right, was instead forced to join the struggle against Rodes and Gordon on Early's left. Sheridan was beside himself.

In spite of Early's grizzled tenacity and Wright's blunder, the sheer weight of Sheridan's numbers and repeating rifles proved too much for the Confederates. Very late in the afternoon, Early found a route to make his escape and his army moved quickly but calmly. To his men this was a redeployment, not a retreat. Twenty miles to the southwest lay the town of Strasburg. Three miles to the west of Strasburg stands Fisher's Hill, a natural setting for building a formidable defense. The "Gibraltar of the Valley," [52] as the locals called it, was a hill on which Old Jube determined was "the only place where a stand could be made" and he built a line of breastworks three miles long on its heights. [53] Sheridan had paid a steep price for his attack at Winchester, losing over 5,000 men, and although hard numbers are not available, it is believed Early lost 30 to 40 percent of his army.

Elisha was jubilant as he watched Early's men being chased down in the streets of Winchester, not knowing that his corps commander had failed the army. Elisha wrote, "the men were wild with joy. I could have knelt and kissed the folds of the old flag that waved in triumph. We captured several Rebel flags which were displayed along the front of our line. I cried and shouted in my excitement and never felt so good before in my life. I have been in a good many battles but never in such a victory as this."[54] The 2nd Rhode Island remained at Winchester while the rest of Sheridan's army continued its pursuit of Early.

Three days after the Battle of Winchester, Early was attacked at Fisher's Hill. Once again, Sheridan's plans *almost* came off. At about six p.m., General Crook successfully flanked a brigade of North Carolinians who broke and fled, sending panic along Early's lines. Early's entire army was in full flight, abandoning 14 irreplaceable cannons in their haste. The general was in serious personal danger of being captured until his cavalry secured an escape route for the army.

Three days after the battle, Early and his battered force, hardly an army at this point, found refuge 60 miles south in the Blue Ridge Mountains at Brown's Gap. But even in the face of the long odds, "Old Jube" wanted one more go at Sheridan.

****

On the morning of the 20th, Captain Elisha Rhodes got some good news. Colonel Edwards informed him that the brigade was being designated as the garrison at Winchester. Elisha, who loved the place, was thrilled and hoped that perhaps the 2nd could winter there. Edwards then stunned Elisha when he told him that for his actions in saving the 37th Massachusetts, he had recommended him for a promotion to major. It was a good day for the young captain. Two days later, the men of the 2nd heard the newswalkers tell of Sheridan's victory at a place called Fisher's Hill.

During the next three weeks, James Sheldon's regiment remained in a kind of military limbo, marching "from point to point," constantly on the move to locate and destroy cavalry and serve as the reserve to a brigade of South Carolinians. The

South Carolinians accomplished the work assigned to them, "so handsomely it was not thought necessary to bring it (Simms' Brigade) into action," Colonel Simms reported. [55] Simms' Brigade lost about eight or ten men who were wounded by sharpshooters or injured in accidents. Half of his men had no shoes when they arrived at Rapidan Station.

Duty at Winchester proved to be as enjoyable as Elisha had anticipated. He was able to borrow some furniture from a family in town and made his headquarters as homelike as possible. But since Sheridan's burnings had begun, the attitude of the locals had turned icy toward Union soldiers. This was particularly true of the young ladies. Young women would often make a "saucy" remark when passing a soldier on the street, prompting the men to doff their caps in mock greeting. At dinner with some townspeople, a couple of girls turned their chairs around so not to face the intruders. Elisha quipped that the insult "did not take my appetite away." [56] Not all of the ladies in Winchester were so inhospitable though, and Elisha and some other officers were invited to spend a few evenings in their company. The fighting seemed far away and Elisha savored his time at Winchester, writing, "it is great fun." [57]

While Elisha was enjoying his time in the northern Shenandoah, James and the 50th Georgia camped at "different places for a short space in time," eventually ending up not far from Elisha near Hupp's Hill between Middletown and Strasburg. [58] The Georgians were eager to get back into the fight but all indications were that they were headed back to Petersburg. The news of Early's defeats at Winchester and Fisher's Hill had cast a pall over James Sheldon and the 50th Georgia and a sense of wasted opportunity ran through Simms' Brigade, as well as Kershaw's entire division. Then, on the 24th, the unexpected happened. The brigade received orders to return to Early. In a driving rain, James retraced his steps, consoling himself with the motto, "Do your duty, therein all honor lies." The men marched through Barboursville and Standardville, crossing the mountain at Swift Run Gap where they camped about a mile from the banks of the Shenandoah River. It had been a brutal march, as one man in Kershaw's Division remembered, "The situation of Early had become so critical, the orders so imperative to join him as soon as possible, that we took up the march next morning at a forced speed, going twelve miles before a halt, a feat never before excelled by any body of troops during the war."[59]

Simms' men, hoping to catch their breath, camped in a pass in the Blue Ridge Mountains called Fisher's Gap. A veteran of the division insisted, "It must be remembered we had been two months cut off from the outside world—no railroad nearer than Staunton, the men being often short of rations and barefooted and badly clad; scarcely any mail was received during these two months, and seldom a paper ever made its appearance in camp. We only knew that Lee was holding his own."[60]

On September 25, Simms' Brigade rejoined General Jubal Early's Army of the Valley. Three days later they were back in action as they moved towards Port Republic via Swift Run Gap where the brigade brushed aside a group of cavalry skirmishers. As October opened, Sergeant James Sheldon was camped near Waynesboro. "It looks like it is to be an ever-lasting war if we have got to have our independence... [But] I think we will whip the Yankees here in the valley yet," wrote a man in his brigade.[61]

James and the 50th were sorely in need of rest and rations. Perhaps the northern Shenandoah would provide both.

15

VERY FINE BUTTERMILK, INDEED

Elisha was enjoying the late September evening and the company, Miss Virginia Wall of Winchester, couldn't have been more pleasant. The music and conversation were equally charming. But to Elisha's astonishment, Miss Wall suddenly mentioned that she knew a man from Rhode Island who was in the Confederate Army. Of course, Captain Rhodes took the bait and asked who the man was. What she told Elisha floored him; "James Sheldon" belonged to a Georgia regiment in Kershaw's Division. Memories came flooding back as Elisha later wrote in his diary, "This is my old schoolmate and neighbor of Pawtuxet. I have written to his family, as this news is only about two weeks old." [1] Elisha must have wondered if Rebecca and Israel Sheldon knew what had become of their son and brother.

****

As October opened in its autumnal grandeur, the armies seemed to pause. At Petersburg, Grant's lines were growing longer every day, causing Lee to stretch his own thin lines to the limit. To the Confederate general's credit, Grant's repeated probes failed to break them.

But the unkindest cut of all for the Confederacy came in the Shenandoah. What had begun in July as a bold stab at Washington by Jubal Early had degenerated into a trail of defeats, and his army was now hiding somewhere between Strasburg and Middletown. "Little Phil" had good reason to believe that his

Valley Campaign was both successful and over, but Early wasn't yet convinced and neither were the civilians of the Valley.

For Elisha Rhodes and the 6th Corps these were good days. "Here, in the enjoyment of lovely weather, pleasant associations, a bountiful supply of lamb and honey, and untold quantities of grapes of delicious flavor, the corps remained several days [near Front Royal], and the men even flattered themselves that in the enjoyment of these luxuries they were to pass the winter." [2] But while the soldiers enjoyed relatively happy times encamped on the outskirts of the town, life in Winchester itself could only be described as bittersweet. The city was filled with hastily dug cemeteries adorned with freshly cut flowers. One morning, Elisha and some officers stumbled into a party assembled at the grave of a Confederate colonel from Winchester and felt compelled to stand with the group, heads bowed and hatless. Earlier, a woman had approached Captain Rhodes, and in an acrid tone told him that she had had three brothers killed in the war and a fourth badly wounded. In spite of these losses, she hoped the war would continue.

On the first Sunday of October, Elisha and a few other men of the 2nd worshipped at the only church in Winchester not in use as a hospital. The city was in mourning, and for that reason some Confederate prisoners were allowed a day of freedom to worship. It was an awkward sight as Union and Confederate men prayed together. The collection box filled with both Confederate and United States dollars.

Being a young officer always brought with it its share of attention, and in Winchester, Elisha got his share. On at least two occasions bouquets of flowers were delivered to his tent, one from an unknown female admirer. Another admirer came in the four-legged variety. A lamb, having wandered the streets of Winchester since the battle, quite simply adopted the Rhode Island captain. Reluctantly, Elisha gave in to his wooly new friend and named him "Dick," claiming, "He follows me or my horse wherever I go." [3]

On the 13th, the newswalkers announced that the 6th Corps would soon be marching back to Petersburg. "I hope not, for I rather like this place," wrote Elisha.[4] It turned out that although the newswalkers were correct; Captain Rhodes would get his wish and as the 6th Corps began making its way south, the 2nd Rhode Island was ordered to remain on provost duty at Winchester.

The 6th Corps men hadn't grown soft during their October stay in the valley, but they had clearly become accustomed to a certain comfort level. On the 13th, the corps marched in the direction of Petersburg. When the men reached the banks of the Shenandoah River, they exchanged grimaces. An officer in the 6th Corps recalled, "the men looked dismally into the cold, dark waters, and shivered at the thought of wading through the stream whose waters would reach nearly to their necks."[5] As the men waited, a courier arrived with a message for General Wright. Word quickly passed throughout the column that Sheridan was ordering them back to rejoin his army at once. An intercepted Confederate dispatch to General Early, believed to be from a recuperated James Longstreet, troubled Sheridan greatly. "Be ready when I join you, and we will crush Sheridan," read the message.[6] Sheridan was summoned to the White House to discuss the campaign with the President, and General Horatio Wright would assume command of the Army of the Valley during his absence. "We turned about, encamped for the night among the hills, started again at three o'clock in the morning, and joined the army again on Cedar creek, in the afternoon of the 14th, where we remained in the enjoyment of undisturbed quiet for several days," wrote a man in the 6th Corps.[7] The war in the Valley was once again alive and well.

Despite the expectation of another fight with Early, life in the 2nd Rhode Island at Winchester could not have been more pleasant. The men began building fireplaces in their huts, assuming they would be wintering there. The pro-Union ladies of Winchester entertained the officers with parties of piano music and sing-a-longs. On one occasion, a group of officers and ladies, including Captain Rhodes, took a cavalry escorted horseback ride into the country. But there was another, much darker, side to many of these smiling natives.

Elisha eyed the locals warily, "The people are honest farmers during the day, but at night they arm themselves and mounting their horses are guerillas and fire upon our pickets and destroy our wagon trains if they can overpower the guards." [8] Part of the 2nd Rhode Island's duties in Winchester and its surrounding farmlands was to search all the houses and barns for hidden weapons and Confederate soldiers. The people of the city were "wild with rage" [9] at these intrusions. The Union Army owned the day while the Confederates owned the night. "Guerilla warfare was a favorite resort of the rebels in the Shenandoah Valley, and many of our men were murdered in cold blood by the cowardly villains who lurked about our camps by day as harmless farmers, and murdered our men at night dressed in Confederate uniform," said one man in the 6th Corps. [10]

The people of the Valley wanted vengeance, and if guerilla war was the means to achieving it, so be it. After all, they believed this war had been thrust upon them. An officer in Elisha's corps remembered, "[We were] burning barns, mills and granaries, driving before us cattle and sheep, and bringing white and black refugees without number…Each day as we marched, dark columns of smoke rose from numberless conflagrations in our rear and on either flank, where the cavalry was at work carrying out the edict of destruction in the valley…Seventy mills, with the flour and grain, and over two thousand barns filled with wheat, hay, and farming implements were thus committed to the flames, and seven thousand cattle and sheep were either driven off or killed and issued to the men." [11] One man in James Sheldon's brigade said, "It is sad, sickening to look upon." [12] "The Burning" was in high gear.

****

At Fishers Hill on October 16, Ben Simms jotted off a quick letter to his sister telling of his brigade's condition. "General Early's cavalry here suffered a disaster last Sunday. They [were] stampeded by the Yankee cavalry and hotly chased for several miles losing eleven pieces of cannon and forty odd wagons and a few prisoners. It was a scandalous affair. Some ran their horses completely down."[13] The rout of the Confederate cavalry became known as the "Woodstock Races."

This fighting took place at Hupp's Hill about a mile and a half from Cedar Creek. Ben Simms explained his brigade's situation, claiming, "After the fight General Early advanced and remained until night then fell back to this hill made famous by his recent ill fortune, when he was flanked and so badly whipped back to Port Republic where our division joined him. Our position here is a magnificent one and I have no idea the enemy can again dislodge General Early."[14]

Ben Simms
(Atlanta Historical Society)

Early's men were despondent. But their mood changed when news reached their camps in mid-October that Kershaw's Division of nearly 4,000 veterans had joined them. A second division, under General Gabriel Wharton, brought the total number of men to 7,000. The new divisions also brought with them 1,500 cavalrymen and 24 cannons.

Commissary Sergeant Sheldon and his regiment enjoyed their short stay in Fisher's Gap, but were suffering badly from the lack of rations, and as Sheridan had his way with the Valley, so did the starving Confederates at Fisher's Gap. One soldier in Kershaw's Division described the looting of the countryside, "The foragers now struck out right and left over the mountains on either side to hunt up all the little delicacies these mountain homes so abounded in—good fresh butter-milk, golden butter—the like can be found nowhere else in the South save in the valleys of Virginia—apple butter, fruits of all kinds, and occasionally these foragers would run upon a keg of good old mountain corn, apple jack, or peach brandy—a 'nectar fitting for the gods,' when steeped in bright, yellow honey...It was astonishing what a change in the morals of men army life occasioned. I have known men who at home was as honorable, honest, upright, and who would scorn a dishonest act, turn out to be veteran foragers, and rob and steal anything they could get their hands on from the citizens, friend or foe alike... While I never countenanced nor upheld foraging, unless it was done legitimately and the articles paid for, still when a choice piece of mutton or pork, a mess tin of honey, or canteen of brandy was hanging on my rifle pole in the morning, I only did what I enjoined on the men, 'say nothing and ask no question.'" [15] One food source was in abundance, and a Confederate officer wrote, "I have just eaten enough apples to make a pig sick." [16]

General John B. Gordon, commanding a division of Georgia, Louisiana and Virginia regiments, was hoping to get Early out of his quandary in the Valley. At 32, the successful attorney led a brigade at Chancellorsville, Gettysburg, and the Wilderness before being promoted to major general on May 14, 1864. He looked every bit an officer, "courtly and impressive," said one observer. [17]

General Gordon wanted to get a look at Sheridan's Army of the Shenandoah and on October 17 he rode to a peak on Massanutten Mountain and peered off into the direction of Sheridan's camps. From this vantage point he got an eyeful.

360

Sheridan's army appeared at rest, lazing about in the warmth of success, doing laundry, cooking meals, and playing cards. Through his fieldglasses, Gordon claimed he could count the number of stripes on a man's sleeve and see sores on the backs of horses. He also saw an opportunity.

Gordon reported to Early that the camps of Sheridan's left flank appeared so relaxed that these men must have been convinced that topography protected them from attack. Sheridan's men had every reason to believe this, as there was no position in their line on which Early could make an advance without terrific loss. As Gordon talked, Early listened.

Gordon proposed taking three divisions on a silent night march south across the Shenandoah River. Having successfully gotten his three divisions across, the men would follow a "dim and narrow pathway," [18] worn by the hooves of wild boar for about three and one-half miles, where they would cross back over to the north side of the river. These three divisions would then slam into the extreme left flank, or the eastern portion of Sheridan's army, while the divisions of Wharton and Kershaw would hit them approximately one or two miles to the west. This surprise attack could send Sheridan's army reeling northward to safety, forced to leave behind miles of wagon trains and tons of supplies. There was even some possibility of capturing Sheridan himself. Further strengthening Gordon's argument for attacking was the belief that Union commanders like Horatio Wright, who believed Early had given up the ghost, had headed back to Petersburg. Knowing he would never get another opportunity like this, Early approved Gordon's plan.

Shortly after dark on the evening of the 18th there were rumblings within the ranks of James Sheldon's camp, and newswalkers spoke of a major battle in the morning. Colonel McGlashan walked through the camps of Simms' Brigade and found himself overcome with sadness. James thought back to the early days in Thomasville where an excited and patriotic Cicero Young was organizing a company in front of the courthouse.

What McGlashan saw in these camps were the tattered remnants of former glory, that would perhaps never be realized again. He estimated that, at best, the entire brigade could muster only about 400 rifles for the coming fight, and explained, "The men, in fact the whole force, were poorly clad and shod, rations being reduced to a minimum, for the whole valley had been gleaned and devastated so long by the contending forces that no further supplies could be obtained...Sheridan boasted, 'that if a crow flew over it he would have to carry his own rations.'" [19]

Sheridan's Army of the Shenandoah was posted on an almost impregnable position on a bluff overlooking Cedar Creek. Behind it was a vast plateau of several square miles. Union breastworks were constructed of strong timbers, with dirt piled against them and a deep trench on the inside allowing men to stand at their full height without being exposed to enemy fire. Several hundred yards to the rear, higher elevations of fifty feet or more above the level of the creek provided ideal positions for artillery batteries. In front of all this firepower was an elaborate array of felled pine trees with needles stripped, limbs cut and pointed five to ten feet from the trunks. These were packed and stacked side-by-side and on top of each other, forty to fifty feet wide, making it difficult for a man to get through even under the best of circumstances. After viewing these works through his fieldglasses, Colonel McGlashan concluded, "This I believe was the most completely fortified position by nature, as well as by hand, of any line occupied during the war, and had the troops not been taken by surprise and stood their ground, a regiment strung out could have kept an army at bay." [20]

Colonel Simms received his orders from General Kershaw early in the evening of October 18. As was Simms' custom, he sought out each of his regimental commanders to give them instructions and offer words of encouragement. Colonel Peter McGlashan was immersed in his thoughts when he saw Simms walking toward him. A few yards away, James Sheldon was attending a prayer meeting and the voice of Chaplain Curry could be heard in the darkness. Simms asked, "Colonel, will you take a walk with me?" [21]

The two men walked in silence toward the prayer meeting and listened with bowed heads. "Poor fellows," Simms commented, "this may be their last meeting, Colonel. We are going to attack the enemy's lines before daybreak, and our brigade has been selected for the post of honor to break the line. [William] Wofford's brigade will support us. Your regiment will be on the right, I depend on you to lead the attack. The men must be in line, ready to move at midnight." The former rivals shook hands and parted. Colonel McGlashan summoned his brother Andrew to discuss their orders. Andrew McGlashan was an experienced old soldier, having served twenty years in the British Army in the Royal Artillery. Andrew listened as his younger brother gave him his orders and at midnight Sergeant James Sheldon and the 50th Georgia struck the Winchester Road, past the waiting columns of troops already there, and took position at the head of the column. Each man was supplied with sixty rounds of ammunition. Generals Gordon and Early, with their staffs, were riding ahead in the direction of Strasburg. Marching through Strasburg the divisions left the turnpike and moved upon a little road on the right, which they followed until coming within sight of the enemy's camp fires.

Colonel McGlashan described the early morning hours of the 19th vividly, saying, "The night was clouded and cold, making it difficult to see any great distance ahead. The horse's feet seemed muffled, and perfect silence maintained. Instructions stated that no orders should be given in the line." Another man described the silent army, saying, "The most profound secrecy, the absence of all noise, from rattling of canteens or tin cups, were enjoined upon the men." [22]

During their silent march to Cedar Creek a sudden clanking noise was heard on the left. James Sheldon and the 50th Georgia halted and listened until a foraging Confederate, with about twenty canteens hanging around him, pushed through the bushes and made his startled appearance. An officer demanded to know what he had in his canteens. "Buttermilk, sir," boasted the cocky soldier. "Pass one of them over here," the officer ordered. Pulling the stopper out he sampled the contents and the fragrant smell of moonshine whiskey wafted through the frosty air, causing James and the other men to sniff expectantly. "Very fine buttermilk, indeed," said the officer, passing it among his comrades. After having his supplies thoroughly tasted, the soldier was dismissed amid frantic pleas from the Georgians begging for just one more swallow of the "good buttermilk." This incident briefly cheered the men of Simms' Brigade and "dispersed the gloom that was gathering over us." [23]

James resumed his silent march as a heavy mist hung in the air, limiting visibility. McGlashan remembered, "All movements conforming to the right, we glided along the road like a procession of specters through the gloom." [24] Phil Sheridan, having returned from his meeting with Lincoln in Washington and confident his campaign was over, slept soundly in Winchester.

Sergeant Sheldon gazed into the distance at what looked like a city. The last embers of the previous night's campfires glowed orange through the fog. Some of Sheridan's men were re-stoking these fires to begin cooking. Coffee, eggs, bacon and all the components that make up a hearty breakfast were abundant in the Army of the Shenandoah and the hungry Confederates knew it. The cheerfulness that had sung down the advancing column disappeared as a hateful mood enveloped the Georgians. Nothing would be more enjoyable than spoiling the breakfast of these burners of the Valley.

The 50th left the road and marched across "some grassy clover fields." [25] They approached "a low range of hills through a gap in which Cedar Creek flowed," and Colonel Peter McGlashan remembered, "Crossing the creek silently, we formed by the right file into line of battle along the edge of the creek. Whispered instructions were now given not to fire under any circumstances." [26] The pounding of hearts could almost be heard as the lifting mist revealed Early's secret.

The faded gray uniforms of the advancing Georgians blended with the color of the October grass and were invisible to the eyes of Sheridan's pickets. "But we could see their dark blue uniforms readily," James' colonel observed. [27] But Sheridan's pickets sensed trouble, and McGlashan observed, "day had not yet broke, yet the pickets were evidently uneasy. They could hear some movements in front, but could not see anything. Finally, one picket, sharper eyed than the rest, cried out: 'I see them,' and fired, when Lieutenant Clayton of the 50th fell forward on the grass mortally wounded." [28] The Battle of Cedar Creek was on.

James and the other men, anxious to respond to their loss, maintained the discipline they had learned over the last three years. McGlashan wrote, "A rattling volley from the picket followed and another man fell out of the ranks. Still the line swept on in utter silence…The whole picket line, now thoroughly alarmed, broke for the woods, but were soon halted by their officers, who [were] cursing the men for running at a false alarm." [29] Sheridan's men had scarcely formed a line before the Georgians were upon them, emerging from the edge of the woods. As they came into full view of the Union men, the rising fog gave the area a ghostly appearance.

Marching quietly into the ravine, the Georgians' line halted. Then came the command: "Now men, fix bayonets. Forward, double quick, *Charge!*" With a wild, Rebel Yell that seemed to reach the clouds, James rushed up the slope toward the entrenchments. [30]

The surprise had been total and Sheridan's men were slow to respond as bleary-eyed Union soldiers stumbled out of their tents, shocked to find themselves under attack. The Union lines were five miles long, representing more of an encampment than a battle line. Men raised their heads above the trenches to fire, regardless of aim or direction, and then fell to the bottom to reload.

As the 50th Georgia charged forward, all the rage from their hunger and the Union's burning of the Valley was unleashed. Colonel McGlashan led the men toward the Union lines and saw, "A slight ravine lay before us and the heights beyond were crowned with a formidable line of entrenchments defined sharply against the camp fires behind, and strengthened by a thicket hedge of abattis, consisting of large branches and young trees, with the smaller branches trimmed and sharpened to a point and laid with the point outward." James could see the terrified pickets scrambling through the abatis and over their entrenchments, alarming the camp with their cries, while half-clad soldiers with muskets rushed out of the tents in all directions.

Within minutes, the Georgians were over the abatis and into the Union trenches. "Such a sight as met our eyes as we mounted their works was not often seen... For a mile or more in every direction towards the rear was a vast plain or broken plateau, with not a tree or shrub in sight. Tents whitened the field from one end to the other for a hundred paces in rear of the line, while the country behind was one living sea of men and horses—all fleeing for life and safety. Men, shoeless and hatless, went flying like mad to the rear, some with and some without their guns. Here was a deserted battery, the horses unhitched from the guns; the caissons were going like the wind, the drivers laying the lash all the while. Cannoneers mounted the unhitched horses barebacked, and were straining every nerve to keep apace with caissons in front. Here and there loose horses galloped at will, some bridleless, others with traces whipping their flanks to a foam. Such confusion, such a panic, was never witnessed before by the troops. Our cannoneers got their guns in position, and enlivened the scene by throwing shell, grape, and canister into the flying fugitives. Some of the captured guns were turned and opened upon the former owners." [31]

James took delight in what he found in the Union camps. One of his comrades said, "The smoking breakfast, just ready for the table, stood temptingly inviting, while the opened tents displayed a scene almost enchanting to the eyes of the Southern soldier, in the way of costly blankets, overcoats, dress uniforms, hats, caps, boots, and shoes all thrown in wild confusion over the face of the earth... [But our] wants were few, or at least that of which they could carry, so they grab a slice of bacon, a piece of bread, a blanket, or an overcoat, and were soon in line again following up the enemy." [32]

Shortly before six a.m. on the morning of the 19th, an officer returning from picket duty near Winchester entered General Sheridan's bedroom and alerted him of artillery fire from the direction of Cedar Creek. The general had his horse saddled and he set off to the front.

Sergeant James Sheldon and his bayonet wielding comrades pushed forward through the trench and into more Union camps, bayoneting and slashing at everything in their path, clearing it of the terrified enemy. Some of the worst fighting took place at and around Belle Grove, a plantation house that Sheridan had been using as his headquarters. But not all of Sheridan's men were ready to run. James could see gunners trying to fire from a Union battery as Confederates swarmed all around them. They only succeeded in firing once, before they were overpowered and bayoneted at their guns. Andrew McGlashan turned the captured guns against the enemy. "In an incredibly short space of time he had formed six gun squads and was sending shell after shell into their broken ranks, completing the rout and hastening their retreat," his brother Peter remembered. [33]

Sheridan's stalwarts quickly won the respect of the Confederates. "The enemy made a stubborn resistance...Some of them were shot down while firing upon our men at the distance of a few feet," stated Colonel Simms. [34] James' brigade was also earning plaudits from those who witnessed its charge. A Confederate brigade commander praised the tenacity with which Simms' Georgians assaulted Sheridan's position, declaring that Simms' Brigade had, "dashed forward across the turnpike, attacking the second line of works with such fierce vigor and determination that the enemy soon fled in the utmost confusion, leaving in our hands a number of prisoners and four pieces of artillery." [35] One man in Kershaw's Division wrote, "Oh, what a glorious victory! Men in their imagination were writing letters home, telling of our brilliant achievements—thirty pieces of artillery captured, whole wagon trains of ordnance, from ten-to-twenty thousand stands of small arms, horses and wagons, with all of Sheridan's tents and camp equipage—all was ours, and the enemy in full retreat!" [36]

As in most battles, the fighting was not without its moments of absurdity, and James and Colonel McGlashan witnessed just such a moment. McGlashan recalled, "In leaping over the earthworks, a young lieutenant discovered a large pot of boiling coffee on one of the camp fires, got ready, doubtless, for some picket's early breakfast. Well, coffee was more than scarce with us. He was excited and thirsty, and the chance to get a good drink of real coffee was a temptation he could not resist, so he sprang over and seized the pot, took a huge swallow and scalded the tongue and roof of his mouth out of his head. Just then, a general officer galloped up and cried: 'What regiment is this?' 'Hell fire and damnation!' screamed the agonized officer, sputtering out the hot coffee. The general stared, but, taking in the situation, rode off, laughing and saying: 'A very good name for your regiment, indeed.'" [37]

The Army of the Shenandoah was forced to evacuate its trenches, leaving behind 2,000 prisoners and 21 guns. Most of all, innumerable commissary and quartermaster stores fell into the hands of the shoeless, starving Confederates. Although these spoils were initially seen as a trophy, they almost immediately became a hindrance to what had so far been a brilliant success at Cedar Creek. The men of the 50th were concerned that too many officers and men remained behind to look after this bounty, leaving only about half of their force to pursue the enemy into the open country. The door of certain defeat that had slammed shut on Phil Sheridan, now creaked open ever so slightly.

"It was at this critical moment that the warning was given to the 6th Corps," remembered a surgeon in that corps. "Staff officers now came riding furiously through the camps, with orders to fall in at once, and proceed at double-quick to the left." [38]

Generals Wright and Ricketts were both wounded, and command of the corps fell upon General George Getty. Getty posted part of his corps on the left of the hastily forming line. "We now awaited the onset of the victorious columns, which were driving the shattered and disorganized fragments of the Eighth and Nineteenth corps, beaten and discouraged, wildly through our well formed ranks to the rear. The hope of the nation now rested with those heroes of many bloody fields," a 6th Corps officer proudly boasted. [39]

The veterans of the 6th Corps waited patiently for their guests—soon to arrive like a hurricane. A 6th Corps surgeon recalled, "The corps, numbering less than twelve thousand men, now confronted Early's whole army of more than thirty thousand men, who, flushed with victory, already bringing to bear against us the twenty-one guns which they had just captured from the two broken corps, rushed upon our lines with those wild, exultant yells, the terror of which can never be conceived by those who have not heard them on the field." [40] He concluded, "It was like the clash of steel to steel." [41]

Early's men fell back stunned. They regrouped and hit the 6th Corps again, but a second countercharge sent them again running in disorder across the creek, the ground now covered with Confederate dead and wounded. Word passed quickly through Early's lines that the men they were fighting were 6th Corps men. Though disheartened by this news, the Confederates hit the 6th Corps a third time but with less zeal.

Knowing he couldn't break through the 6th Corps, Early tried to get around it. The 6th Corps was ordered to fall back to a better defensive position, but one officer made it clear that, "The Sixth corps was not *driven* back." [42] The 6th Corps took up a new position about two miles to the rear, tending to their wounded while somehow managing to cook their morning meals. "It was now ten o'clock; far away in the rear was heard cheer after cheer. What was the cause?" wondered one officer—Sheridan had arrived. [43]

The 50th Georgia and Simms' Brigade had done their job exceedingly well. Joe Kershaw, impressed with Simms' command of his men, decided to recommend the colonel as brigadier general. Ironically, the performance of his competitor for the commission, Peter McGlashan, helped to secure Simms' appointment. But there was still much fighting to be done. "The day was advancing, the heat increasing, and the men, under the tremendous exertions they were making, having driven the enemy over six miles over a rough country, were rapidly becoming wearied and faint. The enemy nowhere made [a] stand against us, but their masses seemed to cover the whole country in our front, retiring sullenly, but in some order, gradually before our advance," remembered Colonel McGlashan. [44] As the tired

Georgians watched thousands of Sheridan's men fleeing in the distance for the safety of Winchester, they couldn't help but visualize a large force of Confederate cavalry charging upon them, cloaking the day in glorious victory. But there was no such cavalry force. Exhausted and out of ammunition, James and the other men of the 50th Georgia looked around, trying to get a head count of who was still with them.

The Confederate attack continued as Sheridan's army sought to right itself, and at about eleven o'clock in the morning Kershaw's Division was ordered to halt and rest. It wasn't until late afternoon that James got the first inkling that things were not what they seemed. Said one soldier, "Here we were halted to better form our columns. But the halt was fatal—fatal to our great victory, fatal to our army, and who can say not fatal to our cause... It was late in the day...I looked in the rear. What a sight! Here came stragglers, who looked like half the army, laden with every imaginable kind of plunder... I saw one man with a stack of wool hats on his head, one pressed in the other, until it reached more than an arm's length above his head." [45]

On his ride to Belle Grove, Sheridan was shocked to find his army on the verge of collapse and he ordered hordes of retreating men to return to the front. Although his army was rallying on its own and in the capable hands of General Wright, his men were inspired by the sight of him. Soon after he arrived, General Wright rode up, his chin bleeding heavily from being grazed by a minie ball. Wright insisted that the day was not lost and by late afternoon, Sheridan was preparing his counterattack.

After ordering units to various points, Sheridan resumed field command and ordered the wounded Wright back to his post as commander of the 6th Corps. Men in blue uniforms were running everywhere but mostly headed for Winchester. Sheridan was angered by this and sent word to Colonel Edwards in Winchester to stretch his brigade across the Valley to stop all fugitives. He also ordered the army's transportation and wagon train to be parked and guarded on the north side of Winchester.

Although not directly involved in the fighting, Captain Elisha Rhodes and the 2nd Rhode Island had their hands full at Winchester. "The Second and the 5th Wisconsin occupied the town, and under command of Captain Rhodes, guarded the trains— nearly two thousand wagons. Some rebel cavalry were hovering about the town, evidently watching an opportunity to strike," said Reverend Woodbury. [46] Elisha described the event of the early part of the day, saying, "At daylight we heard the sound of cannon at the front, and it appeared to draw near. I turned out and had my Regiment form and soon received orders to report in person to Colonel Edwards commanding the post...I was ordered to take command of the 2nd R.I. and 5th Wisconsin Volunteers and look out for the north part of town. I formed my brigade and sent out a line of skirmishers. During the morning our wagon trains came into town pell mell." [47]

James Sheldon and the rest of Simms' Brigade were basking in the glow of apparent victory. As far as the Georgia men knew, everything had gone according to plan and Sheridan was vanquished. Then it happened. Colonel Simms' described Sheridan's counterattack, "[We] rested until about 5 o'clock in the afternoon, when an attack was made upon the troops to our left. They broke and fled in confusion, forcing upon us the necessity of falling back. The line was formed about one-quarter of a mile in rear of the one which had been abandoned, which was held until it was found that the troops on the left of my brigade had abandoned the field. I placed a regiment on my left, formed perpendicularly to the rear to protect the flank. The enemy soon attacked it with such force as it was not able to withstand." [48]

Clearly, Sheridan was back in command. James Sheldon's brigade of Georgians was being pushed back. Confederate cavalry came retreating through their lines and it was clear that the hard won victory had turned into a panic-driven rout. Every soldier who survived the Battle of Cedar Creek had his own version of what happened next. Perhaps the most gripping of these accounts came from the 50th Georgia's own Colonel Peter McGlashan, "The men, acting by a kind of instinct, broke their line formation, and deploying as skirmishers, managed to cover the whole front of the enemy's advance, thus checking their cavalry, but without power and [no] longer [able] to stop the infantry advance. So the huge line of skirmishers fell back rapidly, fighting as they went, every man for himself. By this time every officer was in his place trying to retrieve the lost honors of the day, but too late. All organization was gone, and the men, marching and fighting for eighteen hours, were utterly exhausted and incapable of further effort, and were rapidly falling back to the Shenandoah River.

"[My brother and adjutant, Andrew McGlashan]…was painfully wounded in the left knee, and, during the retreat, was hobbling along supporting himself with his sword. He was a splendid swordsman and always kept his sword sharp as a razor. Being crippled, he was soon over-taken by a squad of pursuing cavalry, one of whom, mounted on a swifter horse, got to him first and called him to throw down his sword and surrender. [He]…would not answer. This enraged cavalry man, who yelled: 'Damn you, surrender, or I will cut you down!' 'Cut away,' said the adjutant, coolly looking back at him over his shoulder. The soldier rode right at him, making a slashing St. George cut at him as he passed. The adjutant waited until the flashing blade was right over him, then, turning suddenly, parried the blow, and, with a heavy counter-stroke, struck the unfortunate soldier on the back of the neck as he passed, nearly hewing the head off the body. As he fell off the horse the adjutant seized it and tried to mount and escape; but his wounded knee preventing him from mounting, he was overtaken and captured." [49]

Throughout Simms' Brigade, the situation was much the same. Union swordsmen cut a swath through the faltering line. James and some of the others not yet captured put up a light fire but fell back, trying to maintain order as Early's men were now breaking and running everywhere. Custer's cavalry chased down groups of fleeing men, taking slower runners prisoner. There was nothing Simms could do but save as much of his crumbling brigade as possible. He later said, "By this time the enemy had gotten completely in our rear and were pressing from the front and flank, and in moving out among the confused masses of troops from other commands our organizations also became confused, and it was impossible to reform the command in proper order." [50]

****

In Winchester, Captain Rhodes' regiment of Rhode Islanders remained vigilant throughout the late afternoon, keeping a sharp eye on Confederate cavalry and protecting Sheridan's trains just outside the town. Adding to the duties of these men was the flood of wounded and hordes of stragglers that had deserted their posts. It was a mob scene, and the streets of Winchester bogged down into one massive traffic jam. Elisha Rhodes remembered, "The Union people were filled with dismay as rumors of a defeat to our Army reached the city, while Rebels were jubilant, and I was told several times during the day as my duty caused me to ride through the city that General Early would send us flying out of Winchester before dark…The Rebel Cavalry were all about the outskirts of town, and I had all I could do looking after the pickets. Many Rebel families prepared food for the expected Rebel Army, but they did not come, and at night we received the news of Sheridan's glorious victory." [51] One of the wounded men was General Wright. Elisha helped carry him from his ambulance into a hotel which was being used as a hospital.

****

The 50th Georgia, numbering slightly over 100, had been crushed. The regiment retraced its steps of earlier that day, traveling a trail of dead and wounded seven miles long. Colonel McGlashan was hit twice, and with a deep flesh wound in each of his thighs had to be carried during the retreat. It wasn't until the Georgians felt protected by darkness and distance that they allowed themselves to tally their losses. Men straggled into the lines in twos, threes or alone. Some would not find their way back to the brigade for days, while for others, the war was over.

Sergeant James Sheldon had miraculously come through another fight unscathed, but ten other men of the 50th were killed during the day's fighting. In addition to Colonel McGlashan, 19 other men were wounded, including their brave color bearer, Sergeant James Bailey. In the storming of Ft. Sanders in Knoxville, Sergeant Bailey had been the first man from the regiment to stand on the parapet of the fort. At Cedar Creek a total of 37 men, almost half the regiment, had been captured. Among them was William Wattles, a 51-year-old private of the Thomas County Rangers. Like James, Wattles was a Yankee by birth, hailing from Newark, New Jersey.

But one of the saddest losses for the men of the 50th was "Gussie" Brack—missing and assumed captured by the enemy. Augustus Brack wanted very much to be a soldier. At the outbreak of the war in April of 1861, the son of John and Jane Brack attended school and worked as a store clerk in the afternoons. He was a good looking young man, standing 6'2" with fair skin and brown hair and eyes. A year later, he was a proud 4th Sergeant in the "Clinch Volunteers," or Company G of the 50th Georgia. Two weeks after he enlisted, his dad, John, joined him in the company as a private, creating a unique situation where "Gussie" was his father's commanding officer. They enlisted in the Confederate Army for "3 years or the war," [52] and each was awarded the impressive sum of $50 (or 4 month's pay) at Camp Davis, outside Savannah when the 50th Georgia was being organized. In July of that same year, "Gussie" fell ill and was sent to a convalescent camp in Whitesville, Georgia. He returned to the 50th later in the year, only to be hospitalized again in February, this time at Richmond. Many of his friends in the regiment didn't expect him to return, but in May of 1863, he was back on the firing line with his father at the Battle of Salem Church. John Brack was severely wounded and died in a Richmond hospital on May 15, leaving behind his wife, Jane, "Gussie," and a daughter, Ann Victoria.

James took it upon himself to look after "Gussie." No one would have faulted "Gussie" for going home to provide for his mother and sister and some, perhaps, encouraged him to do just that. But Sergeant Brack was determined to fulfill his commitment to the Southern cause.

In the fierce fighting of the second day at Gettysburg, "Gussie"was shot in the thigh. Unable to keep up with his friends, he fell into enemy hands. He recuperated from this wound in a hospital for prisoners on David's Island in New York Harbor, and was exchanged as soon as he was well enough to travel. Now at Cedar Creek, he was gone again, presumed captured. James Sheldon and the other men were heartsick over his loss and feared he would be sent to a Northern prison.

The brigade's losses were equally fearful. Simms reported, "In this battle the brigade had about 520 arms-bearing men. Of four regimental commanders three were wounded, two have since died of the wounds…The loss of the brigade was heavy in officers and men about 200 killed and wounded." [53] Furthermore, 112 had been taken prisoner. Among those captured was Private Washington Waters, who had walked home to plant his crops in 1862, and the regiment's chaplain, the popular William Curry. The 50th Georgia now numbered less than 40 men.

Simms' Brigade returned to Fisher's Hill that evening. Twenty-four hours later, the men reached New Market where they rested for a few days. Resuming their march the brigade finally reached a rail line and boarded a train bound for Richmond.

As the Confederate Army dragged itself southward, many of the disheartened soldiers caught a glimpse of General Jubal Early. Colonel Peter McGlashan remarked, "At one place we passed General Early, sitting on his horse by the roadside, viewing the motley crowd as it passed by. He looked sour and haggard. You could see by the expression of his face the great weight upon his mind, his deep disappointment, his unspoken disappointment." [54]

General Grant received the news of Sheridan's victory at Cedar Creek and his army at Petersburg and celebrated with a 100-gun salute. For Sheridan the rewards came quickly, and only a few weeks after the battle he was promoted to major general. But there were some who believed Sheridan received too much credit for the victory at Cedar Creek. One officer in the 6th Corps believed, "Had Sheridan never reached the field, General Wright would have led us against the foe, whose ardor was already lost after the repeated repulses from the single corps."[55]

But Captain Rhodes was enthralled by Sheridan's ride back to Cedar Creek, writing, "Hurrah for Sheridan! He is the man for me."[56] Rhodes was once again proud of his 6th Corps but grateful that he and his men had been spared from the worst of the fighting saying, "The old Sixth Corps has again covered itself with glory. [But] for once the 3rd Brigade has missed a fight."[57]

The Confederate military, from President Davis to the lowliest private, agonized over the events of Cedar Creek. One officer in Kershaw's division accurately summed up the aftermath, "We returned each man to his old quarters, and as the night wore on more continued to come in singly, by twos, and by the half dozens, until by midnight the greater portion of the army, who had not been captured or lost in battle, had found rest at their old quarters. But such a confusion. What was the cause of our panic, or who was to blame, none ever knew…It looked so ridiculous, so foolish, so uncalled for to see twenty thousand men running wildly over each other, as it were, from their shadows, for there was nothing in our rear but a straggling line of Federals, which one good brigade could have put to rout."[58]

A few days had passed since the debacle when Jubal Early felt he needed to get something off his chest. Speaking to his army, Old Jube said, "I had hoped to have congratulated you on the splendid victory won by you on the morning of the 19th at Belle Grove, on Cedar Creek, when you surprised and routed two corps of Sheridan's army, and drove back several miles the remaining corps…but I have the mortification of announcing to you that, by your subsequent misconduct, all the benefits of that victory were lost. Had you remained steadfast to your duty and your colors, the victory would have been one of the most brilliant and decisive of the war. But many of you, including some commissioned officers, yielded to a disgraceful propensity for plunder, deserted your colors to appropriate to yourselves the abandoned property of the enemy... You have thus obscured that glorious fame won in conjunction with the gallant men of the Army of Northern Virginia, who still remain proudly defiant in the trenches around Richmond and Petersburg." [59]

Adjutant Ben Simms, perhaps reflecting the opinion of other officers as well, remarked, "I am looking for one more big fight in the Valley before the campaign closes. General Early I think is very desirous to retrieve his good character as a General and even if the Yanks should not attack—he will be very tempted to assume the offensive and try his skill again." He added, "I am fearful that General Early made his last fight more for self than country, and our disaster was the frowning of an insulted God upon such an unholy act." [60]

After hearing Early's speech, Sergeant James Rhodes Sheldon sat by his campfire and eyed the survivors of his regiment. He had not spent a day in a hospital since leaving Savannah, nor had he enjoyed a day off or furlough of any kind in three years. He was determined to see it through, whatever the outcome. But not everyone in Lee's army still felt the same patriotic zeal. Confederate desertions skyrocketed.

16

WE WERE GENTLEMEN OF LEISURE

It was a sad looking parade. Kershaw's Division, a ragtag collection of broken brigades, marched south through the Shenandoah Valley of lost opportunity. A lot of the men were carrying gear stamped "U.S." or wearing parts of Union uniforms taken in the early hours of October 19. Except for the steady tromp and clanging of canteens, the columns made their way south in relative silence. The spearhead of Kershaw's attack at Cedar Creek, the 50ᵗʰ Georgia Infantry, followed its brigade commander Colonel James Simms, who Sergeant James Sheldon and the 250 or so men of the brigade affectionately referred to as "general." As they passed through little towns and villages, women stood in their doorways, looking on the retreat in silence, causing one of Kershaw's men to remember, "Their sons and husbands had all given themselves to the service of their country, while rapine and the torch had already done its work too thoroughly to fear it much now or dread its consequences." [1]

Reaching New Market, the regiments were once again separated and assigned camping grounds in an attempt to bring order back to Early's routed army. Throughout the night an endless stream of stragglers came through the picket line seeking their comrades. The parade of disheartened men continued for several days. Starvation was the first concern of James Sheldon and other commissary sergeants, and rations of corn were issued and eaten dried, cooked and raw. Some men even tried making coffee from parched kernels.

Kershaw's men remained in camp until the end of October then marched to rejoin Lee. Early's army probed Sheridan's forces one last time in November in a futile attempt to keep him from joining Grant at Petersburg. But without hope of being resupplied, and unable to prevent Sheridan from receiving reinforcements from General Grant, he began his withdrawal from the Shenandoah by returning Kershaw's Division to Petersburg.

When James Sheldon and Simms' Brigade reached Richmond they went to work immediately building winter quarters about seven miles from the city, on the extreme left of Lee's army. According to one officer in Kershaw's Division, "Everything north of the James continued quiet along our lines for a month or more, but we could hear the deep baying of cannon continually, away to our right, in the direction of Petersburg. These were the most comfortable quarters we occupied during the war. They consisted of log huts twelve by fourteen, thoroughly chinked with mud and straw, some covered with dirt, others with split boards. We had splendid breastworks in front of us, built up with logs on the inside and a bank of earth from six to eight feet in depth on the outside, a ditch of three or four feet beyond and an escarpment inside."[2]

Built as a defense against the elements and as a defense against Grant, these winter quarters were different from those of other years. Land mines were sunk in front of Lee's lines, and each of these mines had little sticks about three feet long stuck in the ground, with a piece of blue flannel tied to the end. To confuse Grant's men, hundreds of sticks, exactly like those above the mines, were stuck into the earth every three feet. One man recalled, "Our lines had been so extended that to man our works along our front we had not more than one man to every six feet. Still with our breastworks so complete and the protection beyond the line, it is doubtful whether the enemy could have made much headway against us."[3]

Captain Elisha Rhodes was also concerned about the coming winter, and had his men construct a large hut to be used as his headquarters. Dick, Elisha's pet sheep, continued to entertain the men of the 2nd, despite being "belligerent in his disposition." [4] The men laughed constantly at the tricks they had taught the animal, but Dick's attitude was often no laughing matter, and Elisha warned, "woe be to any who is not on his guard when Dick approaches." [5] So impressive were Dick's dog-like feats that Elisha briefly thought of sending him off to star in P. T. Barnum's circus. The duty at Winchester had been a great diversion for the men of the 2nd and house-building, shopping, and rest was the best medicine for them. But on Friday, October 28, this leisurely life came to an abrupt close.

Elisha received orders to have his regiment ready to march early the next morning, and it was made clear that the 2nd Rhode Island would not be returning to Winchester. Relationships of all kinds had developed between the men of the 2nd and the citizens of Winchester, and Elisha allowed the men to go into town that evening to say their goodbyes. More than a few young hearts were broken at this sad parting, as romance and friendships are often fleeting during wartime. The 2nd Rhode Island was then ordered to rejoin General Wright and the 6th Corps, 20 miles south at Middletown.

As the 2nd Rhode Island marched out of Winchester the locals gave the men a mixed sendoff. The fifes and drums of the regiment's musicians played 'Glory Hallelujah' and 'Oh, Carry Me Back To Old Virginny,' as well as "other tunes painful to the disloyal ear." [6] By three o' clock in the afternoon, the regiment arrived at its new camp in Middletown, and was greeted by General Frank Wheaton who was thrilled to see his "old boys." [7] Wheaton, a native of Providence, now commanded a division in the 6th Corps. They camped on the Cedar Creek battlefield, which, according to Elisha, looked "more like a cemetery than a camp," with fresh graves dotting the fields. [8]

There were other changes for the regiment. Colonel Isaac C. Bassett now commanded their brigade, while Edwards and the 37th Massachusetts remained at Winchester as the provost guard. The 2nd's camp was enclosed by mountains on three sides and Elisha was captivated by their majestic beauty. A cavern was discovered nearby, and some of the soldiers became tourists, exploring its sanctum. Elisha fired his pistol (a gift from Frederick Miller) to hear the effect of the echo.

The Rhode Islanders were back on the road on November 9, as Sheridan moved his entire army down the Valley to Kernstown, about three miles south of Winchester. The 85 officers and men of the regiment were happy to be off the open, wind-swept plain of Middletown. At Kernstown, they found a large oak grove which provided an abundance of firewood, and their proximity to Winchester allowed them to visit their old friends. Early made his last stand near Cedar Creek on November 12. Captain Rhodes' men spent the day with their rifles filled and cartridge boxes loaded, but were never sent into action, although the sounds of the fighting reached their camp, making everyone edgy.

With Early vanquished, this time for good, the 6th Corps began preparing for a long winter. The area Early had vacated was devastated, and as the temperature dropped daily, it became apparent that the fighting of 1864 had drawn to a close. The dreary life of a soldier in winter had begun for Captain Rhodes and his regiment, but no sooner had the men of the 2nd accepted Kernstown as their winter home that they were once again on the road. This time, they were being used to escort a wagon train bound for Martinsburg from Winchester, creating an inviting target for a marauding band of Confederate cavalry led by the daring John Singleton Mosby. The march of November 22 was uneventful, although Elisha noted, "It was one of the coldest nights I ever knew." [9] After several hours of marching in the freezing dark, the 2nd arrived at Winchester and the men were dismissed until morning when they would begin their detail. The order to break ranks was barely out of Elisha's mouth when the men made a mad dash for the warmth of their friends' homes. Elisha found a warm bed at Colonel Edward's headquarters.

The next night was spent near the little town of Martinsburg, and the men were not nearly so comfortable. Forced to bivouac, the brigade huddled around "old-fashioned" [10] campfires, instead of the fireplaces of their shanties that the men had grown accustomed to. The weeklong stay at Martinsburg was harsh and inhospitable, except for a Thanksgiving surprise. A Rhode Island man had brought a gift of 30 cooked turkeys to give to Captain Rhodes' regiment. The feast was just what the regiment needed to make their miserable stay tolerable; there was so much turkey in the Rhode Island camp that the men of the 18th Connecticut were invited to dinner.

****

By mid-November, Grant was eager to have the 6th Corps veterans back with him in front of Petersburg. As the 2nd Rhode Island camped at Kernstown, the newswalkers spoke of the corps being moved to Petersburg. Elisha was warming himself by "a cheerful fire blazing," [11] feeling content, when an orderly tapped on his door around midnight. The 6th Corps was headed back to Petersburg in the morning.

****

While Colonel Peter McGlashan was recuperating from the flesh wounds to his legs, command of the 50th Georgia Infantry was placed in the hands of its highest ranking officer, Major John Spence. When the war began, Spence had been living on his farm in the southeastern part of Coffee County, Georgia. He organized the first and only Confederate company from that county. On March 4, 1862, the "Coffee County Guards" were mustered into the Confederate Army, becoming Company C of the 50th Georgia and the popular Spence was elected captain. Admired by James and the other men for his bravery and valor, he was promoted to major on December 21, 1863. Now, less than a year later the regiment was his—at least temporarily.

But where was Simms' Brigade of Georgians, and where were they going? Grant's scouts weren't quite sure. A Union dispatch dated November 23, stated, "Bryan's brigade is camped on the Williamsburg road. The provost guard of the division came out of Richmond yesterday morning, and these were the last troops that have passed through the town. There was a camp rumor yesterday in Kershaw's division, overheard by our agent, who stopped in Bryan's brigade, that they were going to Georgia, but he learned nothing to justify such an opinion…They say in Richmond that Kershaw's division has been brought down because the enemy (Confederates) expect another attack by us on the north side; and our friends send us word that such is really the opinion."[12] Ben Simms detailed his brigade's activities in a November 14 letter to his sister, "[Since] last Friday morning we have marched forty miles and returned making a distance of eighty miles in four days…We have had several days very cold weather—the ice today is plentiful and thick."[13]

A month later, a private in Simms' brigade explained the whereabouts and well-being of the men. "We are encamped precisely on the same spot we first formed a line of battle on two years ago 8 miles from Richmond. We are in winter quarters and living in fine style [with] no Yanks right in front of us. Wood is very scarce."[14]

James managed to keep his regiment well fed with the exception of bread, which had recently become scarce. Politicians from Georgia visited James' camp and in one night alone the men had to endure five speeches. "They told the sad news of the fall of Savannah. They said there is no chance for peace. They said the only chance is to whip the Yanks to a peace," recalled one man.[15] The newswalkers spoke of the citizens of Richmond giving Lee's army a grand Christmas dinner.

James worried about what was happening at home in Thomasville. But these concerns were unfounded as Sherman's columns stayed well north of Thomasville, preoccupied with the bigger trophies of Savannah and Columbia, South Carolina. But Thomasville was not completely unaffected by his march, and in December of 1864, the city of 2,500 suddenly found itself hosting 5,000 guests. Worried that Sherman might attempt to liberate the prisoners held at Andersonville, Confederate authorities there decided to relocate the more able-bodied prisoners out of his path to Blackshear, Georgia. Logistically, Blackshear could not accommodate such a mob and the men were moved farther south to Thomasville. The prisoners began arriving in Thomasville via the Atlantic & Gulf Railroad in early December.

During this journey, one of the more comical episodes of the war took place. The train's engine was simply on its last legs and required a significant head of steam to get rolling and a shortage of coal didn't help the situation. The train would frequently grind to a halt as the hungry engine demanded to be fed. In these moments, black laborers and slaves would jump off the train with axes, felling any tree or breaking apart any abandoned building near the tracks. Loaded with a fresh stock of wood, the engine would resume hauling its cargo for another half hour or so. On one occasion, the train needed a little extra encouragement to get rolling again and a group of Confederate officers jumped off the train to begin pushing it. Having no success, an officer demanded that the Andersonville prisoners get off the train and join in the effort. "We respectfully, but firmly decline," said a spokesman for the group, explaining later, "We were gentlemen of leisure, we said, and decidedly adverse to manual labor; we had been invited on this excursion by Mr. Jeff Davis and his friends, who set themselves up as our entertainers, and it would be a gross breach of hospitality to reflect upon our hosts by working our passage. If this was insisted upon," the prisoner stated with tongue planted firmly in cheek, "we certainly should not visit them again." [16]

Upon entering their new camp at Thomasville, the prisoners immediately disapproved of the conditions. At the time, the weather was pleasant, but the prisoners were concerned about the rains the approaching winter was sure to bring. The men complained about the lack of shelters, but in fairness to the citizens of Thomasville, no one could have expected their arrival. They were allowed axes and other tools and began constructing what amounted to a small town surrounded by a ditch and guards. At Andersonville, the prisoners had been bored and had no physical activity available to them, but here they enjoyed both the freedom to design their quarters and the exercise the work provided. Rations were scarce, but there was an ample crop of sweet potatoes available and these quickly became a staple of the prisoner's diet. Smallpox broke out and quickly spread around camp, but overall, the conditions were much better than the grim existence at Andersonville, and the excursion was a peaceful diversion for the men who seemed impressed by Thomasville. One prisoner remarked, "the town seemed to have some life… We were told that before the war many rich planters made this place their home. There were some very handsome residences in the place." But there was no doubt that this camp was a prison, however temporary. It was an overwhelmingly depressing existence as one prisoner wrote, "There was little choice between living and dying. If any, it was in favor of the latter…"[17]

The Union prisoners spent two weeks in Thomasville. One night, long past midnight, James Sheldon's sister, Patience, and her husband, Edward Remington, awoke to a rapping at their door. Grabbing a robe and a candle, Edward answered the door to find a man insisting that his presence was urgently needed at the store of fellow merchants Herman and Nathan Wolff.

Edward Remington

Arriving at the store, the 60-year-old Edward was introduced to a skinny, scared prisoner who had managed to escape from the prison camp but had given little thought of what to do next. The man had heard that the Wolff brothers were Masons and he appealed to them as one of their own. The brothers argued over how to resolve this ethical and patriotic dilemma and finally agreed to seek the consul of their wise friend, Edward. In the end, the fraternal bond won out and the man was fitted with civilian clothes and supplied with a sufficient amount of cash to go North. The excited man swore that he would not return to the army and was on his way. Nothing more was ever heard of him.

The citizens of Thomasville, having shared so much with the North, embraced the prisoners, offering what comfort to them they could. One prisoner remembered that upon arriving the townspeople "seemed to be very much affected at the sight they saw, and manifested much sympathy for us." The locals provided the men with "food, barrels of homemade soap, towels, and such clean clothing as could be spared." [18] Not a single prisoner ever complained of being mistreated by the people of Thomasville, and at least one of them moved to Georgia after the war. On December 17, two Confederate regiments arrived at Thomasville to prepare the prisoners for a 60-mile march to Albany, Georgia. The men were issued two crackers apiece as they began their dreary nighttime march. Along the way, they were given some cornbread and fresh beef. Upon reaching Albany, the men were once again put aboard railcars and arrived back at Andersonville on Christmas Eve. Many of these men would not survive the final three months of the war under the brutal conditions of that prison.

****

Captain Elisha Rhodes, and the entire 6th Corps, left Kernstown by train on the first day of December, arriving at the nation's capital about noon the next day. Living on rations in camp, the officers had no need for money and didn't realize until getting to Washington that none of them had any cash. Dick the sheep, who recently had learned to "fall-in" with the men at roll call, had joined the men on the train. But the penniless officers "sacrificed our sentiment and sold poor old Dick to a butcher for $5.00," which Elisha and the other officers used to buy bread and bologna. [19] The regiment boarded a steamer and on December 5 were camped once again near Petersburg along the Weldon Railroad.

It had been five months since the 2nd Rhode Island had left Petersburg, and the men of the 6th Corps immediately noticed the difference between their own appearance and that of the men who had remained there. An officer in the 6th Corps was quick to point out, "our war-worn brothers showed upon their faces the marks of overwork. We were in fresh vigor. We had marched through a blooming valley literally abounding in milk and honey." [20] The 6th Corps men were proud of their service in the Valley, but the stark expressions of their comrades in the Petersburg trenches were hard to look at without a tinge of guilt.

****

Sherman's army reached Savannah on December 10, and with little hope of preventing him from storming the city it was evacuated. Ten days later, Sherman presented Savannah to Lincoln as a Christmas gift. President Lincoln, re-elected a month before, was elated.

****

Lee's Army of Northern Virginia was in bad shape. With winter closing in, sickness increased and desertion rates climbed. Some men, seeing no hope of winning the war, gave up and sneaked away from the trenches to try to make their way home. Those who stayed grew despondent as rations diminished. Some went days at a time with only small amounts of cornbread to appease their aching stomachs. The cold and hungry Confederates huddled in the muddy trenches around Richmond and Petersburg, often comparing their situation to that of Washington's Continental Army—Union men across the field made similar comparisons.

Grant's men were also running away, and both armies were forced to come up with methods of keeping the men in the trenches. The Confederate army offered a $30 reward for the capture and return of any man trying to desert. The Union army, not faced with a manpower shortage, took a harsher approach and offered a twenty-day furlough to any man who shot a deserter. But desertion was a much more serious problem for the Confederacy in the fall and winter of 1864-65. Letters from home, telling of hardships and cruelty at the hands of the enemy, only intensified the temptation to desert. In Georgia, Governor Joe Brown tried to stem the flood of deserters coming back to his state by asking the legislature for the power to seize "the property of persons charged with disloyalty to the Confederacy," and effectively "disenfranchise and decitizenize" these men and their families. [21]

But rations, or lack thereof, remained the bane of Commissary Sergeant James Sheldon and the 50th Georgia's existence. For a time, pickled beef became a staple of the Confederate diet and the men joked that no one really knew for sure what was in the red cans labeled, "made in London." [22] Some men insisted it was dog meat while others laughed and claimed to like it. In Kershaw's Division, sugar, coffee and molasses were occasionally substituted for meat. Rations were issued every other day and most men were so hungry they consumed their allotment immediately. It was better to be hungry only half of the time some men thought. But it was feared that if rations were issued in three or four-day intervals, the men would not control themselves. Kershaw complained of the situation in one of his reports, saying, "The amount allowed even when obtained is not sufficient for the men…To these deficiencies of food I attribute the number of desertions daily occurring and a general feeling of depression existing." [23] Another morale buster was the favoritism often shown to officers when it came to the distribution of foodstuffs and clothing, lowly privates were often given ill-fitting uniforms, stale bread, and worm-infested meat. Commissary Sergeant Sheldon made the most of what he could get his hands on for the men of the 50th. A common trick he would try to pull on the army was to fudge the number of men in the regiment in an attempt to procure more food for them. Gone were the days in the Shenandoah Valley where plunder and foraging filled the bellies of Kershaw's men. In these trenches, the men could only depend on whatever the Richmond government provided them.

If there was any good news for the men of the Army of Northern Virginia during the late fall and winter of 1864, it was the return of James Longstreet. He was eager to get back into the war, although physically the general was a shell of his former self. His once booming voice was reduced to a rasp, and his right arm was a useless appendage. As he rode along his lines for the first time since his wounding, his men cheered wildly.

****

The 2nd Rhode Island's most grueling experience of the winter came immediately after its return to Petersburg. On Friday, December 9, the 2nd took part in a ruse to create a diversion near a place called Hatcher's Run. Thirty miles south of Petersburg, Warren's 5th Corps began operations, and it was hoped that these troop movements would confuse Lee as to Grant's intentions. Reverend Woodbury wrote, "The troops marched in the midst of a severe storm of rain, sleet and snow, and about midnight went into bivouac in a piece of woods, near the run. The storm increased in severity every mile of the way, and when the halt was made the men were 'nearly dead with cold.' It was altogether the severest weather of the season. Of course there were no tents or other means of shelter. Fires were built, but were of little avail in mitigating the rigor of the air. Men and officers walked about or sat down in the snow, wet, cold and miserable, and wished for the day." [24]

The next day, there was a slight thaw and the march resumed through knee-deep mud and water. Occasionally, the air would fill with the buzz and zip of bullets. The men, suffering from exhaustion and exposure, stumbled into their warm huts at Petersburg, three days later.

The year of 1864 closed on a positive note for the men of the 2nd Rhode Island. On Christmas Eve, a company of 70 new recruits arrived and were welcomed as Company "F" into the regiment, its two musicians added to the Christmas cheer. Captain Rhodes got the biggest surprise of all. There was concern that morale of the 2nd was suffering without a colonel, but the regiment was still technically at battalion strength. General Wheaton and Colonel Bassett had written to their superiors citing Elisha's "tact, energy and efficiency," as well as his "conspicuous gallantry in the field." As a result of their recommendations, Elisha became Major Rhodes of the 2nd Rhode Island. [25] Adding even further to Elisha's happy Christmas was a surprise visit from his close friend, T. J. Smith, who had been nearly killed by a sharpshooter several months earlier. Thinking of the sacrifices he had made over the past three and a half years, a philosophical Rhodes decided, "It is all for the Union." [26]

****

As Simms' Brigade of Georgians camped outside of Richmond, Private John Wood, a private in the 53rd Georgia, wrote to his family, "I am afraid this war is bound to last another term of four years or perhaps until the south is subdued or the (illegible) and the men or Yanks exhausted. It will take the North several years to conquer the South if she ever does. I am very tired of this war. I think it is time it would cease. If I can ever get home, and this war will end, I am willing to die there." [27] Ben Simms was equally distressed, and wrote, "I feel almost despondent sometimes in contemplating the future of our Confederacy. I look around and see nothing save a gloomy picture, defeats in Georgia, disaster in Tennessee, and even in

Virginia we sometimes meet with reverses." [28] Most telling was his concern that "the immense amount of blood yet to be shed is sickening." Wood questioned how this could be if God was on the side of the Confederacy. [29]

Although civilian life in Richmond continued as normally as possible, the plight of the men in the trenches was impossible to ignore. "Kershaw's Division is low, awfully hacked from the whipping they got in the valley," said one cavalryman from South Carolina. [30] In November, a movement was begun by the ladies of the city to do something to raise the mood of the dispirited soldiers. Christmas was fast approaching and the holiday, traditionally spent in the company of family and loved ones, would hit the men particularly hard in the midst of their deprivation. The Union Army of the Potomac was notorious for its lavish holiday feasts, and the newswalkers often would describe them in detail to the hungry Confederates. The women of Richmond decided that their own soldiers would enjoy such a feast this Christmas and promptly formed a committee to plan the event.

As always, the newswalkers quickly got wind of the Christmas dinner news, a private in Simms' Brigade told his aunt about it in a letter on December 18. "We are encamped, on the same spot of ground we occupied when we first formed a line of battle before the Seven Days fight, near Richmond [in 1862]. We are in winter quarters, and have a good time to what we have been having of late. We get plenty to eat with the exception of bread which is scarce, though we make out by buying a little. The citizens of Richmond speak of giving us a good dinner Christmas." [31]

It immediately became apparent that logistics prevented the feast from being held on Christmas, so the focus was changed to New Year's Day. But the 1st fell on a Sunday, so the date was changed to January 2 in order to give the organizers an extra day to prepare. The entire city got involved, including the newspapers, which ran pleas for donations and volunteers. When word of the dinner reached James and the 50th Georgia, their gloom lifted. The New Year's feast was on everybody's tongue as the *Richmond*

Examiner boasted of what was going to be "the biggest barbecue ever gotten up on this continent." [32] The menu was argued and debated as the starving men wondered just what delicacies would be crossing their plates. On New Year's Eve, the *Examiner* settled the matter, promising the men, "rounds of beef, saddles of mutton, venisons, whole shoats, hams, sausage of country make, rich with sage and redolent with pepper; turkies, geese, ducks [and] chickens." [33] Aware of the complaints of the lowly private when it came to such matters, the newspaper assured that "the commonest private will be entitled to the first helping and the best." [34] All of this sounded too good to be true to many of the barefoot, famished men. Unfortunately, they were right.

On January 2, most of the men received only a few small loaves of bread. Some got nothing at all. In one case, 1,500 men were issued less than 200 pounds of meat, bread and flour, and four or five bushels of potatoes and turnips. Most of the men had not been able to sleep the night before in anticipation of the big day and were up early in the morning. A man in the 18th Georgia described the events of the day, "And we waited. What a long day that seemed to be! We whiled away the tedious hours by telling stories and cracking jokes! Noon came, then two, four, eight, ten and twelve o'clock, and still no 'goody' wagon. Being still a little weak, I became tired and lay down and went to sleep with the understanding that those on watch would call me when our dinner arrived. It was after three a.m. when a comrade called and told me that a detail had just gone out to meet the precious wagon and bring in our feast. But oh what a disappointment when the squad returned and issued to each man only one small sandwich made up of two tiny slices of bread and a thin piece of ham!" [35]

Some of the men grumbled aloud until a middle-aged man interrupted "God bless our noble women! It was all they could do; it was all they had." The realities of war had come roaring back. Another man remembered, "every man in that old tent indulged in a good cry. We couldn't help it." Silence fell upon the small gathering. [36]

While everyone was disappointed, their reactions varied widely. A Texas Brigade donated their New Year's meal to the orphans in Richmond. Some felt disgust and betrayal after what they had been lead to expect from the newspapers and newswalkers. Others were simply grateful for whatever they were given. These were hard times for the civilians in Richmond as well as the army, and the difficulties facing the organizers of the dinner was understood by many of the disappointed men. But soon, men were deserting from the Army of Northern Virginia at the rate of nearly 100 per day.

James Sheldon and Elisha Rhodes spent New Year's Day in decidedly different fashion. While James consumed his meager Christmas dinner, Elisha entertained the governor of Rhode Island and his staff, who had traveled to Petersburg to present Major Rhodes with a marker and a new set of colors for the 2nd Rhode Island.

****

At year's end, Confederate authorities were able to verify the whereabouts of the approximately 1,000 men taken prisoner at Cedar Creek. James learned that his young friend, "Gussie" Brack, was incarcerated at Point Lookout Prison in southern Maryland and wrote to his brother George at home in Pawtuxet requesting a favor. A veteran himself, George agreed to help "Gussie" and on February 19, wrote to him:

> Friend Brack,
> Having received a letter from my brother James R. Sheldon of the 50th Georgia Regiment a few days since I take the liberty of addressing you. James wants me to either send you 20 or 25 dollars or its equivalent. In doing this I first desire your true address and your wants. He also says you are his friend and wanting to help you he takes this method.

I will forward to you by express or mail anything you desire most if in my power and hope you may receive it.

James says he expects to go home soon as he has not seen his sister for 3 years. He is well and in good spirits, a very good article to have about in the present time.

Hoping to hear from you soon,

I remain truly yours,

Geo. F. Sheldon [37]

While Colonel McGlashan's wounds healed in a Richmond hospital, he had plenty of time to think about what he would face when he returned to his regiment. In spite of the damage Lee had inflicted upon Grant's army, McGlashan had his doubts, saying, "But there the illimitable recuperative energies of the North soon showed themselves. Their ranks were filled up, confidence restored, and the army itself strongly entrenched around Petersburg—new object of the attack." [38]

In mid-January, Simms' Brigade of Georgians simply disappeared, at least as far as the Army of the Potomac was concerned. If Grant was to launch one final assault on Richmond or Petersburg, he could hardly afford to have any Confederate divisions or brigades flying around unaccounted for. On January 16, General George Meade received the following dispatch regarding the movement of Confederate troops to the Carolinas: "It would seem that one of Kershaw's division did not go south— namely, Bryan's (Georgia) brigade, now commanded by Colonel McGlashan. There is also a rumor that Gregg's (Texas) brigade went to North Carolina. Perhaps this brigade went in the place of Bryan's." [39]

With the lines at Petersburg falling into a wintery quiet, Elisha wanted to go home and see his mother Eliza, his family, and former employer, Frederick Miller. Things were certain to heat up when spring returned, and there would be a lot of casualties. Major Rhodes also wanted to meet with Governor Smith to seek promotions for a dozen or so of his sergeants, who he now needed to command companies.

Elisha was upset with the governor after learning that Colonel George Church, of the now defunct 1st Rhode Island, had been appointed colonel of the 2nd Rhode Island. The officers and men of the regiment were also livid. Elisha made no attempt to hide his unhappiness and even considered quitting the army, writing, "I have served for more than three and a half years and have commanded the regiment for six months with rank below other officers who have smaller commands, and it does not seem right to have the Governor send a man from Rhode Island to take command. I might resign, to be sure, but I hope I am serving my country honestly and not for personal ends, and I shall try to see the end of the war." [40]

On January 18, Major Rhodes left his camp on a furlough granted by General Meade. While returning to camp on Sunday, the 5th of February, Elisha carried with him not only the commissions he had requested for his men, but the rank of lieutenant colonel for himself. He remarked, "This promotion was of great service to me as it gave me rank in proportion to my command." [41] It was clear to everyone that Elisha was no longer "only a boy," as he had described himself after the Battle of Antietam. [42]

****

Ulysses Grant was having a hard time waiting for a spring offensive. The winter had been unusually cold, and life for his soldiers in the trenches was miserable. The men were perpetually wet and at times were under shelling around the clock. To alleviate some of this dreariness, and to extend the Union line west of Petersburg, Grant decided to mount his first major offensive of 1865.

On February 4, he ordered four divisions to march southwest from Petersburg to the Boydton Plank Road. As Elisha Rhodes was returning to his regiment he discovered his camp empty, having been sent to join Grant at a place called Hatcher's Run. After sleeping for a few hours, Lt. Colonel Rhodes set off to find his men.

General Lee was attending Sunday services when he received word of the Union movements. He worried that Grant would cut the Southside Railroad, his last supply line to the south and west, and rushed four divisions to meet the new threat. The Battle of Hatcher's Run began in the early afternoon and Grant's men were still erecting earthworks as the Confederates assembled for the attack. Just before four p.m., two Confederate brigades charged the Union entrenchments. Three times these Southern men came on, only to be repulsed. As darkness ended the fighting, men of both sides sought the safety of their trenches. The fight resumed the next day after two Union divisions were ordered northwest to Dabney's Mill. These divisions were met by a single Confederate division and the Yankees got the best of it. The Southerners fell back until reinforced, and then pushed Grant's men back in panic until their own reinforcements arrived, halting the rout of their comrades.

The 2nd Rhode Island, waiting in reserve, bivouacked in the cold. The night brought snow and freezing rain, Lt. Colonel Rhodes said, "I never felt more uncomfortable in my life." [43] Throughout the 7th, there was intermittent skirmishing. The battle was a Confederate victory in terms of casualties, but the war was no longer just about numbers. Grant had extended his line once again. Union casualties were about 1,500, while Lee suffered a total loss of about 750 men.

Two days later, Lt. Colonel Rhodes was back in his old camp and found a surprise waiting for him. While he was on furlough in Rhode Island, his men built him a log hut with a wooden floor and door. In addition, as a token of his regiment's admiration for him, the fireplace was adorned with festive ornamentation.

The despondency in the Confederate trenches was detrimental to the army. Some, including R. O. Davidson, saw it as an opportunity. Davidson believed that he could put a man in flight; in fact, he was sure of it. He claimed his "Bird of Art," or "Artisavis," [44] could put a man in the clouds for prolonged periods of time. His flying machine could serve many useful purposes, such as delivering messages or small quantities of goods. In the spring of 1865, Davidson made the rounds in Richmond, pitching his invention as believers and skeptics alike listened intently. Eventually the skeptics won out. An editorial in the *Richmond Whig* newspaper said about Mr. Davidson's flying machine, "Mr. Davidson's artisavis, as he calls his flying machine…must fail, not from want of ingenuity, but because natural laws are fatally opposed." [45]

Undaunted, Davidson sought a new market. After his plea for funding was rejected by the government, he went directly to the front lines at Richmond and Petersburg where tens of thousands of Confederate soldiers camped throughout the summer and fall. The newswalkers talked of Mr. Davidson and his flying machine and told Simms' Georgians not to miss it. In reality, the flying machine did not materialize—but Davidson certainly did. Part engineer, part huckster, Davidson hawked his idea to the bored men and preyed upon their common desire to go home. In a letter to his sister, Ben Simms wrote that the contraption was "an artificial bird to go by steam through the air that can carry a man to guide it and a number of shells which the man can drop on the Yankees as he passes over them which will soon kill and scare them all away." [46]

As the self-proclaimed inventor handed his business cards to his audience, he told them his "Bird of Art" would "destroy or drive from our soil every hostile Yankee," and tugging on the homesickness that plagued everyone, he added, "and thus soon close the war." [47] As James listened, Davidson explained that one of his machines would cost $20,000, but once proved successful, the Confederate government would certainly provide the funding for several more.

Whether he ever intended to develop the "Artisavis" or not, Davidson managed to collect $1,500 for his efforts, a tremendous sum. When Ben Simms tried to explain his pessimism about the flying machine he said, "I should as soon look for perpetual motion to be invented as one of Davidson's Birds to rise and fly." Simms confessed that others in the brigade were not as cynical, but added, "I never gave him anything, he received from the brigade one-hundred and twenty-seven dollars —pretty liberal patronage for a humbug." [48]

****

On Valentine's Day, Elisha got a new boss—Brigadier General Joseph Hamblin of New York had been put in command of the brigade. Hamblin was born in Yarmouth, Massachusetts, in 1828, and was, for many years prior to the Civil War, a member of the 7th New York militia regiment. At the outbreak of the war, he accompanied the regiment to Washington. He served as lieutenant colonel of the 65th New York Volunteers, commanded his regiment at Chancellorsville, was promoted to colonel and led his regiment at Gettysburg. Recently, he had been severely wounded at Cedar Creek. Elisha and General Hamblin had met before—in the woods of Spotsylvania in May of 1864.

The 2nd Rhode Island spent the balance of the winter keeping warm in their huts. The storms were severe, with one lasting nearly a week. A poetry club was established to help pass the idle hours, often resulting in fits of laughter as men dared to give grand recitals. Just before St. Patrick's Day, the regiment played host to a lady who was the cousin of an officer. The regiment entertained Miss Lena Hunt in grand style, until the party in her honor was interrupted by a Confederate attack. Miss Hunt enjoyed the shooting immensely, clapping wildly as the enemy was driven off. Elisha had his hands full keeping her off the parapet where she might have been killed.

There was little to laugh about on the Confederate side. The health of Lee's men had become critical during the early weeks of 1865. "Starving on its feet," [49] was one description of the army. Daily rations, if available at all, were one to one and one-half pounds of flour or meal, and three-quarters of a pound of meat. The quantity of rations varied from one regiment to the next. The situation became so bad, and at times, so corrupt, that the Commissary General Colonel Lucius Northrop was replaced by Brigadier General Isaac St. John. Malnutrition caused shortness of breath in many men and the slightest physical exertion could be painful. Barefoot men suffered frostbite, and many were without coats or jackets of any kind, despite the often sub-zero temperatures. Even the animals suffered, and nearly a quarter of Lee's cavalry was without horses.

As a private, James had already proven himself as a fighting man and now, in the dark days of February 1865, he proved himself just as valuable as a commissary sergeant. While other regiments suffered for want of food, this was not the case in James' 50th Georgia as one man insisted, "[We are] getting plenty to eat, which constitutes the height of soldiers happiness. We get corn bread and as fine fresh pork as I ever eat in my life – sometimes in addition turnips, potatoes, or peas, which boiled for dinner is splendid." Tongue in cheek, the man continued, "The meals we usually have in camp if eaten from crockery ware six miles off [in a city restaurant] would cost only sixteen dollars per meal." [50]

Perhaps the most heartbreaking ordeal for the men was the stoppage of mail from home. Men were left to imagine the fate of loved ones at home, and most feared the worst. Between February 15 and February 25, 148 men deserted from Longstreet's Corps alone. Of all the division commanders, Kershaw remained among the most successful at keeping men at their posts.

James and the other men of the 50th were in desperate need of some good news in early February, and they got it when their beloved colonel, Peter McGlashan, suddenly returned one day, poised to reassume command of his Georgians. The men were thrilled to have him back, especially Major Spence, who could now go home to visit his family. Spence was granted a leave of absence on February 14, and returned home for the first time since entering the service. It was the last time his men would see him.

By March, the desertion bug had infected James Sheldon's own brigade. The army was falling apart everywhere and even the most distinguished regiments and brigades were subject to desertion. At seven p.m. on Sunday evening of the 19th, Colonel Peter McGlashan, commanding the brigade during a brief absence of the recently promoted General Simms, sought the advice of Richmond in a dispatch, saying, "I have just been informed that a large portion of this brigade and of others intend to leave camp tonight with their arms and fight their way home. Please inform the other brigade commanders and give us your assistance in checking and quelling the threatened danger." [51] On March 25, The *Philadelphia Inquirer* reported, "The largest squad of Rebel deserters that have yet reached here at any one time arrived yesterday evening from City Point. This squad numbers 215, including one officer, Lieutenant J. J. Tillman of the 50th Georgia Regiment." [52] Tillman and the other men sold their muskets to the highest bidders upon their arrival in Philadelphia.

Ben Simms told his sister of the problems within the ranks, writing, "Georgians are very despondent and are behaving disgracefully—I suppose our brigade has lost fifty men by desertion this winter." Letters from home describing the horrors of Sherman's march only led to more desertion. Simms continued, "People at home have done more harm by discouraging the army than they have any idea." He then predicted, "Grant will make a movement of some kind in a very short time, being exceedingly ambitious and zealous to attain for himself, fame, has shown great impatience through the winter." [53]

In this crisis, Peter McGlashan leaned heavily on those he trusted. Believing their colonel had been slighted by the secretary of war, his men insisted on referring to McGlashan as "General." They in turn were often fulfilling the duties of higher ranking officers no longer present. Sergeant James Sheldon took on the duties of the departed John Spence, earning him the title

"Major"[54] with the men of the 50th Georgia. As winter ended, Lt. Colonel Rhodes and Major Sheldon settled into their new ranks. Elisha and James could hardly have imagined this day when they were playing in the streets and yards of Pawtuxet Village.

17

GREAT EVENTS ARE TO HAPPEN IN A FEW DAYS

By April, 1865, only about a third of the 360,000 men enrolled in the Confederate Army were actually present for duty. Considering the abysmal conditions these men had to endure, it may be even more remarkable that so many men stayed. As spring returned to Virginia the outlook of James Sheldon and the other 55,000 men in Lee's army was grim. The best selling novel *Les Miserables* had become a favorite of the men in the trenches and they took to referring to themselves as "Lee's Miserables." [1] But ultimate surrender to Grant's colossal army was never really considered. One officer from Virginia captured the sentiments of Lee's men and their refusal to submit to the Union Army, saying, "Fresh disaster each day did not affect our confidence. We were quite ready to admit, indeed we had already contemplated and discounted anything and everything this side of ultimate disaster; but that—*never!*" [2]

But Lee knew better. Grant was very much in charge of events around Petersburg and Richmond. Peace talks between Washington and Richmond had broken down, and with each passing day Grant's army grew bigger while Lee's shrank with illness and desertion. Grant could either outwait or whip Lee, but staying in these trenches in front of Petersburg would be the death of the Army of Northern Virginia. Lee asked General John B. Gordon to devise a plan that would enable the army to escape from Petersburg and perhaps allow it to join forces with the Confederate army in North Carolina. Gordon came up with a surprise attack that would force Grant to shorten his ever lengthening lines or maybe even pull them back. For at least a couple of hours, Grant's army would be in turmoil and if timed perfectly, Lee's men might escape. The actual attackers would be left on their own and if things went badly the affair could quickly turn into a suicide mission. On March 25, Lee decided it was a risk he had to take.

In the pre-dawn hours, at about three a.m., a group of Confederate sharpshooters claiming to be deserters showed up at a Union fort built to protect a supply depot, believed to be about a mile to the rear on the railroad Grant had built. The men kept the fort's tenants busy trying to figure out what to do with them. The ruse worked, and at about four o'clock the leading elements of Lee's force, comprising perhaps one-quarter of his army, overwhelmed Union pickets and seized the fort, along with some batteries that were posted north and south of the structure.

The attackers promptly turned the fort's guns around and began blasting a wide hole in Grant's line. At about six a.m., General Gordon personally took command of Ft. Stedman, enjoying what appeared to be a striking success. But a sinking feeling filled the general when some of his riders came back to the fort explaining that they couldn't find the depot they were supposed to raid.

Union artillery was suddenly awake and lines of men in blue uniforms were also making inroads toward Gordon's position at the fort. At 7:30 in the morning, Lee ordered Gordon to retreat. The 2nd Rhode Island was roused by the sounds of excited couriers, frantically delivering the news of the attack. Lieutenant Colonel Rhodes' regiment joined its division on a double-quick march of five miles under constant shelling. The Rhode Islanders arrived at the fort just as it was retaken by the Union army, but the Battle of Ft. Stedman was over. By nine o' clock in the morning it was "all quiet within our lines," said Reverend Woodbury.[3] Colonel Rhodes and his men had no way of knowing that a long, difficult day had only just begun for the 2nd Rhode Island.

Returning to their camp, the hungry Rhode Islanders were forced to forego breakfast and ordered to the left of the 6th Corps, in an effort to drive in enemy pickets and extend Grant's lines even further. Elisha's veterans eventually found they were the extreme right flank of their division as they coolly chased the Confederate pickets in front of them. Colonel Rhodes suddenly saw a large force of the enemy closing in on his right flank. He was quick to react, and swung his regiment around and unleashed a vicious volley on the advancing gray line, later recalling, "Our whole line rushed forwards and drove the Rebels from their works."[4] Seeing an opportunity to get out of the war, many of the Confederates surrendered. Elisha took two prisoners at gunpoint. With the fighting over, the Rhode Islanders spent the next several hours digging rifle pits. They staggered back into their camp at three in the morning, 24 hours after the attack had begun.

The Battle of Ft. Stedman only worsened Lee's already dire situation. Grant had actually gained ground further down the line near Ft. Fisher, giving him a staging ground for a breakthrough attack. During the four-hour battle Grant lost 2,100 men, while Lee's own losses approached 4,500—almost half of which deserted or were taken prisoner. The toll this action took on the psyche of men like Major James Sheldon and his brothers-in-arms was profound. Lee became very depressed and knew it was now Grant's turn to call the shots. Grant was overheard saying that he "felt like ending the matter."[5]

****

Four days after the Confederate attack on Ft. Stedman, Grant began what he hoped would be his final campaign. But a steady driving rain made operations difficult, and a full-fledged assault would have to wait. On the 27th and 28th, President Lincoln was staying on a barge on the James River at nearby City Point. He entertained Grant, Admiral Porter and General Sherman—there was plenty to talk about. The President said he was eager to see Lee pressed and on Wednesday, March 29, his wish was answered.

Lee watched the conditions of the roads, desperately hoping to escape and join Joe Johnston. Grant's lines now extended from the north side of the James all the way to the west of Petersburg. Lee's engineers continued to struggle to devise a defense against an enemy more than twice the size of their own army, flooding some sections of trenches with water where manpower was not available. One thing was clear, the Army of Northern Virginia *had* to get out of Petersburg. Grant began threatening Lee's lightly defended right flank, thwarting whatever plans the Confederates might have had of escaping to the west. To counter this move, Lee sent the divisions of Pickett and Fitzhugh Lee to an area which included an intersection known as Five Forks—weakening his lines around Petersburg.

Grant sent Phil Sheridan's cavalry west toward Dinwiddie Court House, and two corps of infantry began marching to support him. A nasty fight decided little, but Grant's intention to break Lee's lines in this area was now out in the open. The next morning the rain continued as both armies concentrated near Five Forks.

On Friday the 31st, Warren's 5th Corps joined forces with Custer's cavalry on the west side of the city. They met Sheridan coming in from the Shenandoah Valley. Grant planned to have Sheridan's horsemen lead the infantry and cut the last Confederate supply line on the South Side Railroad.

General George Pickett was in charge of the Confederate troops in this sector. He managed a successful charge against Custer, but suffered from the lack of support troops—three days of rain had turned the surrounding woods into swamps. Lee could offer Pickett little assistance, and Pickett was ordered to fall back and "Hold Five Forks at all hazards." [6]

About two a.m. the following morning, Warren's 5th Corps engineers completed a 40-foot pontoon bridge across Gravelly Run, and men, artillery and supplies began crossing over toward Five Forks. About an hour before sunrise, Pickett quietly moved to the White Oak Road which passed through Five Forks. His men quickly went to work, piling up dirt and logs as they braced for an attack on their left. This position was referred to as the "Angle."[7] When Custer discovered that Pickett was gone, he sent scouts to find him.

Throughout the day there was skirmishing along White Oak Road. The soaked and flooded terrain created problems for Warren's 5th Corps as officers complained that their maps were wrong. Sheridan instructed Warren to position his men east and south of the "Angle," and to let him know when he was ready to attack. Sheridan waited and fumed. When Warren finally positioned his men he was much further north than Sheridan had intended.

Confident that his fortifications would hold, Pickett gave his lines a brief inspection and rode behind the lines to another general's camp for a shad bake. Throughout the afternoon, the perfumed Pickett gave cursory glances at reports of skirmishing at and around the position of his command.

Still in their camp, the 2nd Rhode Island could hear "the boom of cannon and rattle of muskets."[8] The sky filled with shells bursting like meteors. The regiment stayed under arms, waiting for a battle that never came. They spent the last days of March on picket duty and had fought for and won some enemy rifle pits. Some of the men had not slept for several days and were understandably edgy.

At about 3:45, Warren's 5th Corps was finally ready, and the Union men charged into and over the three-foot high fortifications at the "Angle," taking nearly 1,000 Confederates prisoner within minutes. As the sound of the firing grew closer and more intense, Pickett left the shad bake to rejoin his men. As he rode to the front, some of Warren's men accidentally intercepted and almost captured him. Only a diversion by quick thinking staff officers saved Pickett from a shameful embarrassment.

By five p.m., the fighting was winding down. Sheridan was furious with Warren's less-than-stellar performance at Five Forks, and demanded that the 5th Corps commander report to his headquarters. Sheridan, never an admirer of Warren, used the events of the day to relieve him of command. Pickett managed to escape from Five Forks and his men rejoined the Army of Northern Virginia at Amelia Court House. The infamous shad bake remained a private matter between gentlemen as far as Lee was concerned, but a few days after the incident, Pickett, like Warren, was removed from command.

Grant's losses at Five Forks were about 800 killed, wounded and missing. Confederate losses were about 550 killed and wounded, and at least 2,000 men deserting or surrendering. Lee's right flank was crushed and Grant's army now nearly surrounded Petersburg on the south side of the Appomattox River. That evening Lee notified President Davis that Richmond and Petersburg should be evacuated. In the morning Lee's Confederates retreated to Sutherland Station with Grant in hot pursuit.

****

Although James and the 50th Georgia heard stories of fighting near Petersburg from the newswalkers, they were north of the Appomattox River and not involved in either action. Simms' men had been forced to move their camp to make room for the construction of a moat. Ben Simms explained, "The dam is intended as an aid in the defense of our lines. It will be a monster—one hundred and twenty feet wide at the base, twenty five feet in height, and twenty-five feet wide across the top...the troops required to defend it at present could be spared to operate at some other point as the water will supply the place of men."[9]

Outside Petersburg, the men of the 2nd Rhode Island commented to each other on the significance of Phil Sheridan's arrival. It was as if the last move of Grant's chess match with Lee had put the Army of Northern Virginia in check. "Great events are to happen in a few days," predicted Lt. Colonel Rhodes.[10]

General Edwards was in a good mood on the evening of March 31, and he held a dinner for his regimental commanders and their staff officers. Drinks flowed and cigars were smoked amid a roomful of laughing and smiling officers. Everyone believed the end was at hand and they would soon be going home, although the thought of being killed so near the end of the war was on every man's mind and in everyone's prayers. But on this night it was easy to forget there was still a war going on.

"While the mirth was at its height an officer entered and presented an order to General Edwards." [11] Lieutenant Colonel Rhodes and the other regimental commanders were ordered to report to Edwards' tent immediately. The general got right to the point, saying, "Gentlemen, we attack Petersburg tomorrow morning." [12] The party was over. Rhodes and the other officers knew what to do and readied their regiments for what they believed would be the most desperate fight of the war. Tents struck, the men prepared for battle—then waited. Elisha wrote, "every officer looks anxious." [13]

Just before dawn the 2nd Rhode Island's orders were countermanded. But by the time the sun set late in the afternoon of April 1, the orders were reinstated. Shortly after nine p.m., Lt. Colonel Rhodes' staff walked from hut to hut, ordering the men to awake and prepare to march. Each man was to pack his cups and pans inside his knapsack to maintain absolute silence. Reverend Woodbury remembered, "No lights were allowed, and no horses were to be ridden outside our works. Silently we moved from camp, and taking our place in the column we passed our picket lines and formed in line of battle. The fire from the rebel pickets was deadly, and two of our color-corporals were killed before the advance took place." [14]

At ten p.m. the artillery of the 6th Corps opened upon Lee's trenches in a rage. Confederate artillery responded and the respective gunners sang their hateful duet throughout the night. It was obvious to everyone that this firing was a precursor to the infantry attack. This artillery barrage was among the fiercest anyone had ever witnessed. Lt. Colonel Rhodes thought "it gave us an idea of what we might expect in the morning." [15] Rumors flew through the Union line, but even the newswalkers could only speculate as to what was going to happen next.

The men marched between the opposing picket lines to Ft. Fisher, four miles from their camp. A captain in the 2nd noted, "Here we remained all night before the works we were going to assault in the morning, with a slight elevation to shelter us. As we lay flat upon the ground, the rebel picket fire swept overhead continually." [16] The attack was scheduled for four a.m. and the hours ticked away painfully slow. A fireworks display, worthy of a grand finale, filled the sky; shells seemed to almost collide in mid-flight as they roared and screeched on their missions. The Rhode Islanders, part of the third line of attack, covered their faces with their hands and caps shielding themselves from flying shrapnel and dirt. A dense fog slowly rolled in, reducing visibility to about twenty yards and adding to what was already a surreal and frightening scene. A few minutes before 4 AM, a whispered order "to advance" [17] was passed down the line. All eyes peered into the mist shrouding their front, which was also obscured by hundreds of men that comprised two lines. It seemed to Elisha and the other officers that their presence had gone undetected and they prayed that the surprise would save lives on both sides. But only moments before the signal was to be given there was a loud clanging and commotion from behind the Rhode Island men, drawing the attention of Confederate pickets. A mule, loaded with picks and shovels, had broken loose, and began charging toward the front. The signal went up and with an adrenaline-driven cheer, the 6th Corps unleashed perhaps its most violent attack on Lee's army ever—spearheaded by one terrified mule.

The men of the 2nd charged into the fog and the new men of the regiment braced themselves for their first taste of combat. To avoid friendly fire accidents, Lt. Colonel Rhodes ordered his men to remove their rifle's percussion caps. A captain in the 2nd Rhode Island said of the morning's fighting, "The corps, arranged in three lines, began to move, the Second Rhode Island in the third line, but, as we advanced, the first and second lines became disorganized and seemed to melt away in front, and we passed through." [18] The surprised Confederate pickets fired off a volley at close range but instinctively knew they were being overrun. "Don't fire, Yanks!" begged the Southerners. Lieutenant Colonel Rhodes ordered the prisoners taken to the rear. [19] After taking the picket line without firing a shot, Rhodes' men put percussion caps back on their rifles and charged for the enemy's forts and trenches.

Reaching the abatis, a wagon entrance was found and the entire regiment raced through it, being the first to break through the enemy's lines. At the Confederate fort, Elisha and a group of men leapt into the surrounding ditch as cannon and musketry fire flew over their heads. Throwing a rope up to the top of the fort's wall, "we crawled up the rope and onto the parapet of their works, stepping right among their muskets as they were aimed over the works," said Elisha. "It was done so quick that the Rebels had no chance to fire again but dropped their guns and ran." [20]

The men of the 2nd charged through several Confederate camps, which were in flames, and began moving east toward Petersburg. Now inside Lee's lines, Grant's men could attack the Confederate entrenchments from behind. "In this manner did the army press on all the afternoon, till, finally, the line reached the hills commanding Petersburg. A few shots are now thrown into the works enclosing the city, and the enemy's troops are seen leaving them on the double quick," recalled a Union soldier. [21]

The Rhode Island men piled small mounds of earth and bivouacked for the night. Union brass had watched the actions of the regiment, which only a few months earlier had almost disbanded. They liked what they saw. For his gallant conduct, Lt. Colonel Elisha Rhodes was immediately promoted to full colonel.

The officers of the brigade gathered in the dark, praying and singing. It had been a good day, and the next morning they learned that Lee's Army of Northern Virginia was gone. General Oliver Edwards had the honor of accepting the surrender of Petersburg from the city's mayor. Word quickly spread among the Union troops that Richmond was burning and being evacuated. Both President Davis and General Lee's Army were in flight.

In his report Elisha proudly stated, "I claim that my colors were the first to be planted on that part of the line, and were placed on the parapet while the enemy still occupied their line."[22] This flag was carried and posted upon the captured works by Corporal Thomas Parker, an Englishman. Fifteen men of the 2nd Rhode Island were wounded in the assault at Petersburg. Thirteen of these men were in combat for the first time.

****

Major James Sheldon and his brigade were not involved in the dramatic events at Petersburg, but had their own desperate struggle to contend with. "We were stationed below Richmond, near the extreme left of the line, confronting a powerful division of the enemy," said Colonel Peter McGlashan describing General Ord's 25th Army Corps, "Our line was so attenuated that had we attempted to man the works in continuous line of battle, the line would have had to have been in single rank and the men ten feet apart. Yet so completely were the enemy kept deceived as to our real strength that when we were strengthening our works with chevaux-de-frise and flooding Deep Bottom with water, their pickets called out to ours to know if we thought they were darned fools to charge such lines as that...So depleted were the regiment's numbers that one half of the entire force was on picket duty every night."[23]

Late in the afternoon of April 2, word of Petersburg's surrender and Richmond's evacuation reached the 50th Georgia, but neither Major Sheldon nor Colonel McGlashan took shame in the fall of the two cities. "That this line could have been held at all, as it was for nine months, in the face of the overwhelming force in front, is one of the most wonderful feats of modern arms, and in the last degree honorable to the Southern troops and their noble chief," McGlashan insisted.[24] "On the evening of the 2nd we learned that our lines had been broken in front of Petersburg, that Lee was in retreat southward, and that Richmond must be evacuated."[25] Silently, the Confederate pickets were called in from all along the lines.

James later recalled, "There we were on that bright and tranquil and eventful Sunday... in placid ignorance of the terrific effort and triumphant assault of the enemy on the right of the line, south of Petersburg, some 20 miles away. There was neither sight nor sound that betokened ought but the usual until after noon that day the startling rumor passed from mouth to ear, that we had lost an important position at Hatcher's Run, our troops forced back, our line of earthworks were in the possession of the foe, and Petersburg and Richmond must be evacuated and our army withdrawn...Deep anxiety overshadowed us all. That night orders were received to be prepared to move. Our command was assigned the important and perilous post of protecting the rear." [26]

On Monday, April 3, General Joe Kershaw was summoned by his boss, General Ewell, and received orders to move his division from its position on the lines near Ft. Gilmer through Richmond. Arriving at the city limits, James was shocked at the sight of a mob looting the downtown area. The Georgians crossed a bridge—already in flames.

As Major Sheldon and the 50th marched into Richmond, the faces of the men betrayed the anxiety they felt. Panic stricken civilians rushed wildly about—gangs of crazed men looted stores and government buildings which were on fire. Explosions shook the city as Confederate authorities razed warehouses full of firearms and ammunition. Occasionally, tremendous explosions from gunboats being blown up on the James River added to the din. The despair of the forsaken people and the screams of the crowds made up a scene of horror; barrels of whiskey were rolled out on the sidewalks and the maddened crowd drank the liquor out of the gutter. "There, a wild-looking woman, with a baby in one arm and a bolt of imported brocade cloth in the other she had looted, was flying down the street," recalled Peter McGlashan. "Stumbling over something, womanlike, she held on to the baby, and the cloth rolled off from her. Scrambling to her feet, she again seized one end of the cloth and resumed her flight, with the bolt bouncing and jumping behind her, unwinding and streaming. I sincerely hope she saved it all." [27]

Although the events of this day did not come as a total surprise to those wearing the gray, no one was prepared for the sights that greeted them in Richmond. James described one event, saying, "Just before us marched an armed straggler, with his gun on his shoulder and the bayonet run through a government ham. On nearing him I noticed he had wrapped the ham in a $1000 government bond to keep it from greasing his shoulder. Nothing impressed me so much with the ruin of the government as that single incident did." [28]

Marching out of Richmond, for what everyone knew would be the last time, was a bitter experience for Simms' Brigade. As the men of the brigade approached the Manchester Bridge, they took one last look back upon the burning city. The streets were nearly empty. In the distance, the ear-piercing notes of the fife and the ominous beating of drums announced the approaching enemy. Colonel McGlashan bitterly conceded, "[The Union Army] had gotten into Richmond at last, and the blood of the best and bravest of the South, that had been poured out in torrents for four years in its defense, had been spent in vain." [29]

Mistakenly believing all of its troops were safely across Manchester Bridge, it had been set on fire to slow the enemy's pursuit, nearly trapping Simms' men on the city side. The center span of the bridge was "burning fiercely in the center," recalled McGlashan. "Double-quicking my men through the flames, we gained the other side, being the last troops to leave the city. As we halted for a few moments to rest, an old veteran stepped out in the road, and, looking back, shouted: 'Good-bye, old Richmond, we'll come back; damn 'em, we'll whip 'em yet!'" [30]

James Sheldon's own recollections were similar, "Thousands began that march with empty haversacks and as little in their stomachs. The steady and continuous tramp of troops, and the rumble of ambulances, ordnance and artillery wagons, was the sole and single illustration of order or system. The rest was chaos, and pandemonium reigned.

"Government warehouses were gutted, and here it was discovered that millions of rations were being hoarded for some mysterious reason, and clothing, shoes, and blankets galore, while the faithful, hungry, and ragged men, had been doled scanty feed and less clothes for months... These earnest patriots...marched with firm tread and rapidly, but sadly and silently, across Mayo's Bridge, over the James River, connecting Richmond and Manchester, and bade farewell forever to the Confederate Capital; but here it was we near became separated from the retreating army. [The] bridge had been fired, and had our march been delayed minutes longer, we would have been unable to cross at that point. We were in time, however, and crossed and joined the right wing of the army, with the loss of a few men only." [31]

But Lee's army remained in danger of being destroyed. "There was no time for delay or regret," said Colonel McGlashan. "Only a swift forced march could enable us to avoid the head of General Grant's columns and rejoin the main force under Lee. As we advanced, we saw everywhere the evidences of the terrible nature of the retreat of Lee's army. The road was lined with dead horses and mules in all states of emaciation from want of food; abandoned artillery, half covered with earth, for the time could not be spared to effectually cover them from the gaze of the enemy; foot-sore and half-starved wrecks of soldiers, still clinging to their bright muskets and striving hard to keep up, cheering us as we passed, defiant and resolute to the last, while all over the country behind us streamed the pursuing legions of Grant." [32]

Hearing the news of the fall of Richmond and Petersburg, Governor Smith of Rhode Island honored General Ulysses Grant with a 100-gun salute. But Grant didn't stop to savor his victories. For two days he kept up a relentless pursuit of Lee and his broken army, whose only hope was to miraculously connect with Joe Johnston. But the Army of Northern Virginia was coming apart as it fled west. "The road is filled with broken wagons and the things thrown away in the flight of the Rebels," Elisha wrote two days after the Battle of Petersburg. [33] On the 5th of April, the 2nd Rhode Island plodded along, doggedly following Lee. "Every step we see proof of the demoralized condition of Lee's troops,"

Colonel Rhodes said, convinced that there was a denouement to be played out in the coming days. "[Lee] has often followed us, and we him, but this is the last time," he wrote. [34] The colonel's confidence was buoyed by the presence of Sheridan's cavalry on the march.

Major James Sheldon described the chase from the Confederate perspective, saying, "All through the weary hours, night and day, and day and night again, with but brief intervals of breathing spells, and sleep caught in nods and winks, famished and fighting for one eternal week, did the fragments of Lee's army exist on hopes deferred." [35]

Lee knew his army had to eat if it had any chance of surviving, and his men put on a hard march in pursuit of food. If the men needed any more proof that the end had come, they found it at a sleepy hamlet known as Amelia Court House. "[On the second day's march] we had reason to believe that rations would be issued," James recalled, "General Lee had ordered supplies to be sent from Danville to this point, but demoralization had seized the railroad officials, as it had the Quartermaster's Department, and the trains loaded with provisions had run by our army for whom they were intended, and carried this precious freight to Richmond." [36]

James Sheldon, Peter McGlashan and the other survivors of the 50th Georgia marched on toward Farmville, in a last effort to reach the protection of the hills near Lynchburg. "Horses staggered and fell, no longer able to respond to the overtaxing demand upon their strength and endurance. Men reeled and nodded as they tramped, or went down under the superhuman strain upon their weakened physical powers, and there would be none with heart to disturb them...Yet when these [men] were attacked, they seemed inspired with that same esprit de corps that possessed the whole body in its full pride and glory and heyday of success." [37]

James and Elisha were closing in on parallel roads to a common destination, a little stream that ran through the farm of the Hillsman family called Saylor's Creek, about 30 miles west of Petersburg. The march had been difficult for both armies, even more so for the physically drained Southerners. James and his fellow Georgians pushed themselves until the evening of the 5th, when Simms' Brigade overtook the rear of Ewell's Corps which had been Lee's rear guard. Major Sheldon and the dwindling 50th Georgia lay down beneath the trees and rested until daybreak.

James Sheldon had a surprise for his friends. Colonel McGlashan happily recalled the morning of the 6th when "we were roused up by our faithful commissary, James R. Sheldon driving into the camp with three barrels of flour he had picked up and barely saved from the enemy, who were riding in full sight on parallel roads. It was a welcome addition to our stores, now exhausted, and enabled him to issue rations for the last time, and I will state, in simple justice to a faithful officer, that we never suffered for want of rations in camp or on the fighting line while Commissary Sheldon could get to us, and the commissariat, as every old soldier well knows, is a very vital matter to troops in the field." [38]

It was a sparkling Virginia spring morning, the kind of day one cherishes during peacetime. Colonel McGlashan wanted his men to be ready, and remarked, "While forming to resume our march, I noticed a small body of troops, about 1000 strong, that attracted my attention. They had that air of smartness and military precision of movement, that characterized all through the war our troops from the large cities. Bronzed and soldier-like in appearance, they attracted the attention of my men as they fell in line. Beyond them a body of men in naval uniforms and armed with cutlasses, and evidently fagged out with the severe march, lined up alongside." [39]

Among these men were the old "Savannah Volunteer Guards," known as the 18th Georgia Battalion, commanded by Major William Basinger, who McGlashan knew well. He had seen this group when they were a magnificent 350 strong, camped on the heights below Savannah three years before. Talking with Major Basinger, McGlashan learned that Grant was closing in with the bulk of his force. General Lee was ahead with Longstreet and Gordon, while Ewell, commanding the 3rd Corps, was acting as rear guard. "I hardly think," Basinger warned Colonel McGlashan, "[that] we will escape the day without a fight. Their cavalry have overtaken us and are trying to pass our flanks, while huge masses of their infantry are close behind." [40]

Simms' Brigade was ordered to cooperate with Ewell's Corps, whose ranks were so decimated they were unable to cover all the lines of retreat. Ewell's and Anderson's Corps would make a stand at Saylor's Creek. The 50th Georgia was ordered off the road, following Basinger's Savannah Guards across the creek where they positioned themselves on a slight hill. The Georgians' line faced the rear and overlooked a narrow valley in front through which Saylor's Creek flowed. Their wagon trains were massed on their right and a dense thicket of young pines separated them from the Guards on the left. For some reason this hole in the line was left unoccupied. Further to the left stretched the line of Custis Lee's Division and Ewell's men. Throughout the morning enemy Union skirmishers fired, advanced, and then retreated to the woods, probing the Confederate lines.

Reverend Woodbury of the 2nd Rhode Island remembered the morning from a Union perspective, writing, "bright and early, the army was astir, and pressed on forward. The cavalry and horse artillery were in the advance, and took every occasion to annoy the enemy's trains and rear guard. The route of the army lay toward Prince Edward Court House, on the Danville turnpike. General Lee was between the road to the court house and Appomattox. He had lost the Danville railroad—that was certain." [41] Lee had to get his army onto the turnpike and had only two means of doing so. He could either race for it on the south side of the Appomattox River or cross over to the north side, and then recross back to the south side over the railroad bridges at Farmville. Dividing his forces, he decided to try both. The Union 2nd Corps headed for the river while Elisha's 6th Corps took to the court house road.

Colonel Rhodes had a big responsibility on this day. His regiment was to lead the 6th Corps in its pursuit of the Army of

Northern Virginia's wagon train. An important part of this duty was to secure the homes and families along the route to guard against any possible ambush. To do this, Elisha detailed almost half of his 400 men and officers. In spite of this, 200 Rhode Island men marched throughout the morning and into the afternoon in the warm spring sunshine. They'd heard that a portion of Lee's supply train had already been attacked by Union cavalry and was now waiting for the 6th Corps' infantry to finish the job. At about four o'clock in the afternoon the two opposing columns came in contact near Saylor's Creek. The cavalry immediately attacked.

Major Sheldon was worried. He was responsible for moving the brigade wagon train and if trapped, release the animals and burn the wagons. During the late afternoon, James sought out Colonel McGlashan, feeling that the last day had come. "I preferred to be with the command and share with them whatever might be in store for us. I soon found him with his regiment [or what was left of it] lying on the ground behind a line of rails. We took a seat on the obstruction and I related to him my experience and what I most feared. I did not want to be captured and incarcerated in a Federal prison. To avoid this result I wanted to remain with him and his boys, and help force our way out of it if it became necessary. Fortunately for me, he would not consent to it, saying my post of duty was where I had been ordered to go." Disappointed, the two men parted, hoping to meet again. [42]

Enemy gunfire jolted the Georgians but just as abruptly ceased, while Grant's men formed their lines. Silence fell upon the fields and hills of Saylor's Creek. It was a beautiful spring afternoon and the sun shone brightly, reflecting off the little stream that rippled peacefully by. "The tender flowers of spring were showing above the grass. The hum of the insects and the strange silence all around seemed to cast a drowsy spell over the men, and I could see them, here and there, gradually sinking to the ground, and, pillowing their heads on their arms, fitfully dreaming, perhaps of dear old homes and loved ones in far-off Georgia that many would never see again," Peter McGlashan recalled. [43] The tall Scotsman swallowed hard and ordered his men to *"Attention!"* The line sprang up, and with drill-like precision, brought their rifles to the ready. All eyes looked sternly to the front.

****

Elisha's regiment of Rhode Islanders marched out of the woods and into a clearing beside the creek. Rhodes quickly noticed four men on horseback, engaged in animated conversation. This impromptu conference of Sheridan, Wright, Wheaton and Edwards was an imposing sight to the young colonel, who was surprised when Wright waved him over. Bringing his regiment to a halt, Elisha listened as the generals explained that Lee's wagon train had been stopped and trapped by Union cavalry. Two divisions of infantry had already crossed the creek under a "murderous fire." [44] Now it was time for the 6th Corps to get across. "Being on the extreme left, and without cavalry to guard its flank, the crossing of the stream was a hazardous movement," recalled Reverend Woodbury. The men of the 2nd had watched as the men of the other divisions struggled across the stream, many of whom now floated in the water. "But across the men went with the rest," Woodbury continued, "and, gaining the other bank, immediately reformed and pushed up the slope beyond, the enemy retiring into the woods upon the ridge. But here was a large force of the enemy, lying concealed and awaiting the approach of our troops." [45]

Still full of fight, the Confederates did not wait for their guests and instead fixed bayonets and charged down the slope. "When within about fifty yards of the woods a Rebel officer stepped and shouted: 'Rise up, fire!' A long line of Rebels fired right into our faces and then charged through our line and getting between us and the river," said Elisha. [46] The 2nd Rhode Island entered the creek which in many places, was so deep it ruined their ammunition. Once they reached the opposite bank Colonel Rhodes reformed his line and sent out skirmishers. As his brigade advanced, its left flank became exposed, prompting Elisha to refuse his left wing. With gritty determination the Rhode Islanders pressed the enemy back to the woods in their front, until when within a distance of about thirty yards they received a charge of the enemy, both in front and on the left. The 2nd briefly lost their new United States flag as they were driven back, forced to retire in confusion.

50th Georgia Infantry Flag

Colonel McGlashan took a deep breath. "A beautiful spectacle unrolled itself before us," he said. [47] A line of skirmishers emerged out of the woods on the heights above the 50th Georgia's position. The wave of blue charged down the slope to the creek. Reaching the water's edge, Grant's men received a scattering volley from Simms' rifles, checking their advance and pinning them down in the tall grass. Far away to the left of James' 50th Georgia, Union infantry and cavalry were seen crossing the road the Georgians had just left, forming a line of attack on Custis Lee's division. "It was a magnificent sight," McGlashan insisted. "We had no artillery to hinder their movements, and it looked like a grand field day of parade." [48] The scene mesmerized the men until McGlashan barked the command, "Ready, men! Ready!"

The spell was broken and the men closed up in line. Drawing their cartridge boxes to the front of their belts, they capped their guns, knelt, and waited. "Aim low, men; fire as they cross the creek," McGlashan shouted in a reassuring tone. Grant's men moved steadily to the attack, and as they neared the creek, the colonel let loose the command, "*Commence firing!*" Flame shot from the Georgian rifles as the enemy's line staggered back in confusion. [49] The Union men regrouped and charged into the water again.

"It was a hand to hand fight, the combatants mingling together and freely using bayonets and musket butts," Reverend Woodbury explained, "[The 2nd Rhode Island] tumbled back into and across the creek, the enemy following and planting his colors upon the bank." [50] James' 50th Georgia and Elisha's 2nd Rhode Island were in a fight to the death. In the confusion, no one was in command of Elisha's brigade and General Wheaton entrusted this responsibility to the young colonel. But the 2nd Rhode Island was being smashed and routed as the men fell back across the creek.

Colonel McGlashan remembered, "It was but a moment, however...Quickly rallying they leaped the creek and made a rush up the slope, but the deadly, merciless fire of our men drove them back again, again and again, with terrible loss, until they retreated back across the creek, and the men, throwing themselves down in the grass, refused to advance." [51]

The Savannah Guards struggled on the left of the 50th against overwhelming numbers. Basinger's men became trapped under artillery fire and small arms, and hit the ground struggling to pile up dirt with only their bayonets as tools. The 85 men of the Guards held off two infantry assaults, driving the enemy back with severe loss. "But at this juncture a body of men came up through the pine thicket on our right flank, in much disorder from having to make their way through the woods," Major Basinger stated. [52]

The enemy charged the Guards a third time, only to be repulsed again. But another wave of blue came through the pines and again attacked their right flank. The Georgians fell back to some low grounds in the rear. "On looking to the right and left of me I saw no men left but the non-commissioned officers with their swords alone," Basinger remembered, "Desiring to spare the lives of the few remaining survivors, I tied my handkerchief to my sword, already broken by a bullet, and waved it. Immediately they came out from behind the trees and began to fire on the wounded men as they lay on the ground... I charge and assert, on my honor as an officer and a gentleman, that they fired on and slaughtered my wounded men after we had surrendered, and without an effort on the part of their officers to prevent it" [53] The men of the 50th Georgia watched and would bitterly remember the desperate last stand of the Savannah Guards.

But Simms and McGlashan had their own problems. McGlashan recalled, "The enemy, failing to dislodge us with their infantry, brought up artillery to complete the work. Battery after battery rolled out of the woods until I counted over twenty guns commanding our position at grape shot range... the men who were falling fast from the constant fire, glanced anxiously at me as the cannon unlimbered in front." [54] In the distance, the sounds of battle had faded away.

An officer in a Virginia battery described the desperation of the fighting, saying, " I saw numbers of men kill each other with bayonets and the butts of muskets, and even bite each others throats and ears and noses, rolling on the ground like wild beasts." [55]

****

Colonel Rhodes calmly but urgently reorganized his regiment. He sent for his horse, and after reforming his lines ordered his men to cross the stream. Once reaching the opposite bank, the 2nd Rhode Island drove the enemy from the woods, capturing a wagon train. A sergeant in the brigade suddenly had a distinguished looking Confederate prisoner on his hands claiming to be General Richard Ewell. Not quite believing his luck, the sergeant led the general's horse by the bridle, taking him to the rear of the fighting. "Before our capture I saw men eating raw fresh meat as they marched in ranks," reported General Ewell. [56]

General Joseph Kershaw had also watched his command melt around him and saw Colonel Simms trying to save his brigade. Kershaw observed, "Unfortunately his attempt had failed, and the enemy made his appearance in rear of Simms' brigade at the same time he was engaged in front and flank. That officer attempted to extricate his command, but found it impossible to do so without confusion, as he was attacked on all sides." [57] Minutes later, Joe Kershaw and James Simms joined General Ewell as prisoners of war. Colonel McGlashan wasn't sure what was happening other than what he saw directly in front of him. "Just then a shout from the rear attracted my attention; looking back I saw a staff officer calling to me; going towards him he cried: 'Why don't you stop firing? Ewell has surrendered his entire force, and you must cease firing.' I was astounded, but soon made up my mind not to surrender my men if I could help myself." [58]

McGlashan walked his line and ordered his men to cease firing. In retreat march, the colonel directed his men to a low wooded ground in the rear where they were momentarily sheltered from enemy fire. Originally over eleven hundred strong, only ninety remained. As they stood at attention, McGlashan looked keenly at them. "They were cool and steady, ready to obey any order," he remembered. "Men, General Ewell has surrendered his force, we are cut off and surrounded, yet I cannot, will not, surrender you. Bring me the colors." The color guard advanced and placed the colors in the colonel's hand. The men watched in silence as he pulled the banner from its staff, broke the staff against a tree, and tore the flag into fragments. Peter McGlashan scattered the shreds in the shrubs, turned and gave his regiment a final order— "Men, I will dismiss you right here, in the hope you may succeed in escaping and joining the army under Lee. Break ranks, March!" The men looked at McGlashan for a moment, then the line wavered, broke, and disappeared into the brush. Suffering from unhealed wounds, their colonel couldn't follow his men. [59] Moments later, he was taken prisoner. He had no way of knowing that his rival, James Simms, along with his brother Ben, had also been captured.

****

James Sheldon was alone. Realizing that his regiment had scattered through the fields and forests around the creek, he determined to escape and find the right wing of the army. As canister, shrapnel and minie balls whistled around him, James ordered the teamsters, or what were left of them, to release the animals and make their escape. Standing alone, he reflected on his next move as a friend, Sergeant J. D. Campbell of the 10th Georgia Infantry, appeared and asked what they should do. James told the sergeant, "We will cross the creek and relieve ourselves of this stampede, and await events." [60]

But the waters of the creek were swift and its depth uncertain. Some drivers had failed in an attempt to cross at this point, and six or eight mules lay where they had struggled and drowned attempting to reach the opposite bank. "This was our opportunity. I told Campbell we will use their carcasses for a bridge." They succeeded, emerging on the opposite bank wet but alive. Out of immediate danger, Sheldon and Campbell rested and thought about the day's events. "Imagine, if you can, the view before us: Wagon upon wagon on fire, thousands of men captured, an army corps dissolved." [61]

The 2nd Rhode Island had played their part in the destruction of James' wagon train. "We set fire to the wagons which appeared to be loaded with potatoes and sorgham molasses, which our boys enjoyed," Elisha proudly claimed. [62]

As the sun disappeared behind a hill, James and J. D. frantically searched for what was left of their army. Advancing up the slope, they reached some woods in which 100 or 150 Confederates had gathered. Somehow these men had managed to haul two pieces of artillery with them. Major Sheldon and the other officers decided to form a command and make an attempt to hold their position with the field guns. Rolling the guns to the brow of the hill, a body of Union cavalry could be seen across the creek to the east. "We opened fire, more for the purpose of deceiving them as to our number than any damage our guns could do. To our chagrin they ran out a battery of six field pieces, and before our second round was fired they opened fire in reply, and our little battery was soon left without a wheel to stand upon." [63]

James and J. D. continued to search for the army in the gathering darkness. Five of the men they had met in the woods joined them. After hiking a few miles, the party decided to lie down and sleep for about thirty minutes. James volunteered to take the first watch. After rousing the sleeping party, James and the six other soldiers resumed their search for Lee's army. It was at this moment that hunger and exhaustion finally caught up with Major Sheldon and he collapsed, unconscious.

About midnight, James awoke, lying against a fence and alone. Startled, he stepped into the road and listened. A stony silence gave him a chill. "Where had my companions gone? Why had they left me?" he wondered. [64] Concluding that they must have headed west, he started in that direction, following the road until reaching the Appomattox River at Highbridge. James couldn't believe his eyes. Before him stretched hundreds of camp fires—Grant's army. Wagons were crossing on a pontoon bridge. James knew he had to cross this bridge to reach the Army of Northern Virginia, but to do this he would have to pass through the Union camp. He thought about his chances and decided to go through the camp. To his amazement, no one noticed a Confederate soldier walking through the sleepy camp.

Nearly frozen with fear, James reached the river without interference, just as a wagon rolled onto the pontoon. Suddenly, a voice in the darkness shouted, "Halt," stopping him in his tracks. "Throwing my eyes toward the direction the sound came from I saw a shadow. Hoping that some other unfortunate was between the sentry and myself, I pushed up into the shadow of a wagon, and moved quicker, thinking that if he shot I would get some protection by placing myself in that position. No other challenge came. The guard must have felt satisfied, and I rejoiced. My heart stopped beating a tattoo as I reached the open field to the right."[65]

****

By ten o' clock, Colonel Rhodes and his regiment sat down to rest. Exhausted and hungry, the men were stunned by the day's events. It had been their most tragic day, and Elisha thought, "So near the end and yet men must die." [66] Out of the less than 200 men of the regiment who took part in the fighting at Saylor's Creek, five were killed and 39 were wounded. Among those killed was James Seamans, a 43-year-old painter from Scituate, who began the war at 1st Manassas where he was taken prisoner. Also killed was Captain Charlie Gleason of Warwick. Elisha liked the captain and recalled that as the day's fighting began, Gleason remarked to him that if all went well on this day they would all be going home. Gleason was shot through the head. First Manassas, Salem Church, and The Wilderness all ranked among the bloodiest days in the storied career of the 2nd Rhode Island. Now a fourth, Saylor's Creek, could be placed on the list of the 2nd Rhode Island's worst regimental losses.

****

The morning of April 7 found James in the company of the 50th's assistant surgeon, Dr. William Pue, and both men were comforted by the reunion. Convinced they were near the Confederate Army, they marched until late in the afternoon when they were joined by the 50th's surgeon, Dr. Henry Parramore. The trio continued on in a westerly direction until after dark, when they finally reached Lee's lines.

"The 8th was a repetition of the previous day with the weary men, except that the monotony was unbroken by the annoyingly pressing attention of our confident antagonist, who now knew that they had us like cattle penned in, with the

James River on our right and their line of march converging. It could be but a question of hours, the end inevitable," predicted James. "Circumstances had so changed matters with me, that I was forced to the conclusion that if we must surrender, I would remain with the army, survive or perish." [67]

18

HOME? I HAD NONE.

The 2nd Rhode Island, staggered by their losses, rested until the early evening of April 7 when the regiment took up the chase once again. Colonel Rhodes found his brigade at Farmville, where it crossed the Appomattox River and joined its division in what was now more of a hunt than a pursuit. Unknown to Elisha Rhodes and James Sheldon, momentous events were taking place out of view of the two armies.

General Grant had arrived at Farmville and set up his headquarters at the town's hotel. According to Union General Horace Porter, Grant was told that one of his famous prisoners, General Ewell, had expressed an opinion that "[the South's] cause was lost when they crossed the James River, and he considered that it was the duty of the authorities to negotiate for peace then, while they still had a right to claim concessions, adding that now they were not in condition to claim anything. He said that for every man killed after this somebody would be responsible, and it would be little better than murder. He could not tell what General Lee would do, but he hoped he would at once surrender his army." [1] Grant decided it was time. At five p.m. on Friday, April 7, a message was sent through the lines to General Lee at his headquarters:

> "The results of the last week must convince you of the hopelessness of further resistance on the part of the Army of Northern Virginia in this struggle. I feel that it is so, and regard it as

my duty to shift from myself the responsibility of any further effusion of blood by asking of you the surrender of that portion of the Confederate States army known as the Army of Northern Virginia." [2]

Lee wrote a reply within an hour of receiving Grant's olive branch, but it didn't reach the Union general's hands until after midnight:

"I have received your note of this date... I reciprocate your desire to avoid useless effusion of blood, and therefore, before considering your proposition, ask the terms you will offer on condition of its surrender." [3]

****

On the morning of April 8, as he was preparing to leave Farmville, Grant sent a second message to Lee:

"Your note of last evening in reply to mine of the same date, asking the conditions on which I will accept the surrender of the Army of Northern Virginia, is just received...I will meet you, or will designate officers to meet any officers you may name for the same purpose, at any point agreeable to you, for the purpose of arranging definitely the terms upon which the surrender of the Army of Northern Virginia will be received." [4]

General Grant spent most of the day with his army's leading column pressing Lee's rear guard. This kept him close to Lee should the Confederate general send another message. After dark the army halted and the general-in-chief closed his eyes. At midnight, he was awakened by his adjutant telling him that another letter for him had arrived from Lee. Fighting off the pain of a headache, Grant read the short note:

> "I received at a late hour your note of to-day. In mine of yesterday I did not intend to propose the surrender of the Army of Northern Virginia, but to ask the terms of your proposition…I should be pleased to meet you at 10 A. M. to-morrow on the old stage road to Richmond, between the picket-lines of the two armies."[5]

General Grant shook off his headache and after downing some coffee, penned a dispatch to Lee:

> "By the South laying down their arms, they would hasten that most desirable event, save thousands of human lives, and hundreds of millions of property not yet destroyed. Seriously hoping that all our difficulties may be settled without the loss of another life…"[6]

****

Major James Sheldon and Lee's other surviving men knew full well what they were facing. Another battle was suicide, but they would do their duty no matter how their fate was to be played out. James was issued a horse and ordered to secure cattle of any kind, from any source, to feed the army. James was accompanied by a major from the 51st Georgia and as the two men rode forward, they discovered Gordon's line of Georgians was engaged. "It was then I heard the report of the last gun at Appomattox," James sadly remembered.

Every Confederate soldier understood the situation. The James River was their right, Ord stood on the left, Meade blocked the rear, and Sheridan's cavalry was poised in their front. With his troops famished and exhausted, Lee saw only one reasonable option. "On the night of the 8th we went into camp within a short distance of Appomattox Court House," recalled James, "and doubtless each worn and wearied soul thought, if he did not in his devotions repeat, 'Blessed be the man that invented sleep.'" [7]

Simms' Brigade had been shattered. Its half-starved, delirious men staggered around lost and terrified at Highbridge, Farmville, Burkeville, Harper's Farm, Frazier's Farm and Amelia Court House. In all, 44 men of the 50th Georgia had been rounded up by the Union Army. One man, Corporal John Register, was shot in the neck at Saylor's Creek. Miraculously, no one in the regiment had been killed during the rout of April 6. Simms' Brigade reported total casualty figures of 43 wounded and 174 taken prisoner. Three men in the 53rd Georgia were killed, including its colonel.

Sunday grew unusually hot for early April, even by Virginia standards, and although the two men were corresponding, Grant was going to press Lee's army until the Southern commander surrendered. The Union general was riding his favorite horse, Cincinnati, heading out to meet Sheridan, when he was overtaken by an officer of Meade's staff, who carried with him a new message from Lee:

> "I received your note of this morning on the picket-line...I now ask an interview, in accordance with the offer contained in your letter of yesterday, for that purpose." [8]

The officer also presented Grant with a note from General Meade, who had taken it upon himself to grant Lee's request of a short truce while peace negotiations were being conducted. Grant immediately sat down on a shady knoll and wrote a reply:

"I am at this writing about four miles west of Walker's Church, and will push forward to the front for the purpose of meeting you." [9]

Grant pressed on, and about one o'clock the little village of Appomattox Court House came into view. Generals Sheridan and Ord rode out to greet the general-in-chief and exchanged pleasantries. "Is Lee over there?" asked General Grant, pointing up the street. "Yes, he is in that brick house," answered Sheridan. "Well, then, we'll go over," said Grant. [10]

Hours earlier, Lee had been lying down on a blanket under an apple tree, about a half a mile from Appomattox. Over the years, thousands of wagon wheels had rumbled past the base of this tree exposing its root base and Lee's boots rested on these roots. Lee was suffering from mental and physical exhaustion, but when Grant's latest message reached him, he knew he had one last duty to fulfill. He mounted Traveller and accompanied by his secretary, started for Appomattox Court House. They were followed by an officer and a mounted orderly. Arriving at Appomattox they met Wilmer McLean, a prominent resident of the village. Lee asked McLean where a room suitable for an important meeting could be borrowed for a short time and McLean offered his own home. The men sat and awaited General Grant's arrival. Grant mounted the steps and entered the house about 1:30.

The demise of Lee's generalship saddened Grant deeply, and he tried to soften the meeting with small talk, but Lee insisted that they stick with the business at hand. After carefully reading Grant's proposal, Lee asked an aide to draw up a letter of acceptance. A few minutes later, Lee silently read these notes, and after making a few minor changes, inked his signature:

"I received your letter of this date containing the terms of the surrender of the Army of Northern Virginia as proposed by you. As they are substantially the same as those expressed in your letter of the 8th inst., they are accepted." [11]

The terms were simple and clear:
APPOMATTOX COURT HOUSE, VA.,
April 10th, 1865.

Agreement entered into this day in regard to the surrender of the Army of Northern Virginia to the United States authorities:

First. The troops shall march by brigades and detachments to a designated point, stack their arms, deposit their flags, sabres, pistols, etc., and from thence march to their homes under charge of their officers, superintended by their respective division and corps commanders, officers retaining their side-arms and the authorized number of private horses.

Second. All public horses and property of all kinds to be turned over to staff-officers, designated by the United States authorities.

Third. Such transportation as may be agreed upon as necessary for the transportation of the private baggage of officers, will be allowed to accompany the officers, to be turned over at the end of the trip to the nearest United States quartermaster, receipts being taken for the same.

Fourth. Couriers and mounted men of the artillery and cavalry, whose horses are their own private property, will be allowed to retain them

Fifth. The surrender of the Army of Northern Virginia shall be constructed to include all the forces operating with that army on the 8th instant, the date of the commencement of negotiations for surrender, except such bodies of cavalry as actually made their escape previous to the surrender; and except, also, such pieces of artillery as were more than twenty (20) miles from Appomattox Court House at the time of the surrender on the 9th instant.

With the formalities completed, Lee reminded Grant that he was holding over a thousand Union prisoners, saying, "I shall be glad to send them into your lines as soon as it can be arranged, for I have no provisions for them. I have, indeed, nothing for my own men." [12]

Grant turned to Sheridan instructing him to return any captured Confederate supply trains to Lee's army. The Union commander then asked Lee how many men he had left, and in this touching exchange between the two generals, Lee admitted that he didn't know. "Suppose I send over 25,000 rations, do you think that will be a sufficient supply?" asked Grant. "I think it will be ample and it will be a great relief, I assure you," responded a grateful Lee. [13]

With those words the two men parted. Grant and his staff began their ride back to their headquarters when they heard the firing of salutes celebrating the surrender. "Some time in the afternoon we heard loud cheering at the front," recalled Colonel Rhodes, "and soon General Meade commanding the Army of the Potomac rode like mad down the road with hat off shouting: 'The war is over, and we are going home!' Such a scene only happens once in centuries." [14]

Word of Lee's surrender spread throughout the armies in minutes. "The batteries began to fire blank cartridges, while the Infantry fired their muskets in the air. The men threw their knapsacks and canteens into the air and howled like mad," a delighted Colonel Rhodes wrote. Grant promptly ordered that the celebratory firing cease, saying, "The war is over, the rebels are our countrymen again, and the best sign of rejoicing after the victory will be to abstain from all demonstrations in the field." [15]

Like everyone else near Appomattox, James Sheldon wondered what was going on. The newswalkers were having a field day, but no one had any more information than the man next to him. As James sat on a horse, he saw a flag of truce come from Grant's line in search of General Lee. The newswalkers said the war was over. Lee suddenly appeared, silently and sadly riding Traveller. James was struck by how dignified the old general looked, even in this dark hour. Men crowded around him, each man reaching to shake his hand. Slowly, Lee turned to his soldiers and with a quivering voice said, "Men we have fought through the war together. I have done my best for you. My heart is too full to say more." [16]

For James and the other Confederate soldiers at Appomattox, the moment filled them with a mixture of relief and anxiety as no one knew what surrender would bring. The answer came almost immediately as according to James, "There was no exhibition of vaunting, exultation, or triumph; no manifestation of superiority; no show of enmity, from General Grant, commanding, down to the privates. Magnanimity ruled the hour. Rations were issued to our hungry band, and we learned of the generous, liberal, and honorable terms of capitulation, and which were honestly conformed to and complied with." [17] The healing process had begun.

James and Elisha felt both joy and great sorrow. Warm memories and friendly faces came rushing back as thoughts of men like John Slocum, the 2nd's first colonel, Charlie Gleason and John Sedgwick filled Elisha. The memory of Cicero Young, the impassioned first captain of the "Thomas County Rangers," urging men on the courthouse steps to join his company, came roaring back to James and the other survivors of that company. What would Paul Semmes and Frank Kearse think of this day? "I cried and laughed by turns," Elisha said. "I was never so happy in my life." [18]

The war had ended almost four years to the day of Beauregard's firing on Ft. Sumter in Charleston. The majority of Union men now saw their vanquished foe as fellow American soldiers who needed help. Elisha Rhodes commented, "The Rebels are half starved, and our men divided their rations with them. The 2nd Rhode Island had three days' rations and after dividing their rations with the Rebels will have to make a day and a half's rations last for three days. But we did it cheerfully." [19]

"On the 10th, the last farewell address from our illustrious commander, as he stood surrounded by his skeleton command, was delivered," remembered James, adding, "I was one of the number of attentive listeners." [20] James and the other men strained to hear General Lee as he explained his reasoning for, and terms of, the surrender. In closing his remarks Lee said, "With an unceasing admiration of your constancy and devotion to your country, and a grateful remembrance of your kind and generous consideration of myself, I bid you all an affectionate farewell." [21] The soldiers stood quieted. "And then, in silence, with uplifted hat, he rode through a sorrowing, weeping army to his home in Richmond," James recalled. [22] Soldiers with heads bowed reached out to touch and stroke Traveller as he pushed through the crowd.

****

Before Grant left Appomattox, it was made clear that no Union soldier should enter the Confederate camps, although Elisha did get a chance to talk with some of them. "They all seem surprised at our kind treatment of them…they are as glad as we that the war is over," he observed. But Elisha had no desire to visit the Confederate camps. "I have seen all the Rebels I want to see for my life time." [23] Both Elisha and James had a hard time sleeping. A night of rest without being disturbed by an attack or artillery bombardment felt unnatural to the men.

****

"On the 11th the sun rose and cast its rays upon the Army of Northern Virginia, prisoners of war bivouacked, eating, sleeping, resting and renewing its strength for the events to come, whatever they might be," James Sheldon remembered. [24] General Grant left Appomattox at noon the following day and at no point did he enter the Confederate lines. Lee quietly set out for Richmond. The war was over, finally. Although Grant's terms of surrender had been generous, he insisted that there be a ceremony in which the Army of Northern Virginia would surrender to its Union antagonist. Confederate General John B. Gordon and Union General Joshua Chamberlain were chosen to represent their respective armies. It had rained almost continuously since the surrender, but on Wednesday, April 12, it stopped. James recalled, "About mid-day, the last parade and folding of colors, and stacking of arms, was made, characterized by a dignified and delicate consideration throughout." [25]

The men of the Army of Northern Virginia were up early and every attempt was made to create a proud appearance. All that remained of Lee's army were 28,000 dirty, often barefoot, men who assembled on the north side of the Appomattox River. The regiments which still had flags carried them on their staffs, while other poles were empty, their banners having been captured or wrapped around the waist of the color bearer, concealed beneath his shirt to be carried home. Confederate battle flags flew proudly as the column made its slow march toward Appomattox. There were no bands, as their musicians' instruments were long since lost. The long line moved in silence as the men shouldered their muskets one last time. As the Confederates approached the village, the two Union columns lined each side of the road, in awed silence. "The regimental battle flags crowded so thick by thinning out of men, that the whole column seemed crowned with red," one Union soldier observed. [26]

As James made this final march, he looked ahead and saw two full Union brigades. Under the flag of the United States was a small group of officers, including General Joshua Lawrence Chamberlain. With a quick burst of a bugle, the Union men shifted from "order arms" to "carry arms." [27] Gordon solemnly rode up to Chamberlain—the moment was spellbinding. There was no roll of the drums or blaring of trumpets "but an awed silence rather, and breath holding, as if it were the passing of the dead." [28]

Grim faced Confederates with tear-filled eyes, stacked their rifles, pressed their battle flags to their lips and gently laid them down. "Sitting on my horse in the midst of them, I spoke to them for the last time as their commander. In all my past life I had never undertaken to speak where my own emotions were so literally overwhelming," General Gordon said. [29]

James could see Gordon, chin drooped to his chest, heartbroken almost beyond description. But when Chamberlain ordered his men to attention, the snap of arms returned the Confederate general to the soldierly business at hand. Similarly, Chamberlain was also deeply moved by the grim pageantry, "He wheeled his horse facing me, touching him gently with the spur, so that the animal slightly reared, and as he wheeled, horse and rider made one motion, the horse's head swung down with a graceful bow, and General Gordon dropped his swordpoint to his toe in salutation...And it can well be imagined, too, that there was no lack of emotion on our side, but the Union men were held steady in their lines, without the least show of demonstration by word or by motion. There was, though, a twitching of the muscles of their faces, and, be it said, their battle-bronzed cheeks were not altogether dry." [30]

****

By company, the survivors of the 50th Georgia Infantry were issued paroles, guaranteeing their safe passage home. A man captured in the morning of April 9 would spend several months in a federal prison, while a man surrendering at Appomattox was paroled. More precious than money, each man guarded this document with his life, as losing it could be a fatal mistake. There were less than two dozen men left in the regiment, only five of which claimed to be the remnants of the gallant "Thomas County Rangers." They were Privates Lenny, David Stephenson, Aaron J. Donaldson, James Spears and Major James Rhodes Sheldon.

Commanding Simms' Brigade was Captain George Washington Waldron of the 50th Georgia. Only 190 men remained of the 5,100 who had served in the brigade.

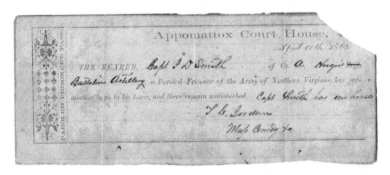

Parole Pass
(courtesy of National Park Service)

Souvenir hunting began as soon as the surrender was final. The McLean house was stripped bare by Union officers who paid Wilmer McLean cash for the tables, chairs and anything else he would part with. The apple tree where Lee had rested was cut up —every limb and twig was carried off by the men.

The day after the folding of the colors, private citizen James Rhodes Sheldon mounted his horse. "The hour arriving for me to start, I mounted my animal, and as I seated myself the thought came to me, to what point was I to head for? Home, Home, Sweet Home? No. You can never experience the feeling that took possession of me that moment. Home? I had none. 'Tis true, I could have gone to my mother's home in the state of Rhode Island, but that was within the lines of the Government I had borne arms against. It is true that my mother would have welcomed me with the love which only a mother has for her child, but I knew not what changes had taken place there. Mother might be absent. So I turned my horse's head Southward towards the state of my adoption." [31]

Men returned to their hometowns in pairs or in small groups. Many made the trip alone. James' long journey was mostly solitary as he hiked along the base of the mountains across Virginia, North Carolina, and South Carolina. At a railroad station in Athens, Georgia, he boarded a train taking him through Atlanta, Macon and Albany, where the tracks ended. From there, he made another lonely march of 60 miles, finally reaching Thomasville on the 13th day of May, 30 days after the surrender. Sister, Patience, and her husband, Edward, rushed to greet the ragged, dirty man as he approached their front gate. James was "home." "A merciful Creator had spared and blessed me, and I bowed my head in humble praises for His protection and kindness," he wrote to his mother, Rebecca, in far away Pawtuxet. [32]

On April 11, two days after the surrender of the Army of Northern Virginia, Colonel Rhodes and the 2nd Rhode Island marched out of Appomattox. Elisha recalled, "We left camp near Appomattox Court House this morning with the 6th Corps and after marching 20 miles are now on the road to Burkesville, if anybody knows where or what it is. The marching is fair, and the men are in good spirits." [33]

****

A Union General passed through Saylor's Creek on his return from Appomattox, and remembered, "One week after the battle I visited the field and could then have walked on Confederate dead for many succeeding rods along the face of the heights held by the enemy when the battle opened." [34] The hot weather caused the natives of the area to worry that disease would fester from the unburied dead and the citizens of the community collected the corpses and buried them as respectfully as possible. The scene was not unlike dozens that had come before, from Manassas to Chickamauga, Vicksburg to Cedar Creek.

A half century later, an old Confederate veteran reminisced with other war survivors about the last battle of the great conflict. As if the deeds and sacrifices of so many were soon to be forgotten, the old soldier shook his head, surrendering to the passage of time saying in a whisper,

"But it is all gone now. Fifty years have passed since the sound of guns of Saylor's Creek died away on the gentle breeze of that April day long ago. Kindly nature has healed up the scars of the battle field and when the spring comes again, green grass and sweet flowers will wave over the last resting place of the unreturning brave of both armies, who there await alike the judgment day, but whose spirits have long made peace on the camping ground of the brave and the just." [35]

EPILOGUE

On Christmas Eve, 2007, I received a Christmas card from my friend Robert Hunt Rhodes, Elisha's great-grandson. Along with a warm Christmas greeting the card included a message worthy of Santa Claus considering this book was finished and off to the publisher. Bob told me of a small leather bound notebook entitled: "A Trip Through The South & West And What I Saw" by E. H. Rhodes, Providence, R. I.. He explained, "Elisha was traveling via railroad and steamboats to New Orleans and then up the Mississippi and visiting mills for his mill supply business in Providence with Frederick Miller, his employer and mentor before the war. They sold leather harnesses and belts for running mill machinery. Elisha became his partner and then took over the business later on. In 1868 Elisha was 26 and wrote quite humorously about the South, almost like Mark Twain… He spent the night at the Pulaski House in Savannah."

The next morning, Wednesday, March 11, 1868, Elisha wrote, "Savannah in its better days must have been a fine city. The streets are wide and well laid out, but not paved. They cross at right angles, and at every crossing there is a small park or open square.

"The Police are uniformed in Confederate gray with U. S. officers' hats and make a fine appearance with their clubs and pistols in their belts.

"I found my old schoolmate James R. Sheldon and was introduced by him to several prominent merchants. The state of politics was the principal subject of conversation, which I avoided as much as possible but found myself called on for an opinion, which I gave but did not give very good satisfaction.

I was treated very kindly however. In the afternoon my friend Sheldon and myself took a long ride into the country and took a look at the fortifications which surround the City. On our return we took tea together and then sorted ourselves for a talk. Soon a young man (James R. Finegan) joined us and was introduced to me by Sheldon as a lieutenant on his father's staff, [Brigadier General Joseph Finegan, CSA], and supposing me to be a good Reb, he told me some of his exploits. The way they whipped the Yanks at Hatchers Run. (As I was there I knew better.) One of his friends killed several Yanks with a pistol. Finegan then fired and missed a man at thirty yards. This last story I believed, for Finegan looked as if he might miss at HALF THE DISTANCE. Major General Mansfield Lovell who surrendered New Orleans to the U. S. troops is a guest here."

"Thursday, March 12—Said goodbyes to my friends and started for Augusta with Rev. Dr. Berry, wife and boy from New York...".[1]

Elisha Hunt Rhodes was never officially mustered into the army as a colonel. The 2nd Rhode Island returned to Providence on July 17. A huge crowd stood on the platform to welcome home their sons, brothers, husbands and fathers. Although the train was delayed by seven hours, the midnight arrival of the regiment did not dim the crowd's enthusiasm. Elisha wrote that his "eyes were full of tears" as his men gave him one last rousing cheer.[2] On July 28, the 2nd was paid and disbanded; its flag furled for the last time. Colonel Rhodes told his men:

"Comrades; The time has come for us to part, after serving together for over four years. Before bidding you farewell, I wish to express my gratitude to you all for your uniform kindness toward me, and your attention to duty. Nobly have you served your country, gallantly have you followed our battle-scarred flags through the fiercest of the fight. You have never allowed the good name of our native state to suffer, but have added to its historic fame. You may well be proud of the part that you have taken in preserving the Union. Your commanding officer will ever be proud to say, that he served through the rebellion in the Second Rhode Island Volunteers, and will remember with pleasure the brave men who so nobly supported him during the time that he had command. We are now to commence a new career. We are to become citizens. Show to the nation that you can be good citizens as well as gallant soldiers. Be true to your God, your country and yourselves. Farewell!"[3]

On June 12, 1866, Elisha married his sweetheart, Caroline Pearce Hunt, at the First Baptist Church in Providence. Together they had two children, Frederick Miller and Alice Caroline.

Elisha bought out his former employer, Frederick Miller, and changed the name of the firm to the Dunham & Rhodes Company. He engaged in other business ventures, first, as a grocer with his army buddy, T. J. Smith, and later as a real estate agent. He was a member of the Pawtuxet Baptist Church and the Central Baptist Church of Providence where he served as a deacon and superintendent of the Sunday school.

He belonged to several fraternal organizations, including the Masons, and became commander of the Rhode Island Department of the Grand Army of the Republic, vice president of the Army of the Potomac Society, and founder and first president of the Soldiers and Sailors Historical Society. He attended the Gettysburg Reunion of 1913 and was active in the raising of funds for Civil War monuments. Working on behalf of veterans who had fallen on hard times, Elisha was also a member of the State Board of Soldier's Relief. In 1879, he was elected brigadier general of the Rhode Island Militia.

Elisha was also a member of the Providence School Board and was appointed collector of Internal Revenue by President Ulysses Grant. He was also chairman of the Home for Aged Men and Couples in Providence. In spite of the urging of others to run for governor, he declined.

On Sunday evening, January 14, 1917, Elisha Hunt Rhodes finished his dinner and sat in his favorite chair. A heart attack took his life, and the last man to command a Rhode Island regiment in the Civil War was gone. General Elisha Rhodes and his wife, Caroline, are buried at Swan Point Cemetery, Providence.

Graves of Elisha & Caroline Rhodes
Swan Point Cemetery, Providence, RI

The Community Church of Providence, formerly the Central Baptist Church, on Wayland Avenue, has a large photo of Elisha taken shortly before he died. It is in Rhodes Hall, the reception room at the church. Elisha was the chairman of fundraising for the church, which was completed a few months after his death. There is also a stained glass window and flag holder to the right of the chancel in his memory.

Elisha Hunt Rhodes (in his later years)

James Rhodes Sheldon returned to Thomasville but did not remain there long, saying, "it was not a home, only a resting place for a time, without employment, no prospect, no money." [4] In October of 1865, until the fall of the following year, he held a clerical position in Madison, Florida. Then, in 1870, James tried his luck in the big city, taking a low level clerk's position at a cotton brokerage in Savannah, while living in a rooming house. In 1880 he was one of the three organizers of the Savannah Guano Company, a fertilizer processing firm, erecting a plant on the east side of the city and eventually turning it into a flourishing business. He served as the vice president of the company from its inception and invested wisely in various interests throughout the city. Several years later, he opened a brokerage of his own. He also became a prosperous rice planter.

On Monday morning, March 17, 1862, *The Daily Morning News* of Savannah ran this news story: "Foreseeing the necessity of larger facilities for the care of the sick, Hiram Roberts, Esq, tendered the use of his elegant private residence, as a free hospital." [5] Private James Sheldon was ill at that time and is listed as recuperating in Savannah. Whether James was treated at the Roberts home is not known, but on April 7, 1875, at Saint John's Church, James married Miss Louisa Caruthers Roberts, daughter of Hiram Roberts. Six years after they married, on March 31, 1881, Louisa gave birth to Louise Roberts Sheldon. Sadly, there were complications following this birth and two months later, Louisa died.

On November 16, 1882, in New York City, James remarried. His new bride was 25-year-old Elizabeth Evelyn Roberts, Louisa's sister. But tragedy struck the Sheldon family again when four-year-old "Little Louise" [6] died on August 16, 1885. Louise was buried with her mother Louisa in Laurel Grove Cemetery in Savannah. Nearly ten years later, on November 5, 1893, James Rhodes Sheldon, Jr. was born. In 1915, the bodies of Louisa and Louise were disinterred from Laurel Grove Cemetery and interred at Bonaventure Cemetery in Savannah.

James retired from business after the turn of the century. Although his interest in politics was limited (having once served as an alderman) his role in public affairs was not. When a neighboring city was crippled by a yellow fever epidemic, Savannah's mayor turned to James Sheldon to organize and maintain an effective quarantine. His reputation as fair and politically unbiased allowed him to successfully ward off a potential disaster. He was an avid horseman well into his seventies and was a daily fixture around Savannah, driving his buggy with all the expertise of a former commissary sergeant. He was the oldest member of Savannah's Oglethorpe Club and an active Mason, being a master of the Ancient Landmark Lodge and a thirty-second degree Mason of the Scottish Rite. But of all his accomplishments, he was most proud of his career as a soldier. During his service in the Army of Northern Virginia, he never once applied for or received a furlough of any kind.

James maintained his independent political status but gave his support to candidates and referenda that he deemed appropriate. He served on the Savannah Health and Sanitary Board for six years and was an active member of the Savannah Volunteer Guards. Although he never became a member of any religious organization, James attended services at St. John's Protestant Episcopal Church, where his wife was a communicant. He was very active in the Confederate Veterans Association and was the last surviving veteran of the Army of Northern Virginia in Savannah. In 1909, James was offered the position of Chief of Staff of the Georgia Division of the United Confederate Veterans at the rank of colonel. Replying to the offer, James wrote, "I thank you but decline. I am not partial to such titles not earned." [7]

James did see his mother again. According to his grandson, Irving C. Sheldon, "In 1869 Grandpapa's mother was apparently going downhill and it didn't seem that she would live much longer. He decided to visit her and set off to the North. They often traveled to New York by sea, the Savannah Line offering excellent service. He arrived in Providence, whether by the night boat or train I do not know, and was met by a friend who told him that his brothers would not allow him in Pawtuxet. This was, of course, due to the bitter feelings engendered by the War, and they did not want to be in the same town with him. I do not know what sort of parleys were held but eventually an agreement was reached whereby his brothers would leave Pawtuxet for the period of his visit with his mother."[8]

Throughout his life, Major Sheldon had enjoyed remarkable health, but in mid-June of 1928 he fell and broke his hip. In a weakened state, he developed pneumonia, succumbing a few days later on June 28 at his home on East Gaston Street. Besides his wife he was survived by his son, James Rhodes Sheldon, Jr., and five grandchildren. The flag over Savannah City Hall flew at half-staff in honor of his memory. Lafayette McLaws, grandson of James' old division commander, was one of his pallbearers. James was buried with Louisa and Louise at Bonaventure Cemetery. Bessie died toward the end of World War II on August 6, 1944 and is also buried at Bonaventure.

Major James Rhodes Sheldon never applied for a Confederate pension.

James Rhodes Sheldon
(in his later years)

Graves of James Rhodes, Louise, Louisa and Bessie Sheldon
– Bonaventure Cemetery, Savannah, GA

Augustus "Gussie" Brack was released from federal prison in 1865. Nothing else is known of him.

Goode Bryan returned to Georgia and engaged in various business ventures until his death at Augusta in 1885.

J.D. Campbell survived the war. Nothing else is known of him.

John T. Chastain fell in love while working as a nurse in Farmville, Virginia. Before returning to Thomasville, he married Martitia "Tishia" Davis of Farmville. The hospital where he was detailed surrendered to Union forces, and John was paroled on April 11, 1865. He returned to his position at *The Southern Enterprise* and when the paper merged with the *Times*, Chastain retired and purchased the old homestead which had belonged to his grandfather. John and Tishia Chastain raised 6 children and lived out their last years in their beautiful home amid a grove of live oaks, magnolias, holly and pecan trees. John and his wife devoted their free time to work in the Missionary Baptist Church. His good friend, James Sheldon, was a witness to his Confederate Pension application. He is buried in Thomasville.

Thomas Drayton farmed in Dooly County, Georgia, after the war before entering the insurance business in 1872. In 1878, he moved to South Carolina and became president of the South Carolina Immigration Society. He died at Florence on February 18, 1891.

William O. Fleming returned to his family at Bainbridge, Georgia. After the war he was appointed solicitor general of the Albany circuit court in 1876. Shortly before his death in 1881 at the age of 46, he was elected judge by the state legislature.

Joseph Kershaw was held prisoner at Ft. Warren, Boston, until August 12, 1865. He returned to his law practice in South Carolina. Later that year, he was elected to the State senate. In 1874 he was a candidate for congress and three years later, was elected circuit judge. In 1893, he resigned his judgeship because of failing health and returned to his practice as an attorney. In February, 1894, he was commissioned postmaster of Camden, South Carolina. He died only two months after this appointment.

John McCall was transferred into the Veterans Reserve Corps on December 12, 1864 and returned to Brooks County, Georgia, as a recruiting officer. He died there in 1921.

William Manning had been a large land owner and slaveholder in Coffee County until 1861, when he moved to Lowndes County and bought lands near Valdosta, Georgia. He suffered several financial setbacks after the war and died nearly broke in October 1871.

Andrew McGlashan died in Rome, Georgia on October 6, 1886.

Peter Alexander Selkirk McGlashan was imprisoned on Johnson's Island in Ohio until July 25, 1865. In 1866, he was elected mayor of Thomasville. He was active in the affairs of

Confederate veterans in Thomasville and continued to be after he moved to Savannah in 1885. In Savannah, he returned to his craft as a saddler and served as the city's plumbing inspector. While swimming near his home in June of 1908, Peter McGlashan suffered a heart attack and drowned at the age of 77. He went to his grave swearing that Union soldiers fired upon his men after they had surrendered at Saylor's Creek. Some believe that President Davis' last official act was to commission McGlashan brigadier general, although no evidence of this survived the fall of Richmond. His life was the stuff of legends.

Frederick Miller died at his home, 80 Congdon Street, Providence, on August 18, 1880 of Typhoid Fever. He was 56 years old.

Tom Parker, Medal of Honor recipient of the 2nd Rhode Island, died on April 27, 1872 in Philadelphia, Pennsylvania. He is buried at Mechanics Cemetery.

Tillie Pierce published an account of her experiences during the Battle of Gettysburg in 1888. She married Horace P. Alleman in 1871 and they had three children. Tillie lived in Selinsgrove, Pennsylvania, until she died in 1914. She is buried in Trinity Lutheran Cemetery in Selinsgrove.

George Randolph was promoted to Chief of Artillery of the 3rd Corps in April of 1863. He resigned from the army in January of 1864 at the rank of colonel. He died in Colorado in 1912.

Edward Remington died in Thomasville in 1878 at the age of 73. He is buried in the Old Cemetery.

Patience Remington, James' sister, outlived her husband by eight years. She was 56 years old when she died in Thomasville.

Eliza Rhodes died on May 3, 1885 at 79 years of age. She is buried at Pawtuxet Memorial Cemetery in Warwick, Rhode Island.

Grave of Eliza Rhodes
Pawtuxet Memorial Cemetery
Warwick, RI

Horatio Rogers was promoted to brigadier general in March of 1865. After the war, he returned to his law practice and served as Rhode Island's attorney general. Rogers enjoyed a career as a writer for several newspapers and magazines and was known for his exciting lectures on the Civil War. Later, he served as a judge on the Rhode Island Supreme Court. Rogers was the featured speaker at the unveiling of the Ambrose Burnside monument in Providence. Rogers' wife, Lucia, died from childbirth complications in 1867. He remarried in 1869 and was the father of three children.

Paul Semmes was buried with a simple board for a grave marker. Three years after the war, his body was exhumed and carried back to his hometown of Columbus, Georgia, and given a funeral amid so much pomp and circumstance that the occupying Union authorities cringed. During the ceremony, a covered photograph of a uniformed

General Semmes rested above his flag draped coffin, prompting an unknown woman to rise from the crowd and remove the shroud. Over 150 veterans escorted the body to the cemetery, along with a throng of women. As angry authorities watched Semmes' funeral, full military honors were bestowed upon him. Surveying the crowd, one Union officer was heard saying to another, "we dare not molest them." [9] Today, General Paul Semmes' bloodstained uniform is on display at the Museum of the Confederacy in Richmond.

Israel Sheldon resumed working in the jewelry business with his partners Nathan Mathewson and W.C. Greene. He and **Alma** resided with her parents on Post Road in Pawtuxet. They had one child, William, born in 1855. Their house, also known as the Carder Tavern, is extant. Israel died in 1885 at the age of 53. Alma survived him by 27 years.

George Sheldon was employed as a clerk in a mill after the war and later worked as a bookkeeper until retiring in 1900. In 1910, he was a part time janitor at Pawtuxet's Commercial Street School. His wife, Hannah, was named for the little sloop that enticed the HMS *Gaspee* onto a sandbar in 1772. George died in 1916 at the age of 75; Hannah had died 12 years earlier. They are buried in the Sheldon lot at Pawtuxet Burial Ground a few hundred yards from their former home which still stands on Post Road next to the Carder Tavern. In recent years, the house has been rental property, and several residents have insisted that the home is haunted by a sea captain, an old woman and a little girl.

George Sheldon's home
Pawtuxet, RI

Rebecca Sheldon never remarried. She died at her home in Pawtuxet on April 17, 1869 at 63 years of age. She is buried at Pawtuxet Burial Ground.

Arthur Benjamin "Ben" Simms was captured at Saylor's Creek on April 6, 1865, and was a prisoner of war at Johnson's Island, Ohio. It was his second incarceration there. After his release he resumed his law practice in Covington, Georgia. He died on June 6, 1887.

James Phillip Simms was held prisoner at Ft. Warren in Boston, Massachusetts, until July 24, 1865. He returned to his home in Covington, Georgia, where he practiced law. He died in 1887 at the age of 50.

Simeon Alexander Smith died in 1846 at the age of 67 in Thomasville.

Thorndike Jameson Smith entered into the grocery business after the war with his good friend Elisha Rhodes. Smith died at the age of 26 at Webster, Massachusetts, in 1869.

John Spence, of Coffee County, served in the Georgia House of Representatives from Coffee County in 1871-72. He died about 1904, and was buried in the Spence family cemetery near his home.

William Stilwell was wounded at the Battle of Cedar Creek, requiring the amputation of a leg below the knee. He was 24 years old at the time.

John Wood was captured at Saylor's Creek. After his release from prison he returned to Newton County, Georgia, where he lived out his life as a farmer. He and his wife, Nancy, had six children together.

Augustus Woodbury returned to his avocation of a civilian clergyman after the war. He was the pastor of the Westminster Unitarian Church in Providence until 1892 when he and his wife, Rebecca, retired to Concord, New Hampshire. Reverend Woodbury died on November 19, 1895. The Woodbury Union Church in Warwick, Rhode Island, is named in his honor.

Cicero Holt Young, the first captain of the Thomas County Rangers, is buried in Winchester, Virginia. Today there is a little iron pot on display in a library in Thomasville. A tag on it reads: "THIS LITTLE POT WAS USED BY CAPTAIN CICERO HOLT YOUNG OF THOMAS COUNTY, GEORGIA, TO MELT LEAD TO MAKE BULLETS FOR USE IN THE WAR BETWEEN THE STATES. HE WAS KILLED IN THE CONFEDERATE ARMY IN VIRGINIA AND BURIED THERE."

The 50th Georgia left its mark upon the families of all who served in it, and some families suffered more than most.

- Richard G. Kirkland and his brothers, Timothy and Zean, all joined the 50th Georgia in the spring of 1862. Only Zean would come home from the war.
- Parrish and Sarah Lankford watched their sons Hardy, Tarlton and Parrish, Jr. march off to the front. None would return.
- Letters from home describing families' hardships tempted many soldiers to desert. Washington Wayne Waters of Company C, the Coffee County Guards, typified the worried men of the 50th Georgia. One Waters family member remembered, "The story was told that while he served in South Carolina, Grandma & Aunt Sallie were having a heartbreaking time trying to keep their families fed, and the farms going with both of their husbands away at the war. So, he walked away from his outfit and back to south Georgia in the spring to help get a crop into the ground. Then, he

walked back and rejoined his unit." [10] Waters was captured at Cedar Creek October 19, 1864. He was paroled at Point Lookout, Maryland and was later transferred for exchange on February 13, 1865.

The flag of the 50th Georgia is on display at the Jefferson Davis Memorial Historic Site in Irwinville, Georgia.

Thomasville today has a population approaching 20,000 people. Its historic homes, fine restaurants, and annual Rose Show and Festival attract thousands of tourists each year.

Downtown Thomasville, GA (today)

Pawtuxet Village retains the charm of the mid-18th century. Sheldon Street, across from the site of James' childhood home, stills bears that name today. In 2005 the remnants of a hurricane caused the river to flood its banks. The little waterfall was turned into a roaring torrent. All the residents of the village came out to watch and eat ice cream on the bridge. Pawtuxet is a great place to be a kid—some things never change.

Pawtuxet Falls (as it appears today)

MAYORAL PROCLAMATIONS

As a direct result of the information discovered while researching for this book the following proclamations were issued:

RESOLUTION
WARWICK, RHODE ISLAND

WHEREAS, *it has been called to the attention of the Mayor and Council of the City of Thomasville, Georgia, and Warwick, Rhode Island, that they share an interesting historical relationship dating back to the early 1800s, when Edward Remington and Simeon Smith, both of Warwick's Pawtuxet Village, settled in the area that was to become the City of Thomasville; and,*

WHEREAS, *after the Civil War, the City of Thomasville flourished as a popular resort for Northerners who appreciated its pleasant climate, majestic oaks, and Southern hospitality, many of whom were Rhode Islanders, thus building a more extensive connection between the two cities; and,*

WHEREAS, *in addition to sharing early settlers, Thomasville and Pawtuxet Village presently share characteristics including streets named for Remington and Smith, and common architectural features; and,*

WHEREAS, *on May 13ᵗʰ, 2000, His Honor Scott Avedisian, Mayor of the City of Warwick, did proclaim Thomasville, Georgia, a Sister City of Warwick, Rhode Island.*

NOW, THEREFORE, BE IT RESOLVED *that the Mayor and the Council of the City of Thomasville do hereby proclaim Warwick, Rhode Island a Sister City of Thomasville, Georgia. SO DONE, this 10ᵗʰ day of July 2000.*

Roy Campbell, Mayor

CITY OF WARWICK

MAYORAL PROCLAMATION

WHEREAS, *Thomasville, Georgia and Warwick, Rhode Island share a significant historical relationship that dates back to the early 19*[th] *Century; and,*

WHEREAS, *Edward Remington and Simeon Smith - both from Warwick's Pawtuxet Village - moved to Georgia in the early 1800s, helping to establish the City of Thomasville; and,*

WHEREAS, *Remington's brother-in-law, James, moved to Thomasville at age 18. He joined the 50*[th] *Georgia Regiment during the Civil War, meeting the Second Rhode Island Regiment - of which his life-long Pawtuxet friend, Elisha Hunt Rhodes, was a part - on the battlefield eleven times during the war; and,*

WHEREAS, *after the war, Thomasville became a vacation retreat for many Rhode Islanders, especially those from Pawtuxet - further solidifying the two towns' relationship; and,*

WHEREAS, *in addition to sharing early settlers, Thomasville and Pawtuxet Village still share several characteristics, including street names and some architecture, making them "twin cities."*

461

NOW, THEREFORE, BE IT RESOLVED THAT I, SCOTT AVEDISIAN, MAYOR OF THE CITY OF WARWICK DO HEREBY PROCLAIM THOMASVILLE, GEORGIA, A SISTER CITY OF WARWICK, RHODE ISLAND, AND PROCLAIM, MAY 13, 2000 AS:

THOMASVILLE, GEORGIA HERITAGE DAY IN THE CITY OF WARWICK,

AND ENCOURAGE ALL ITS CITIZENS TO JOIN ME IN RECOGNIZING THIS IMPORTANT OCCASION.

SCOTT A. VEDISIAN, MAYOR

END NOTES

Beginning

1. Horace Belcher Papers
2. Henry A.L. Brown (interview)
3. Horace Belcher Papers

Chapter 1. Little Falls

1. Scott, Joseph E. Brown.
2. Sheldon, The Ship "Hanover" of Providence, 1-5.
3. Mathews, Linda. Pawcatuck, Pawtucket, Pawtuxet: Three Places in Rhode Island?
4. Rogers, Ante-Bellum Thomas County, 20.
5. Ibid., 20.
6. Ibid., 66.
7. Ibid., 67.
8. Ibid.
9. Cranston Historical Society, William Sprague of Rhode Island.
10. Ibid.

Chapter 2. "It seemed as though the Union Army melted away"

1. Brown, Joseph. Governor Joseph Brown's Open Letter.
2. Ibid.
3. Ibid.
4. Ibid.
5. Woodbury, The First Rhode Island Regiment, 10-14.

6. Rhodes, All For The Union, 12.
7. Ibid., 13.
8. Ibid., 14.
9. Woodbury, The Second Rhode Island Regiment, 40.
10. Rhodes, All For The Union, 13-14.
11. Ibid., 14.
12. Ibid., 20.
13. Official Records of the War of Rebellion, Series 1, Volume 2, Chapter IX, 7.
14. Rhodes, All For The Union, 20.
15. Ibid., 20.
16. Woodbury, The Second Rhode Island Regiment, 25.
17. Rhodes, All For The Union, 23.
18. Official Records of the War of Rebellion, Series 1, Volume 2, Chapter IX, 308.
19. Ibid., 326.
20. Ibid.
21. Ibid., 319.
22. Ibid., 316.
23. Ibid., 396.
24. Ibid., 320.
25. Woodbury, The Second Rhode Island Regiment, 36.
26. Official Records of the War of Rebellion, Series 1, Volume 2, Chapter IX, 397.
27. Ibid., 321.
28. Ibid., 400.
29. Ibid., 399.
30. Ibid., 404.
31. Rhodes, All For The Union, 30.
32. Sears, To the Gates of Richmond, 17.
33. Rhodes, All For The Union, 44.
34. Long, The Civil War Day by Day, 128.
35. Rhodes, All For The Union, 47.
36. Boatner, The Civil War Dictionary, 432.
37. Rhodes, All For The Union, 49.
38. Ibid., 50.

Chapter 3. "We are living as fine as you ever saw"

1. Bucklyn, The War of the Rebellion, Wickford/North Kingstown Standard Times.
2. Sheldon, The 1862 War Diary of Israel Sheldon.
3. Wheeler, Sword Over Richmond, 64.
4. Rhodes, All For The Union, 54.
5. Boatner, The Civil War Dictionary, 857.
6. Sheldon, The 1862 War Diary of Israel Sheldon.
7. Ibid.
8. Ibid.
9. Harden, John Chastain File, USGenWeb Archives.
10. Rogers, Thomas County During The Civil War, 15.
11. Sheldon, The 1862 War Diary of Israel Sheldon.
12. Bucklyn, The War of the Rebellion, Wickford/North Kingstown Standard Times.
13. Rhodes, All For The Union, 59.
14. McCall, Letters from John G. F. McCall, 3/20/62 Camp Davis, Guyton, GA.
15. Life In A Civil War Camp, Website.
16. McCall, Letters from John G. F. McCall, 4/1/62 Camp Davis, Guyton, GA.
17. Bucklyn, The War of the Rebellion, Wickford/North Kingstown Standard Times.
18. Sheldon, The 1862 War Diary of Israel Sheldon.
19. Rhodes, All For The Union, 60.
20. McCall, Letters from John G. F. McCall, 3/20/62 Camp Davis, Guyton, GA.
21. The Augusta Constitutionalist, March 7, 1862.
22. Woodbury, The Second Rhode Island Regiment, 70-71.
23. Wheeler, Sword Over Richmond, 20.
24. Long, The Civil War Day by Day, 192.
25. McCall, Letters from John G. F. McCall, 4/3/62 Camp Davis, Guyton, GA.
26. Sheldon, The 1862 War Diary of Israel Sheldon.

27. McCall, Letters from John G. F. McCall, 3/20/62 Camp Davis, Guyton, GA.
28. Ibid., 4/3/62.
29. Long, The Civil War Day by Day, 197.
30. Manning, National Archives.
31. Ibid.
32. Rhodes, All For The Union, 63.
33. Sheldon, The 1862 War Diary of Israel Sheldon.
34. Ibid.
35. Long, The Civil War Day by Day, 207.
36. Griess, Atlas for The American Civil War, 11.
37. Bucklyn, The War of the Rebellion, Wickford/North Kingstown Standard Times.
38. Sheldon, The 1862 War Diary of Israel Sheldon.
39. Bucklyn, The War of the Rebellion, Wickford/North Kingstown Standard Times.
40. Ibid.
41. Ibid.
42. Ibid.
43. Ibid.
44. Robertson, Standing Like A Stone Wall, 122.
45. Long, The Civil War Day by Day, 210.
46. Rhodes, All For The Union, 65.
47. Sears, To the Gates of Richmond, 94.
48. Rhodes, All For The Union, 67.
49. Ibid.
50. Long, The Civil War Day by Day, 216.
51. Ibid., 216-217.

Chapter 4. "Why not?"

1. Dyer, Adjutant Generals Report 1861-65, Volume 1, 476.
2. Ibid.
3. Ibid.
4. Ibid.
5. Ibid., 477.

6. Ibid.
7. Spicer, Ninth and Tenth R. I. Volunteers and Tenth R.I. Battery, 126.
8. Ibid., 130.
9. Dyer, Adjutant Generals Report 1861-65, Volume 1, 477.
10. Spicer, Ninth and Tenth R. I. Volunteers and Tenth R.I. Battery, 134.
11. Ibid., 136.
12. Dyer, Adjutant Generals Report 1861-65, Volume 1, 477.
13. Spicer, Ninth and Tenth R. I. Volunteers and Tenth R.I. Battery, 141-142.
14. Gragg, The Illustrated Confederate Reader, 46.
15. Long, The Civil War Day by Day, 217.
16. Sears, To the Gates of Richmond, 117.
17. McCall, Letters from John G. F. McCall, 5/29/62 Near Savannah, GA.
18. Sheldon, The 1862 War Diary of Israel Sheldon.
19. Ibid.
20. Sears, To the Gates of Richmond, 154.
21. Rhodes, All For The Union, 69.
22. Freeman, R. E. Lee, 608.
23. Rhodes, All For The Union, 69.
24. Ibid.
25. Douglas, I Rode With Stonewall, 89.
26. Boatner, The Civil War Dictionary, 812.
27. Sheldon, The 1862 War Diary of Israel Sheldon.
28. Ibid.
29. Ibid.
30. Rhodes, All For The Union, 71.
31. Ibid., 72.
32. Sheldon, The 1862 War Diary of Israel Sheldon.
33. Ibid.
34. Ibid.
35. Rhodes, All For The Union, 72.
36. Freeman, Lee's Lieutenants, Volume 1, 590.
37. Freeman, R.E. Lee, 207-208.

38. Boatner, The Civil War Dictionary, 506.
39. Sheldon, The 1862 War Diary of Israel Sheldon.
40. Douglas, I Rode With Stonewall, 114.
41. Sheldon, The 1862 War Diary of Israel Sheldon.
42. Rhodes, All For The Union, 73.
43. Wheeler, Sword Over Richmond, 344.
44. Sheldon, The 1862 War Diary of Israel Sheldon.
45. Ibid.
46. Rhodes, All For The Union, 73.
47. Sheldon, The 1862 War Diary of Israel Sheldon.
48. Ibid.
49. Ibid.
50. Rhodes, All For The Union, 74.
51. Sheldon, The 1862 War Diary of Israel Sheldon.
52. Rhodes, All For The Union, 76.
53. Jones, History of Decatur County Georgia, 383.
54. The Augusta Constitutionalist, August 14, 1862.
55. Rhodes, All For The Union, 77.
56. Dyer, Adjutant Generals Report 1861-65, Volume 1, 481.
57. Spicer, Ninth and Tenth R. I. Volunteers and Tenth R.I. Battery, 307.

Chapter 5. "Where is you? Where is you?"

1. Sheldon, The 1862 War Diary of Israel Sheldon.
2. Ibid.
3. Official Records of the War of Rebellion, Series 1, Vol.12 (Part II), Chap. XXIV, 437.
4. Sheldon, The 1862 War Diary of Israel Sheldon.
5. Pendleton, Confederate Memoirs, 27.
6. Rhodes, All For The Union, 79.
7. Official Records of the War of Rebellion, Series 1, Vol.12 (Part II), Chap. XXIV, 420.
8. Sheldon, The 1862 War Diary of Israel Sheldon.
9. Lewis, The History of Battery E, 103.
10. Rhodes, All For The Union, 79.

11. Official Records of the War of Rebellion, Series 1, Vol.19 (Part II), Chap. XXXI, 602.
12. Boatner, The Civil War Dictionary, 17.
13. Fleming, scrapbook of M.J. Solomon, Duke University, Durham, North Carolina.
14. Ibid.
15. Rhodes, All For The Union, 81.
16. Ibid.
17. Sheldon, The 1862 War Diary of Israel Sheldon.
18. Rhodes, All For The Union, 82.
19. Ibid., 84.
20. Long, The Civil War Day by Day, 274.
21. Ibid., 275-276.
22. Ibid., 278.
23. Rhodes, All For The Union, 85.
24. Ibid., 86.
25. Long, The Civil War Day by Day, 281.
26. Rhodes, All For The Union, 86.
27. Long, The Civil War Day by Day, 282.
28. Rhodes, All For The Union, 87.
29. McCall, Letters from John G. F. McCall, 12/3/62 Near Fredericksburg, VA.
30. Long, The Civil War Day by Day, 284-285.
31. Sears, George B. McClellan, 341.
32. Curtis, McClellan's Last Service to the Republic, Part II, 474.
33. Rhodes, All For The Union, 88.
34. Sheldon, The 1862 War Diary of Israel Sheldon.
35. Rhodes, All For The Union, 88.
36. Semmes In America
37. Long, The Civil War Day by Day, 292.
38. Rhodes, All For The Union, 89.
39. Wood, Letters from John L.G. Wood, 12/18/62 and 12/29/62 Near Fredericksburg, VA.
40. Official Records of the War of Rebellion, Series 1, Vol. 21, Chap. XXXIII, 536.

41. Ibid.
42. Freeman, Lee's Lieutenants, Vol. 2, 378.
43. Faust, Historical Times Illustrated Encyclopedia of the Civil War, 18.
44. Official Records of the War of Rebellion, Series 1, Vol. 21, Chap. XXXIII, 537.
45. Rhodes, All For The Union, 92.
46. Wood, Letters from John L.G. Wood, 12/18/62 and 12/29/62 Near Fredericksburg, VA.
47. Ibid.
48. Ibid.
49. Ibid.
50. Ibid.
51. Ibid.
52. Augusta Constitutionalist
53. Rhodes, All For The Union, 93.
54. Holland, Keep All My Letters, 61.

Chapter 6. "They were a savage looking set of blue birds"

1.   Stilwell, The Stilwell Letters, 101.
2.   Long, The Civil War Day by Day, 314
3.   Holland, Keep All My Letters, 63.
4.   Boatner, The Civil War Dictionary, 409.
5.   Ibid., 410.
6.   Rhodes, All For The Union, 98.
7.   Ibid., 98.
8.   Ibid.
9.   Holland, Keep All My Letters, 64.
10. Ibid., 67.
11. McCall, Letters from John G. F. McCall, 2/27/63 Near Fredericksburg, VA.
12. Rhodes, All For The Union, 101.
13. Holland, Keep All My Letters, 73.
14. Ibid., 78.
15. Ibid., 79.

16. McCall, Letters from John G. F. McCall, 4/22/63 Near Fredericksburg, VA.
17. Ibid.
18. Holland, Keep All My Letters, 82.
19. Wood, Letters from John L.G. Wood, 5/10/63 New Camp, 8 miles from Fredericksburg, VA.
20. Official Records of the War of Rebellion, Series 1, Vol. 25 (Part I), Chap. XXXVII, 833-834.
21. Fergurson, Chancellorsville 1863, 127.
22. Ibid., 140.
23. Sears, Chancellorsville, 233.
24. Boatner, The Civil War Dictionary, 433.
25. Freeman, Lee's Lieutenants, Volume 2, 547.
26. Henderson, Stonewall Jackson and the American Civil War, 668.
27. Douglas, I Rode With Stonewall, 202.
28. Sheldon, The 1862 War Diary of Israel Sheldon.
29. Ibid.
30. Freeman, Lee's Lieutenants, Vol. 2, 567.
31. Wood, Letters from John L.G. Wood, 5/10/63 New Camp, 8 miles from Fredericksburg, VA.
32. Boatner, The Civil War Dictionary, 254.
33. Rhodes, All For The Union, 106.
34. Wood, Letters from John L.G. Wood, 5/10/63 New Camp, 8 miles from Fredericksburg, VA.
35. Official Records of the War of Rebellion, Series 1, Vol. 25 (Part I), Chap. XXXVII, 835.
36. Confederate Veterans Association. Addresses Delivered Before The Confederate Veterans Association of Savannah, Ga. 1898-1902, 90-91.
37. Ibid., 91.
38. Ibid.
39. Ibid.
40. Ibid.
41. Official Records of the War of Rebellion, Series 1, Vol. 25 (Part I), Chap. XXXVII, 835.

42. Rhodes, All For The Union, 106.
43. Confederate Veterans Association. Addresses Delivered Before The Confederate Veterans Association of Savannah, Ga. 1898-1902, 91.
44. Wood, Letters from John L.G. Wood, 5/10/63 New Camp, 8 miles from Fredericksburg, VA.
45. Ibid.
46. Woodbury, The Second Rhode Island Regiment, 170.
47. Confederate Veterans Association. Addresses Delivered Before The Confederate Veterans Association of Savannah, Ga. 1898-1902, 92.
48. Official Records of the War of Rebellion, Series 1, Vol. 25 (Part I), Chap. XXXVII, 838.
49. Ibid.
50. Confederate Veterans Association. Addresses Delivered Before The Confederate Veterans Association of Savannah, Ga. 1898-1902, 92.
51. Ibid., 92-94.
52. Ibid.
53. Ibid.
54. Official Records of the War of Rebellion, Series 1, Vol. 25 (Part I), Chap. XXXVII, 835.
55. Wood, Letters from John L.G. Wood, 5/10/63 New Camp, 8 miles from Fredericksburg, VA.
56. Ibid.
57. Confederate Veterans Association. Addresses Delivered Before The Confederate Veterans Association of Savannah, Ga. 1898-1902, 93-94.
58. Ibid.
59. Wood, Letters from John L.G. Wood, 5/10/63 New Camp, 8 miles from Fredericksburg, VA.

Chapter 7. "It was a sad list"

1. Confederate Veterans Association. Addresses Delivered Before The Confederate Veterans Association of Savannah, Ga. 1898-1902, 94.
2. Rhodes, All For The Union, 107.
3. Gallagher, The Fredericksburg Campaign: Decision on the Rappahannock, 175.
4. Rhodes, All For The Union, 108.
5. Lewis, The History of Battery E, 178.
6. Rhodes, All For The Union, 112.
7. Holland, Keep All My Letters, 88.
8. Rhodes, All For The Union, 113.
9. Stilwell, The Stilwell Letters, 181-182.
10. Rhodes, All For The Union, 114.
11. Ibid., 115.
12. Alleman, At Gettysburg, 21.
13. Ibid, 21-23.
14. Clark, The Civil War, Gettysburg, 59.
15. Ibid., 66.
16. Ibid., 65-66.
17. Boatner, The Civil War Dictionary, 336.
18. Pendleton, Confederate Memoirs, 34.
19. Rhodes, All For The Union, 115.
20. Ibid.
21. Freeman, Lee's Lieutenants, Volume 3, 114.
22. Alexander, Fighting for the Confederacy, 227.
23. Official Records of the War of Rebellion, Series 1, Vol. 27 (Part II), Chap. XXXIX, 367.
24. Pendleton, Confederate Memoirs, 35.
25. Rhodes, All For The Union, 115.
26. Ibid., 115-116.
27. Official Records of the War of Rebellion, Series 1, Vol. 27 (Part I), Chap. XXXIX, 683.
28. Woodbury, The Second Rhode Island Regiment, 195.
29. Pendleton, Confederate Memoirs, 35.

30. Ibid.
31. Confederate Veterans Association. Addresses Delivered Before The Confederate Veterans Association of Savannah, Ga. 1898-1902, 22-23.
32. Official Records of the War of Rebellion, Series 1, Vol. 27 (Part I), Chap. XXXIX, 372.
33. Stilwell, The Stilwell Letters, 185.
34. Official Records of the War of Rebellion, Series 1, Vol. 27 (Part I), Chap. XXXIX, 369.
35. Ibid., 370.
36. Pendleton, Confederate Memoirs, 36.
37. Wert, General James Longstreet, 290.
38. Clark, The Civil War, Gettysburg, 119.
39. Woodbury, The Second Rhode Island Regiment, 195.
40. Pendleton, Confederate Memoirs, 36.
41. Ibid.
42. Ibid.
43. Rhodes, All For The Union, 116.
44. Clark, The Civil War, Gettysburg, 136.
45. Rhodes, All For The Union, 116.
46. Freeman, Lee's Lieutenants, Volume 3, 166.
47. Official Records of the War of Rebellion, Series 1, Vol. 27 (Part I), Chap. XXXIX, 684.
48. Clark, The Civil War, Gettysburg, 144.
49. Official Records of the War of Rebellion, Series 1, Vol. 27 (Part I), Chap. XXXIX, 684.
50. Rhodes, All For The Union, 116.

Chapter 8. "Kiss This Corner"

1. Alexander, Edward Porter, Fighting For The Confederacy, 279-280.
2. Alexander, Military Memoirs of A Confederate, 436.
3. Ibid., 437-438.
4. Washington Evening Star, 7/6/63.
5. The Philadelphia Inquirer

6. The Charleston Courier
7. Washington Evening Star, 7/6/63.
8. Alleman, At Gettysburg, 81.
9. Rhodes, All For The Union, 117.
10. Semmes In America, Gettysburg National Military Park, Collection.
11. Ibid.
12. Alexander, Military Memoirs of A Confederate, 438.
13. Ibid.
14. Ibid.
15. Pendleton, Confederate Memoirs, 37.
16. Rhodes, All For The Union, 117.
17. Strater, The Life and Times of a Rebel Surgeon.
18. Ibid.
19. Rhodes, All For The Union, 117.
20. Ibid.
21. Ibid.
22. Long, The Civil War Day by Day, 381.
23. Rhodes, All For The Union, 118.
24. Pendleton, Confederate Memoirs, 38.
25. Ibid.
26. Woodbury, The Second Rhode Island Regiment, 202.
27. Rhodes, All For The Union, 118.
28. Stilwell, The Stilwell Letters, 185-186.
29. Rhodes, All For The Union, 118.
30. Pendleton, Confederate Memoirs, 39.
31. Woodbury, The Second Rhode Island Regiment, 202.
32. Alexander, Military Memoirs of A Confederate, 440-441.
33. Pendleton, Confederate Memoirs, 39.
34. Long, The Civil War Day by Day, 385.
35. Ibid., 386.
36. Ibid., 387.
37. Jones, History of Decatur County Georgia, 384.
38. Rhodes, All For The Union, 120.
39. Pendleton, Confederate Memoirs, 39.
40. Rhodes, All For The Union, 120.

41. Ibid.
42. Pendleton, Confederate Memoirs, 41.
43. Wood, Letters from John L.G. Wood, 8/13/63 Camp near the Rapidan River, in Orange County.
44. Ibid.
45. Rhodes, All For The Union, 120.

Chapter 9. "We all stand as hearty as bucks"

1. Woodbury, The Second Rhode Island Regiment, 206.
2. Ibid.
3. Holland, Keep All My Letters, 96.
4. Ibid., 97.
5. Rhodes, All For The Union, 123.
6. Ibid.
7. Ibid.
8. Holland, Keep All My Letters, 99.
9. Stilwell, The Stilwell Letters, 201.
10. Holland, Keep All My Letters, 101.
11. Stilwell, The Stilwell Letters, 208.
12. Wert, General James Longstreet, 299.
13. Life In A Civil War Camp.
14. Wert, General James Longstreet, 303.
15. Ibid.
16. Pendleton, Confederate Memoirs, 41-42.
17. Ibid., 42.
18. Holland, Keep All My Letters, 106.
19. Pendleton, Confederate Memoirs, 44.
20. Ibid., 43.
21. Long, The Civil War Day by Day, 412.
22. Richmond Daily Dispatch
23. Ibid.
24. New York Times
25. Jones, History of Decatur County Georgia, 384-386.
26. Holland, Keep All My Letters, 107.
27. Long, The Civil War Day by Day, 414.

28. Ibid., 415.
29. Ward, The Civil War, 90.
30. Rhodes, All For The Union, 125.
31. Pendleton, Confederate Memoirs, 44.
32. Ibid.
33. Stilwell, The Stilwell Letters, 217.
34. Woodbury, The Second Rhode Island Regiment, 207.
35. Rhodes, All For The Union, 127.
36. Ibid.
37. Ibid.
38. Pendleton, Confederate Memoirs, 44.
39. Wood, Letters from John L.G. Wood, 10/12/63 Camp in line of battle in Dry Valley, 3 miles from Chattanooga.
40. Ibid.
41. Rhodes, All For The Union, 127.
42. Ibid., 128.
43. Ibid.
44. Long, The Civil War Day by Day, 424.
45. Rhodes, All For The Union, 129.
46. Woodbury, The Second Rhode Island Regiment, 208.
47. Rhodes, All For The Union, 131.
48. Woodbury, The Second Rhode Island Regiment, 208.
49. Ibid., 208-209.
50. Rhodes, All For The Union, 132.
51. Woodbury, The Second Rhode Island Regiment, 204.

Chapter 10. "They Were Brave Men"

1. Boatner, The Civil War Dictionary, 397.
2. Catton, A Stillness At Appomattox, 39.
3. Stiles, Four Years Under Marse Robert, 239.
4. Pendleton, Confederate Memoirs, 44.
5. Ibid., 44-45.
6. Ibid., 45.
7. Ibid., 46.
8. Ibid.

9. Ibid., 47.
10. Boatner, The Civil War Dictionary, 51.
11. Civil War Times Illustrated, Great Battles of the Civil War, 421.
12. Pendleton, Confederate Memoirs, 47.
13. Ibid.
14. Ibid.
15. Ibid., 48.
16. Humphreys, Official Records of the War of Rebellion, Series 1, Vol.31 (Part I), Chap.XLIII, 521.
17. The Southern Drummer, Knoxville, TN, Vol. 2, 2/16/1887.
18. Kelly, "...On They Came With A Yell..."
19. Pendleton, Confederate Memoirs, 48.
20. Burnside, Official Records of the War of Rebellion, Series 1, Vol.31 (Part I), Chap. XLIII, 278.
21. Seymour, Divided Loyalties, 207.
22. Burnside, Official Records of the War of Rebellion, Series 1, Vol. 31 (Part I), Chap. XLIII, 278.
23. Seymour, Divided Loyalties, 211.
24. Ibid., 212.
25. Pendleton, Confederate Memoirs, 48.
26. Rhodes, All For The Union, 133.
27. Ibid.
28. Woodbury, The Second Rhode Island Regiment, 210.
29. Ibid., 211.
30. Rhodes, All For The Union, 134.
31. Woodbury, The Second Rhode Island Regiment, 211.
32. Ibid.
33. Ibid.
34. Rhodes, All For The Union, 134.
35. Woodbury, The Second Rhode Island Regiment, 212.
36. Rhodes, All For The Union, 135.
37. Ibid.
38. Woodbury, The Second Rhode Island Regiment, 212.
39. Rhodes, All For The Union, 135.
40. Ibid., 136.

41. Ibid.
42. Pendleton, Confederate Memoirs, 49.
43. Ibid., 49-50.
44. Ibid., 49.

Chapter 11. "A Wonderfully Tenacious Life"

1. The Richmond Whig
2. Dickert, History of Kershaw's Brigade, 291.
3. Ibid., 292.
4. Ibid.
5. Ibid.
6. Holland, Keep All My Letters, 113.
7. Wood, Letters from John L.G. Wood, 1/3/64 Camp near Russellville, TN.
8. Woodbury, The Second Rhode Island Regiment, 219.
9. Ibid.
10. Ibid., 219-220.
11. Ibid., 222.
12. Ibid.
13. Ibid., 223.
14. Ibid., 224.
15. Ibid., 225.
16. Ibid., 226.
17. Ibid.
18. Ibid.
19. Ibid.
20. Ibid.
21. Ibid., 227.
22. Ibid., 228.
23. Boatner, The Civil War Dictionary, 459.
24. Official Records of the War of Rebellion, Series 1, Vol. 32 (Part III), Chap. XLIV, 83.
25. Wert, General James Longstreet, 357.
26. Catton, A Stillness At Appomattox, 39.
27. Pendleton, Confederate Memoirs, 51.

28. Holland, Keep All My Letters, 111.
29. Wood, Letters from John L.G. Wood, 3/31/64 Bristol, VA.
30. Pendleton, Confederate Memoirs, 54.
31. Wood, Letters from John L.G. Wood, 4/8/64 Camp Near Bristol, TN.
32. Pendleton, Confederate Memoirs, 54.
33. Holland, Keep All My Letters, 117.
34. Ibid., 119.
35. Woodbury, The Second Rhode Island Regiment, 231.

12. "A Lick And A Promise"

1. Boatner, The Civil War Dictionary, 509.
2. Pendleton, Confederate Memoirs, 55.
3. Dickert, History of Kershaw's Brigade, 340-341.
4. Pendleton, Confederate Memoirs, 55.
5. Catton, A Stillness At Appomattox, 62.
6. Simms, A Georgian's View of the War in Virginia, 105.
7. Rhodes, All For The Union, 144.
8. Woodbury, The Second Rhode Island Regiment, 234.
9. Ibid.
10. Rhodes, All For The Union, 146.
11. Woodbury, The Second Rhode Island Regiment, 235.
12. Civil War Times Illustrated, Great Battles of the Civil War, 434.
13. Dickert, History of Kershaw's Brigade, 344-345.
14. Freeman, Lee's Lieutenants, Volume 3, 356.
15. Ibid., 357.
16. Dickert, History of Kershaw's Brigade, 341.
17. Ibid., 345.
18. Pendleton, Confederate Memoirs, 56.
19. Ibid.
20. Ibid.
21. Dickert, History of Kershaw's Brigade, 347.
22. Pendleton, Confederate Memoirs, 56.
23. Ibid., 57.

24. Dickert, History of Kershaw's Brigade, 347.
25. Pendleton, Confederate Memoirs, 57.
26. Ibid., 56-57.
27. Freeman, Lee's Lieutenants, Volume 3, 510.
28. <u>Swinton</u> Campaigns of the Army of the Potomac, 429.
29. Rhodes, All For The Union, 146.
30. Ibid., 147.
31. Woodbury, The Second Rhode Island Regiment, 236-237.
32. Freeman, Lee's Lieutenants, Volume 3, 365.
33. Woodbury, The Second Rhode Island Regiment, 239.
34. Ibid., 237.
35. Catton, A Stillness At Appomattox, 89.
36. Ibid.
37. Ibid., 90.
38. Stevens, Three Years in The Sixth Corps, 313.
39. Catton, A Stillness At Appomattox, 90.
40. Woodbury, The Second Rhode Island Regiment, 239.
41. Freeman, Lee's Lieutenants, Volume 3, 372.
42. Rhodes, All For The Union, 146.
43. Woodbury, The Second Rhode Island Regiment, 240.
44. Boatner, The Civil War Dictionary, 14.
45. Freeman, Lee's Lieutenants, Volume 3, 380.
46. Pendleton, Confederate Memoirs, 58.
47. Dickert, History of Kershaw's Brigade, 357.
48. Pendleton, Confederate Memoirs, 58.
49. Woodbury, The Second Rhode Island Regiment, 241.
50. Rhodes, All For The Union, 149-150.
51. Pendleton, Confederate Memoirs, 58.
52. Ibid., 59.
53. Ibid.
54. Rhodes, All For The Union, 150.
55. Catton, A Stillness At Appomattox, 109.
56. Ibid.
57. Rhodes, All For The Union, 150.
58. Woodbury, The Second Rhode Island Regiment, 243.
59. Catton, A Stillness At Appomattox, 117.

60. Stiles, Four Years Under Marse Robert, 254.
61. Ibid., 255.
62. Woodbury, The Second Rhode Island Regiment, 245-246.
63. Ibid., 246.
64. Ibid., 246-247.
65. Civil War Times Illustrated, Great Battles of the Civil War, 445.
66. Boatner, The Civil War Dictionary, 70.
67. Woodbury, The Second Rhode Island Regiment, 247.
68. Rhodes, All For The Union, 147.
69. Ibid.
70. Ibid.
71. Stevens, Three Years in The Sixth Corps, 334.
72. Benedict, Vermont in the Civil War, Vol. 1, 448.
73. Pendleton, Confederate Memoirs, 59.
74. Ibid.
75. Ibid.
76. Stilwell, The Stilwell Letters, 257-258.
77. Rhodes, All For The Union, 149.
78. Simms, A Georgian's View of the War in Virginia, 106.
79. Rhodes, All For The Union, 149.
80. Woodbury, The Second Rhode Island Regiment, 251.
81. Rhodes, All For The Union, 149.
82. Pendleton, Confederate Memoirs, 60.

13. "The angry features of the foe!"

1. Pendleton, Confederate Memoirs, 60.
2. Ibid., 61.
3. Woodbury, The Second Rhode Island Regiment, 254.
4. Pendleton, Confederate Memoirs, 61.
5. Ibid.
6. Ibid.
7. Woodbury, The Second Rhode Island Regiment, 255.
8. Pendleton, Confederate Memoirs, 61.
9. Boatner, The Civil War Dictionary, 748.

10. Catton, A Stillness At Appomattox, 45.
11. Ibid.
12. Ibid., 100-101.
13. Woodbury, The Second Rhode Island Regiment, 256.
14. Ibid.
15. Furgurson, Not War But Murder, 76-77.
16. Pendleton, Confederate Memoirs, 63.
17. Stevens, Three Years in The Sixth Corps, 347.
18. Woodbury, The Second Rhode Island Regiment, 256-257.
19. Rhodes, All For The Union, 157.
20. Pendleton, Confederate Memoirs, 63.
21. Ibid., 64.
22. Stevens, Three Years in The Sixth Corps, 349.
23. Catton, A Stillness At Appomattox, 152.
24. Stevens, Three Years in The Sixth Corps, 350.
25. Ibid., 351.
26. Catton, A Stillness At Appomattox, 158-159.
27. Ibid., 159.
28. Woodbury, The Second Rhode Island Regiment, 258.
29. Pendleton, Confederate Memoirs, 64-65.
30. Ibid., 65.
31. Boatner, The Civil War Dictionary, 165.
32. Stevens, Three Years In The Sixth Corps, 353.
33. Pendleton, Confederate Memoirs, 65.
34. Furgurson, Not War But Murder, 119.
35. Simms, Official Records of the War of Rebellion, Series 1, Vol. 36 (Part I), Chap. XLVIII, 1065.
36. Catton, A Stillness At Appomattox, 163.
37. Simms, A Georgian's View of the War in Virginia, 108.
38. Rhodes, All For The Union, 158.
39. Ibid.
40. Woodbury, The Second Rhode Island Regiment, 261.
41. Ibid., 265.
42. Ibid., 267.
43. The Providence Journal, June 10, 1864.
44. Woodbury, The Second Rhode Island Regiment, 279.

45. Pendleton, Confederate Memoirs, 66.
46. Simms, A Georgian's View of the War in Virginia, 109.
47. Ibid.
48. Woodbury, The Second Rhode Island Regiment, 281.
49. Pendleton, Confederate Memoirs, 66.
50. Ibid.
51. Official Records of the War of Rebellion, Series 1, Vol. 36 (Part I), Chap. XLVIII, 1065.
52. Stevens, Three Years in The Sixth Corps, 356.
53. Rhodes, All For The Union, 161.
54. Long, The Civil War Day by Day, 523.
55. Dickert, History of Kershaw's Brigade, 67.
56. Simms, A Georgian's View of the War in Virginia, 110.
57. Dickert, History of Kershaw's Brigade, 380.
58. Rhodes, All For The Union, 162-163.
59. Pendleton, Confederate Memoirs, 67.
60. Simms, Official Records of the War of Rebellion, Series 1, Vol. 40 (Part I), Chap. LII, 768.
61. Pendleton, Confederate Memoirs, 67.
62. Rhodes, All For The Union, 163.
63. Simms, A Georgian's View of the War in Virginia, 111.
64. Ibid.
65. Ibid., 112.
66. Catton, A Stillness At Appomattox, 202, 204.
67. Ibid., 203.
68. Ibid.
69. Pendleton, Confederate Memoirs, 68.
70. Ibid.
71. Simms, A Georgian's View of the War in Virginia, 112-113.

14. "Early was Late"

1. Rhodes, All For The Union, 168.
2. Ibid., 169.
3. Ibid.

4. Freeman, Lee's Lieutenants, Volume 3, 770.
5. Catton, A Stillness At Appomattox, 263.
6. Stevens, Three Years in The Sixth Corps, 372-373.
7. Ibid., 374.
8. Rhodes, All For The Union, 170.
9. Ibid.
10. Ibid., 171.
11. Simms, A Georgian's View of the War in Virginia, 113.
12. Ibid., 114.
13. Official Records of the War of Rebellion, Series 1, Vol. 40 (Part I), Chap. LII, 768.
14. Pendleton, Confederate Memoirs, 69.
15. Official Records of the War of Rebellion, Series 1, Vol. 40 (Part I), Chap. LII, 768.
16. Dickert, History of Kershaw's Brigade, 387-388.
17. McGlashan, Recollections of Petersburg, Virginia, June, 1864, 67-69.
18. Dickert, History of Kershaw's Brigade, 383.
19. Official Records of the War of Rebellion, Series 1, Vol. 40 (Part I), Chap. LII, 768.
20. Pendleton, Confederate Memoirs, 70.
21. Official Records of the War of Rebellion, Series 1, Vol. 40 (Part I), Chap. LII, 768.
22. Pendleton, Confederate Memoirs, 70.
23. Dickert, History of Kershaw's Brigade, 405.
24. Hassler, Commanders of the Army of the Potomac, 227.
25. Catton, A Stillness At Appomattox, 271.
26. Rhodes, All For The Union, 23.
27. Woodbury, The Second Rhode Island Regiment. 291.
28. Wood, Letters from John L.G. Wood, 8/5/64 Camp Near Petersburg, VA.
29. Pendleton, Confederate Memoirs, 72.
30. Dickert, History of Kershaw's Brigade, 417-418.
31. Rhodes, All For The Union, 178.
32. Ibid., 179.
33. Simms, A Georgian's View of the War in Virginia, 119.

34. Dickert, History of Kershaw's Brigade, 418.
35. Pendleton, Confederate Memoirs, 73.
36. Ibid.
37. National Archives.
38. Ibid.
39. Simms, Letter to his sister, Atlanta Historical Society, 8/23/64 Near Charlestown, VA.
40. Official Records of the War of Rebellion, Series 1, Vol. 43 (Part I), Chap. LV, 590.
41. Pendleton, Confederate Memoirs, 74.
42. Simms, A Georgian's View of the War in Virginia, 120.
43. Rhodes, All For The Union, 181.
44. Ibid.
45. Wood, Letters from John L.G. Wood, 9/9/64 Camp At Winchester, VA.
46. Official Records of the War of Rebellion, Series 1, Vol. 43 (Part I), Chap. LV, 590.
47. Boatner, The Civil War Dictionary, 216.
48. Pendleton, Confederate Memoirs, 76.
49. Boatner, The Civil War Dictionary, 938.
50. Freeman, Lee's Lieutenants, Volume 3, 578.
51. Rhodes, All For The Union, 183-184.
52. Lewis, The Shenandoah In Flames, 122.
53. Official Records of the War of Rebellion, Series 1, Vol. 43 (Part I), Chap. LV, 555.
54. Rhodes, All For The Union, 185.
55. Official Records of the War of Rebellion, Series 1, Vol. 43 (Part I), Chap. LV, 590.
56. Rhodes, All For The Union, 186.
57. Ibid., 187.
58. Official Records of the War of Rebellion, Series 1, Vol. 43 (Part I), Chap. LV, 590.
59. Dickert, History of Kershaw's Brigade, 436.
60. Ibid., 438.
61. Wood, Letters from John L.G. Wood, 9/29/64 Camp near Waynesborough, VA.

15. "Very fine buttermilk, indeed"

1. Rhodes, All For The Union, 189.
2. Stevens, Three Years In The Sixth Corps, 412.
3. Rhodes, All For The Union, 190-191.
4. Ibid., 191.
5. Stevens, Three Years In The Sixth Corps, 412-413.
6. Sheridan, The Personal Memoirs of P. H. Sheridan, 314.
7. Stevens, Three Years In The Sixth Corps, 413.
8. Rhodes, All For The Union, 189.
9. Ibid., 189-190.
10. Stevens, Three Years In The Sixth Corps, 410.
11. Ibid., 410-411.
12. Simms, A Georgian's View of the War in Virginia, 123.
13. Simms, Letter to his sister, Atlanta Historical Society, 10/21/64 Near New Market, VA.
14. Ibid.
15. Dickert, History of Kershaw's Brigade, 443-445.
16. Simms, A Georgian's View of the War in Virginia, 123.
17. Boatner, The Civil War Dictionary, 349.
18. Gordon, Reminiscences of the Civil War, 336.
19. Confederate Veterans Association. Addresses Delivered Before The Confederate Veterans Association of Savannah, Ga. 1898-1902, 50-51.
20. Ibid.
21. Ibid.
22. Dickert, History of Kershaw's Brigade, 445.
23. Confederate Veterans Association. Addresses Delivered Before The Confederate Veterans Association of Savannah, Ga. 1898-1902, 51.
24. Ibid.
25. Ibid.
26. Ibid.
27. Ibid., 51-52.
28. Ibid.
29. Ibid.

30. Ibid., 52.
31. Dickert, History of Kershaw's Brigade, 448-449.
32. Ibid.
33. Confederate Veterans Association. Addresses Delivered Before The Confederate Veterans Association of Savannah, Ga. 1898-1902, 52-53.
34. Official Records of the War of Rebellion, Series 1, Vol. 43 (Part I), Chap. LV, 591.
35. Ibid., 593.
36. Dickert, History of Kershaw's Brigade, 450.
37. Stevens, Three Years In The Sixth Corps, 418.
38. Ibid.
39. Ibid., 419.
40. Ibid.
41. Ibid., 419-422.
42. Ibid., 421.
43. Ibid., 422.
44. Confederate Veterans Association. Addresses Delivered Before The Confederate Veterans Association of Savannah, Ga. 1898-1902, The Battle of Cedar Creek, 53-54.
45. Dickert, History of Kershaw's Brigade, 450.
46. Woodbury, The Second Rhode Island Regiment, 308.
47. Rhodes, All For The Union, 192-193.
48. Simms, Official Records of the War of Rebellion, Series 1, Vol. 43 (Part I), Chap. LV, 591.
49. Confederate Veterans Association. Addresses Delivered Before The Confederate Veterans Association of Savannah, Ga. 1898-1902, The Battle of Cedar Creek, 54-55.
50. Official Records of the War of Rebellion, Series 1, Vol. 43 (Part I) Chap. LV, 591.
51. Rhodes, All For The Union, 192-193.
52. National Archives.
53. Official Records of the War of Rebellion, Series 1, Vol. 43 (Part I), Chap. LV, 591-592.
54. Dickert, History of Kershaw's Brigade, 469.
55. Stevens, Three Years In The Sixth Corps, 423.

56. Rhodes, All For The Union, 193.
57. Ibid.
58. Dickert, History of Kershaw's Brigade, 454-455.
59. Woodbury, The Second Rhode Island Regiment, 314-315.
60. Simms, A Georgian's View of the War in Virginia, 126.

16. "We were gentlemen of leisure"

1. Dickert, History of Kershaw's Brigade, 470.
2. Ibid., 471.
3. Ibid., 471-472.
4. Rhodes, All For The Union, 194.
5. Ibid.
6. Ibid.
7. Ibid., 195.
8. Ibid.
9. Ibid., 197.
10. Woodbury, The Second Rhode Island Regiment, 318.
11. Rhodes, All For The Union, 198.
12. Official Records of the War of Rebellion, Series 1, Vol. 42 (Part III), Chap. LIV, 686.
13. Simms, A Georgian's View of the War in Virginia, 126-127.
14. Wood, Letters from John L.G. Wood, 12/17/64 Camp Near Richmond, VA.
15. Ibid., 12/18/64.
16. Rogers, Thomas County During The Civil War, 85-88.
17. Ibid., 85-86.
18. Ibid., 90.
19. Rhodes, All For The Union, 199.
20. Stevens, Three Years In The Sixth Corps, 429.
21. Weitz, Mark A. More Damning Than Slaughter, 241.
22. Power, Lee's Miserables, 258.
23. Ibid., 259.
24. Woodbury, The Second Rhode Island Regiment, 319-320.
25. Ibid., 321-322.

26. Rhodes, All For The Union, 201.
27. Wood, Letters from John L.G. Wood, 12/17/64 Camp Near Richmond, VA.
28. Simms, A Georgian's View of the War in Virginia, 129.
29. Ibid.
30. Power, Lee's Miserables, 228.
31. Wood, Letters from John L.G. Wood, 12/18/64 Camp Near Richmond, VA.
32. Power, Lee's Miserables, 231.
33. Ibid.
34. Ibid.
35. Freeman, Lee's Lieutenants, Volume 3, 620-621.
36. Ibid., 621.
37. National Archives.
38. Confederate Veterans Association. Addresses Delivered Before The Confederate Veterans Association of Savannah, Ga. 1898-1902, 59.
39. Official Records of the War of Rebellion, Series 1, Vol. 46 (Part II), Chap. LVIII, 146.
40. Rhodes, All For The Union, 208.
41. Ibid., 209.
42. Ibid., 82.
43. Ibid., 212.
44. Power, Lee's Miserables, 264.
45. Richmond Whig, March 19, 1864, p. 1, c. 3.
46. Simms, A Georgian's View of the War in Virginia, 132-134.
47. Power, Lee's Miserables, 265.
48. Simms, A Georgian's View of the War in Virginia, 132-134.
49. Freeman, Lee's Lieutenants, Volume 3, 621.
50. Simms, A Georgian's View of the War in Virginia, 130.
51. Power, Lee's Miserables, 262.
52. The Philadelphia Inquirer, March 25, 1865, p. 1.
53. Simms, A Georgian's View of the War in Virginia, 133-134.
54. Savannah Morning News, June 19, 1928.

17. "Great events are to happen in a few days"

1. Stiles, Four Years Under Marse Robert, 252.
2. Ibid., 317-318.
3. Woodbury, The Second Rhode Island Regiment, 332.
4. Rhodes, All For The Union, 222.
5. Woodbury, The Second Rhode Island Regiment, 339.
6. Freeman, Lee's Lieutenants, Volume 3, 661.
7. Boatner, The Civil War Dictionary, 283.
8. Rhodes, All For The Union, 223.
9. Simms, A Georgian's View of the War in Virginia, 131-132.
10. Rhodes, All For The Union, 223.
11. Woodbury, The Second Rhode Island Regiment, 341.
12. Ibid.
13. Rhodes, All For The Union, 224.
14. Woodbury, The Second Rhode Island Regiment, 341.
15. Rhodes, All For The Union, 225.
16. Woodbury, The Second Rhode Island Regiment, 343.
17. Ibid.
18. Woodbury, The Second Rhode Island Regiment, 343-344.
19. Rhodes, All For The Union, 225.
20. Ibid., 226.
21. Woodbury, The Second Rhode Island Regiment, 343-344.
22. Official Records of the War of Rebellion, Series 1, Vol. 46 (Part I), Chap. LVIII, 951.
23. Confederate Veterans Association. Addresses Delivered Before The Confederate Veterans Association of Savannah, Ga. 1898-1902, 59-60.
24. Ibid.
25. Ibid., 60.
26. Ibid., 84
27. Ibid., 60.
28. Ibid., 60-61.
29. Ibid., 61.
30. Ibid.

31. Ibid., 84-85.
32. Ibid.
33. Rhodes, All For The Union, 227.
34. Ibid.
35. Confederate Veterans Association. Addresses Delivered Before The Confederate Veterans Association of Savannah, Ga. 1898-1902, 85-86.
36. Ibid., 86.
37. Ibid.
38. Ibid., 61.
39. Ibid., 62.
40. Ibid.
41. Woodbury, The Second Rhode Island Regiment, 349.
42. Confederate Veterans Association. Addresses Delivered Before The Confederate Veterans Association of Savannah, Ga. 1898-1902, 87.
43. Ibid., 62-63.
44. Woodbury, The Second Rhode Island Regiment, 351.
45. Ibid., 350.
46. Rhodes, All For The Union, 229.
47. Confederate Veterans Association. Addresses Delivered Before The Confederate Veterans Association of Savannah, Ga. 1898-1902, 63.
48. Ibid.
49. Ibid.
50. Woodbury, The Second Rhode Island Regiment, 351.
51. Confederate Veterans Association. Addresses Delivered Before The Confederate Veterans Association of Savannah, Ga. 1898-1902, 63.
52. Ibid., 64.
53. Ibid.
54. Ibid.
55. Stiles, Four Years Under Marse Robert, 333.
56. Southern Historical Society Papers.
57. Official Records of the War of Rebellion, Series 1, Vol. 46 (Part I), Chap. LVIII, 1284.

58. Confederate Veterans Association. Addresses Delivered Before The Confederate Veterans Association of Savannah, Ga. 1898-1902, 65.
59. Ibid.
60. Ibid., 87.
61. Ibid., 87-88.
62. Rhodes, All For The Union, 229.
63. Confederate Veterans Association. Addresses Delivered Before The Confederate Veterans Association of Savannah, Ga. 1898-1902, 88.
64. Ibid.
65. Ibid.
66. Rhodes, All For The Union, 227.
67. Confederate Veterans Association. Addresses Delivered Before The Confederate Veterans Association of Savannah, Ga. 1898-1902, 89.

18. "Home? I had none."

1. Porter, Appomattox, 138.
2. Ibid., 139.
3. Ibid.
4. Ibid.
5. Ibid., 140.
6. Ibid., 141.
7. Confederate Veterans Association. Addresses Delivered Before The Confederate Veterans Association, of Savannah, Ga. 1898-1902, 89.
8. Porter, Appomattox, 141.
9. Ibid.
10. Ibid., 142.
11. Ibid., 148.
12. Ibid.
13. Ibid., 149.
14. Rhodes, All For The Union, 230.
15. Ibid.

16. Confederate Veterans Association. Addresses Delivered Before The Confederate Veterans Association of Savannah, Ga. 1898-1902.
17. Ibid.
18. Rhodes, All For The Union, 230.
19. Ibid.
20. Confederate Veterans Association. Addresses Delivered Before The Confederate Veterans Association of Savannah, Ga. 1898-1902.
21. Ibid.
22. Ibid.
23. Rhodes, All For The Union, 230.
24. Confederate Veterans Association. Addresses Delivered Before The Confederate Veterans Association of Savannah, Ga. 1898-1902.
25. Ibid.
26. Freeman, Lee's Lieutenants, Volume 3, 746.
27. Ibid., 747.
28. Ibid.
29. Gordon, Reminiscences of The Civil War.
30. Chamberlain, Details of the Surrender of General Lee at Appomattox Courthouse, April 9th, 1865, Lenient Terms of General Grant.
31. Confederate Veterans Association. Addresses Delivered Before The Confederate Veterans Association of Savannah, Ga. 1898-1902.
32. Ibid.
33. Rhodes, All For The Union, 230.
34. Southern Historical Society Papers, New Series. No. IV, Vol. XLII, Richmond, VA, September 1917, 149-150.
35. Ibid., 150.

Epilogue

1. Rhodes, Elisha H. A Trip Through The South & West And What I Saw.
2. Rhodes, Elisha. All For The Union, 247.
3. Woodbury, The Second Rhode Island Regiment, 365-366.
4. Confederate Veterans Association. Addresses Delivered Before The Confederate Veterans Association of Savannah, Ga. 1898-1902, 94.
5. Daily Morning News, Savannah.
6. Sheldon Family Papers.
7. Sheldon, James, Letter.
8. Sheldon, Irving C., Tales My Mother Told Me.
9. Semmes In America. Gettysburg National Military Park. Collection.
10. Cassel, Allie Waters, Wiregrass Allie, 60

BIBLIOGRAPHIES

Archives, Historical Societies and Libraries

Adams County Historical Society
Appomattox Court House National Historical Park
Bonaventure Cemetery, Savannah, Georgia
Gettysburg National Military Park
Jefferson Davis Memorial Historic Site, Irwinville, Georgia
The Cranston Historical Society
The Georgia Historical Society
The Knoxville Civil War Round Table
The Providence Public Library
The Rhode Island Historical Society Library
The Rhode Island State Archives
The Thomasville Genealogical, History and Fine Arts Library
The University of Tennessee, Special Collections, John Watkins
Papers.
The Warwick Public Library
Thomas County Historical Society

Primary Sources

Bonnes, Marguerite Schaezler. The 1862 Diary of Israel
Sheldon, Corpus Christi, Texas.

Brown, Henry A.L. The Horace G. Belcher Papers. From
the collection of Henry A.L. Brown, courtesy of Henry A.L.
Brown.

Brown, Henry A. L. The Henry A.L. Brown Historical Papers and Photograph Collection, courtesy of Henry A. L. Brown.

Gettysburg National Military Park. Semmes In America, Collection.

Grow, Gerald, ed. March 23, 2003. Milo Grow: Letters from the Civil War. Website. http://www.longleaf.net/milo (accessed April 21, 2006).

Peacock, Jane Bonner, ed. "A Georgian's View of the War in Virginia," Atlanta Historical Society Journal, 1979.

Rhodes, Elisha H. A Trip Through the South & West and What I Saw. Unpublished.

Sheldon, Irving C. Tales My Mother Told Me.

Solomon, M. J. William O. Fleming's letter on Crampton's Gap from newspaper article, Duke University.

Newspapers

Boston Journal, "The Last Salute Of The Army Of Northern Virginia," May, 1901

Daily Morning News, Savannah, Wednesday Morning, March 17, 1862.

Daily Morning News, Savannah, Wednesday Morning, March 19, 1862.

Richmond *Dispatch*, "Last Sad Days," March 4, 2001.

Savannah *Morning News*, Savannah, May 4, 1996.

Savannah *Morning News*, Savannah, June 19, 1928.

Savannah *Republican*, February 26, 1862, p. 2, c. 6.

Savannah *Republican*, August 14, 1862, p. 2, c. 2.

Savannah *Republican*, December 14, 1862, p. 2, c. 2.

The *Providence Journal*.

The Richmond *Sentinel*, May 2, 1864, p. 2, c. 3.

The Richmond *Whig*.

The Southern Drummer, Knoxville, TN.

Official Reports and Government Publications

Dyer, Elisha, Adjutant General. *Adjutant Generals Report 1861-65*. E.L. Freeman & Son, Providence, RI, 1893, Vol. I.

Dyer, Elisha, Adjutant General. *Annual Report of the Adjutant General of the State of Rhode Island and Providence Plantations for the Year 1865*. Corrected, revised, and republished in accordance with provisions of chapters 705 and 767 of the public laws. By Brig.Gen. Elisha Dyer. E.L. Freeman & Son, Printers to the State, Providence, RI, 1895.

Georgia, State of. *Roster of the Confederate Soldiers of Georgia 1861-1865*. 7 vols., Confederate Pension and Record Department, Hapeville: Longino & Porter, 1955-58.

National Archives and Records Administration, Soldiers Service Records.

The Union Army, A History of Military Affairs in the Loyal States 1861-65 – Records of the Regiments in the Union Army – Cyclopedia of Battles – Memoirs of Commanders and Soldiers. 8 vols., Madison: Federal Publishing, 1908.

United States War Department. *Official Records of the War of Rebellion: A Compilation of the Official Records of the Union and*

Confederate Armies. 128 vols., Washington, GPO, 1880-87.

United States Census

Published Primary Sources

Alexander, Edward Porter. *Fighting For The Confederacy, The Personal Recollections of General Edward Porter Alexander.* The University of North Carolina Press, Chapel Hill/London, 1989.

Alleman, Tillie Pierce. *At Gettysburg: Or What a Girl Saw and Heard at the Battle.*

Brown, Joseph. *Governor Joseph Brown's Open Letter.* Website. http://hometown.aol.com/jfepperson/jbrown.html(accessed May 21, 2006).

Bucklyn, John Knight. "The War of the Rebellion." Wickford/North Kingstown *Standard Times*, July 15, 1892 to April 1906.

Chamberlain, J.L. *Details of the Surrender of General Lee at Appomattox Courthouse, April 9th, 1865, Lenient Terms of General Grant.* Website. http://www.civilwarhome.com/chamberlainsurrender.html (accessed May, 2006).

Chamberlain, J.L. *"Bayonet! Forward":My Civil War Reminiscences.* Gettysburg, PA: Stan Clark Military Books, 1994.

Civil War Extra. Arno Press, New York, NY, 1975.

Civil War Front Pages. Fairfax Press, New York, NY, 1989.

Confederate Veterans Association. *Addresses Delivered Before The Confederate Veterans Association of Savannah, Ga. 1898-1902.* To which is added: The President's Annual Reports, Presentation of Southern Cross of Honor, Memorial Resolutions, Tributes and List of Officers and Members. Published by the Association, 1902. Savannah Morning News Print, Savannah, GA., 1902.

Dickert, D. Augustus. History of Kershaw's Brigade. With Complete Roll of Companies, Biographical Sketches, Incidents, Anecdotes, etc., Press of Morningside Bookshop, 1973.

Douglas, Henry Kyd. I Rode With Stonewall. Mockingbird Books, Inc., St. Simons, GA, 1989.

Evans, Clement A. Confederate Military History. 18 vols., Extended Edition. Broadfoot, Wilmington, North Carolina, 1987, (reprint of 1899 edition).

Evans, Clement A. Confederate Military History. A Library of Confederate States History, 12 vols. Written by Distinguished Men of the South, and edited by Gen. Clement A. Evans of Georgia, vol. VI., Confederate Publishing Company, Atlanta, Ga., 1899.

Gordon, John B. Reminiscences of the Civil War. New York, C. Scribner's Sons, 1903.

Grant, Ulysses S. Ulysses Grant describes the life and environment of the West Point Academy to his cousin R. McKinstry Griffith, Sept. 22, 1839. A Website to Complement C-SPAN's 20th Anniversary Television Series, American Presidents: Life Portraits, March-December 1999. Website. http://www.americanpresidents.org/letters/18.asp.html (accessed April 21, 2006).

Holland, Katherine S. *Keep All My Letters, The Civil War Letters of Richard Henry Brooks, 51st Georgia Infantry.* Mercer University Press, Macon, Georgia, 2003.

Longstreet, James. *From Manassas to Appomattox: Memoirs of the Civil War in America.* Philadelphia, J.B. Lippincott Company, 1896.

McClellan, George B. *McClellan's Own Story: The War for the Union, the Soldiers Who Fought It, the Civilians Who Directed It, and His Relations to It and to Them.* Charles L. Webster, New York, NY, 1887.

Moseley, Ronald, ed. *The Stilwell Letters, A Georgian in Longstreet's Corps, Army of Northern Virginia*. Foreword by Herman Hattaway, Mercer University Press, 2002.

Pendleton, Constance, ed. *Confederate Memoirs, Early Life and Family History*, William Frederic Pendleton, Mary Lawson Pendleton. Supplement by Amena Pendleton Haines, Bryn Athyn, Pennsylvania, 1958.

Porter, Horace. *The Surrender At Appomattox Court House*. By Horace Porter, Brevet Brigadier General, USA, from the internet –"General Horace Porter" American Civil War Primary Sources. Ed. UXL-Gale, 2005. eNotes.com. 2006. Website. http://www. civilwarhome.com/surrender.html (accessed on April 22, 2006).

Reid, Whitelaw. *A Radical View: The "Agate" Dispatches of Whitelaw Reid, 1861-1865*, Volume 1. Memphis University Press, Memphis, Tennessee, 1976.

Reid, Whitelaw. *A Radical View: The "Agate" Dispatches of Whitelaw Reid, 1861-1865*, Volume 2. Memphis University Press, Memphis, Tennessee, 1976.

Rhodes, Elisha Hunt. *All For The Union, The Civil War Diary and Letters of Elisha Hunt Rhodes*. Edited by Robert Hunt Rhodes. Foreword by Geoffrey C. Ward. Orion Books, New York, 1991.

Sheridan, Philip Henry. *Personal Memoirs of P. H. Sheridan*. Da Capo Press, 1992.

Simon, John Y. *Last Months of the Civil War, On the Road to Appomattox – Grant and Lee from War to Peace*. Southern Illinois University, editor, The Papers of U.S. Grant.

Spicer, William A. *Ninth and Tenth R. I. Volunteers and Tenth R.I. Battery*. Providence: Snow & Farnham, 1892.

Stevens, George T. *Three Years in the Sixth Corps: A Concise Narrative of Events in the Army of the Potomac, from 1861 to the Close of the Rebellion, April, 1865*. Time-Life Books, 1984.

Stiles, Robert. *Four Years Under Marse Robert.* Morningside, Dayton, OH, 1988.

Strater, Terrance. *The Life and Times of a Rebel Surgeon.* Dr. George Rogers Clark Todd, brother of Mary Todd Lincoln, by permission of the author.

Woodbury, Augustus. *A Narrative of the Campaign of the First Rhode Island Regiment in the Spring and Summer of 1861.* Sidney S. Rider, Providence, 1862.

Woodbury, Augustus. *The Second Rhode Island Regiment: A Narrative of Military Operations in which the Regiment was engaged from the beginning to the end of the War for the Union.* Valpey, Angell and Company, Providence, 1875.

Secondary Sources

Allardice, Bruce S. *More Generals In Gray.* Louisiana State University Press, Baton Rouge and London, 1995.

Barker, Harold R. *History of the Rhode Island Combat Units in the Civil War (1861-1865),* edited by Alfred H. Gurney, 1964.

Boatner, Mark Mayo III. *The Civil War Dictionary.* Random House, New York, 1988.

Cassel, Allie Waters. *Wiregrass Allie: A Link in the Chain.* (Washington Waters) Vantage Press, New York, 1991.

Catton, Bruce. *The Army of the Potomac: Mr. Lincoln's Army.* Doubleday & Company, Inc., 1951.

Catton, Bruce. *The Army of the Potomac: A Stillness At Appomattox.* Doubleday & Company, Inc., Garden City, New York, 1953.

Clark, Champ, and the eds. of Time-Life Books. *The Civil War, Gettysburg: The Confederate High Tide.* Time-Life Books, Alexandria, Virginia, 1981.

Dunkelman, Mark H. *Brothers, One And All: Esprit de Corps in a Civil War Regiment.* Louisiana State University Press, Baton Rouge, Louisiana, 2004.

Elson, Henry William. *History of the United States of America.* Chapter IV pp. 93-97, transcribed by Kathy Leigh. (Oglethorpe) The MacMillan Company, New York, 1904.

Encyclopedia Britannica 1913.

Fergurson, Ernest B. *Chancellorsville, 1863: The Souls of the Brave.* Alfred A. Knopf, New York, NY, 1992.

Fox, William F. *Regimental Losses in The American Civil War 1861-1865.* 18th ed., Morningside House, Dayton, Ohio, 1985.

Frassanito, William A. *Antietam: The Photographic Legacy of America's Bloodiest Day.* Charles Scribner's Sons, New York.

Freeman, Douglas Southall. *Lee's Lieutenants: A Study In Command.* Volume 1. C. Scribner's Sons, New York, NY, 1970.

Freeman, Douglas Southall. *Lee's Lieutenants: A Study In Command.* Volume 2. Touchstone, New York, NY, 1995.

Freeman, Douglas Southall. *Lee's Lieutenants: A Study In Command.* Volume 3. C. Scribner's Sons, New York, NY, 1972.

Harden, William. *A History of Savannah and South Georgia.* Volume II. Illustrated. The Lewis Publishing Company, Chicago and New York, 1913.

Henderson, G. F. R. *Stonewall Jackson and the American Civil War.* Da Capo Press, New York, NY, 1988.

Henderson, Lillian. *Roster of the Confederate Soldiers of Georgia 1861-1865.* Vol. 5. Compiled for the State of Georgia. Longino & Porter, Inc., Hareville, GA, 1960.

Huxford, Folks. *Pioneers of Wiregrass Georgia*. Vol. VII. Huxford Genealogical Society, Homerville, Georgia, 1982.

Jones, Frank S. *History of Decatur County Georgia*. With New Index by Ann Gometz Foshee. The Reprint Company, Spartansburg, South Carolina, 1980.

Kelly, Dorothy E. "...On They Came With A Yell..." One Man's View of the Battle of Fort Sanders. Website. http://www.discoveret.org/kcwrt/history/hw-text.html (accessed on April 22, 2006). Copyright 1988.

Kerlin, Robert H. *Confederate Generals of Georgia And Their Burial Sites*. Americana Historical Books, Fayetteville, Georgia, 1994.

Long, E. B., with Barbara Long. *The Civil War Day by Day, An Almanac, 1861-1865*. Foreword by Bruce Catton. Da Capo Press, New York, 1971.

Marvel, William. *Burnside*. The University of North Carolina Press, Chapel Hill & London, 1991.

Power, J. Tracy. *Lee's Miserables, Life in the Army of Northern Virginia from the Wilderness to Appomattox*. The University of North Carolina Press, 1998.

Rogers, William Warren. *Thomas County During The Civil War*. The Florida State University Press, Tallahassee, FL, 1964.

Sears, Stephen W. *To The Gates Of Richmond, The Peninsula Campaign*. Ticknor & Fields, New York, NY, 1992.

Seymour, Digby Gordon. *Divided Loyalties, Fort Sanders and the Civil War In East Tennessee*. University of Tennessee Press, Knoxville, Tennessee, 1963.

Sifakis, Stewart. *Who Was Who In The Civil War*. Facts on File, 1988. (Bio of Beauregard).

Smith, Timothy H. *The Story of Lee's Headquarters*. Thomas Publications, Gettysburg, Pennsylvania, 1995.

Staples, William R. *Documentary History of the Destruction of the Gaspee*. Compiled for the *Providence Journal* by entered according to Act of Congress, by Knowles, Vose and Anthony, in the Clerk's Office of the District of Rhode Island, 1845.

Swinton, William. *Campaigns of the Army of the Potomac: A Critical History of Operations in Virginia, Maryland and Pennsylvania from the Commencement to the Close of the War 1861-65*. The Blue and Grey Press, Secaucus, New Jersey, 1988.

Tucker, Glenn. *Chickamauga: Bloody Battle In The West*. The Bobbs-Merrill Company, Inc., A Subsidiary of Howard W. Sams & Co., Inc. Publishers, Indianapolis & New York, 1961.

Weitz, Mark A. *More Damning Than Slaughter: Desertion in the Confederate Army*. University of Nebraska Press, 2005.

Wert, Jeffrey D. *General James Longstreet: The Confederacy's Most Controversial Soldier, A Biography*. Simon & Schuster, New York, NY, 1993.

Wheeler, Richard. *Sword Over Richmond: An Eyewitness History of McClellan's Peninsula Campaign*. Harper Perennial, New York, NY, 1986.

Wiggins, David N. *Remembering Georgia's Confederates*. Arcadia Press, 2005.

Internet Sources

The American Civil War Home Page. http://www.civilwarhome.com

The American Civil War Research Database. http://civilwardata.com (Duxbury, Massachusetts).

The Civil War Biography Page. Website. http://www.civilwarhome.com/biograph.html (accessed on April 22, 2006).

Cranston Historical Society. *William Sprague of Rhode Island.* Website. http://www.geocities.com/rilydia/william.html (accessed on April 22, 2006).

The Generals of the American Civil War. Website. http://www.generalsandbrevets.com (accessed on April 22, 2006).

Goddard, Ian Williams. *Roger Williams, Champion of Liberty.* Website. http://www.iangoddar.net/roger.html (accessed on April 22, 2006).

Gordon, John B. *Reminiscences Of The Civil War.* Website. http://www.civilwarhome.com/endofwar.html (accessed on April 22, 2006).

Harden, William. John Chastain File, USGenWeb Archives, pp. 1042-1045.
The American Civil War Home Page. http://www.civilwarhome.com (accessed on April 22, 2006).

Kelly, Dorothy E. and the Knoxville Civil War Roundtable. "... *On They Came With A Yell...*" One Man's View of the Battle of Fort Sanders. An article commemorating the 125th anniversary of the Battle of Fort Sanders. Copyright 1988. Website. http://www.discovret.org/kcwrt (accessed on April 26, 2006).

Life In A Civil War Camp. Website. http://www.usgennet.org/usa/ga/topic/military/CivilWar/lifeincamp.html (accessed on April 21, 2006).

Scott, Carole E. *Joseph E. Brown, a North Georgia Notable.* Website. http://www.ngeorgia.com/people/brown.html (accessed on April 21, 2006).

Sheridan, Philip H. *Personal Memoirs of P. H. Sheridan.* Volume 1. Website. http://www.pattonhq.com/militaryworks/sheridan.html (accessed on April 22, 2006).

Tumblin, J. C. *Knoxville In The Civil War.* Website. http://www.discoveret.org/kcwrt/history/hk-text.html (accessed on April 21, 2006).

ABOUT THE AUTHOR

Les Rolston was born in 1954 and has studied American history for most of his adult life. His greatest interest is in the lives of ordinary people, who in times of crisis go on to do extraordinary deeds.

Mr. Rolston is a frequent contributor to the *Providence Journal* and his work has appeared in the *South Reporter, Civil War Times Illustrated, Our Heritage,* the *New Orleans Times–Picayune* and other publications.

Photo by Erika-Lee Slaughter

His first book, **_Lost Soul: A Confederate Soldier In New England_** (Mariner 2007 (second edition), described his efforts to preserve the unmarked grave site of the only Confederate soldier known to be buried in Rhode Island. As a result of this book Rolston gained national attention, telling his story through the Associated Press and television programs. He has received citations from the Rhode Island House of Representatives and a letter of commendation from former United States Senator Claiborne Pell. He was also awarded the Jefferson Davis Medal, the United Daughters of the Confederacy's highest award.

In 1999, Rolston solved the mystery of the "soldier in the cane field" in Bayou Goula, Louisiana, when he identified Private

David Ingraham, 3rd Rhode Island Cavalry, as being buried in a makeshift grave there. This grave is now marked as a Louisiana Historic site.

In 2000, after an inquiry by 91-year old Vera Harris, Les located the grave of Marzy Van Howland Lincoln, 11th United States Heavy Artillery (Colored). In a modest ceremony, only months before her own death, Mrs. Harris visited her father's grave for the first time.

In 2001, Rolston secured a military burial for Harold Brown. Mr. Brown had been machine-gunned to death in a lifeboat eight miles off the coast of Virginia after his cargo ship was sunk by a German U-Boat during the opening days of World War II. After months of negotiations with the United States government, Brown, a merchant marine, was recognized as a war veteran. Acknowledging Rolston's efforts was United States Senator Jack Reed (D) Rhode Island.

In 2004, Les was instrumental in restoring and preserving the vandalized gravesite of General George Sears Greene, hero of Gettysburg.

In addition to his writings, he serves the City of Warwick, Rhode Island (pop. 85,000) as its Building Inspector. Warwick has three Historic Districts and scores of Colonial era buildings and cemeteries.

Rolston recently completed ***Home Of The Brave: Selected Short Stories Of Immigrant Medal Of Honor Recipients Of The Civil War***. He is now working on his fourth book, ***No Place For Christians: The Civil War Imprisonment Of Michael Dougherty.*** Les lives in Warwick with his wife, Mary, and son, Derek.

Printed in the United States
213224BV00002B/4/P

MAY _ - 2013